This work meticulously examines the concept of benefaction and patronage in the Pastoral Epistles in ways that are relevant to the needs of the global church. Anyone who undertakes to understand the communities in Africa will find this work a necessary resource.

David Ngaruiya, PhD
Associate Professor and Director of Theological Studies PhD Program,
International Leadership University, Nairobi, Kenya

Nathan Nzyoka Joshua breaks new ground in the study of the Pastoral Epistles by carefully and responsibly locating them within the ancient practice of benefaction and patronage. His work has added benefit by applying his findings to ecclesial structures in his own East African context. An eye-opening and challenging work.

James C. Miller, PhD
Professor of Inductive Biblical Studies,
Asbury Theological Seminary, Wilmore, Kentucky, USA

Benefaction and Patronage in Leadership

A Socio-Historical Exegesis of the Pastoral Epistles

Nathan Nzyoka Joshua

MONOGRAPHS

© 2018 Nathan Nzyoka Joshua

Published 2018 by Langham Monographs
An imprint of Langham Publishing
www.langhampublishing.org

Langham Publishing and its imprints are a ministry of Langham Partnership

Langham Partnership
PO Box 296, Carlisle, Cumbria, CA3 9WZ, UK
www.langham.org

ISBNs:
978-1-78368-501-1 Print
978-1-78368-502-8 ePub
978-1-78368-503-5 Mobi
978-1-78368-504-2 PDF

Nathan Nzyoka Joshua has asserted his right under the Copyright, Designs and Patents Act, 1988 to be identified as the Author of this work.

All rights reserved. No part of this publication may be reproduced, stored in a retrieval system or transmitted, in any form or by any means, electronic, mechanical, photocopying, recording or otherwise, without the prior written permission of the publisher or the Copyright Licensing Agency.

Unless otherwise stated, Scripture quotations are from the New Revised Standard Version Bible, copyright © 1989 National Council of the Churches of Christ in the United States of America. Used by permission. All rights reserved.

Scripture quotations marked RSV are from Revised Standard Version of the Bible, copyright © 1946, 1952, and 1971 National Council of the Churches of Christ in the United States of America. Used by permission. All rights reserved.

Translations of the Greek New Testament are the author's own.

British Library Cataloguing-in-Publication Data
A catalogue record for this book is available from the British Library

ISBN: 978-1-78368-501-1

Cover & Book Design: ProjectLuz.com

Langham Partnership actively supports theological dialogue and an author's right to publish but does not necessarily endorse the views and opinions set forth here or in works referenced within this publication, nor can we guarantee technical and grammatical correctness. Langham Partnership does not accept any responsibility or liability to persons or property as a consequence of the reading, use or interpretation of its published content.

To
God
my wife, Regina Muthoki
our children, Irene Mwende, Nason Ngila and Nehemiah Musembi
my late father, Joshua Kieti Munyao
late father-in-law, Jackson Muia Masai
mother, Alice Kieti
mother-in-law, Jane Muia
the late Rev Daniel Mulemba
the late ex-senior chief, Paul Munguti
and the entire church fraternity in Africa

Contents

List of Tables xi

Acknowledgements xiii

Abstract xv

Abbreviations xvii

Chapter 1 1
General Introduction and Modern Scholarship on Benefaction and Patronage
    1.1 General Introduction 1
    1.2 Intended Contribution to Biblical Scholarship 5
    1.3 Delimitations 6
    1.4 Methodology 7
    1.5 Authorship of the Pastoral Epistles 9
    1.6 Modern Scholarship on Benefaction and Patronage 15
        1.6.1 Frederick W. Danker: *Benefactor* 17
        1.6.2 John M. G. Barclay: *Jews in the Mediterranean Diaspora* 19
        1.6.3 D. A. deSilva: *Honor, Patronage, Kinship and Purity* 21
        1.6.4 Andrew Wallace-Hadrill: *Patronage in Ancient Society* 26
        1.6.5 Stephan J. Joubert: "One Form of Social Exchange or Two?" 26
        1.6.6 Zeba A. Crook: *Reconceptualising Conversion* 31
        1.6.7 Two Works on Specific NT Books 36
        1.6.8 Sources Specifically on PE 37
        1.6.9 Bruce W. Winter: "Providentia for the Widows" 37
        1.6.10 Reggie M. Kidd: *Wealth and Beneficence in the Pastoral Epistles* 40
        1.6.11 Commentaries 45

Chapter 2 47
Socio-Historical Background of Benefaction and Patronage
    2.1 Introduction 47
    2.2 Ancient Sources 47
        2.2.1 Cicero: *De Officiis* (On Duties) 48
        2.2.2 Seneca: *De Beneficiis* (On Benefits) 49
        2.2.3 Sets of Laws on *Patronicium* 56

  2.2.4 Philo and Josephus 58
 2.3 Benefaction and Patronage in the Greek, Roman and
 Jewish Contexts 60
  2.3.1 In Greek Context 61
  2.3.2 In Roman Context 67
  2.3.3 In Jewish Context 80
 2.4 Conclusion 89

Chapter 3 93
Benefaction, Patronage, and Leadership in the Pastoral Epistles Text
 3.1 Introduction 93
  3.1.1 Benefaction and Patronage in the New Testament 93
  3.1.2 God the Father and Christ on Benefaction
  and Patronage 94
  3.1.3 NT Authors on Benefaction and Patronage 100
 3.2 Benefaction and Patronage in the Pastoral Epistles 103
 3.3 Pastoral Epistles Characters as Benefactors and Patrons 111
  3.3.1 God as Benefactor and Patron 112
  3.3.2 God as Benefactor in the Context of Prayer and
  Salvation, 1 Tim 2:1–7 118
  3.3.3 Christ as Benefactor, Patron and Mediator 134
 3.4 Humans as Benefactors and Patrons 146
  3.4.1 Paul, Timothy, Titus and the Church 146
  3.4.2 Benefaction and Patronage between Various
  Individuals and Groups 153
  3.4.3 Benefaction and Patronage between Church
  Officers and the Other People 156
  3.4.4 Qualifications of the Church Officers
  (1 Tim 3:1–13; Titus 1:5–9) 160
  3.4.5 Benefaction for Widows by the Church
  (1 Tim 5:3–16) 211
  3.4.6 Remuneration for Church Officers (1 Tim 5:17–18) 217
  3.4.7 Masters and Slaves (1 Tim 6:1–2; Titus 2:9–10) 221
  3.4.8 The Rich and the Needy (1 Tim 6:17–19) 227
 3.5 Conclusion 237

Chapter 4 243
Influences of African Benefaction and Patronage on Africa Inland Church Leadership
 4.1 Introduction 243
 4.2 Faith and Moral Character of Church Leaders 245

4.3 Management Skill 256
　　4.4 Economic Status 261
　　4.5 Conclusion 275

Chapter 5 279
　Summary and Conclusions
　　5.1 Summary 279
　　5.2 Conclusions 280
　　5.3 Recommendations 286
　　　　5.3.1 Benefaction...286
　　　　5.3.2 Patronage..286
　　　　5.3.3. Appointment of Leaders 287

Appendix A 289
　Questionnaires

Appendix B 293
　Interviewees for Chapter 4

Bibliography.. 297
　　Primary Sources 297
　　Secondary Sources...300

List of Tables

Table 1. Differences between εὐεργεσία and *Patronicium*...................................75

Table 2. Customized Outline of the Pastoral Epistles......................................108

Table 3. Qualifications of Church Officers versus Qualifications of Leaders, Benefactors and Patrons in the Graeco-Roman Societies...........164

Acknowledgements

My utmost gratitude is to God for enabling me to do this study. Heartfelt thanks to Dr Margaret G. Sim, Professor I. Howard Marshall and Professor Samuel M. Ngewa for your faithful supervision with godly patience and encouragement in my writing. Sincere thanks to the Fraser-Peckham Trust through Jeremy and Jan; to Lamb Foundation through Martha Johnston; to Wayfarers Ministries Inc. through Betty Wagner; to Overseas Council International; to Professor Chester and Dolores Wood; to Christian Leaders for Africa; to all family members; and to friends, for your sacrificial financial benefaction to us. Gratitude to my wife and our children; to the pioneer PhD cohort of Africa International University (AIU), its faculty and support staff; to the second PhD cohort, and all other doctoral studies cohorts, and their teaching and support staff; to all AIU faculty members, administration and staff; to all other AIU academic cohorts and friends, for your prayers, patience, sacrifice, positive challenge and constant encouragement throughout my writing.

Abstract

This work is a development from my PhD dissertation titled "Benefaction and Patronage in the Pastoral Epistles: Influences on the Author." It is a historical analysis of the epistles in the social context of benefaction and patronage in the first century AD. The core proposition is that, *as Paul formulated and promulgated the instructions for guidance and administration of the Pastoral Epistles (PE) churches, he either deliberately or subconsciously utilized the ideologies of Greek benefaction (εὐεργεσία), Roman patronage (patronicium) and Jewish kinship benefaction systems.* That fact is portrayed in his employment of principles and expressions that were common in those systems. Some previous studies have focused on what the scholars view as PE author's biased support for the "corrupted systems." In this study however, the discussion is on how Paul interacted prudently with both the positive and negative principles of material and nonmaterial benefaction and patronage. Prime among other arguments is that, Paul encouraged PE churches to function as good benefaction and patronage associations. His portrayal of God as "the only God and saviour of all people" and Christ as "the only mediator between God and humans" had patronal nuances. Likewise, from a patronal perspective, as the false teachers had abandoned sound doctrine and were destroying the faith and conduct of believers, they were rejecting and causing others also to reject dependence on God and loyalty to him as "the Chief Patron," and denying loyalty to Paul as a "secondary patron." In PE churches also, there apparently was laxity in giving benefaction, and in reciprocation for it. Hence, together with confronting heresy and exhorting believers to adhere to sound faith, Paul exposed and confronted malpractice in the benefaction systems, and, instead, encouraged participation in the positive aspects of the systems.

This study also assesses how the positive and negative principles of ancient and modern African benefaction and patronage have influenced the Africa Inland Church (AIC), especially its leadership philosophy. AIC acknowledges PE as the basis for its administrative philosophy. The study about Paul's interaction with the positive and negative aspects of the first century benefaction and patronage systems enables the African biblical scholarship and church fraternities to read and apply PE instructions with better understanding of the relationship between patronage and church leadership.

Abbreviations

1 Apol.	Justin Martyr, *First Apology*
2 Apol.	Justin Martyr, *Second Apology*
ACC	Area Church Council
AIC	Africa Inland Church
AIM	Africa Inland Mission
AIU	Africa International University
ALGNT	Mounce, *The Analytical Lexicon to the Greek New Testament*
Alleg. Leg.	Philo, *De Allegoriis Legum (The Allegories of the Legislative)*
Ant	Josephus, *Antiquities of the Jews*
ATR	*Anglican Theological Review*
BD	Blass, F., and Debrunner, A., *A Greek English Grammar of the New Testament* (trans. by R. W. Funk), Chicago/Cambridge, 1961 (Same as BDF below.)
BDAG	Walter Bauer, F. W. Danker, W. F. Arndt, and F. W. Gingrich. *A Greek-English Lexicon of the New Testament and Other Early Christian Literature*
BDF	F. Blass, A. Debrunner, and R. W. Funk, *A Greek Grammar of the New Testament*
CCC	Central Church Council (of AIC)
CIL	*Corpus Inscriptionum Latinarum* (Berlin, 1863–)
D-C	Dibelius and Conzelmann, *The Pastoral Epistles: A Commentary on the Pastoral Epistles*
DCC	District Church Council (of AIC)
De Ben	Seneca, *De Beneficiis (Seneca III: Moral Essays III [On Benefits])*
De Cor	Demosthenes, *De Corona (On the Crown)*

De Off	Cicero, *De Officiis* (*On Duties*)
De Plant	Philo, *De Plantatione* (*On Noah's Work as a Planter*)
De Vit Mos	Philo, *De Vita Mosis* (*On the Life of Moses*)
Det Pot Ins	Philo, *Quod Deterius Potiori Insidiari Soleat* (*That the Worse Is Wont to Attack the Better*)
Ep Ar	*The Epistle of Aristeas*
G-R	Graeco-Roman
I.Eph.	*Die Inschriften von Ephesos* I–VIII
ILS	*Inscriptiones Latinae Selectae*, ed. H. Dessau (Berlin, 1892–1916)
IPE	*Inscriptiones Antiquae Orae Septentrionalis Ponti Euxini Graecae et Latinae*
LSJ	*The Liddell, Scott and Jones Greek-English Lexicon*
NEGST	Nairobi Evangelical Graduate School of Theology, Nairobi, Kenya
Nic Eth	Aristotle's *Nicomachean Ethics*
NIDNTT	*New International Dictionary of New Testament Theology*
NTS	*New Testament Studies*
PE	Pastoral Epistles
PMich V	*Michigan Papyri V*
P Oxy	*Oxyrhynchus Papyri*
Pol	Plutarch, *Precepts for Politicians*
Praem Poen	Philo, "De Præmiis et Pœnis" (*The Rewards and Punishments*)
RCC	Regional Church Council (of AIC)
Rer Div Her	Philo, *Quis Rerum Divinarum Heres* (*Who Is the Heir of Divine Things*)
Rhet	Aristotle, *The Art of Rhetoric*
SEG	*Supplementum Epigrephicum Graecum*, ed. J. J. E. Hondius. (Leiden, 1923–)
TDNT	*Theological Dictionary of the New Testament*
TLNT	*Theological Lexicon of the New Testament*
War	Josephus, *The Jewish War*
WUNT	*Wissenschaftliche Untersuchungen zum Neuen Testament*

CHAPTER 1

General Introduction and Modern Scholarship on Benefaction and Patronage

1.1 General Introduction

A close survey of the material written on the Pastoral Epistles reveals that although there have been good studies on the Epistles in the perspective of benefaction, before this study there still remained a need to re-examine significant sections in them in view of εὐεργεσία (benefaction), *patronicium* (patronage) and "kinship benefaction" as distinct systems, the features of which are reflected therein. It is also apparent that most of the previous studies on PE favour "benefaction" (Greek εὐεργεσία, or Graeco-Roman[1] benefaction in general) and greatly overlook (or are outrightly against) Roman *patronicium*. Additionally, not much study has been done on Jewish "kinship benefaction." Conspicuously also, the studies have highlighted material forms of benefaction and generally neglected the nonmaterial forms, such as the role that the positive principles of nonmaterial benefaction played in the mission and administration of PE churches. Hence, in this book, the benefaction and patronage systems are studied with a special interest on how their operations were related to leadership, especially church leadership.

Likewise, in my reading on the subject so far, I have never come across any study that juxtaposes the influences of the ideologies of the first-century

---

1. Hereafter referred to as G-R.

benefaction and patronage systems on Paul[2] and PE churches with the influences of the principles of the ancient and modern benefaction and patronage systems of any African community. Hence, I have presented a case study on how the principles of the ancient and modern benefaction and patronage systems of the Akamba[3] community have influenced the leadership system of the Africa Inland Church.[4] Thus, this study fills evident gaps that have been in existence for a long time.

Such long-existent lacunae have resulted in a scenario in which lay people and leaders in AIC – and other African churches that mainly base their leadership philosophy on PE – have been reading and applying PE instructions without knowledge of their historical and social background. They have been doing it unaware of or acknowledging how Paul interacted with the principles and practices of those contemporary systems and how his interactions with them are featured in his expressions in the epistles. Similarly, the occurrence of this oversight has led to a situation in which believers apply PE instructions, such as the qualifications of church leaders, on the African church unaware of how ideologies of African benefaction and patronage, that are comparable to the first-century G-R and Jewish counterparts, relate with the biblical principles. Consequently, it has been difficult to separate the good influences of the African systems from the bad. This has resulted in syncretistic church leadership philosophy and practice. In the chapter on the influences of African benefaction and patronage, this study discusses the twofold hazard facing some Akamba believers, namely, (1) lack of knowledge about Paul's reflection about and interaction with the ideologies of G-R and

---

2. The ongoing debate on the authorship of PE, that is, the author, the recipients, dates, and other related matters and their relevance to this writing is discussed below in this chapter, in section 1.5 titled "Authorship of the Pastoral Epistles." The purpose of PE is discussed later in section 3.2 titled "Benefaction and Patronage in the Pastoral Epistles" in the introduction of chapter 3 in this writing.

3. The Akamba (plural term, singular is Mũkamba) are the fifth largest tribe in Kenya. Kĩkamba is their language. Ũkambanĩ is the general region where the Akamba live. Kĩkamba orthography has two unique vowels, ĩ (capital is Ĩ) and ũ (capital Ũ). Ĩ is pronounced as the i in "hill" and ũ is pronounced as the double o in "look."

4. The Africa Inland Church, hereafter referred to as AIC, is one of the oldest and most dominant evangelical churches in Kenya, Tanzania, eastern Democratic Republic of Congo and South Sudan. It is also found in Uganda, Rwanda and Burundi. It was founded originally among the Akamba of eastern Kenya by missionaries of Africa Inland Mission (AIM) in 1895 and became the most dominant church in Ũkamba. From there it spread into other regions of Kenya and the other East African countries.

Jewish benefaction systems in his writing of the instructions, and (2) unawareness of the influences of African benefaction and patronage principles on church leadership. The discussion in chapter 4 on influences of African benefaction and patronage on AIC leadership provides a new and better way of reading and applying the instructions in PE in the African setting with fuller understanding, identifying and avoiding the bad influences of those systems and adopting the good ones.

Connected to the concerns stated above, this study answers two important and related questions: (1) As reflected in the advice and instructions[5] that he issued in the epistles, how did Paul interact with the ideologies and practices of Greek εὐεργεσία, Roman *patronicium* and Jewish "kinship benefaction" systems in the first century AD? (2) On the African scene, in relation to the insights gained from study of PE text in chapter 3 of this work, how have Christians in AIC been interacting with the ideologies of the ancient and the modern African benefaction and patronage systems? Specifically, how have the ideologies influenced the church's leadership philosophy? First, the study focuses on the socio-historical background of the three systems. Then it studies PE text in view of the systems, focusing on the expressions related to the systems. Finally, based on the insights derived from PE text, the study deals with the influences of the ideologies of African benefaction and patronage on AIC church leadership, especially in the appointment of leaders.

At the time of Paul's writing, benefaction and patronage were social trends that influenced significantly how people interrelated in the socioeconomic spheres of the G-R world. Throughout history, it has been normal, common and inevitable for various social systems to adopt principles and features from each other. Therefore, it was not unusual for the church to incorporate some of the good values from the benefaction systems of that time. As Verner says, the church, as presented by PE author, valued highly the good

---

5. In *The Pastoral Epistles*, ICC (London: T & T Clark, 1999), 12, Howard Marshall prefers the term "mandates" as the most appropriate genre especially for 1 Timothy and Titus because the instructions given in them, especially 1 Timothy, are "almost totally lacking in personal touches." He says that although those letters are addressed to individuals, some of their content indicates that they were "implicitly overheard by the Christian believers associated with the named recipients, presumably the members of the congregations for which they were responsible." Nevertheless, in 2 Timothy, the bulk of content is personal instructions to Timothy.

opinions of the larger society.⁶ The opposite could also be true. It is possible that at some stage, the benefaction and patronage systems also borrowed some characteristics from the church that already had been in existence for some decades before PE were written. Christianity itself borrowed many values from Judaism. However, by the time of writing PE, some principles and practices that were unique features of the Greek and Roman systems were already fairly established. By the time the church became an established organization, the unique features were prominent in those systems which were older than the church itself.

It is therefore logical to conclude that the church borrowed and modified some of its values from those systems. Such values included the practice of exchanging material and nonmaterial resources and services observing some protocols that had become unique to benefaction and patronage. For example, there were relational principles to observe between people of various social classes (*ōrdinēs*) especially in patronage. There were particular expressions for use in the social, economic, political and religious transactions of the systems. There were also specific categories of resources to be exchanged, rules to be adhered to in the selection of beneficiaries and clients, and specific reciprocation methods. Another reality that had unique connotations especially in the patronage system, although it was also found in other systems, was the feature of mediation. Those values were also found in other social systems in which interpersonal exchange of resources was practised. Nevertheless, in the benefaction and patronage systems of the first century AD, they had special connotations and usage.

This study of the epistles in view of the benefaction and patronage systems joins other approaches that scholars have accepted as appropriate for study of the same epistles. The benefaction systems were working in conjunction with other coexistent social systems, especially the G-R household and Jewish kinship systems. Paul's terminologies in the epistles reflect amicable

---

6. David C. Verner, *The Household of God: The Social World of the Pastoral Epistles*, SBL Dissertation Series 71 (Chico, CA: Society of Biblical Literature, 1983), 182. Nevertheless, similar to Dibelius, Verner turns around against PE church's esteem of the good values of the current systems. He views that act of the church as an indication of having turned against the first-generation early church's strong eschatological stand against the systems of this world. His conclusion was that the second-generation church had developed unhealthy support for leadership by the bourgeois class against the lower classes (of women, slaves, young men and children).

interconnection with the good features of those systems. As Judge observes, the church of the first century consisted primarily of households that were composed of the household head (who belonged to the "owner" and "patron" class), blood relatives, slaves and other dependents.[7] My argument is that, as household features were prominent in the church system, so also were features of benefaction and patronage. Therefore, this treatise about the benefaction and patronage systems provides another approach that is harmonious and coactive with the household and kinship systems in the study of PE, leading to fuller understanding of the epistles. My view about them rhymes with deSilva's observation, "Even its [NT's] use of family imagery connects with the image of the patron who brings a host of clients into the household, although now with the special status of daughters and sons."[8]

Verner's divergent view is that PE author presents the image of the household not only for descriptive purposes but more so for prescriptive purposes, that the church should conform to the hierarchical structure of the elite circles.[9] However, my argument is that as Paul utilizes principles of benefaction and patronage he does not suggest that the church should conform to them without sifting off what is bad and retaining what is good. He certainly utilized their good principles but also confronted, corrected and discarded the bad ones. Evaluation of this argument is the core task of this book, especially in chapter 3, on study of PE text.

1.2 Intended Contribution to Biblical Scholarship

In this book, the reader will gain more insights on sections of PE that have not been previously studied in much detail distinctly in the G-R and Jewish benefaction contexts. The reader will understand better the sections in which explicit and implicit terms and concepts that were common in those systems are used. As said above, before this study, scholars have covered sections that are mainly on material benefaction. Others, such as Zeba Crook and Reggie

---

7. E. A. Judge, *The Social Pattern of Christian Groups in the First Century: Some Prolegomena to the Study of New Testament Ideas of Social Obligation* (London: Tyndale, 1960), 75. This observation of Judge is also supported by Verner, Kidd, deSilva, and others.

8. D. A. deSilva, "Patronage," in *Dictionary of New Testament Background*, eds. Craig A. Evans and Stanley E. Porter (Downers Grove: InterVarsity, 2000), 769.

9. Verner, *Household of God*, 182.

Kidd,[10] have done commendable study but they have not highlighted the differences between the principles of benefaction and those of patronage as reflected in PE. Still, as stated above also, scholars who have distinguished between the systems in the NT, seem to favour εὐεργεσία above *patronicium*. For that reason, without neglecting or opposing what has been covered already, this study discusses Paul's interaction with both the positive and the negative aspects of material and nonmaterial benefaction and patronage, especially focusing on the positive aspects.

This book is intended to be a source of reference in Christian institutions of various levels of learning throughout the English-speaking world wherever there is interest in the study of PE, starting with Africa. It is also purposed to be a guide in churches in practical Christian life and church administration. The chapter on the influences of Akamba benefaction and patronage ideologies on AIC leadership will particularly help believers to be aware and assess carefully the relationship between biblical church leadership and African benefaction and patronage values. This will help them to decide intelligently which ideologies to adopt from those system and what to reject for general life and church administration.

1.3 Delimitations

There also were other social institutions which were closely related to the systems of εὐεργεσία, *patronicium* and kinship benefaction at the time the NT was written. Some of those were the φιλία (friendship) and the household systems. However, this study centres only on features of εὐεργεσία, *patronicium* and "kinship benefaction" which this writer considers applicable in the study of PE. The other systems are therefore discussed only whenever absolutely necessary. Second, although my study covers both material and

---

10. In *Reconceptualising Conversion: Patronage, Loyalty, and Conversion in the Religions of the Ancient Mediterranean* (Berlin: de Gruyter, 2004), Crook's opinion is that although patronage and benefaction are not perfectly synonymous they are very closely-related practices and therefore their terminologies can be used interchangeably without much obscurity encountered. Thus in his book he uses them interchangeably, unlike Stephan Joubert and Alicia Batten who highlight the differences more clearly. In *Wealth and Beneficence in the Pastoral Epistles*, SBL Dissertation Series 122 (Atlanta, GA: SBL), although Reggie Kidd exhibits commendable knowledge about the difference between the two systems, he does not outline them clearly in his writing. Crook's and Kidd's works are further reviewed later in this chapter under "Modern Scholarship on Benefaction and Patronage."

nonmaterial benefaction and patronage in PE, my focus is on nonmaterial benefaction and the positive features of both εὐεργεσία and *patronicium*, especially as they relate to church leadership. Another area where delimitation is applied is that, although some scholars, including myself, agree that Titus is historically older than 1 and 2 Timothy, throughout this book, whenever such order is applicable, scripture references from 1 and 2 Timothy are listed before those from Titus. The order of the epistles as listed in the Nestle-Aland *Novum Testamentum Graece* 27 (NA27) is retained. Similarly, on African benefaction and patronage, I limit myself specifically to the influences of the ideologies of the Akamba systems on AIC leadership only. I focus on those communities because I am a member of both and because AIC which is predominant in Ũkamba confesses dependence on PE as reference for guidance, especially in the appointment of leaders.

1.4 Methodology

To write this book, I have used the three closely-related systems of first-century Greek benefaction, Roman patronage, and Jewish kinship benefaction as necessary context for the study of PE. The interpretive method that I have used is social scientific historical criticism.[11] *Encyclopaedia Britannica* describes historical criticism in conjunction with social context as,

> . . . literary criticism in the light of historical evidence or based on the context in which a work was written, including facts about the author's life and the historical and social circumstances of the time. This is in contrast to other types of criticism, such as textual and formal, in which emphasis is placed on examining the text itself while outside influences on the text are disregarded.[12]

Εὐεργεσία and *patronicium* are contextual themes that are usually used in the study of the social relationships of mutual interdependence between

---

11. The use of the patronage theme as background for interpretation of the NT is highly recommended by the Context Group. You will get a detailed explanation of the theme in David deSilva's book, *Honor, Patronage, Kinship and Purity: Unlocking New Testament Culture* (Downers Grove: InterVarsity Press, 2000), 95–119.

12. *Encyclopedia Britanica*, s.v. "Historical Criticism," accessed 29 September 2018, https://www.britannica.com/art/historical-criticism-literary-criticism.

people in various spheres of social life, such as in religious, political and economic associations. In the first century AD, they were systems of interpersonal relationship in which there was reciprocal exchange of various goods and services between individuals or specific groups of people of varying social status. In benefaction and patronage, the relationship was usually between superiors and inferiors. However, asymmetrism was more pronounced in patronage. In those systems, one party, the benefactor or the patron, met the needs of the beneficiary or the client in a specified manner. Similarly, the recipient responded to the provider in a specified manner. The entire transaction was supposed to be carried out in an atmosphere of willingness, mutual understanding, grace (χάρις), and trust (πίστις or *fides*).

With a sincere and favourable attitude (χάρις, grace), the provider gave the material or nonmaterial gift or favour (χάρις, grace) and the beneficiary responded in turn with gratitude (χάρις, grace). Thus, grace dominated the entire transaction. The beneficiary was expected to express gratitude in various specific ways, such as by verbal and non-verbal expression of honour, praise, and through other services to the benefactor or patron. Crook says that patronage and benefaction worked in harmony with the values of honour and shame in that, without the importance attached to achieving honour within one's lifetime, patronage and benefaction would not have existed in the form or to the extent that it did. He cites a scenario that was highlighted by Dio Chrysostom (in *1 Glor.* 2; *De lege* 7) where benefaction was so much connected with honour that people could spend all their wealth or sell all their belongings with the singular aim of gaining honour through grand benefactions.[13] Another element that was present specifically in *patronicium* is that sometimes there was involvement of a third party broker, that is, a mediator who facilitated the transaction between the primary parties.

In the flow of argument in this book, chapter 1 is the general introduction, including modern scholarship on Greek, Roman and Jewish benefaction and patronage in the NT, especially what is specifically related to PE. Then, based especially on ancient sources, chapter 2 deals with the sociohistorical background of the three benefaction systems that are focused on. Chapter 3 is exegesis of significant sections of PE that I assess as having some

---

13. Crook, *Reconceptualising Conversion*, 68.

content related to those systems. After that, based on chapter 3, the discussion in chapter 4 is on the influences of African benefaction and patronage on AIC leadership philosophy and practice. The final chapter, 5, is the grand conclusion of the subject.

Library research is mainly the basic resource for the discussion in chapters 1 to 3. The Greek texts on which the study is based on are NA27, as main text, and UBS fourth edition, as supplementary. The English translation used is the New Revised Standard Version (NRSV), and my own translation of the Greek NT. For chapter 4 on African benefaction and patronage, the study is based on field research and literature on African culture, especially of the Akamba. My own knowledge and experience as a member of the Akamba community, as a member of AIC, and as a trained translator of the Bible into the Kikamba language are also put into use. Qualitative data was gathered through field research by means of two questionnaires. The people who were interviewed consisted of active and retired church leaders and lay church members, active and retired civic leaders, and political leaders, mainly from the Akamba community.

1.5 Authorship of the Pastoral Epistles

Scholars hold divergent views on the authorship of PE, such as who the actual author is, who the recipients were, and the dating of the epistles.[14] Concerning the author and the date, some scholars argue that a pseudonymous author wrote the epistles to fictional addressees at the end of the first century or at the beginning of the second century.[15] They say that the epistles

---

14. Paul's authorship of seven of the thirteen epistles that explicitly introduce themselves as having been written by Paul is not disputed at all. The seven letters that are not disputed are: Romans, 1 and 2 Corinthians, Galatians, Philippians, 1 Thessalonians and Philemon. However, for various reasons, his authorship of Ephesians, Colossians and 2 Thessalonians is moderately disputed. The three that are strongly disputed are 1 Timothy, 2 Timothy and Titus.

15. Gerald F. Hawthorn, Ralph P. Martin, and Daniel G. Reid, eds., *Dictionary of Paul and His Letters: A Compendium of Contemporary Biblical Scholarship* (Downers Grove, IL: InterVarsity Press, 1993), 659. Hawthorn, Martin and Reid present F. C. Baur (*Die sogenannten Pastoralbriefe*, of 1835), and others whom they call "The Baur School" (such as Donelson, Goodspeed, Gealy and von Campenhausen) as arguing that PE are post-Pauline second-century forgeries. H. J. Holtzmann summed their objections to Pauline authorship as based on: (1) the historical situation, (2) the Gnosticizing false teachers condemned, (3) the stage of church organization, (4) the vocabulary and style, and (5) the theological

were written by more than one author generally to church leaders rather than to the actual historical Timothy and Titus. Another argument that they propose is that the letters are an attempt to be true Pauline letters. In this group, some, such as Dibelius and Conzelmann, argue that PE contain only fragments of genuine letters of Paul put together by a pseudonymous author.[16] Others of the same persuasion are K. A. Credner, P. N. Harrison and B. S. Easton. I. H. Marshall's opinion is that, although the author based his theology on Paul, he was "his own man and not a mere repeater of Paul's ideas."[17] Towner says that it is impossible to know whether the epistles are genuinely Pauline or pseudonymous. Nevertheless, throughout his most recent commentary on PE he refers to the author as Paul.[18] Those who argue strongly for Pauline authorship say that he wrote them in mid first century AD.[19]

Key among the arguments that scholars raise against Pauline authorship are that there are major differences in the literary style between PE and the

---

views and themes. Others who have argued strongly against Pauline authorship include Helmut Koester, A. Malherbe, Howard C. Kee, Rudolf Bultmann, B. S. Easton, G. Lohfink, E. F. Scott, P. N. Harrison, M. Dibelius, H. Conzelmann, R.W. Wall, A. T. Hanson, D. G. Meade, and D. Horrell.

16. Martin Dibelius and Hans Conzelmann, *The Pastoral Epistles: A Commentary on the Pastoral Epistles*, Hermeneia: A Critical and Historical Commentary on the Bible (Philadelphia: Fortress, 1972), 4.

17. Marshall, *Pastoral Epistles*, 57–108.

18. See Philip H. Towner, *The Letters to Timothy and Titus,* NICNT (Grand Rapids, MI; Cambridge, UK: Eerdmans, 2006), from page 94 onwards.

19. Hawthorn, *Dictionary of Paul*, 659. Hawthorn, Martin and Reid cite J. B. Lightfoot and T. Zahn as countering F. C. Baur and others who disputed Pauline authorship and an early date for PE. They said that, (1) the changed historical situation and (2) the more advanced church organization of PE were accounted for if some years separated Paul's earlier letters from the time of writing PE, that is, after release from his first Roman imprisonment, which is attested in *1 Clement* (of about AD 95). (3) About the Gnosticizing false teachers, Lightfoot and Zahn argue that they were already present during the ministry of Paul. (4) On changes of vocabulary, style, and (5) theological emphasis, they attribute them to normal change in the last years of Paul's ministry. In addition to Lightfoot and Zahn, those who support Pauline authorship include W. M. Ramsay, W. Michaelis, J. A. T. Robinson, D. Guthrie, F. Danker, B. Malina, G. Fee, J. N. D. Kelly, R. Kidd, S. E. Porter, L. T. Johnson, G. W. Knight and W. D. Mounce. See also Brandon Carter, "The Authorship of the Pastoral Epistles," (A Senior Honours Thesis in partial fulfillment of the requirements for graduation from the Honours Program of Liberty University, Liberty University, 2007). More details are provided in my discussion in this section on "Authorship of the Pastoral Epistles." See also William D. Mounce, *Pastoral Epistles*, WBC 46 (Nashville, TN: Nelson Reference & Electronic, 2000), cxviii–cxxix, for more details on authorship.

undisputed Pauline epistles. They say that the *vocabulary of PE is very different* from that of the undisputed Paulines;[20] that the language and the style of PE are different from Paul's. For example, Harrison says,

> In addition to the number of *Hapax Legomena* [such as Θεοσέβεια in 1 Tim 2:10] and other non-Pauline words shared between two or more of the Pastorals . . . they are connected by a series of characteristic phrases which seem collectively to favour strongly the impression that, in their present form at any rate, they are the work of one mind, and that mind, another than Paul's.[21]

Harrison also says that the syntax of PE is different from the Paulines. For example, from the 214 particles that occur in the ten accepted Paulines,[22] 112 are nowhere in PE.[23] Those who argue against Pauline authorship also say that the PE are not included in the earliest codex of Pauline writings that stops at 1 Thessalonians 5:5. They also argue that Marcion did not include PE in his canon, the epistles are not in the Chester Beatty Papyri (P 46), and that in the Muratorian Canon of the second century AD they are included only as an appendix to the Pauline corpus.[24]

Another issue that they raise is that the *church structure* that is reflected and promoted in PE indicates that the epistles were written much later after Paul's time. Those who oppose Pauline authorship based on the difference of church structure say that the level of institutionalization of church life in PE is more advanced,[25] and therefore it is non-Pauline. Another point

---

20. See also Barry D. Smith, "Paul's Pastoral Letters," *First Timothy*, accessed 28 February 2011, http://www.abu.nb.ca/courses/ntintro/1Tim.htm. See also Percy Neale Harrison, *The Problem of the Pastoral Epistles* (London: Oxford University Press, 1921).

21. Harrison, *Problem of the Pastoral Epistles*, 17. See further discussion on Θεοσέβεια in chapter 3 of this book under sub-section 3.5 titled "Benefaction and Patronage in the Pastoral Epistles."

22. Note that some scholars also dispute Pauline authorship of some of the ten accepted letters, such as, Ephesians, Philippians and Colossians.

23. Harrison, *Problem of the Pastoral Epistles*, 34–38.

24. See Dibelius and Conzelmann, *Pastoral Epistles*, 1–4.

25. Such as in that there is an apparent structured system of bishops (elders), deacons, women deacons, and widows with an order of qualifications, duties and remunerations (unlike in the earlier Paulines), as listed in 1 Tim 3:1–13; 5:3–16, 17–22 and Titus 1:5–9. For more details on this, see Philip H. Towner, *Letters to Timothy*, 16, and Dibelius and Conzelmann, *Pastoral Epistles*, 4.

of opposition is based on the particular false teachings that the author was refuting in PE, that the *false teachings and practices that are addressed in PE* were those of the second-century Gnosticism. Yet another argument against Pauline authorship is the theological content of the epistles. It says that *the theology of PE is very different* from that of Paul. For example, the disputants say that the theological expressions in PE are more formulaic and more creative than Pauline expressions.

In response to the opponents, scholars who support Pauline authorship give several reasons for the differences in language, ecclesiastical, ethical, and theological content of PE. For example, on dating, because it is not easy to reconcile the evidence that is in PE with what is in Acts, most scholars rely on Eusebius's *Ecclesiastical History* of c. AD 325 and date the writing of Titus and 1 Timothy after Paul's release from his first imprisonment. Titus is viewed as having been written earlier than 1 Timothy, as implied by the fact that, there were probably no mature Christians in the Cretan church when the instructions on appointment of its church leaders were given. They date the writing of 2 Timothy during Paul's second imprisonment in Rome. Robinson has a different order of the dates, and places 1 Timothy before Titus. He dates 1 Timothy in early 56, Titus in late spring 57 and 2 Timothy in autumn 58, during Paul's imprisonment in Caesarea.[26] These scholars have no accord on the dates, but they agree that the PE are Pauline.

On *linguistic evidence*, their view is that the *difference in vocabulary* does not necessarily point to non-Pauline authorship but rather proves how much remains unknown about the conditions in which all the Paulines (the undisputed and the disputed epistles) came into being. The response to the argument on the numerous hapaxes in PE is that Paul could have used a different amanuensis to write the three Pastorals. Concerning the argument that the *church structure in PE is different* from and later than Paul's time, the answer is that such church structure as is in PE was there even before Paul's time.[27] In answer to the argument that the *false teachings* that are addressed in PE were second-century Gnosticism, they admit that

---

26. John A. T. Robinson, *Redating the New Testament* (London: SCM, 1976), 61, 352.

27. Such an order in the early church is seen in Acts 6 and 15 on the institution of the seven deacons and the settlement of the Gentile conversion dispute by the Jerusalem Council that was composed of Apostles and elders.

there are indications of proto-Gnosticism in PE, although it was not the highly-developed Gnosticism of the second century. On the contention that *the theology of PE is very different* from the Paulines, the response is that this occurrence is not beyond the ordinary. For example, Childs says that even among the undisputed letters there are differences in theological content, and that even in PE there are elements of genuine continuity with the undisputed epistles.[28]

From the summarized arguments above, much evidence has been proposed against Pauline authorship. Similarly there is much evidence in support of Pauline authorship. Nevertheless, as Kidd observes, "there is more that unites the Pastorals and Paul than there is that divides them."[29] My conclusion on the authorship is that, if the author was other than Paul but claimed to be him, that in itself would have been malicious pseudonymity that would have destroyed the credibility of PE and made the epistles unacceptable to the early church. Wall also observes,

> Since the canonical approach to differences between the Pastorals and the undisputed Pauline letters is not adversarial but complementary, I ask what are the implications when considering the Pauline corpus as a whole? The answer is that the teaching of Paul, preserved and collected in his canonical letters, must continue to be treasured from generation to generation ("from faith unto faith") as the normative witness to God whose salvation is present for us in Christ Jesus and by his Spirit . . . The church's recognition of the Pastoral Epistles as apostolic and divinely inspired – and thus canonical – is the result of their actual performance in forming an infallible understanding of God within faithful readers.[30]

The fact that the early church accepted PE as apostolic and divinely inspired assures us that they accepted that they were certainly written by Paul

---

28. Brevard S. Childs, *The New Testament as Canon: An Introduction* (London: SCM, 1985), 387.

29. Kidd, *Wealth and Beneficence*, 195.

30. R. W. Wall, "Pauline Authorship and the Pastoral Epistles: A Response to S. E. Porter," review of *Pauline Authorship and the Pastoral Epistles: Implications for Canon*, by Stanley E. Porter, *Bulletin for Biblical Research* 5 (1995): 128.

as each of them openly indicates from the beginning. This leaves us with no other option than to accept them as genuinely Pauline and therefore trustworthy. There is evident continuity between the undisputed Paulines and PE. The expressions in PE that have something to do with benefaction and patronage also find continuity and support in the unquestioned epistles. The elements of benefaction and patronage featured in the undisputed Paulines are not in conflict with similar elements in PE but are complementary. That fact is attested and elucidated by the relevant cross references from those epistles in this writing. From the very beginning to the end of PE, Pauline tradition is upheld. Therefore, being fully aware of the on-going debate on the authorship of the epistles, throughout this book, based on the weightier evidence in support of Pauline authorship, I acknowledge and refer to the author as Paul.

On the question of the real addressees of the letters, just as Paul does, and mainly based on the internal and external evidence in support of them being the real historical Timothy and Titus, throughout this writing I also acknowledge and refer to them as Timothy and Titus. Concerning dating, as discussed earlier in this section on authorship, mid-first century AD is the most viable time of writing the three letters. Titus and 1 Timothy were written after Paul's release from his first imprisonment, and 2 Timothy was written during his second and last imprisonment, being the last epistle of Paul before his execution by Emperor Nero in AD 67.

Important studies that have been done on PE on the subject of benefaction include "Providentia for the Widows,"[31] "Can Slaves Be Their Masters' Benefactors?"[32] and *Wealth and Beneficence in the Pastoral Epistles*.[33] My current study introduces an African voice to this discussion and thus enriches it more. Highlighting aspects of the three systems as distinctly as possible, this study covers miscellaneous sections of the epistles that contain explicit and implicit content that can be viewed confidently as containing material associated with those systems. Some of those sections have not been studied at all with the principles of the systems as crucial historical and social background.

---

31. Bruce W. Winter, "Providentia for the Widows," *Tyndale Bulletin* 39 (1988): 83–99.

32. Philip H. Towner, "Can Slaves Be Their Masters' Benefactors?," *Current Trends in Scripture Translation* 182/183 (1997): 39–52.

33. Kidd, *Wealth and Beneficence*.

Without any bias, the study highlights how Paul interacted concurrently with the good and the corrupted features of the systems. In connection with that, in *De Beneficiis*, Seneca showed that there were material and nonmaterial forms of exchange operating simultaneously in the benefaction systems of the G-R world of the first century. Similarly, in his article, "God, Benefactor and Patron: The Major Cultural Model for Interpreting the Deity in Greco-Roman Antiquity," Neyrey says that the common media of exchange were power, knowledge and material benefaction,[34] implying that in the G-R systems there was material and nonmaterial benefaction. However, most scholars of PE have focused on material benefaction and barely explored the nonmaterial forms. And, even with that, some of the views on material benefaction and patronage are outrightly, and unfairly, negative. For this reason, alongside material benefaction, this writing highlights nonmaterial benefaction and patronage, especially their positive aspects.

1.6 Modern Scholarship on Benefaction and Patronage

In this section are summaries and reviews of some key works on benefaction and patronage in the Mediterranean world around the first century AD. Those whose interest is to study the New Testament in general in the social sciences perspective will learn much from the insights of members of the Context Group, such as Bruce Malina, Jerome Neyrey, Stephan Joubert and Alicia Batten, to name few. Some of their works are reviewed below. Fredrick Danker's *Benefactor*,[35] and John Barclay's *Jews in the Mediterranean*

---

34. Jerome H. Neyrey, "God, Benefactor and Patron: The Major Cultural Model for Interpreting the Deity in Greco-Roman Antiquity," *Journal for the Study of the New Testament* 27, no. 4 (2005): 465. See also Talcott Parsons, *Politics and Social Structure* (New York: Free Press, 1969) who says that the media of exchange were power (236–262), commitment (439–472), material goods, and influence (405–429). Similarly, Shmuel Noah Eisenstadt and Luis Roniger, *Patrons, Clients, and Friends: Interpersonal Relations and the Structure of Trust in Society* (Cambridge: Cambridge University Press, 1984), 43–64 say that, in the benefaction systems, the various types of resources that were simultaneously exchanged were above all instrumental, economic and political.

35. Frederick W. Danker, *Benefactor: Epigraphic Study of a Graeco-Roman and NT Semantic Field* (St. Louis: Clayton, 1982).

Diaspora[36] are also reviewed. In a way, Barclay supplements and expands Danker's work especially on Jewish benefaction from the Intertestamental Period to early second century AD. DeSilva's *Honor, Patronage, Kinship and Purity*[37] is equally helpful. It builds largely on the world-view of specific social systems, including benefaction and patronage around the first century AD. As with Barclay's book, deSilva can be viewed as complementing Danker; Danker focuses on inscriptions whereas both Barclay and deSilva deal mainly with other literary evidence.

Similarly, the 1989 book by Wallace-Hadrill,[38] is helpful. In it, various scholars give insights on a variety of aspects of the Roman patronage system from classical Greece times to late Antiquity in the Mediterranean world. Stephan Joubert's article[39] also provides us with valuable insights especially on the similarities and differences of the two systems. Before looking at literature specifically on PE, it is helpful in this section also to examine the treatise by Zeba Crook in which he discusses Paul's transformation in view of patronage, loyalty, and conversion in the religions of the ancient Mediterranean world.[40] Last in my reviews of modern literature are two works specifically on PE. First we discuss Winter's article on benefaction to widows, which is based on 1 Timothy 5:3–16.[41] The discussion is closed with a review of Reggie Kidd's dissertation, *Wealth and Beneficence in the Pastoral Epistles*.

The second main discussion on modern literature is a brief assessment of some commentaries on PE. Some of the latest commentaries have shown interest in exegeting sections of PE in view of the benefaction and patronage institutions. Those commentaries are reviewed very briefly in this chapter but are consulted extensively and their views commented on in detail in chapter 3, on exegesis of the PE text. Detailed review of the ancient sources is done at the beginning of chapter 2.

---

36. John M. G. Barclay, *Jews in the Mediterranean Diaspora: From Alexander to Trajan (323 BCE–117 CE)* (Edinburgh: T & T Clark, 1996).

37. deSilva, *Honor*.

38. Andrew Wallace-Hadrill, ed., *Patronage in Ancient Society* (London: Routledge, 1989).

39. Stephan J. Joubert, "One Form of Social Exchange or Two? 'Euergetism,' Patronage, and Testament Studies," *Biblical Theology Bulletin* 31, no. 1 (Spring 2001): 17–25.

40. Crook, *Reconceptualising Conversion*.

41. Winter, "Providentia."

1.6.1 Frederick W. Danker: *Benefactor*

Danker provides to us an excellent collection of fifty-three original texts and honorary inscriptions that contain terms that were common in the benefaction networks in the Mediterranean regions in and around the first century AD. Several inscriptions contain evidence of the existence and operations of the system in the Greek, Roman and Jewish contexts. Most of those inscriptions were made as memorial of good deeds that benefactors did to individuals and communities. For each one of them, he has given helpful background, a list of the key manuscripts that contain the texts, and even secondary literature. He also has provided his own extensive commentary on each inscription. Most helpful to NT readers, he has devoted a large portion of the book, over two hundred pages, on discussion about the usefulness of the texts in the study of benefaction in the NT.

As he states, the book is important in that it brings to the notice of scholars a subject that was hitherto largely ignored. He offers us the most profound collection of inscriptions on the benefactor phenomenon, inscriptions which were not previously collated and published by any other scholar. In his collection, there are inscriptions in honour of kings, medical doctors, benefactors of voluntary associations, and many other people in general who performed good deeds of benefaction.

Danker has shown the importance and relevance of using the benefaction theme as a necessary context for NT study. He has shown that for some concepts in the NT to be understood well, the reader has to take into account the existence of the benefactor phenomenon. However, he helpfully cautions us to be careful not to fall into the temptation of carrying over too much significance of some of the terms from the prevailing Greek culture into the NT Christian usage of the same terms. Understanding the expressions in their original settings is crucial for our understanding of their usage in the NT.

One of his arguments that I differ with is that the title σωτήρ and other titles and attributes that were given to people in acknowledgement of their good deeds of physical salvation did not have any metaphysical significance in the character of the persons so labelled. My argument is that the behaviour of some benefactors and the treatment that they received implies that they regarded themselves (and their beneficiaries also regarded them) as having divine supernatural attributes, which affirms metaphysical implications. Some emperors and even lower officials were viewed and honoured as deities. The deification and worship of both dead and living emperors, especially due to benefaction to their subjects, began early in the Roman times. A fitting example is that of Herod Agrippa I (AD 37–44) who is on record as having been struck down by God because he did not reject the flattery directed to him that he was superior to mortal nature but accepted to be honoured as God.[42] The metaphysical connection may not be evident or significant in the opinion of many in the modern western world, but it was significant in the ancient Greek, Roman and Jewish worlds of the first century. On the same issue, the Greek understanding of εὐεργέτης, that is, "a doer of good," and ἀνὴρ ἀγαθός, which means, "a good man," had ethical and metaphysical significance in the Greek world because good deeds were significantly viewed as guarantee of a good life after death and benefactors therefore participated in good works to secure their future. Being good and engaging in doing good works of benefaction to ensure for oneself a good afterlife had strong metaphysical connotations. Of course, benefactors also did good works to benefit needy people and to get honour and other services in this life, but the metaphysical motivation was significant.

For the convenience of those interested in studying the NT from the perspective of the benefaction context, Danker has summarized how the concept can be used. Some of the prominent terms in the original texts that he highlights as having been used in reference to benefactors and are found in the NT text are σωτήρ, χαρίς, εὐεργέτης, ἀρετή, ἀνὴρ ἀγαθός, and others. He says that before their usage in the NT, the terms were common in the conventional benefaction transactions. Such terms and expression, especially those that are found in PE, are discussed in chapter 3 of this book. However, Danker did not discuss some of the significant terms which were also related to the benefactor phenomenon in the NT, such as, τιμή (including διπλῆς τιμῆς).

In the book he does not mention the patronage phenomenon which was a close counterpart and was operating contemporaneously with the benefaction phenomenon especially among the Romans. In a converse manner, that

---

42. Flavius Josephus, *Josephus: Complete Works*, trans. William Whiston (Grand Rapids: Kregel, 1978), *Antiquities of the Jews* 19.8.2 (cf., Acts 12:22, 23).

is a strength of his book for his focus is on the Greek benefactor semantic field. However, the book would have been more helpful if it included some Latin inscriptions on patronage as well. Another thing that would have been helpful to the reader is an index of the main Greek and English terms that are used in the book; it would aid the reader to trace them easily. Nevertheless, overall, the original texts that Danker has provided on the benefactor phenomenon equip the scholarship fraternity that has interest on the subject with very important evidence. Judging from the frequency of allusions from the book in works that have been written subsequent to it, it is evident that since its publication it has continued to be a goldmine on various aspects of the benefactor phenomenon.

1.6.2 John M. G. Barclay: *Jews in the Mediterranean Diaspora*

Most modern scholars who have written about ancient benefaction and patronage have concentrated on the Greek and Roman contexts. For example, as seen immediately above, Danker has dealt with the benefactor phenomenon specifically in the Greek context. Although the systems were also operative among the Jews, not many authors have given attention to the Jewish context. Among the few who have done so, along with other information on the social life of the Jews as a minority group struggling to survive in the Diaspora, Barclay gives us important facts on Jewish benefaction and patronage (such as, page 290). For example, he informs us that, just as for Diaspora Jews, Judaism was not uniform throughout the various Mediterranean Jewish communities, so the scope of their involvement in the benefaction and patronage systems in their respective locations was also varied.

One of his core arguments is that Jewish communities in Asia integrated well with the local communities, adapting to their culture while at the same time not losing their Jewishness. Nevertheless, despite their substantial caution as they participated in the cross-cultural socioeconomic activities of the societies around them and retention of their unique Judaistic faith and customs, their culture was inevitably affected by the elements of assimilation, acculturation and accommodation.[43] Hence, it was Hellenized. Barclay's

---

43. Barclay, *Jews in the Mediterranean*, 4, 13.

assertion that Jews in Diaspora adopted and assimilated to the features of the G-R benefaction and patronage that they did not find to be against their Jewish distinctives, and that they abhorred whatever was against their traditions is supported by ancient writings such as *The Letter of Aristeas*, such as in 1:135–138; 4 Macc 8:12, 28; and in Josephus's *Antiquities of the Jews*, 11.6.8.

Although Jews were warned not to participate in practices that were contrary to their religion, it is apparent that some were doing as the nations did, as is implied in Jesus's prohibition in Matthew 23:9 and Luke 22:25–27. He prohibited them from calling anyone πατήρ (father or patron) or being lords over others and from desiring to be called εὐεργέτης (benefactor). Nevertheless, for their own survival, they adhered to the principles of the non-Jewish benefaction and patronage systems that were functioning wherever they were. In their religious teachings, for example Jeremiah 29:7, Jews were required to participate actively in the welfare of the cities where they lived. They did so in various ways, such as when they gave military support to the Romans as they were fighting the Ptolemaic dynasty to gain power in Egypt. That fact is attested in a stele (in Josephus's *Contra Apionem* 2.37, 61) in which Emperor Augustus publicly acknowledged their support for Rome.

Based on Josephus's writing, Barclay also gives several examples of Roman patronal support to the Jews, such as in *Antiquities of the Jews*.[44] He views Josephus's apologetic inclination as overstretching the reality about Roman patronal favour to the Jews. However, although his inclination is viewed and interpreted by some scholars as bending the truth, my view is that in the benefaction and patronage contexts of that time his behaviour was conventional, logical and acceptable. Beneficiaries were required to reciprocate benefaction by honouring and elevating the patron's/benefactor's reputation verbally and in writing, often with flattery. The modern repugnance that is directed against that behaviour is anachronistic for it is using current post-modern views and values to judge an ancient custom. It is therefore misguided and unfairly directed against Josephus for he was acting within the precincts of the prevailing ethos.

Overall, Barclay's account on the participation of the Diaspora Jews in the prevailing benefaction and patronage setups is outstanding. More than

---

44. Barclay, *Jews in the Mediterranean*, 262–277.

others, what he has written on the subject in the Jewish context helps us to understand better the scope of influence of the ideologies and practices of those systems on the Jews. This in turn helps us to understand better the influences of those systems on the early church that was composed of Jews at first (in Jerusalem) and then Jews and Gentiles (such as the churches in Ephesus and Crete). Thus, Barclay's book helps us much in the study of PE and the other NT texts that contain elements of benefaction and patronage.

1.6.3 D. A. deSilva: *Honor, Patronage, Kinship and Purity*

In *Honor, Patronage, Kinship & Purity: Unlocking New Testament Culture*, deSilva discusses four basic aspects of cultural environment that help the modern reader to study and apply the teachings of the NT being aware of their origin in the context of those social systems.[45] His discussion centres on the G-R and Jewish social systems of interpersonal relationship. A very helpful feature of his book is that, similar to Danker before him, he does extensive consultation of primary extra-biblical sources to deduce the meanings of many NT statements. The eight aspects discussed in the book, all of which are in four pairs of two related aspects each, are honour and shame, patronage and reciprocity, kinship and family, and purity and pollution. As stated above, the focus of my writing is on Greek, Roman and Jewish benefaction and patronage. Therefore, my exclusive interest is in what deSilva says on patronage and reciprocity, and, slightly, on honour, as it relates to patronage.

DeSilva bases his arguments mainly on Seneca. He points out that giving and receiving of assistance was not only essential but was expected in the G-R world.[46] He even proposes that Jesus's disciples were operating within the patronage and friendship networks which were common in Palestine, Greece, Asia-Minor, Rome and Africa.[47] Some scholars may interpret this view as reading too much into the NT text, which Danker cautions about. However, deSilva's observation is justifiable. As elaborated in chapter 3 of this writing, my argument is that the gospel records and the epistles contain explicit and implicit expressions which indicate that the benefaction and patronage systems were not strange phenomena during their writing.

---

45. deSilva, *Honor*, 17.
46. deSilva, 96.
47. deSilva, 121.

Some scholars find fault with deSilva's claim that around the first century AD, G-R patronage was widespread and had clearly established codes that governed the system.[48] Westbrook, for example, doubts that patronage was as widespread and well-established in the Mediterranean world in the Middle and Late Roman Republic eras (BC 264–133, BC 123–27 respectively) and in the Early Empire era (27 BC–AD 284).[49] However, in the study of ancient sources on patronage in the first century AD, my inference is that deSilva is right. For example, in the second half of the century, there were clear legal codes that were made for governing Roman municipalities, including stipulations on the appointment of patrons for the cities. Those codes, such as Lex Ursonensis, for the city of Urso in Spain, and Lex Irnitana, for Irni, were inscribed on bronze tablets during the Flavian dynasty (AD 69–96). Their contents support deSilva's argument that the first century patronage had some well-established codes and was fairly widespread.[50] For example, in Lex Irnitana chapters 23 and 97 some rights of a patron over a freedman are clearly listed.[51]

Scholars concur on the view that there was no patronage on mainland Greece during the Greek era. Nevertheless, that does not mean that there was no patronage at all in the empire. DeSilva states that it was practised in Athens. It was only during the Athenian democratic revolution in 462 BC that open patronage was muted as the basic model for structuring society in the city.[52] However, secret patronage continued. Open patronage was revived about 359 BC and it continued during the time of Philip of

---

48. deSilva, 122.

49. Raymond Westbrook, "Patronage in the Ancient Near East," *Journal of the Economic and Social History of the Orient* 48, no. 2 (2005): 200.

50. See Bart D. Ehrman, *The Apostolic Fathers*, Loeb 1 (Cambridge, MA and London: Harvard University Press, 2003), 338–341. See also Julian Gonzalez, and Michael H. Crawford, "The Lex Irnitana: A New Copy of the Flavian Municipal Law," *Journal of Roman Studies* 76 (1986): 147–243 (by the Society for the Promotion of Roman Studies). The laws were established earlier but they were inscribed on bronze tablets in the reign of Emperor Hadrian (AD 117–138). M. H. Crawford also cites material that are in support of deSilva's view in *Roman Statutes I*, BICS Supplement 64 (London: Institute of Classical Studies, University of London, 1996), 427, 431. *Lex Coloniae Genetivae* and *Lex Ursonensis*, jointly called *Colonia Genetiva Iulia Ursonensis*, also were laws governing Roman provinces and colonies of the Roman Empire, including laws for regulating patronage.

51. Gonzalez and Crawford, "Lex Irnitana," 183, 199.

52. deSilva, *Honor*, 102.

Macedonia and his son, Alexander the Great (356–323 BC). DeSilva points out some examples of such open patronage in Athens, such as between citizens and metics (from μέτοικος).[53] A metic was required to have προστάτης (a patron) who helped him to have access to the services of the city for non-citizens.[54] LSJ also says that προστάτης-μέτοικοι arrangements were common in Athens where patrons cared for the interests of the metics. Citing Plutarch, LSJ says that the μέτοικοι were required to choose patrons under whose protection they would live and in whose name they would be registered. Otherwise, if they did not have such patrons, they could not have access to the city's services.

Concerning patronage and mediatorship in the first century AD, deSilva raises a point which is of special interest in this study. Through examples from history, he provides evidence that affirms that both direct patronage and patronage through brokers were common in NT times.[55] For example, he points out that sometimes the most important gift that a patron could give to a client was to provide access for him to a patron who had more power over the benefit that he was seeking. He cites an example of Pliny's letters to Trajan.[56] In the letters Pliny tried to procure imperial favours for his own friends and clients, such as Voconius Romanus. DeSilva also points out that numerous other examples of brokerage can be found in some earlier letters of Cicero (106–43 BC). This is valuable insight into the benefaction and patronage implications of Paul when he writes of Jesus's position and function in the patronal relationship between God the Father and humans, such as in 1 Timothy 2:5.[57]

Another contentious issue that deSilva raises is that God was conceptualized as a public benefactor due to his creation and sustenance of all life, and that he was viewed as a personal "patron" because of his gifts to individual

---

53. In Greek antiquity μέτοικος was a sojourner, an immigrant, an alien resident in a Grecian city, a non-citizen.

54. deSilva, *Honor*, 103.

55. deSilva, 97–98.

56. Pliny lived from 61 to 113 and the letters are dated from AD 111 to 113 when Trajan was governor of Bithynia.

57. Details are in chapter 3 of this study in the section titled "Christ as Benefactor, Patron and Mediator."

believers for church development.[58] Some scholars such as Alicia Batten have questions about Silva's (and other scholars') view of God as a "patron" to individuals. Instead, they view him as a communal and individual "benefactor." In her article titled "God in the Letter of James: Patron or Benefactor?"[59] she asserts that in James God is presented more appropriately as a communal benefactor rather than a patron. Her article builds on Joubert's view that benefaction and patronage were distinct social systems. She asserts that the author of the epistle of James presented God as a "frank friend" rather than a patron. She also argues that the author condemned patronage. Together with other scholars, she concludes that as depicted in the use of friendship vocabulary, the author confronted the audience's dependence on a rich patron and criticized "the sort of behaviour that patronage could breed."[60] She also refutes the view of scholars who assert that the author encouraged the replacement of human patrons with God as a divine patron. Because of the numerous abuses that gave Roman patronage negative reputation and from comparison of the characteristics of a benefactor with those of a patron, it is understandable why Batten says that it is better to view God as a benefactor rather than patron.[61] However, her implication that patronage was altogether bad is not correct.

It is better to see God as both a good benefactor and patron. For example, as benefactor, God gives unconditional help to all types of people, irrespective of their status and relationship to him. As a good patron, he does not misuse his power for self-interest at the expense of human clients as some patrons do. Also as a good patron, he faithfully gives his clients whatever they ask (Matt 6:8).[62] God's benefaction and patronage is pure and does not have any abuses that are in human benefaction systems, as what were in the ancient systems.[63] Nevertheless, Batten is right in her observation that

---

58. deSilva, *Honor*, 126–127, 132–133.

59. Alicia Batten, "God in the Letter of James: Patron or Benefactor?," *New Testament Studies* 50, no. 2 (April 2004): 257–272.

60. Batten, "God in the Letter of James," 258.

61. The differences and the similarities between the characteristics the two systems and their stakeholders are elaborated in chapter 2 under the discussion on the contexts of the Greek, Roman and Jewish benefaction and patronage systems.

62. I have discussed more on God as benefactor and patron in chapter 3.

63. My disagreement is elaborated further in chapter 2 and 3.

in James and other NT records, God is not to be depicted as a replacement patron, replacing the wayward Roman human and divine patrons. In the entire Bible we have records of God's good benefaction and patronage to communities and individuals. Although Paul emphasizes God's benefaction to all people, his writing also contains material that depict him as a good patron.[64]

Another point that deSilva highlights more than other modern scholars is that he assigns the feature of reciprocation a prominent position in the patronage and benefaction systems.[65] In highlighting it, he is faithfully following Seneca. In *De Beneficiis* Seneca highlighted reciprocation as one of the Three Graces that are essential in benefaction. DeSilva's elaboration of the ancient G-R and Jewish benefaction, patronage and reciprocity systems is helpful in identifying and understanding the operations of those systems in the NT in general. However, in his quest to identify and unlock the culture of patronage in the NT, it is not clear why he did not discuss Romans 16:2 in which the only explicit term on patronage, namely προστάτις, is found in the entire NT. As the epistle to the Romans was written to Christians in Rome (the capital of the Roman Empire) at a time when patronage by wealthy men and women was common, the usage of προστάτις in Romans 16:2 is significant. Phoebe was a deacon of the church at Cenchreae as well as a patron to many. This is significant and it agrees with the reference to women as deacons (servant-leaders) in PE churches.[66]

Overall, what deSilva has written about patronage is very profitable for understanding the dynamics of that system in the NT records. The discussion helps us to approach NT texts with more awareness and understanding, especially those that contain expressions related to the benefaction and patronage systems. Compared to Barclay, deSilva has less material on benefaction and patronage in the Jewish context. Nevertheless, he has provided us with many valuable insights on benefaction, patronage and reciprocity in general. My assessment of his book is that, like Danker, deSilva shows that

---

64. This argument is elaborated further in chapter 3 in section 3.6.1 titled "God as Benefactor and Patron."

65. deSilva, *Honor*, 96.

66. Details are in chapter 3 in the subsection titled "Qualifications of Women, γυνή: 1 Timothy 3:11; cf. Titus 2:3–6."

the NT contains more material that is related to benefaction and patronage in the first century AD than many people have previously acknowledged.

1.6.4 Andrew Wallace-Hadrill: *Patronage in Ancient Society*

Patronage in Ancient Society is a collection of articles on patronage edited by Wallace-Hadrill. In the articles, the authors give insights on the system in the ancient Mediterranean world, especially the Roman society, from Classical Athens (510–323 BC) to late Antiquity (AD 250–750). They enlighten us on the patron-client relationships in those times. The first article by Millet highlights the fact that although the *cliens/patronus* vocabulary that was common in the Roman world was very scarce in classical-age-Greece, this does not mean that patron-client relationships were absent altogether.[67] Millet gives various examples based on historical evidence. The examples that he and the other authors give are supported by original sources, such as Aristotle's *Politics*. He says that the vocabulary was scarce in Greece because Greeks, especially in Athens, preferred εὐεργεσία over *patronicium*. The relationships were common after classical Greece but they were operating alongside euergetism relationships. Thus, although they were individual systems, each with unique features, their operations and vocabularies were shared, just as the Greek and Roman cultures intermingled and shared in other aspects. For example, as indicated by Cloud in chapter 10, the benefits that patrons gave to the clients were called *beneficia* (or *patronicium*).[68] *Beneficia* was a Latin term equivalent to εὐεργεσία, which means a "good work," "good deed" or "benefit." All the articles are valuable in their discussion on various aspects of the patronage system.

1.6.5 Stephan J. Joubert: "One Form of Social Exchange or Two?"

Joubert's essay[69] challenges the scholarly status quo that sees ancient Roman patronage and Greek "euergetism" as one and the same form of social

---

67. Paul Millett, "Patronage and Its Avoidance in Classical Athens," in *Patronage in Ancient Society*, ed. Andrew Wallace-Hadrill (London; New York: Routledge, 1989), 15–47.

68. Duncan Cloud, "The Client-Patron Relationship: Emblem and Reality in Juvenal's First Book," in *Patronage in Ancient Society*, ed. Andrew Wallace-Hadrill (London; New York: Routledge, 1990), 210.

69. Joubert, "One Form of Social Exchange," 17–25.

exchange relationship whose only difference is in substance. In this study, the conclusion is that the generalization is unjustified. Some scholars have addressed the two systems indiscriminately as if they are entirely the same entity with different names. Basing his arguments on ancient Greek and Roman authors such as Aristotle, Cicero, Seneca, and Lucian,[70] who have significant content on Greek euergetism and Roman patronage in their writing, Joubert asserts that Greek euergetism is different from Roman patronage. For example, using Aristotle's *Rhet* 1361a28–43 and 1361a43–1361b3, Joubert's view is that euergetism was the practice where a person of means, for example a noble by birth or wealth, did good works by providing collective benefits from his own pockets to his community or city. The nobles were expected to provide various services to their communities collectively and to individuals in exchange for public honour from the beneficiaries.[71] Euergetism was a form of social dependence relationship that was prevalent in the Greek society even before the Hellenistic period and extended beyond the early Christian era in the near East.[72]

Joubert describes patronage further as one of the most important and enduring forms of socio-political systems of exchange and control "between people of unequal social status" in the ancient Roman Republic and imperial eras.[73] The difference is seen, for example, in the three types of "friends" that the patrons transacted with.[74] Concerning the types of goods that were exchanged between the patrons and their friends and clients, Joubert says that

---

70. Aristotle especially in *Nicomachean Ethics* and *The Art of Rhetoric,* Marcus Tullius Cicero, *On Duties,* ed. G. P. Goold, trans. Walter Miller, Loeb Classical Library XXI (Cambridge, MA: Harvard University Press, 1913), translation of *De Officiis*; Lucius Annaeus Seneca in *Seneca III: Moral Essays III,* ed. G. P. Goold, trans. John W. Basore, Loeb Classical Library (Cambridge, MA: Harvard University Press, 1989), translation of *L. Annaei Senecae Ad Aebutium Liberalem: De Beneficiis*; and Lucian in *Nigrinus*. Adhering to scholarly standards, references to Cicero's *On Duties* will be referred to as *De Officiis* or *De Off*, whereas Seneca's book , *Seneca III: Moral Essays III* will onwards be recorded as *De Beneficiis* or in short as *De Ben* in the main text. In short footnotes they are listed respectively as Cicero, *On Duties*, and Seneca, *Seneca III*.

71. Joubert, "One Form of Social Exchange," 18.

72. According to *The World Book Encyclopedia* 9 (London, Sydney, Tunbridge Wells, Chicago: World Book International, 1994), 144, the Hellenistic period lasted for nearly 200 years in Greece itself from 323 BE and for nearly 300 years in the Middle East.

73. Joubert, "One Form of Social Exchange," 19.

74. Joubert, 20.

individuals and groups exchanged "material goods" and services.⁷⁵ However, my argument is that "material goods" were not the only commodities exchanged. My argument is based on ancient sources, such as Seneca and Cicero, which affirm that the "goods" that were exchanged were in various forms, both material and nonmaterial. Significant examples of the nonmaterial goods are advice and protection from oppression, that were provided mainly through rhetoric. Similarly some modern scholars, such as Neyrey,⁷⁶ also agree that the media of exchange included both material and nonmaterial goods, such as power, knowledge, commitment.

In the essay, Joubert gives us several differences between the two forms of exchange. As stated earlier, those differences and others that are encountered are highlighted later in chapter 2 in the discussion on the Greek and Roman contexts of benefaction and patronage. Among the distinctives of Roman patronage, Joubert highlights the fact that although Roman aristocrats exercised patronage in their respective locations of political and military leadership, the most prominent form of patronage was that of the emperor to all the citizens of the empire. Another prominent feature that Joubert highlights, citing Malina, is that brokerage became increasingly important during the Roman Principate.⁷⁷ Brokerage was necessary in Roman *patronicium* where the patron was usually high above the prospective client and there was needed someone in between, for example, to provide a letter of introduction or recommendation. When the two parties were not so far apart socially, it was not necessary, as in some φιλία (friendship) and εὐεργεσία systems. As pointed above in the review of deSilva, this highlight helps us to see another possible implication of the term μεσίτης in 1 Timothy 2:5, in addition to the Jewish view of the same.

One notable feature of his essay is that he cites numerous scholars of the Greek period, such as Hans-Josef Klauck, E. Rawson, J. Touloumakos, John Harvey Kent and I. E. M. Edlund, who provide numerous honorary inscriptions in Greek phraseology and historical examples that testify to the

---

75. Joubert, 19.
76. Neyrey, "God," 465.
77. Joubert, "One Form of Social Exchange," 20.

importance of patrons.⁷⁸ For example, they show their importance in private voluntary associations of people of various vocations.⁷⁹ One important aspect that he points out is that the term προστασία was at times used by Greek authors to refer to patronage (*patronicium*).⁸⁰ However, this should not be understood as implying that Greek εὐεργεσία was similar to Roman *patronicium*. Joubert himself asserts strongly with evidence (as backed by Alicia Batten) that εὐεργεσία and προστασία were understood as different kinds of relationships in parts of the Roman Empire. Thus, although some vocabulary from both systems found their way into each other, they were used with understanding and caution, unlike some scholars who do not show distinction of the two systems. Citing Touloumakos, Joubert points out that the term προστασία was not widely used in Asia Minor and the Greek cities there.⁸¹ However, my argument is that Joubert's assertion should not be understood as meaning that there was no patronage at all in the East. Historical records attest differently. For example, in the Flavian period, fountains that patrons built in Rome were quickly emulated in Asia Minor by local patrons. Such were the Fountain of Pollio, which was erected at Ephesus in AD 97 in honour of Caesar Sextilius Pollio. Pollio had constructed the Marnas aqueduct earlier through governor Offilius Proculus. In the dedicatory inscriptions to such fountains, the emperor was given prominent mention.⁸²

Joubert gives examples of how the Greeks understood and practised euergetism and patronage respectively. He also summarizes clearly the similarities and the differences between the systems.⁸³ A point that he highlights in the summary about Roman patronage is that for someone to qualify to

---

78. Hans-Josef Klauck, *Alte Welt und neuer Glaube* (Freiburg: Universitätsverlag, 1994); E. Rawson, "The Eastern Clientelae of Clodius and the Claudii," *Historia* 22 (1973): 219–239; J. Touloumakos, "Zum römischen Gemeindepatronar im griechischen Osten," in *Hermes* 11 (1988): 304–324; John Harvey Kent, "The Inscriptions 1926–1950," *Corinth* 8, no. 3 (1966): 1–258; I. E. M. Edlund, "The Invisible Bonds: Clients and Patrons through the Eyes of Polybios," *Kilo* 59 (1977): 129–136.

79. Joubert, "One Form of Social Exchange," 21–22.

80. Joubert, 22.

81. Joubert, 22.

82. See more examples in Brenda Longfellow's dissertation, *Roman Imperialism and Civic Patronage: Form, Meaning, and Ideology in Monumental Fountain Complexes* (Cambridge; New York: Cambridge University Press, 2011) and Naci Keskin, *Ephesus* (Istanbul: Keskin Color, 2013).

83. Joubert, "One Form of Social Exchange," 23.

be an official patron in the Roman communities he had to possess certain necessary qualifications.[84] His argument finds support in the sets of laws that governed Roman municipalities in the first century AD, such as the *leges Ursonensis* and *Malacitana*.[85] For example, for anyone to be appointed as a patron in the city he had to be either the founder of the city, a relative or friend of the founder. This is developed further later in our discussion.

It is helpful that Joubert highlights the fact that in the first century AD, Roman patronage coexisted with other forms of social exchange relationships such as the family, friendship, charity and euergetism.[86] That assertion finds support in the NT epistles in which we find interplay of the ideologies of those different systems. Joubert asserts that it is only by the late Empire[87] that the Roman ideology of patronage had become so embedded into the social life of people in the Mediterranean G-R world that it could rightly be considered a universal phenomenon that had usurped all the functions of civic benefaction.[88] However, that does not mean that its ideologies were not strong and dominant before that time. As indicated above, Roman patronage had spread notably throughout the Roman Empire in the first-century AD.

In his conclusion Joubert says that in patronage and in the various forms of public and private euergetism, the exchange of gifts often led to the establishment of long-term relationships between the transactors. He ends his essay by giving a timely and justified caution that there needs to be detailed analysis of the distinct nature and functions of euergetism and patronage in early Christian circles to get rid of the high levels of abstraction about those important forms of social reciprocity.[89] My overall assessment of the essay is that, unlike other writings on the closely-related subjects of benefaction and patronage, it clearly elaborates the difference between Greek εὐεργεσία and Roman *patronicium*. On grammar and general literary εὐεργεσία precision, apart from the omission of the crucial comparative conjunction "than" in the thesis statement in the abstract and lack of translation of some crucial

---

84. Joubert, 23.
85. Briefly reviewed in chapter 2 below.
86. Joubert, "One Form of Social Exchange," 23.
87. Late Roman Empire is approximately said to have been from AD 250 to 550.
88. Joubert, "One Form of Social Exchange," 24.
89. Joubert, 24.

expressions that are not in English or the other fairly understood scholarly languages in the essay, the general flow of his argument is clear.

1.6.6 Zeba A. Crook: *Reconceptualising Conversion*

At the beginning of his discussion, Crook points out that although he highlights Paul's conversion his study is not about the Apostle to the Gentiles, but rather uses his conversion as a point of comparison in the discussion about ancient conversion. He argues that, contrary to the claims of the Christian tradition Paul was not a paradigm-setting convert without peer or parallel in the ancient world but he "was like his peers when it comes to how he talked about and how he envisioned his conversion experience."[90] He says that he uses Paul's example only because it is the most accessible example of conversion from the ancient world.

In chapter 1,[91] Crook shows the problem with the assumption that Paul's conversion can be transported into a modern cultural setting whereby we can speak about his personal experience as if he were living in our time, in which the emotional and introspective dimension of conversion is emphasized. Chapters 2 to 4 establish the extent to which Paul's conversion narratives were consistent with his cultural paradigm of communal patronage, benefaction and reciprocity, which is different from the individual and emotional emphasis of conversion in the modern Western world. Chapter 5 introduces the loyalty dimension to the equation of conversion to prevent the misconception that ancient conversion was entirely an emotionless transaction. Crook says that by his emphasis on the philosophical approach to ancient conversion he is not undermining the prevailing psychological reading of Paul's conversion experience but that he is providing an alternative approach to the widely discussed subject. However, his statement that introspective and emotional markers are absent in Paul's conversion narratives and that in their place are markers of patronal exchange, benefaction and gratitude is too extreme.[92] Nevertheless, in the ultimate conclusion of his writing Crook exonerates himself from the extreme of rationalism by

---

90. Crook, *Reconceptualising Conversion*, 1.
91. Titled, "The Influence of Psychology on Contemporary Society and Scholarship."
92. Crook, *Reconceptualising Conversion*, 8.

arguing that conversion is both rational and psychological.[93] It is true that Paul's own conversion accounts, as recorded by Luke in Acts, and his daily life before God, have allocentric philosophical and social elements,[94] but they also have idiocentric, internal and emotional elements, as portrayed in his writing, such as in Romans 7:15–25.

Chapter 3 is discussion on five rhetorical conventions that occur consistently within the language of patronage and benefaction, which were adhered to regardless of whether the patron or benefactor was human or divine. The five conventions can be employed to throw more light on the ancient conversion experiences in the Mediterranean world. They are: (1) The call of the patron. He says that contrary to the view that normally the clients approached patrons to be benefitted, human and divine patrons were reputed as approaching clients and initiating the patron-client relationship. This, therefore, explains the motif of "the call" by gods and philosophers. (2) The philosopher's teaching and rhetorical delivery was a benefaction in and of itself. Crook says that it was common for disciples and sympathetic writers to refer to philosophical teachers and their teaching in the language of patronage and benefaction, because "a philosopher's lessons were a benefaction to humanity, designed to save people from ignorance and death."[95] A disciple's response to a philosopher's teaching was equivalent to a client's response to a patron. (3) Prayer, praise and proselytism were the primary ways for a client to communicate with a patron or benefactor. For example, praise was a way of honouring the divine patron whereas prayer was both a way of honouring him and making a request to him. Praise and proselytism were an expected behaviour of clients of human patrons to publicize the generosity of a patron in an attempt both to increase the reputation of the patron and to attract new clients, for the logic was that the more clients a patron had the more his public honour. Thus "patron evangelization" was not uncommon behaviour among clients/worshippers. In the discussion in

---

93. Crook, 253.

94. As in 2 Cor 1:6 where Paul says, "If we are being afflicted, it is for your consolation and salvation; if we are being consoled, it is for your consolation, which you experience when you patiently endure the same sufferings that we are also suffering."

95. Crook, *Reconceptualising Conversion*, 6.

chapter 3 below, Paul's exaltation of God the Father and Christ in PE, such as in 1 Timothy 1:17 and 2:5–6, is nothing short of "patron evangelization."

(4) Patronal synkrisis was common, whereby one drew comparison of life (*bios*) before with life after his encounter with philosophy (or conversion). For example, in patronage and benefaction clients were used to comparing their lives before and after encounter with their patrons in a way that always honoured the current patron/benefactor. (5) The vocabulary of ancient patronage (such as the χάρις, εὐεργ – and πίστις words) found its way into the conversion narratives. For example, χάρις in G-R benefaction context had both a concrete and an abstract sense of "favour." Crook supports the view that emphasis was on the concrete sense of benefaction, whereby although in the NT χάρις may be translated abstractly as "gratitude," it should be translated more as "benefaction." It expresses the relationship of a client to a divine patron, as reflected in Paul's language.

Against the modern Western psychological concept of prioritising idiocentric, emotional or sentimental introspective conscience in conversion, Crook argues that Paul's conversion was pegged on external, collective and allocentric ethical standards of the ancient G-R world. He argues that the behaviour of people in the ancient Mediterranean world (including the conversion experience) was governed more by external than by internal forces.[96] Crooks observation finds support in the African setting because the scenario in the ancient Mediterranean world is equivalent to what we find in some contemporary African societies where although conversion is an individual experience, it is mainly dominated by external forces.[97] Taking patronage and clientage as one of the foremost keys of interpreting human interaction in the ancient Mediterranean setting, he says that many ancient sources both literary and material suggest that people in G-R antiquity framed their conversion experience in the language of ancient patronage and benefaction, and Paul did so as well.[98] His view is that we need to maintain a healthy balance between the psychological and the philosophical aspects of

---

96. Crook, 253.

97. Such as where allegiance to Christianity and other faiths is catalyzed by external pressure to conform to the prevailing culture.

98. Crook, *Reconceptualising Conversion*, 4, 5, 8.

conversion. We should not over-personalize, over-emotionalize ancient conversion, nor should we view it as a mechanical transaction involving automatons.

It is true that sometimes the bond that united some clients to their patrons involved psychological elements beyond the rational choice factor, such as when the client was ready to die for the patron and vice versa, but the personal or emotional element should not be overemphasized. The false assumption that there is continuity of meaning between the concept of ancient conversion and conversion in the modern Western perspective should be understood and avoided. Similarly, although much in the ancient conversion narratives emphasized the balance sheet of what was to be gained by joining a certain patron, the conversion experience should not be over-mechanized. It should not be understood as if the key thing in the entire transaction was computing the costs and benefits of converting from one patron or benefactor to another, on the basis of the principle of "what's in it for me?"

It is notable that throughout his discussion Crook uses the words "patronage" and "benefaction" interchangeably. On whether there is any difference between the two systems, his argument is that patronage and benefaction are not perfectly synonymous but they are very closely-related practices. Citing Harrison's *Paul's Language of Grace*, he points out that although the vocabulary of both Greek benefaction and Roman patronage was distinct in earlier times, it began to overlap in the Greek East.[99] He mentions the on-going debate on the differences between the two systems as highlighted by Stephan Joubert and Alicia Batten. Assessing Joubert's list of similarities and differences, Crook concludes that if we cancel the similarities between the two systems, the differences lie in the fact that patronage was more political, exploitative and elitist than euergetism. He says that it is difficult to distinguish patronage and benefaction because the same person could be called a patron and a benefactor simultaneously. That is true. However, as highlighted in my discussion in chapter 2 below, Greek εὐεργεσία and Roman *patronicium* were distinct systems and they should be viewed and addressed as such.

---

99. Crook, 60n13.

About divine patronage and benefaction in Hellenistic Judaism, Crook says that unlike Greeks and Romans who had clearly demarcated social institutions of benefaction and patronage, pre-common-era Palestine did not have a patron-client of a benefactor-client social structure. Instead, Jews had a system of covenantal exchange that shared many features in common with generalized reciprocity but had a formalized agreement, which made it different from patronage and benefaction for it[100] did not have any formal features of agreement. Citing Weinfeld's "*Berit*–Covenant Vs. Obligation," Crook says that the expectations and obligations between patrons/benefactors and clients were not enshrined in a formal contract but were socially enforced informally. Nevertheless, as discussed below in the section on the systems in the Roman world, my argument is that in the first century AD, especially in the cities, some principles of *patronicium* had become formal and were even inscribed on bronze tablets during the Flavian dynasty.

Similarly, Crook's conclusion that "it would be difficult to claim that Jews thought of their God as a patron or a benefactor since they lacked any social model or vocabulary which might serve as a metaphor" is not entirely true.[101] My argument is that he is right in saying that Jews did not view their God as a patron or benefactor in the same way as Greeks and Romans. However, he is not right in saying that they did not view God as a patron or benefactor at all simply because they lacked a social model and vocabulary. As confirmed below in my discussion on the systems in the Jewish world, although they did not have exactly the same terminology, from their inception as a nation the Jewish community viewed their God specifically and exclusively as their founder and protector, namely, as their divine patron. That fact is attested in their records, from the call of Abram through the exodus experience and afterwards. That perspective is purely patronal.[102] Nevertheless, overall, Crook has argued well that the modern Western Christian world generally goes overboard as it talks about, understands and frames the ancient allocentric

---

100. Crook uses the singular neuter pronoun "it" for both systems for he sees little difference between them.

101. Crook, *Reconceptualising Conversion*, 79.

102. Later in chapter 3 on PE passages, especially in subsection 3.3.1 titled "God as Benefactor and Patron," and 3.3.2 titled "God as Benefactor and Patron in the Context of Prayer and Salvation, 1 Tim 2:1–7" is discussed how Paul depicted God the Father, Jesus Christ and the Holy Spirit in view of benefaction, patronage and mediatorship.

conversion experience in the perspective of the modern idiocentric motifs. His stress on the application of the philosophical approach to the study of the conversion narratives in the NT in conjunction with the psychological approach is tenable.

1.6.7 Two Works on Specific NT Books

In his study of the epistle to the Hebrews in the context of G-R benefaction and reciprocity,[103] Whitlark used "authorial audience criticism" method. His main conclusion is that in Hebrews fidelity is secured and maintained through human reciprocity, a system that was common in the ancient Mediterranean world. However, the problem with that argument is that it tends to promote human effort as acting alongside, or without God's enablement. It is true that Hebrews focuses rather strongly on the danger of turning away from the true faith (10:38, 39) and refusing to heed the gospel message of salvation by faith in the blood of Jesus (12:22–25). However, it could also be argued that although human reciprocity has a prominent place in the fidelity cycle, as stated in Hebrews 9:14 and 10:24, the most prominent argument in the epistle is the teaching that fidelity toward God is achieved and maintained through divine enablement, as 12:2 implies. In a similar way, Paul ascribes to the notion of divine enablement of fidelity, as indicated in the testimony of his own salvation, that it was prompted and accomplished by God's special mercy to him, not by anything that he had done (cf. 1 Tim 1:12–17; 2 Tim 1:13; 3:15; Titus 1:2).

Jonathan Marshall also has done a similar study to determine the extent of the influences of the ideals of Hellenistic and Roman benefaction and *patronicium* in Luke.[104] His dissertation is a response to the lack of interaction with classical scholarship on the subject in the past two decades. Using new insights of modern classicists on Luke's writing and Jesus's social relationships, his endeavour was to determine whether Jesus used the prevailing benefaction and *patronicium* terminology and conceptions in his ministry. To gain insight on the subject, he evaluated physical and literary

---

103. Jason A. Whitlark, *Enabling Fidelity to God: Perseverance in Hebrews in Light of Reciprocity Systems in the Ancient Mediterranean World*, Paternoster Biblical Monographs (Milton Keynes: Paternoster, 2008).

104. Jonathan Marshall, *Jesus, Patrons, and Benefactors: Roman Palestine and the Gospel of Luke* (Tubingen: Mohr Siebeck, 2009).

evidence on Galilee and the surrounding regions and cities and personality profiles of particular Jewish rulers. His conclusion about the gospel is that some passages should be studied in light of reciprocity and benefaction, and not *patronicium*.

1.6.8 Sources Specifically on PE

As stated earlier, among the few writings on benefaction and patronage specifically on PE, Winter's article, Marshall's and Towner's commentaries are significantly helpful.[105] Nevertheless, Kidd's dissertation is the most extensive and enlightening. Winter and Kidd are the only writings reviewed here. Marshall's and Winter's insights are discussed extensively in chapter 3 where views from other commentaries on PE are also cited.

1.6.9 Bruce W. Winter: "Providentia for the Widows"

Winter wrote this article to clarify the puzzling subject of the Graeco-Roman and Jewish social and legal context on provision (*providentia*) for widows, as addressed in 1 Timothy 5:3–16. Winter asserts that in the Greek, Roman, and Jewish social settings of the first century AD, there were clear legal guidelines on how to provide for widows, such as through the κύριοι who were in charge of their dowry.[106] He observes that, in contrast, there was no support for widows from the lowest economic ladder who had no provision from any households. In the G-R world, especially in the imperial period after Caesar Augustus, there were ad hoc helps for the poor by the rich of the cities. The Jewish synagogue also had a permanent arrangement for support of the poor, including widows.[107] However, both the Roman and Jewish help systems were polluted by various abuses. For example, during the principates of the Flavian emperors, sometimes widows' benefits and exemptions from taxes and liturgies were exploited by the officers in charge of their administration.[108] Similarly, extended family members (including Christians) who were the official "lord of the dowry" for the widows failed

---

105. Winter, "Providentia," 83–99; Marshall, *Pastoral*; Towner, *Letters to Timothy*.
106. Winter, "Providentia," 83–86.
107. Winter, 86–87.
108. Bruce W. Winter, *Roman Wives, Roman Widows: The Appearance of New Women and the Pauline Communities* (Grand Rapids, MI: Eerdmans, 2003), 127. See document number 458 in M. McCrum and A. G. Woodhead, *Select Documents of the Principates of the Flavian Emperors, A.D. 68-96* (Cambridge: Cambridge University Press, 1961).

to fulfil the financial commitment given to them.[109] Therefore, the church took up the responsibility of caring for widows who had become Christian without abuse.[110] Winter says that is what Paul addressed in chapter 5 of 1 Timothy.

The non-Christian world's culture of caring for widows influenced church's practice of *providentia* for widows, but it is not clear "how much" the influence was. Winter says that it is not clear whether the guidelines for *providentia* for widows in 1 Timothy 5:3–16 were modified from the earlier guidelines on widow-support in the Jerusalem church, to take care of the changing culture within and around the Ephesian churches.[111] It is apparent that the church did not originate the idea and come up with rules on how to help widows. In keeping with pre-existent legal requirements, the Christian household lord was responsible for offering *providentia* not only to members of his immediate household but also to members of the extended family who were not living within his household.[112] Winter discusses the injunction for children and grandchildren to honour (provide for) their parents and cites the example of a tombstone inscriptions that indicates that Christian children supported their widowed parents.[113]

Although the system of helping widows was not new, Winter says that the exhortation in 5:16 for believing women to care for widows was a new development in the early church. It was not based on any previous legal or ecclesiastical precedent. The believing women were either rich women or women appointed by the church to care for widows.[114] Apart from the fact that Winter's reference to "ecclesiastical" precedent is not clear because there was no church before the Jerusalem congregation, his argument that support of widows by believing women was an innovation in PE church is viable. However, general care for them was common in Israel, as indicated in Deuteronomy 10:18, where God is presented as the ultimate supporter of the widow, and in 14:29 and 26:12–13 where it is stated that every third

---

109. Winter, *Roman Wives*, 127.
110. Winter, "Providentia," 86–88.
111. Winter, 89–90.
112. Winter, 90–91.
113. Winter, 93.
114. Winter, 94.

year Israelites were required to give their tithes to the Levites, orphans, widows and aliens among them. Widows were also allowed to glean other people's farms for support, as the case of Naomi and Ruth confirms (Ruth 2:2–3, 15–16; cf. Deut 24:21). In other cases, the care for widows lay in the hands of kinsmen redeemers, as also attested in the story of Ruth (3:1–4:13). Nevertheless, these provisions were frequently ignored and therefore the church saw the necessity to institute a better system.

According to Roman law, a widow of below fifty was considered capable of marriage and of bearing children. Thus she was not entitled to receive any inheritance. The reason for the new rule in PE that she should be sixty is not explained.[115] The exclusion of some widows from the church's *providentia* does not indicate that the church was reverting to the secular society's hierarchical and patriarchal structures of social office (where men only ascended to leadership and where widows of below fifty years were the only ones considered as eligible for support).[116] As Paul advised in 1 Timothy 5:16, the church needed to act wisely to cushion itself from being taken advantage of by the widows or the lords and relatives who were required by the law and the social order of the day to support the widows from their dowry and from family resources. The new guideline was for the church to support only the widows who had no dowry or able relatives to depend on.

My overall assessment of Winter's article is that, *providentia* for widows by the household lords in charge of their dowry could not be considered as benefaction or patronage for they were performing a legal requirement, unless the help that they gave surpassed the legal requirement. Similarly, *providentia* by children or grand children cannot be viewed as benefaction or patronage in the G-R sense if it was given as discharge of the filial requirement only. However, if done as an act of free will, then it qualified to be beneficence. Seneca reiterated that when a child's support for the parents surpassed what he had received from the parents, then he was a better benefactor than the parents.[117] Similarly, when the aid that benefactors gave in support of festivals and warfare in their official capacity surpassed what was required officially, it qualified from being λειτουργία (liturgy or offering)

---

115. Winter, 95.
116. Winter, 97.
117. Seneca, *Seneca III*, III.XXIX.1–XXXVIII.3.

to be εὐεργεσία and merited more honour to the giver.[118] In the G-R world as well as the Judaistic world, poor people in the society, including widows who had no dowry or relatives to rely on, were provided for through the benefaction and patronage systems. *Providentia* to widows by the church has to be regarded more as benefaction than patronage because it was done out of good will by people not required to give it by law or as dictated by filial relations. Although Winter has not clarified which system Paul was depending on as he instructed the church to support widows, my suggestion is that he was relying on a Christianized form of benefaction that had a mixture of principles of both Judaistic kinship benefaction (as seen in the instruction that believing relatives should care for their widows) and G-R εὐεργεσία and *patronicium*.[119]

1.6.10 Reggie M. Kidd: *Wealth and Beneficence in the Pastoral Epistles*

Kidd's dissertation is the only extensive material that we have come across so far that deals specifically with the subject of benefaction in PE. Others have written brief articles based on single episodes in the epistles, specifically in 1 Timothy, such as Winter that are reviewed above. Kidd's dissertation is a response to the ambiguousness and superficiality exhibited in the incidences where some scholars have branded PE Christianity as "bourgeois." Dibelius was the first scholar to make prominent the label of PE Christianity as *bürgerlich* (bourgeois). His view is considered as being the product of a situation in Germany when socioeconomic life was dictated by bourgeois-proletariat principles. He therefore viewed PE Christianity as having developed into a middle-class existence, a condition that made it to seek little more than to live comfortably in the world. Thus, he saw the ethical instructions in the epistles as aimed at promoting *christliche Bürgelichkeit* (Christian good-citizenship or bourgeois Christianity) in the contemporary world.[120] Kidd's dissertation is aimed at establishing whether

---

118. D. D. Walker, "Benefactor," in *Dictionary of New Testament Background* 1, eds. Craig A. Evans and Stanley E. Porter (Downer Grove, IL: InterVarsity Press),157.

119. Further discussion on this subject is in chapter 3 of this book, under "Benefaction for Widows."

120. Philip H. Towner, *The Goal of Our Instruction: The Structure of Theology and Ethics in the Pastoral Epistles* (Sheffield: JSOT Press, 1989), 9.

the epithet "bourgeois"[121] is an appropriate description of PE Christianity. He looks at what degree PE churches were accommodating and/or critical about how people of wealth were living in relation to the norms of first-century Greek and Roman culture. He has also evaluated the conservative ethics reflected in PE in comparison with the more apocalyptic ethics in the undisputed Paulines.

His argumentation is in the form of answers to a series of questions: (1) Whether the social status of PE Christians was really middle class or not; (2) whether the principles of beneficence depicted in PE portrayed a type of Christianity that was compromised and too accommodative to the cultural values of that time and (3) whether or not the theology and ethics presented in PE are focused on the here and now, unlike the eschatology that is presented in the accepted Paulines, which is heaven-focused. His findings led him to conclude that the Christianity depicted in PE is not different from what is depicted in the Paulines. Therefore, it does not deserve the negative title of "bourgeois" at all.

Concerning the bourgeois epithet labelled on PE Christianity, just like Kidd, Spicq's assertion is more tenable than that of Dibelius. Spicq disagrees with Dibelius that bourgeois Christianity in PE "connotes a static Paulinism that uncritically makes its peace with the world."[122] Spicq's view is that the term "bourgeois Christianity" is the description of "a community of prosperous Christians who are in a position to be taught that the gospel ennobles human existence, and that it does so at many points by affirming values that are already familiar."[123] The PE affirm that there were affluent middle class people who had become Christians, as seen in the instruction about the rich in 1 Timothy 6:17–19. Viewed diachronically, it is possible that some of the rich, for example, slave-owners (1 Tim 6:1–2; Titus 2:9–10), had behaviour that can be regarded as equivalent to that of the bourgeois of Germany. Nevertheless, there also were poor members in PE churches, such as the helpless widows (1 Tim 5:3–16), some of the elders (1 Tim 5:17–18),

---

121. Martin Dibelius was the first scholar to highlight the "bourgeois" epithet about early Christianity. Ceslas Spicq contested certain features of Dibelius' use of the term and explained it further.

122. Kidd, *Wealth and Beneficence*, 29.

123. Kidd, 29.

and the slaves (1 Tim 6:2; Titus 2:9–10). It is implicit also that even Paul himself was not affluent (1 Tim 6:6–10).

By presenting early Christians as belonging to various distinct social classes, just as the situation was in the Roman world, Kidd refutes Dibelius' view that they belonged to the bourgeois class only. Also, unlike Dibelius and Spicq who asserted that PE Christians had ascended the social ladder from proletariat to the bourgeois' class, Kidd observes that they were at the same social level as the Christians depicted in the undisputed letters of Paul. The person who reads the undisputed Pauline letters carefully acknowledges that the rich people addressed in PE were not an emergent class but they were similar to those addressed in the accepted letters, as in 1 Corinthians 11: 20–22. However, Kidd somehow contradicts his own argument when he says that the concern of Paul is largely with helping social superiors (especially, prosperous household heads) to relate well with the rest of the community of faith. Kidd says that PE do not depict a bourgeois Christianity in the modern connotation of the term, as Rostovtzeff argues anachronistically, but they address a people of municipal upper class in society.[124] That is not entirely true. In fact the opposite is true.

As manifested in the epistle, Paul also targeted those at the bottom of the social and economic ladder. For example, in the instructions on remuneration for certain church elders it is implicit that the socioeconomic status of the church leaders was varied. Kidd admits that at least church elders and deacons were not necessarily drawn exclusively from the aristocratic class of Christians in the church but that they consisted of the wealthy, who did not need any financial honour (support) from the church, and those who needed material support.[125] Another example that Paul addressed the poor is as explicitly portrayed in 1 Timothy 6:1–2 and Titus 2:9, where he directed his instructions exclusively to the slaves. He did not address the masters. Slaves were not social superiors. Additionally, despite having been written a bit later, in early second century AD, a credible example that the poor also were prominent church officials is found in *Epistles of Pliny* 10:97, 97. Pliny, the governor of Pontus from AD 111 to 113 says that he selected and tortured

---

124. Kidd, 197.
125. Kidd, 77, 106–108.

two slave girls, whom he identified as "deaconesses" attempting to find out the truth about Christianity.[126] Their selection implies their prominence in the church despite their poor socioeconomic status.[127]

In response to Dibelius' accusation that PE Christianity had assimilated and accommodated negative cultural values of the bourgeois society in which it lived, Kidd says that although the epistles retained the bürgerlich language, they depict a strong deliberate departure from accommodative cultural integration. He gives an example in support of his argument by saying that just as it is in the accepted letters of Paul, in PE Christian benefactors are exhorted not to expect payment for their benefaction in the present life.[128] Kidd observes correctly that "cultural notions of the role of benefactors are shared in part and repudiated in part – the content of the ideal is transformed even as its language is appropriated."[129] Nevertheless, Kidd does not elaborate much how the content of the benefaction ideal was transformed in PE, namely, how Christian benefaction differed from what was in the prevailing G-R systems.

In *De Beneficiis*, Seneca exhorted G-R benefactors to give their benefaction not expecting anything in return because a person of noble mind enjoys the fruits of giving without expecting return.[130] In the prevailing non-Christian societies, people were already practising giving supposedly "without expecting recompense." What Kidd failed to observe is that Paul comparatively placed Christian benefaction as much higher than the prevailing non-Christian counterpart for it exhorted that Christians practise their benefaction in reference and reverence to the only true God and in gratefulness for God's mercy and salvation in Christ (1 Tim 6:17–19; 2 Tim 1:8–12; Titus 3:1–8). In effect, Paul's exaltation of Christian benefaction was a rebuttal against practicing benefaction as the surrounding non-Christian world was doing it. Instead, he recommended that Christian benefaction

---

126. Pliny, "Pliny, Letters 10.96-97: Pliny and Trajan on the Christians," *Letters - Pliny and Trajan on the Christians*, accessed 30 September 2018, http://web.archive.org/web/20021208163238/http://hadrians.com:80/rome/romans/sources/pliny.html.

127. There is more detailed discussion on this issue in chapter 3 of my writing, under 3.4.7 Masters and Slaves.

128. Kidd, *Wealth and Beneficence*, 200.

129. Kidd, 200.

130. Seneca, *Seneca III*, I.I.9–13.

and patronage should be practised for the benefit of others, not merely for personal enjoyment, although the Christian benefactor also received something in return in the present life (1 Tim 2:6; 5:10; 6:18; 2 Tim 2:2, 14; Titus 2:14; 3:14). Eternal rewards in the afterlife (not merely the temporal honour) were another main motivation for Christians to participate in benefaction and patronage (1 Tim 6:19; 2 Tim 1:12, 18; 4:8).

It is notable that Kidd's dissertation discusses leadership in PE church era, although it does so very briefly.[131] Kidd agrees with Countryman and Verner[132] on the description of some church officers as identical to the local elite (the leading citizens), in such characteristics as being householders who were known to be hospitable, sober, self-restrained and had the ability to keep their households under control.[133] Somehow, he agrees with Verner's view that Paul's description of the overseer's office as καλὸν ἔργον (or *noblesse oblige*, as Spicq called it) equated it to a charitable deed performed by a well-to-do person on behalf of the less fortunate.[134] His unsubstantiated argument is that the office of overseer was possibly occupied by a wealthy patron.[135] Similarly, he also agrees with Verner that the requirement for the deacons to be good managers of their own households indicates that some of them were drawn from the comparatively well-to-do ranks, because only those who were wealthy could afford to have households composed of more than a nuclear family.[136] Thus, notably emphasizing material benefaction, Kidd categorizes some of the leaders as benefactors. However, his observation that church leadership was not the exclusive preserve of the wealthy saves him from the pitfall of Dibelius, Verner, Hanson and others who accuse PE author of being biased in support of that view.[137] Another related problem is as Fee observes in his review that, ". . . especially because of

---

131. Such as on pages 77, 83–86,185–188.

132. However, as in *Household of God*, 184, Verner's view is that church leadership was entirely the preserve of the wealthy elite, such as PE author himself, and they did what they could to preserve their wealth and their status from would-be social climbers (as in 1 Tim 6:9–10).

133. Kidd, *Wealth and Beneficence*, 77.

134. Kidd, 84.

135. Kidd, 108.

136. Kidd, 83, 108. However, this observation is from the perspective of a modern Western mind and is not true.

137. Kidd, 87, 108.

the significant role of the passages on wealth, church leadership, wealthy women, and households, one might have wished for a bit more precision on the relationship of the false teachers to wealthy householders as leaders of the community."[138]

Another notable element in Kidd's dissertation, which is also found in other works on benefaction in PE is that, there is lack of comprehensive exegesis on certain sections of the epistles in which explicit and implicit features of benefaction and patronage are found. Similarly, as is also common with several studies on the subject of benefaction and patronage, although Kidd exhibits profound knowledge about the difference between the two systems, he has not outlined them clearly, as Joubert and Batten have done.

Overall, compared to the other scholars on the subject, Kidd has given the scholarship world a more trustworthy view of the status of PE Christianity. His vivid description and refutation of the contentions of Dibelius and those who support his view of bourgeois Christianity in PE helps us to understand and appreciate more the content of the early Christian era. His exposition and dependence on original sources on the subject of wealth and benefaction in PE is very insightful.

1.6.11 Commentaries

There are numerous commentaries on the Pastorals. One of the noticeable features of the older commentaries is that they acknowledge that the household motif is obviously featured in the epistles. However, they do not acknowledge presence of the benefaction/patronage motif. Nevertheless, the good news is that some of the modern commentaries recognize that PE contain expressions that were associated with those ancient systems also. Some of the commentaries that stand out in their highlight of content that is connected with benefaction and patronage in PE are those by Dibelius and Conzelmann (D-C), Mounce, Marshall and Towner.[139] For example, in his comment on the phrase τοῦ σωτῆρος ἡμῶν θεοῦ in Titus 1:3, Marshall says that the title "our saviour God" is used in the sense of God being a

---

138. Gordon D. Fee, "Review of Reggie Kidd, *Wealth and Beneficence in the Pastoral Epistles: A Bourgeois Form of Early Christianity?*" SBL Dissertation Series 122, *Journal of Biblical Literature* 111, no. 2 (Summer 1992): 352–354.

139. I have listed them by order of date, not by merit of intensity on coverage of the subject.

"deliverer, preserver from illness and calamity." He adds that the same title was applied to many gods including Zeus and Asclepius and to deified rulers "as the protectors [patrons] of cities and the helpers of the distressed."[140]

Among the commentaries, Towner's most recent edition (of 2006) is the most reflective on the subject of benefaction and patronage in PE. Whenever he encounters expressions that he judges as related to the systems, he points them out and gives brief but insightful comments on them. For example, in his comment on 1 Timothy 3:4, 5, he says that management of one's own household included the "maintenance of important relationships with benefactors/patrons or clients."[141] He also highlights the fact that some gods attained undying honour and fame because of their benefaction to humankind. He also points out that divinity was conferred on some humans because of their benefaction to fellow humans.[142] There are more expressions on benefaction that he highlights in the commentary. It is notable that in his earlier smaller commentary on PE, he did not highlight benefaction and patronage context as he has done in the latest.

Although the comments that the commentaries give on material related to the subject of benefaction in PE are brief (such as on χάρις in 1 Tim 1:12, 14; 2 Tim 1:3, 9; Titus 3:7), the insights that they give are very helpful. Some terms related to the systems that are discussed briefly or not at all in some of the commentaries are: (1) τιμή in 1 Timothy 1:17; 5:17; 6:1, and 16; (2) δόξα in 1 Timothy 1:17; 2 Timothy 2:10; 4:18 and Titus 2:13; (3) μεσίτης in 1 Timothy 2:5; and (4) ἔργων ἀγαθῶν in 1 Timothy 2:10, ἔργοις καλοῖς and its cognates in 1 Timothy 5:10; 5:25 and 6:18; Titus 2:7, 14; 3:8, and 14. Although they do not highlight benefaction and patronage issues, other good commentaries on PE are by John Calvin, Raymond Collins, Gordon Fee, Donald Guthrie, A. T. Hanson, Luke-Timothy Johnson, J. N. D. Kelly, G. W. Knight, Walter Liefeld, Walter Lock, S. Ngewa, Lorenz Oberlinner, Jerome Quinn, Jürgen Roloff, Ceslas Spicq and Ben Witherington. These and other commentaries are alluded to mainly in chapter 3.

---

140. Marshall, *Pastoral Epistles*, 131.
141. Towner, *Letters to Timothy*, 254.
142. Towner, 659–661.

CHAPTER 2

Socio-Historical Background of Benefaction and Patronage

2.1 Introduction

In this chapter, an overview of the background and the general features of εὐεργεσία, *patronicium* and kinship benefaction is given. We begin with reviews of some key ancient sources on the systems around the first century AD. Then we discuss the existence and operations of the systems, (1) in the Greek context, (2) the Roman context, and (3) the Jewish context. The rationale for this section is that knowing the socio-historical background of the systems in the Mediterranean regions in the first century AD is necessary for identifying the presence and influences of their features and ideologies in PE as discussed in chapter 3 of this dissertation.

2.2 Ancient Sources

On ancient sources, we give more attention to Cicero's *De Officiis*, Seneca's *De Beneficiis*, Philo's and Josephus's writings on προστασία, *patronicium* and kinship benefaction systems around the first-century AD. Then we also discuss briefly the codes of laws that governed social, political, economic and religious systems in the Roman municipalities, such as, *Lex Irnitana* (similar to *Lex Malacitana*) and *Lex Coloniae Genetivae* (or *Lex Ursonensis*). Extensive allusions to these sources are found in the main section on the contexts of the systems in this chapter and in chapter 3.

2.2.1 Cicero: *De Officiis* (*On Duties*)

Cicero (106–43 BC) was a renowned Roman orator who wrote essays on various subjects. In some of the essays, he provides us with insights on benefaction and patronage in his days. One such essay is *De Officiis* (*On Duties*). It was Cicero's second-to-last contribution to literature, which was written between 46 and 43 BC just before his death. In the introduction, it is described as a product of Cicero's student days' passion of Greek philosophy which he had then adapted to suit his Roman inclination to a practical approach to life.[1] To Cicero, praxis was the primary goal of philosophy, as opposed to the Greek notion of gnosis as the primary goal of philosophy. *De Officiis* was written based on the moral philosophy of the Greek Stoic philosopher, Panaetius. Nevertheless, Cicero so tailored what he wrote to meet the needs of his audience to the extent that his treatise reflected the mind-sets and the behaviour of the Romans of his day. To him, the most important department of philosophy was ethics. That fact is reflected in *De Officiis* which is a treatise on rules for personal conduct. In the writing, he has covered a broad spectrum of topics on moral duties. However, my interest is on his views on the moral duties of benefaction and patronage.

Cicero gave the subject of patronage considerable attention. For example, being an orator himself, he highlighted the fact that orators were essential benefactors, especially as they championed the needs of the common people and defended the rights of the community. For example, in Book II section XIX.66, he speaks of orators as defenders of the common people's rights. Without reluctance and without demanding compensation, orators advocated for the community's needs through their eloquence.[2] In our days, such a statement, coming from an orator in praise of orators can be easily categorized as excessive and offensive self-praise and thus its credibility regarded as questionable, especially among Christians. Ancient ethicists also viewed self-praise by benefactors as questionable. In *De Ben*, for example in V.VII.2, Seneca denounced self-praise, "*Quomodo nemo se portat, quamvis corpus sum moveat et transferat, quomodo nemo, pro se dixerit, adfuisse sibi dicitur, nec statuam sibi tamquam patrono suo ponit . . .*" (Just as no one carries

---

1. Cicero, *On Duties*, ed. G. P. Goold, trans. Walter Miller, Loeb Classical Library XXI (Harvard University Press, 1913), i.
2. Cicero, *On Duties*, 240, 241.

himself, although he moves his body and transports it from place to place; as no one, though he may have made a speech in his own defence, is said to have stood by himself, or erects a statue to himself as his own patron . . .)[3] Nevertheless, in the first century AD, praise of others who were in the same profession, and genuine pride in one's work were considered legitimate and acceptable.[4] Despite the pitfall of self-praise, throughout history, oratory has been a useful tool for defence of human rights. In Cicero's time, orators gave nonmaterial benefaction/patronage in form of verbal defence and they were often paid with material reciprocation.

Although Cicero gives the subject of patronage a general coverage in various sections of his writing, judging from the frequency of its appearances in the essay, one can deduce that both material and nonmaterial patronage was a significant practice in his time. For example, in Book I section IX.35, he describes patrons as people who were protectors of the states and nations that they had conquered. In Book II section XX.69–70, he exhibits his disgust with the situation where people accepted someone as their patron and themselves as clients not based on mutual favour but based on slavish subservience. Seneca's view agrees with Cicero's on that point.[5] Although the cases and statements that Cicero provides on patronage are quite scattered throughout his writing, careful study of the texts reveals that among other social systems of interpersonal relationship, oratory was a form of patronage in the Roman Empire in the years immediately before the first century AD.

2.2.2 Seneca: *De Beneficiis (On Benefits)*

This section is a summary and review of Seneca's writing popularly known as *De Beneficiis* (*On Benefits*, *De Ben* in short) or *Seneca III: Moral Essays III* in the Loeb Classical Library series. In the seven part essay (Book I to VII), written between AD 58 and 65, Seneca gives advice to Aebutius Liberalis[6] on the morality of giving and receiving, in other words, on the ethics of

---

3. Seneca, *Seneca III*, V.VII.2.

4. Kate C. Donahoe, "From Self-Praise to Self-Boasting: Paul's Unmasking of the Conflicting Rhetoric-Linguistic Phenomena in 1 Corinthians," (PhD diss., The University of St. Andrews, Scotland, 2008).

5. Cicero's dates are given as 106–43 BC whereas Seneca's are 4 BC–AD 65.

6. Aebutius Liberalis was a member of an elite and wealthy family in the Roman Empire who, most likely, was Seneca's patron.

benefaction and gratitude. During his time, benefaction and gratitude were regarded not as private graces but as social virtues that needed to be exercised by everyone with great care and genuineness.[7] He wrote the essay as an attempt at pointing out and correcting one of the greatest errors of the people of his time, which is present in the modern world also, namely, lack of discernment and grace in giving and receiving benefits.[8] The essay is an attempt at restoring benefaction and patronage back to its original purposes, as good means of necessary socioeconomic inter-dependence and egalitarianism among people of all classes in the society.

Book I (I.I.1–XV.6) addresses the need for care in choosing the right recipients of beneficence, that is, people who would indeed be helped by the benefactor's support. In the essay, he highlighted gratefulness as one of the essential elements expected in benefaction.[9] He also advised that gratitude was not to be pursued or demanded from the recipients of benefaction.[10] However, this advice is a bit controversial. In a setting where benefactors were entitled to receive honour and other services as reciprocation for their benefaction, demanding gratitude from reluctant clients who had benefited from the benefactors' generosity would have been acceptable, especially in the secular community, for that was the rightful privilege of the patrons. Therefore, to advise patrons not to demand gratitude as rightful recompense for their help was contrary to the accepted etiquette.

In Book I also, Seneca pointed out that benefits could be given in various forms: money, credit, influence, advice, and sound precepts.[11] This affirms that both material and nonmaterial benefits were given. He categorizes the benefits in a descending order as (1) the necessary, (2) the useful, and (3) the pleasurable.[12] According to Seneca, public office, such as leadership, belonged to the second category, namely, the useful but not necessary benefits.[13]

---

7. Seneca, *Seneca III*, Introduction, vii.
8. Seneca, I.I.1–2.
9. Seneca, I.X.3–4.
10. Seneca, I.I.9–13.
11. Seneca, I.II.4.
12. Seneca, I.XI.1–3.
13. Seneca, *Seneca III*, I.XI.5. Seneca elaborates the useful benefits as: (1) enough money (not excess) for a reasonable standard of living; (2) public office; and (3) advancement, for those striving for higher positions.

However, this is debatable. My argument is that, as affirmed in history, due to the vital role that leaders have played in all sectors of society since the inception of time to the present, their office and services rightly belong to the first category, namely, the necessary benefits.

Book II (I.1–XXXV.5) deals with the right manner in which a benefit should be given; giving in a way that the benefit would have been acceptable to the giver were he the recipient.[14] The attitude and the ability of the benefactor in giving beneficence are highlighted in this part of the essay. In it also, Seneca points out that patrons of voluntary associations were generally required to be financially stable so that they could support their households, give aid to the needy members of the associations and pay any fines that they would incur in their tenure of service.[15] That requirement implies that in the G-R benefaction and patronage systems there was preference for materially wealthy elites over people who did not have much. That trend has continued throughout history to the present, in both secular and religious organizations.

In Books III (I.1–XXXVIII.3) and V (I.1–XXV.6), Seneca revisits and highlights the virtue of gratitude that he introduced in Book I. He especially encouraged gratitude of offspring to their parents. His advice was that all benefaction, even benefaction between relatives, should be based more on goodwill rather than filial or legal obligation.[16] That was good advice there is difficulty in its applicability in that throughout history, even in Seneca's time, it has not been easy to establish a clear demarcation between doing good deeds to relatives based purely on goodwill and doing them as dictated by filial obligation.

Seneca defined a benefit in the same book, III.XIX.1, as, "*Beneficium enim id est, quod quis dedit, cum illi liceret et non dare,*" (A benefit is something that some person has given when it was also within his power not to give it). He also highlighted and gave examples that benefaction could be given amicably by people of all classes. For example, masters could be benefactors to their slaves and vice versa. Similarly, captors could be benefactors to their victims and vice versa. Such noble benefaction finds support in Polybius's

---

14. Seneca, *Seneca III*, II.I.1.
15. Seneca, VI.XIX.4–5.
16. Seneca, III.XI.1–3, III.XXIX.1–XXXVIII.3.

book, *The Histories*, in which there are examples of slaves who became benefactors to their masters.[17] Seneca's advice could have encountered resistance from those who had become corrupt in the manner they used the system.

In Book VI[18] Seneca said that the benefits that were given out freely to people in groups were likewise to be reciprocated through corporate thanksgiving[19]. However, in Book V Seneca advised against the potential scenario where a benefactor might demand gratitude from the people he was helping. He said that it was disgraceful for the givers to crave for or wrench gratitude from beneficiaries.[20] Although most of Seneca's advice was prescriptive rather than descriptive, what he wrote had support in real life in his time. For example, as scholars point out, Emperor Caligula (AD 37–41) was the first emperor to demand to be worshiped, although he did it due to insanity.[21] Emperor Domitian (AD 81–96) was the first emperor, who with full sanity took his divinity seriously and demanded Caesar worship.[22] It is apparent that in Seneca's time it was difficult for some benefactors and patrons to observe the protocol of free and fair voluntary benefaction and gratitude.

Book IV (I.1–XI.5) advises against bequeathing benefits for the sole purpose of receiving gratitude from the recipients. To Seneca, good deeds were not to be done with the view of self-profit, such as, for the pleasure that someone would get from doing them. For him, they were to be done for the sake of the deeds themselves; simply because it was good to do them.[23] We may infer Seneca's prescription as targeted against the thought of earlier

---

17. Polybius, *Polybius: The Histories*, Loeb Classical Library V (Cambridge, MA: Harvard University Press, 1926), 9:8–10.

18. My jump from Book III to VI is not a mistake. My intention here is to maintain a smooth flow of my review for there are materials in book VI that are similar to those in Book III. Book IV follows after and then Book VI is revisited. Note also that I discussed Book V before Book IV earlier with Book III.

19. Seneca, *Seneca III*, VI.XVIII.2.

20. Seneca, V.XX.6–7.

21. Jacob Neusner and William Scott Green, eds., *Dictionary of Judaism in the Biblical Period: 450 B.C.E. to 600 C.E.* 1 vol. (Peabody, MA: Hendrickson, 1996 [2002]), 238. See also *Encyclopaedia Judaica* 5 (Jerusalem, Israel: Keter, 1971), 59–60. See also Moshe David Herr, "Ancient History: Jews in the Land of Israel from Cyrus to Mohammed," in *Encyclorama of Israel* 1, ed. Arie Serper, 7 vols. (Jerusalem: Pierre Illouz, 1986), 211. Caligula ordered for erection of a statue of himself as Emperor-God in the Temple at Jerusalem.

22. Neusner and Scott Green, *Dictionary of Judaism*, 173.

23. Seneca, *Seneca III*, IV.I.2–3.

philosophers such as Epicurus who taught that pleasure is one of the main purposes of human life.[24] Seneca's views were in line with the views of stoic philosophers of his day who taught that pleasure to the human material body is not good. Gauged against the teachings of Jesus, who was his contemporary in Palestine, Seneca's views were different: (1) Jesus did not oppose deriving pleasure from doing good,[25] (2) He also did not exhort his followers to do good deeds merely because it was good to do them or merely because they derived pleasure from doing them. On the contrary, (a) they were to do good primarily as expression of love and obedience to God, for his glory,[26] and (b) in love and for the benefit of others.[27] Jesus's philosophy for the purpose of doing good was different from what Seneca suggested.

In Book VI (I.1–XLIII.3), Seneca answered the philosophical question on whether it was possible to retrieve a benefit that had already been given. His argument is that it was possible to take away or give back a gift but not the benefit that the recipient had already earned from the gift. However, that argument is contradictory to what he said earlier in Book I about the dance of the three Graces. He said that if one goddess stopped dancing, the whole dance would be disrupted.[28] Similarly, he said that the real benefit is not only the material given and received but the goodwill (intention) of the giver.[29] That being so, it is not possible to retrieve the material gift and leave intact and unaffected the benefit it has already given. Retrieving a gift or being forced to give back without consent any one of the essential material or nonmaterial elements invalidates the rest of the components of the gift and turns sour whatever initial benefits it may have already incurred. However, in case the intended recipient returns an unwanted gift,

---

24. See Epicurus's, "Letter to Menoeceus" contained in Diogenes Laertius, *Lives of Eminent Philosophers*, Book X. Epicurus is dated from 341 to 270 BC.

25. For example, in Luke 19:6, καὶ σπεύσας κατέβη, καὶ ὑπεδέξατο αὐτὸν χαίρων, Jesus did not rebuke Zacchaeus for rejoicing because of being accorded the honour of doing the good deed of hosting him in his house.

26. See for example Matt 5:16 "let your light shine before others, so that they may see your good works and give glory to your Father in heaven."

27. In Luke 6:27, ἀγαπᾶτε τοὺς ἐχθροὺς ὑμῶν, καλῶς ποιεῖτε τοῖς μισοῦσιν ὑμᾶς, Jesus even went a step further and told his disciples that their good deeds should exceed that of sinners by loving and doing good to their enemies.

28. Seneca, *Seneca III*, I.III.1–IV.6.

29. Seneca, I.V.1–6.

as sometimes happens nowadays in the UK and elsewhere, there is no loss of the merit (honour) that is immediately gained by the giver because of his goodwill at the moment of giving.

In Book VII (I.1–XXXII.32), Seneca concluded his writing on the rules that governed the cycle of giving and receiving benefits by dealing with miscellaneous aspects that he had not discussed in the earlier sections. One of the new elements that he dealt with is criticism against hoarding things for oneself and failing to help others.[30] He also gave more reasons for incessant giving even to the ungrateful recipients.[31] Those reasons resonate with the rationale of the NT authors for they also encouraged believers to be always generous and not greedy, as they encouraged them to store through generosity their possessions where moths and rust do not destroy (Matt 6:19–20; cf. Acts 20:35). In 1 Timothy 6:17–19, Paul told Timothy to urge the rich members of the Ephesian church that being generous and sharing with the needy would result in a secure foundation for them in the future. Seneca concluded by encouraging Aebutius, his addressee, to keep on giving and receiving benefits in the right way, as guided in the essay.

In conclusion, Seneca himself admitted that his writing might have been laboriously repetitive, like a long-drawn song, and that it contained some details that seemed to be unnecessary.[32] However, my assessment is that Seneca needed not be concerned at all that he was repetitive, because some readers find the repetition useful. For example, to many Africans, repetition is natural and beneficial for a repeated statement sticks better in the mind than what is stated once only;[33] although, conversely, too much repetition is detrimental.[34] The extensive details that Seneca gives on the art of proper

---

30. Seneca, VII.IX.1–6.

31. Seneca, VII.XXXI.1–5.

32. Seneca, VII.I.1.

33. In the section titled "Repetition," *Repetition*, accessed 12 July 2012, http://hum.lss.wisc.edu/jazz/repetition.html University Course: Jazz Improvisation 331 and 530. Joan Wildman says that repetition is deeply embedded in the call-response of African music, and that music uses repetition in a particularly sophisticated manner. She explains that repetition provides emphasis and is effective in the medium of musical pitches as in the spoken word.

34. As Roy M. Mūtīsya, *Kikamba Proverbs and Idioms: Nthimo sya Kĩkamba na Myasyo* (Nairobi: Roma Publishers, 2002), 8, indicates in the Kĩkamba idiom, "Soo wa mwĩnzĩo ndwambaa," translated as "A trumpet that is blown insistently loses its vitality." The meaning is that a warning or a statement that is repeated too often is taken less seriously.

giving and receiving of benefits agree with the Christian principles of giving as depicted in the NT epistles. As stated above, Seneca was a non-Christian philosopher who was a contemporary of Christ and his Apostles in early first-century AD. Therefore, it is not surprising that some of the principles of social life that he knew and taught were similar to the principles that those early Christians upheld. However, following the teachings of Christ, Christians revolutionized the principles that were taught in the non-Christian world. For example, the teaching that exhorts Christians to help their enemies was built on a similar principle as that on which Seneca's principle to give benefaction to ungrateful people was built, the principle of doing good from a noble heart.[35] However, Christians made that principle a lot more advanced by exhorting that helping enemies should be based on love and devotion to God and on love and compassion for the needy recipient. In helping enemies, Christians were exhorted to value the recipient as much as they valued themselves, even though he was an enemy.

Seneca, highlighted the fact that it was necessary for someone to possess a substantial amount of money before he was chosen as senator.[36] That rule was instituted as a new requirement in the patronage system before Seneca, when Augustus became emperor and principal senator in 27 BC. The reason for the requirement was that the person had to prove that he was wealthy and solvent. As a senator, he was forbidden from involving himself directly in commercial ventures. Possession of wealth also enabled him to give material benefaction to the needy under his jurisdiction.

Overall, from the early church times to the present, Seneca's treatise remains a masterpiece on the subject of benefaction. Early fathers of the church and of the Middle Ages, such as Jerome, Tertullian, Augustine, Lactantius, St Ambrose, Martin of Bracara and others liked very much the moral teachings of the essay because they closely resembled the teachings of

---

35. Seneca, *Seneca III*, III.XV.5; VII.XXXII.

36. Seneca, VI.XIX.4, 5. In a note, John Basore, the translator of *Seneca III*, says that the potential senator was required to have 1,000,000 sesterces. The qualification required of someone vying for the position of a decurion in the local aristocracy (or for magistracy in the local council) was 100,000 sesterces, a tenth of what was required of a Roman senator. See Kidd, *Wealth and Beneficence*, 85–86, (where he cites Ramsey MacMullen, *Roman Social Relations 50 BC to A.D. 284* [New Haven; London: Yale University Press, 1974], 90 and Richard Duncan-Jones, *The Economy of the Roman Empire: Quantitative Studies*, 2nd ed. [Cambridge: Cambridge University Press, 1982], 243, 304).

the early church.³⁷ Together with other ancient writings, the extensive and comprehensive essay provides very valuable insights to the modern enquirer on the social transactions of benefaction and patronage in the G-R world of the first century AD.

2.2.3 Sets of Laws on *Patronicium*

As mentioned briefly above in the review of deSilva, certain sets of laws or *leges* were instituted to govern the social, economic, political and religious interactions between various people in the G-R world of the first century AD. Because patronage was an important intricate network of socioeconomic interdependence, there were laws that the imperial leaders instituted to govern it directly and indirectly. Such sets of laws were as those contained in *Lex Irnitana, Lex Salpensana, Lex Malacitana*, and *Lex Coloniae Genetiuae Iuliae*, which is also called *Lex Ursonensis*.³⁸

Some of *leges* included laws on honesty; laws on elections, for example, stipulations on who was fit to be elected as a patron by decuriones or senators; laws on financial matters; on hoarding; and laws on games and operas, for example, on participation and sponsorship of entertainment theatres. The laws for governing the Roman provinces were close to those that governed the respective municipalities. As in the writings of Cicero, the information that is contained in the numerous sets of laws is scattered all over, but the information that we get about the existence, features and operations of the patronage in the first century AD helps us to know how it was regulated. Although the laws in *Lex Irnitana* were inscribed in the later part of the first century AD, they had been in operation in oral unwritten forms from earlier times. The information is very helpful to us today as we read and attempt to understand some NT terms and constructions that have a bearing on the ideologies of the system.

---

37. For example, see M. Spanneut, "Seneca, Lucius Annaeus," in *New Catholic Enyclopoedia* 13 (SCU TEX), ed. John P. Whalen (Washington, DC: Catholic University of America), 80–81. See also Leighton Durham Reynolds, Miriam T. Griffin and Elaine Fantham, "Annaeus Seneca (2), Lucius," in *The Oxford Classical Dictionary* 1, eds. Simon Hornblower and Anthony Spawforth (Oxford: Oxford University Press), 96–98.

38. See Gonzalez, "Lex Irnitana," and M. H. Crawford, *Roman Statutes I*.

The information in chapter 6 of *Lex Irnitana* (for the city of Irni, in Spain; similar to *Lex Ursonensis* of Urso, also in Spain)[39] concerning the co-opting of a patron for a city[40] sheds light on the fact that there were principles that were put in place to regulate the system. The stipulations in *Lex Irnitana* about co-opting a patron are very similar to those in *Lex Flavia Malacitana* (for Malaga, Spain).[41] In the first century AD, Malaga became a municipality governed by Roman law that was enacted in AD 81. *Lex Flavia Malacitana* was inscribed on five tablets, but only part of it was discovered in 1851 in the El Ejido district of the city of Malaga.[42] Chapter

---

39. The *Lex Irnitana*, as cited in Gonzalez, and Crawford, "Lex Irnitana," 166, says: De patrono [c]ooptando. Ne quis patronum public{a}e municipibus municipi Flaui Irnitani cooptato patrociniumue c{i}ui deferto, nisi ex maioris par-tis decurionum decreto, quod decretum factum erit, cum duae partes non minus decurionum adfuerint et iurati 30 per tab[el]lam se[n]tentiam tulerint. Qui aliter aduersusue ea patronum public{a}e municipibus municipi Flaui Irni-tani cooptaueri{n}t patr[olciniumue cui detulerit, is HS(sestertium) X(milia) in pub-licum municipibus municipi Flaui Irnitani d(are) d(amnas) e(sto), isque, qui aduersus h(anc) l(egem) *patronus* cooptatus cuiue patrocinium dela- 35 tum erit, ne magis ob eam rem *patronus* municipum mu-nicipi Flaui Irnitani esto. Its translation on page 190 of Gonzalez and Crawford says:
Concerning the co-opting of a patron. No one is publicly to co-opt a patron for the municipes of the Municipium Flavium Irnitanum or to confer the power of patronage on anyone, except by a decree of the majority of the decuriones, which has been passed when not less than two thirds of the decuriones are present and they have cast their votes by ballot on oath. Whoever publicly co-opts otherwise or contrary to these rules a patron for the municipes of the Municipium Flavium Irnitanum or confers the power of patronage on anyone, is to be condemned to pay 10,000 sesterces to the public account of the municipes of the Municipium Flavium Irnitanum; and whoever has been co-opted a patron against this statute or had the power of patronage conferred on him, is not thereby to be a patron of the municipes of the Municipium Flavium Irnitanum.

40. Ex masters automatically became patrons to their manumitted slaves (those who were freed by the owner or on payment of a sum of money), but for one to be acknowledged as a municipal patron he had to be elected by not less than two thirds of the decuriones.

41. Armin U. Stylow, "LA LEX MALACITANA, DESCRIPCIÓN Y TEXTO," CIL II (2001): 45. See also Nicols' discussion about *Lex Malacitana* on co-opting a patron, John Nicols, "Patronum cooptare, patrocinium deferre: lex malacitana, 61," accessed 1 October 2018, https://scholarsbank.uoregon.edu/xmlui/bitstream/handle/1794/5058/Nicols_PatronumCooptareDeferre.txt?sequence=3&isAllowed=y.

42. For some details on the municipal laws for Malaca (or Malaga), see Nicholas Purcell, "Municipium," *The Oxford Classical Dictionary: The Ultimate Reference Work on the Classical World*, 1001. For details on the discovery and dates of *Lex Malacitana* see "MÁLAGA UNTIL ANTIQUITY," accessed 1 October 2018, http://www.malagaturismo.com/en/pages/malaga-until-antiquity/300. For *Lex Irnitana* see Michael H. Crawford, "Tabula Irnitana," *The Oxford Classical Dictionary: The Ultimate Reference Work on the Classical World*, 1467.

97 of *Lex Irnitana* also speaks of the powers of a patron over freedmen.[43] These and other similar inscriptions help us to know some of the principles of the Roman *patronicium* system. The laws are plausible evidence that in the first century AD, *patronicium* was a well-established system, at least in some parts of the Mediterranean region.

2.2.4 Philo and Josephus

Philo's (20 BC–AD 50) and Josephus's (30–100 AD) accounts on the social status of the Jews in the first century AD are insightful. They contain some details on Jewish benefaction and patronage, although not as detailed as Seneca's discussion about the systems in *De Beneficiis*. Scholars argue that Josephus's and Philo's records had certain biases towards Judaistic, Hellenistic, and Roman interests. Such biases are encountered, for example, in what Josephus wrote touching on patronage as recorded especially in *The Life of Flavius Josephus*,[44] *Antiquities of the Jews*, and *The Jewish War*. Josephus, himself a Jew living in Rome at the time of his writing, is believed to have fabricated some details in his historical accounts to favour his Roman patrons.[45] For example, that bias is seen in his accounts about the good deeds that King Agrippa II did as benefaction to the Jews in many cities in Asia

---

43. See Gonzalez, "Lex Irnitana," 181, LXXXXVII R(ubrica). Vt in libertos libertas ciuitatem Romanam consecu- 20 tos consecutas per honores liberorum suorum aut uirorum patroni it ius habeant, quod antea habu-erunt. Qui libertini quaeue libertinae ex h(ac) l(ege) per honores liberto-rum suorum aut uirorum ciuitatem Romanam consecuti 25 consecutae erunt, in eos eas inque bona eorum earum is qui eos manumiserint, si non et ipsi ciuitatem Romanam conse-cuti erunt, idem ius esto quod fuisset si ei eae ciues Romani Romanae facti factae non essent. Si ciuitatem Romanam pa-troni patronae consecuti consecutae erunt, idem ius in [eos] 30 libertos easque libertas inque bona eorum earum esto, quQd esset si a [ciui] bus Romanis manumissi {manumissa} manumis-sae egsent.

Its translation on page 199 of Gonzalez reads: That patrons should have the same rights as they had before over freedmen or freedwomen who have obtained Roman citizenship as a result of the offices of their sons or husbands. If any freedmen or freedwomen have obtained Roman citizenship under this statute as a result of the offices of their sons or husbands, PErsons who manumitted them are to have the same rights over them and their goods, even if they themselves have not obtained Roman citizenship, as they would have had if they had not been made Roman citizens. If the patrons, male or female, have (also) obtained Roman citizenship, they are to have the same rights over those freedmen and freedwomen and their goods as they would have if they had been manumitted by Roman citizens.

44. Flavius Josephus, *Josephus*, 1–21.

45. Richard Laqueur, *Der jüdische Historiker Flavius Josephus: ein biographischer Versuch auf neuer quellenkritischer Grundlage* (Darmstadt: Wissenschaftliche Buchgesellschaft, 1970 [1920]). Cited by Peter Kirby in *Early Jewish Writings* at http://www.earlyjewishwritings.com/josephus.html.

around the first century AD, as recorded in *Ant.* 14, 16.2.2 and other sections. Although it was not acceptable in Christian circles, flattery in oral speech and in writing was common behaviour that was somehow acceptable in the general society, especially from beneficiaries/clients to their benefactors/patrons (cf. Plutarch, *How to Tell a Flatterer from a Friend*). Most of what Josephus and Philo wrote is confirmed as fact by other authors of their time. The fact that Jews had patrons in Asian cities who fought for them, such as Marcus Alexander in Halicarnassus, as shown in *Ant.* 14.256, and Prytanis in Miletus, as in *Ant.* 14.425, is supported by the writings of Apollonius Molon in Eusebius's *Praeparatio Evangelica* 9: 19.1–3, and those of Nicolas in *Ant.* 16.31–57.

Some important information that is missing in what Philo and Josephus wrote on patronage is that they did not write much on Jewish patronage to fellow Jews or to people of other nations. They wrote mainly about the patronage that the Romans gave to the Jews.[46] However, we cannot discredit their accounts because of that weakness. Throughout history there are authors who focus their writing on the social situation of some sections of their society but that does not make their accounts invalid.[47] What Philo and Josephus wrote about the benefaction and patronage of the Romans and the Jews from antiquity to their times is credible. What can be deduced from what they wrote especially about the Jews gives a useful hint that although Jews maintained their social distinctives in Palestine and in the Diaspora, they were also caught up in the prevailing G-R benefaction and patronage networks of the first century AD.

For example, their statements on the cosmological and soteriological nuances of mediatorship and its use in non-religious and religious contexts gives us a glimpse of the concept of μεσίτης. From a religious perspective, Philo perceived the angel who arbitrated between Haggar and Sarah and the angel who led Israelites into Canaan as mediators of God's protection

---

46. However, as seen in my discussion on benefaction and patronage in the Jewish context below in this chapter, Jews both received from and gave support to fellow Jews and non-Jews in places where they were in Diaspora.

47. For example, see David Bearinger, "Sustaining Local History: Honoring Virginia's Community Historians," *vfh Views: The Newsletter of the Virginia Foundation for the Humanities*, accessed 1 October 2018, https://www.virginiahumanities.org/wp-content/uploads/2011/11/news_spring_2011.pdf.

and guidance to his people. In addition, in *Antiquities*, Josephus provides examples of episodes of religious and non-religious mediation and that way helps us to know the existence of that aspect of G-R and Jewish benefaction and patronage at the time of his writing. The detailed accounts that Philo and Josephus give us about the Jews on benefaction and patronage are close to some of the NT accounts. For example, Josephus's account of the Herod's death in Caesarea when he accepted honour and praise that belongs to God alone is similar to Luke's account in Acts 12:20–23.[48] Hence, their accounts are very valuable resources in the study of the principles of benefaction and patronage in PE. Additionally, the Apocrypha, for example Maccabees, and other writings of before and around the first century AD, for example, the writings of Polybius, Aristotle and Lucian also provide us with valuable accounts of Greek, Roman and Jewish benefaction and patronage. Valuable background information based on the ancient sources that are reviewed above and others that contain insights on the systems in the Greek, Roman and Jewish contexts, is discussed in the following section.

2.3 Benefaction and Patronage in the Greek, Roman and Jewish Contexts

Chronologically the study should begin with the Jewish world for, in accessible recorded history, it is older than the Greek and Roman worlds. However, my study begins with the Greek and Roman worlds because in the first century AD the Greek and Roman cultures were dominant in the Mediterranean region. Domination of the Greek culture especially through the spread of Koine Greek as a lingua franca of the post-Alexander era in the eastern Mediterranean region[49] occurred earlier than that of the Roman culture. The influence of Greek culture was still strong among the Mediterranean populations in the first century AD although the Roman Empire was the dominant political power at that time. Historically the domination of the Greek empire and its culture in the Mediterranean world was earlier than that of the Romans. When the Romans took over later, they

---

48. See *Ant.* 19.8.2 in *Josephus: Complete Works*.
49. See also Jeremy Duff, *The Elements of New Testament Greek* (Cambridge: Cambridge University, 2005), 9.

did not suppress or replace Greek culture totally. Therefore, Greek εὐεργεσία and other traditional systems were still flourishing in the first century. Roman *patronicium* became prominent during the reign of Caesar Augustus, but it did not replace Greek εὐεργεσία. Instead, the two systems operated alongside each other. Εὐεργεσία operated more in the eastern side of the empire while *patronicium* was more in the west. Jewish kinship benefaction also was functioning simultaneously with the other systems, especially among the Jews. Although some of the principles of the three systems were similar, each system was distinct. When the Christian church came into existence, for its benefaction endeavours, it mainly adopted and Christianized principles of the Jewish kinship benefaction. It also adopted and utilized some of the language and principles of the Greek and Roman benefaction systems. The similarities and differences are elaborated below in the discussion on the Greek, Roman and Jewish contexts respectively.

Benefaction is a broad term that covers various systems of good deeds or benefits that various beings do to others. For example, divine beings do good to humans, and humans do good things to one another. Among humans, they are modes of socioeconomic relationships in which those who are endowed more with material and nonmaterial resources help those who are less endowed. In the first-century Greek, Roman and Jewish societies, εὐεργεσία, *patronicium* and kinship benefaction were such systems. The particular terms used in reference to the features and transactions of each one of the three systems are defined and elaborated comprehensively below, in the respective sections on their contexts.

2.3.1 In Greek Context

Among the Greek communities of the ancient world, gods and people who had resources used them for the good of people who did not have. What they did was known as εὐεργεσίαι, that is, "acts of kindness" or "good service," that is, "good deeds."[50] The gods and the people who did those acts of kindness were called εὐεργέται (singular εὐεργέτης). Εὐεργέτης was "doer of good" or "benefactor." The term was an honorary title used for wealthy and influential men in high positions who used to provide support (for

---

50. With the coming of Roman culture in the ancient world, εὐεργεσία sometimes was called *benefactus*, which is past participle of benefacere: *bene*, well/good + *facere*, to do.

example, political power and financial aid) for others. Various cognates of εὐεργέτης occur in the NT in Luke 22:25 (εὐεργέται); Acts 4:9 (εὐεργεσίᾳ); 10:38 (εὐεργετῶν) and 1 Timothy 6:2 (εὐεργεσίας). What qualified to be εὐεργεσία is what was done based on the free decision and goodwill of the εὐεργέτης. Good deeds were provisions in various material and nonmaterial forms: money, credit, influence, protection, advice and good precepts. In *De Beneficiis* I.VI.1, Seneca describes a benefit (*beneficium*, pl. *beneficia*) as doing an act of kindness that gives joy to the recipient and also achieves joy for the giver who grants it "from the prompting of his own will." The term εὐεργέω and its cognates are not discussed at all in *TDNT*. Its mention in *NIDNTT* III, 1147, 1152, is very slight. As it is with the older commentaries, the importance of the benefaction and patronage language was presumably not recognized at the time when these dictionaries were compiled.

In the Anchor Bible Dictionary,[51] Danker defines "benefactor" as a person or deity who was considered to be of outstanding merit (ἀρετή, that is, "moral excellence,"[52] "goodness," "redemptive acts") because of benefits conferred on others.[53] He calls him εὐεργέτης, that is, "one who does good." He describes him further as the truly public-spirited citizen or benefactor who aspires to the highest of virtues, especially uprightness (δικαιοσύνη). He gives examples of such benefactors as the Stoic philosophers who helped to popularize the democratization process in the G-R world. He also says that recognition of ἀρετή and beneficence was across gender boundaries, and gives evidence of that in biblical and non-biblical examples of women who were recognized and honoured for their contribution. A striking example that he gives is that of Kaikilia Tertylla who was honoured for benefaction and leadership of elders, young men and boys.[54] He gives many significant terms in the Greek NT that describe those who qualified for special

---

51. Frederick W. Danker, "Benefactor," in *Anchor Bible Dictionary*, vol. 1: A–C, ed. David Noel Freedman (New York: Doubleday, 1992), 669–671.

52. Note that here "moral" does not mean "godly" or "spiritual." It is excellence in reference to G-R ethical standards.

53. ABD does not have any article on προστάτης (patron) or προστάσια (patronage) because the terms are nowhere in the NT. Nevertheless, there is προστάτις in Rom 6:2, but Danker does not discuss it.

54. As in J. J. E. Hondius, ed., *Supplementum Epigrephicum Graecum*, SEG no. 696, (Leiden: Brill 1923).

recognition or express their beneficent actions. Ἀρετή and ἀνὴρ ἀγαθός lead the list. In the list also are "one who is generously kind" (χρῆστος), "one who functions as a saviour" (σωτήρ), "one who is noted for righteousness" (δικαιοσύνη), "one who is eager to render service" (φιλοτιμέομαι), "one who does good works" (εὐεργέτης), and others. It is notable that Danker misses other terms that also have significant use in benefaction, such as χάρις, τιμή and πίστις, among others.

Several writings of ancient Greek and Roman authors contain material on G-R εὐεργεσία and *patronicium* respectively. For example, as seen above in their reviews, Cicero's *De Officiis* and Seneca's *De Beneficiis* give us valuable insights on those distinct systems. Lucian's *Nigrinus*, Aristotle's *Nicomachean Ethics,* and *The Art of Rhetoric* also are helpful. According to Aristotle, for example *Rhet.* Book I.V.5–9, Greek εὐεργεσία was the practice in which a person of means, for example a noble by birth or wealth, did good works by providing benefits from his own resources to his community. In *Nic Eth* Book IV Aristotle wrote about two basic types of benefactors in Greek system of εὐεργεσία: (1) the "magnificent man" who did collective good works for the common good of all his fellow citizens, and (2) the "great-souled man" from an upper social stratum who, based on a reciprocal interchange agreement, engaged in good deeds of a more personal nature with people of equal stratum, or near equal stratum.[55] Collective and reciprocal εὐεργεσία was more common. In *De Ben* I.III.3, Seneca gives three types: (1) those who bestow benefits (2) those who repay them, and (3) those who both receive and repay them.

In section III.X.7 of Aristotle's fourth century BC book, *Politics*, on the Greek society of that time, he states that some men of eminent virtue were made kings because of their goodness that was portrayed through acts of εὐεργεσία.[56] In III.V.7, he states that in the Greek society, the rich were few and the poor were many. That factor created a system of benefaction, which although not as clearly defined as in the Roman patron-client system, there was a struggle as the many poor strove to get support from the few rich. That

---

55. Aristotle, *Nicomachean Ethics*, ed. Roger Crisp, Cambridge Texts in the History of Philosophy, (Cambridge: Cambridge University Press, 2000), 65–73.

56. Aristotle, *Politics*, ed. G. P. Goold, trans. H. Rackham, Loeb XXI (Cambridge, MA: Harvard University Press, 1932 [350 AD]), 258, 259.

phenomenon has been the same for many societies because in an unequal world humans need some reciprocal system in order to survive.

As indicated by Seneca, the nobles were expected to provide various material and nonmaterial helps to their communities collectively and to individuals in exchange for the public honour they received from the beneficiaries.[57] Honour was sometimes given before the benefaction was given by the benefactor, whereas, at other times, the benefit was given first and then the honour followed as reciprocation for the benefit. A credible example of Greek benefaction by a renowned leader in the Intertestamental Period is the Seleucid ruler, Antiochus IV, that is, Antiochus Epiphanes, as affirmed by Livy[58] and Polybius.[59] Epiphanes is said to have given benefaction to Greek cities and paid honours to the Greek gods. His benefaction is said to have surpassed the benefaction that his predecessors had given.[60]

In the first century AD, the Greek title εὐεργέτης still had its primitive sense and was given to someone who gave general benefaction in the society. However, it also acquired a new technical meaning of "protector" and was used in reference to benefactor of a particular city or group of people.[61] Because of this development, sometimes Greek benefaction was not distinguishable from Roman patronage. When used in reference to the gods, the term meant that the gods were the benefactors or protectors of the whole world.[62] Honorary statues and inscriptions were made and titles, like "saviour" or "benefactor" were given to benefactors by the citizens who had benefited from the generosity of the benefactors. For example, Emperor Claudius was given the title "saviour" on coin inscriptions

---

57. Seneca, *Seneca III*, I.II.4.

58. Livy, *Ab Urbe Condita*, LCL Book 41: Livy Vol. 12 (Cambridge, MA: Harvard University Press, 1938). Titus Livius (Livy) lived ca. 60 BC–AD 17.

59. Polybius was born about 208 BC and died in 126 BC (*Polybius: The Histories*, Loeb Classical Library I [Cambridge, MA: Harvard University Press, 1922], vii, x).

60. See Livy, *Ab Urbe Condita*, 41.20.5, and Polybius, *Polybius*, XXVI.I.10.

61. Susanne Ebbinghaus, "Protector of the City, or the Art of Storage in Early Greece," *JHS* 125 (November 2005): 51–72.

62. See εὐργέτ-εια in Henry George Liddell, and Robert Scott, *A Greek-English Lexicon*, revised supplement ed. (Oxford: Clarendon, 1996), 712.

of AD 41. Numerous honorary inscriptions in Greek phraseology attest to the importance of benefactors in the G-R world.[63]

An example of such honorary reciprocation is what was given to Emperor Claudius (AD 41–54). He received the accolades of "saviour and benefactor" and was elevated to the position of a god worthy of worship because he improved administration and curbed extortion in the empire.[64] Greeks honoured their Roman benefactors using the Roman terminology of patronage. A good example is an inscription for Marcus Antonius Promachus in Corinth in which he is called φίλος καὶ προστάτης, "friend and patron"[65] which is equivalent to the Latin *amicus et patronus*. Additionally, the term προστασία was at times used by Greek authors to refer to patronage. Similarly, inscriptions were made in honour of Junia Theodora, who was a regional patron living in Corinth about AD 43 or 57.[66] She was honoured for her patronage to Lycian cities. The provisions that she gave were referred to as προστασία, for example, in line 77 of *A Decree of the Lycian City of Telmessos*.

Competition among benefactors was common. As depicted in the ancient honorary inscriptions, in the benefaction systems, the language of excess was typical. Benefactors competed in the exhibition of certain virtues, such as goodwill (εὔνοια), benevolence (φιλανθρωπία), courage (ἀνδρεία), love of glory (φιλοδοξία), love of honour (φιλοτιμία), greatness of mind (μεγαλοφροσύνη), and moderation (σωφροσύνη). They competed to outdo one another in the provision of benefactions so that they would be honoured by the beneficiaries more than their fellow competitors. For example, in an honorary inscription by the council of Carallia, as a benefactor, Conon, son of Cendeas (who was also called Longinus), is said to have eclipsed the honour of his ancestors. In an eastern Mediterranean context, it was essential that the ἀνὴρ ἀγαθός (good man, benefactor) replicate and surpass ancestral

---

63. See Danker, *Benefactor*, 56–313 for such inscriptions that date from 241 BC to the first century AD and after.

64. See Danker, *Benefactor*, 223.

65. Inscription number 265 in J. H. Kent's book, *The Inscriptions 1926–1950. Corinth: Results of Excavations. VIII/3* (Princeton, NJ: Princeton University Press, 1966).

66. Inscriptions about her were found on a stele by a French archaeological team in 1954. The inscriptions are published in Pallas, Bulletin de correspondence hellenique (1959): 496–508.

glory, as it was for the *nobilis* in the Roman west.[67] Similarly, a Greek legend has it that Athens was named after the goddess Athena (Minerva in Roman culture, the goddess of wisdom and skill) as honour for offering to Athens patronage that was more valuable than what was offered by her competitor god, Poseidon (Neptune, the god of seas). Athena is said to have been the provider of useful advice and skills for men and women respectively and she provided protection and victory in such times as during the decisive war with Persia. Such evidence provides clues to us that benefaction was efficient in some Greek cities from antiquity.

Simply stated, in Greek εὐεργεσία benefits were communally given rather than individually bestowed. Those who received the benefits regarded themselves as equals or near-equals to the givers. The benefits were given face-to-face rather than through brokers. The relationship between the benefactor and the beneficiaries was based on free association and therefore permanence of the benefaction relationship was not guaranteed but sometimes the relationship acquired permanence. The benefactors were expected to be willing, to be timely and faithful in giving benefaction, whereas the beneficiaries were highly expected to be loyal in reciprocation of the benefits they had received.

Εὐεργεσία was a noble system. However, over time, it acquired a negative characteristic because of negative reciprocity where there was self-interest at the expense of the other person. For example, the demand for benefaction and for reciprocation became a vicious cycle, where pursuit of self-interest by one party, or both, became paramount. In some instances, the beneficiaries became too focused on benefit-loving, and the benefactors on honour-loving.[68] As Dionysius of Halicarnassus indicates in *Roman Antiquities* II.IX.2, another abuse that developed was that some Greek benefactors, such as the Thessalians and Athenians, abused their clients by treating them with haughtiness. In a derogatory manner, Athenians called their clients θῆται or "hirelings" because they served for hire. Thessalians called theirs πενέσται or "toilers" thus reproaching them for their condition. Because of that and

---

67. J. R. Harrison, "Excels Ancestral Honours," in *New Documents Illustrating Early Christianity*, vol. 9, *A Review of the Greek Inscriptions and Papyri Published in 1986-87*, ed. S. R. Llewelyn (Grand Rapids, MI: Eerdmans, 2002), 20.

68. Aristotle, *Art of Rhetoric*, ed. Jeffrey Hendersen and G. P. Goold, trans. John Henry Freese, LCL XXII: LCL 193 (Cambridge, MA; London, England: Harvard University Press, 1926), 59–69.

other negative practices, the systems became polluted. However, it did not become as polluted as *patronicium*, as shown in the following section. Even so, without the abuses, the two systems were noble ways of bringing some equilibrium in the society, especially in facilitation of access to necessary resource to the less privileged.

Although explicit patronage terminology is scarce in ancient Greek materials, that fact does not mean that patron-client relationships were non-existent in the Greek world as has been detailed above.[69] In the ancient Jewish context also, explicit G-R benefaction and patronage terminology is scarce. However, that does not mean that there was no benefaction or patronage among the Jews.

2.3.2 In Roman Context

Patronicium was the Roman counterpart of the Greek εὐεργεσία system. *Patronicium* means "patronage, protection, defence (in court)." *Patrocinium* was a system in which a *patronus* (patron) took up the responsibility of protecting, sponsoring or meeting the various needs of a *cliens* (plural *clienten*) from the lower class of *plebeians* (of Roman citizens, distinguished from slaves) or people from outside Rome. Generally, a *patronus* (plural *patroni*) was the most senior member in one of several social relationship networks. *Patroni* were normally drawn from the *patricians*, that is, class of elite citizens. A *patrician* was a natural or adopted member of one of the dignified families of the ancient Roman Republic. Before the third century BC, those families had exclusive rights to the senate and the magistracies. In Late Roman Empire, the patrician class broadened to include high council officials. In the first century AD, the term *patronus* referred to "defender," "protector," and "advocate."[70] The closest Greek equivalent term for *patronus* was προστάτης. *Patronatus* was the status or position of the patron. The term *patronus* was derived from *patr-*, *pater*, that is, "father." A deity or a person was recognized and honoured as a father for the provision and care that he gave to those over whom he had responsibility.

---

69. Wallace-Hadrill, *Patronage*, 16.

70. Philip Babcock Gove and The Merriam-Webster Editorial Staff, eds., *Webster's Third New International Dictionary of the English Language Unabridged* (Springfield, MA: G. & C. Merriam, 1961), 1656.

From antiquity, Roman society was highly stratified. Concerning patronage, Saller points out that, more so in Imperial Rome, every citizen was either a patron or client because patron-client relationships were found in one form or another in most societies in and outside Rome.[71] The stratification was so intricate that a patron could also have a patron of his own and a client have his own clients. The larger the number and the higher the status of his clients are what determined a patron's prestige. Whenever Romans of equal high status held a patronage relationship for reciprocal benefits, they acquired the label *amicus* (friend) and they operated as equals,[72] not as superior and inferior. In the relationship of unequals, the patron helped the client in various ways, such as offering protection for him and his family in legal matters, giving financial help, and providing other resources. In return for benefaction, the clients became indebted to patrons. For example, they owed their votes to their patrons. Therefore, in any case, the social stratification was beneficial to all parties.

According to legend, the *patronus-cliens* relationship was invented by Romulus, the founder of Rome. He invented it to introduce cordiality and get rid of the abrasiveness and insensitiveness that previously dominated the relationships between benefactors and beneficiaries.[73] Citing Dionysius of Halicarnassus, Neyrey says that cordiality was introduced when Romulus wished that the relations between patrons and client in Rome would not be dominated by harshness like what was displayed in Greek relationships. As hinted to by Dionysius in *Roman Antiquities* II.IX.2, some Greek benefactors, such as the Athenians and Thessalians, treated their clients with haughtiness and imposed on them duties that were not fit for free men. He says that "they beat them and misused them in all other respects as if they had been slaves they had purchased." Therefore, Romulus recommended that there be changes and the entire benefaction transaction be referred to by the honourable name of "patronage."[74] Hence, some semblance of kinship

---

71. Richard P. Saller, *Personal Patronage under the Early Empire* (Cambridge: Cambridge University Press, 1982), 3.

72. Nevertheless, Saller points out on page 11 of *Personal Patronage under the Early Empire*, the title *amicus* was also used between people of unequal status to avoid the abrasiveness that was sometimes found in *patronus-cliens* relationships.

73. Neyrey, "God," 468.

74. Neyrey, 468.

and friendship developed between the two unequal parties.[75] For example, the relationship acquired other dimensions, such as familial and friendship language. Such was the case in the first century AD, for example, as seen in John 19:12, where Pilate was called Caesar's friend although Pilate was inferior to Caesar in political status.

Patronus-cliens (patron-client) vocabulary became more defined in the Roman world during the early empire period,[76] from 27 BC to AD 96. The *patronus-cliens* relationship was an asymmetrical reciprocal relationship between two parties of unequal social and economic status in which there was exchange of various sorts of goods and/or services, respectively, for a long time, and, sometimes, permanently. The relationship was largely controlled by the party of superior status.[77]

Patronicium was one of the most important and enduring forms of sociopolitical and economic systems of exchange and control between people of unequal social status in the early, middle and late Roman republic and the early and late imperial eras. In those periods, individuals and groups were exchanging material and nonmaterial goods and services. In the Middle Roman Republic (264–133 BC) and Late Republic (123–27 BC) eras, the difference in power and status between the parties in the exchange transaction was acknowledged and emphasized.[78] As in εὐεργεσία, some of the relationships between patrons and clients were mainly based on *fides*, that is, faith (trust) and loyalty, and not on any written, formal or legally binding contracts. In relation to patronage, Crook defines *fides* (πίστις) as "an action of the client that reflects well upon or supports the patron."[79] Thus, the relationships could be broken easily. However, some forms of patronage were long-term and legally binding, for example, the *patronus-libertus* (patron-freedman) type where the masters remained in permanent *potestas* (power) as patrons

---

75. Wallace-Hadrill, *Patronage*, 154.

76. Wallace-Hadrill, *Patronage*, 15–16; Citing Saller (*Personal Patronage*, 8–11) and Garnsey and Saller (*The Roman Empire* [Oakland, CA: University of California, 1987], 148–159).

77. Wallace-Hadrill, *Patronage*, 16.

78. That was unlike in the Greek εὐεργεσία where superiority of the benefactor was not emphasized.

79. Crook, *Reconceptualising Conversion*, 215.

over the freedmen and even over their children as required by the law.[80] As one of the trademarks of the Roman Empire, Rome maintained direct and indirect patronage over citizen and non-citizen subjects in cities and provinces where the Empire had political influence in the Mediterranean world.

Although Roman aristocrats exercised patronage in their respective locations of political and military leadership, the most prominent form of patronage was that of the emperor over all the citizens of the empire. The emperor had control over important resources such as land, money, status, positions, and honour. He had direct patronage influence over some individuals while also maintaining the relationship indirectly through intermediary figures or brokers (μεσίται). Although sometimes the μεσίται acted as patrons to the clients, their main role was that of providing access to the more powerful patrons.[81] Some of the brokers, for example, were the family members and friends of the emperor. The *principes* (governors) of the cities and provinces, the senators and other people who were close to the emperor, also played the role of brokers or mediators between the emperor and the citizens. Evidence of the existence and operations of the Roman patronage system towards the end of the first century BC is also found in Horace's odes.[82] For example, in a poem titled *To Maecenas* in Horace's cluster of poems titled *Echoes from the Sabine Farm*, Horace addresses Maecenas as friend and patron and invites him to come and share with him in drinking his home-made Sabine wine. Thus, it is evident that from the era of Roman Republic to the era of Roman Empire, patronage was an integral part of the Roman social world. Brokerage became increasingly important during the Roman Principate (27 BC–AD 284, that is, in the early imperial period). Although in Roman *patronicium* brokerage was common, in Greek εὐεργεσία, direct benefaction was common.

According to *De Beneficiis* VI.33.3–34.5, it was customary for kings and their imitators to classify into three groups the people who depended on them for support. (1) The first-class of friends consisted of those who were most select and were received privately by the patron. (2) The second-class friends were more select and were received collectively during the customary

---

80. See also Joubert, "One Form of Social Exchange," 19.
81. deSilva, "Patronage," 767.
82. Horace, whose real name is Quintus Horatius Flaccus, lived from 65 to 8 BC.

morning salutations. (3) The "never true friends" were the clients proper, who generally gathered at the patron's compound every morning to receive monetary handouts or so that they would be available for service to the patron. The third group was also referred to as protégés or *amicitiae inferiores*, that is, inferior-friends.

Some specific forms of Roman patronage were unique and different from Greek εὐεργεσία. For example, patronage between a master and a freedman, and patronage between the emperor and Roman citizens were very formal. In Roman patronage, there were prominent differences between the social status of the patron and the client. The patron normally belonged to a higher dominant elite class while the client belonged to a lower subservient class. Another difference is that in Roman patronage, in some cases, failure to honour obligations on both the side of the patron and the client did not affect much the relationship between the two as in Greek εὐεργεσία εὐεργεσία. That was so because in those cases the relationship was based on a permanent binding agreement whereas in εὐεργεσία the relationship was mainly voluntary and temporary. Additionally, for someone to be designated as an official patron in some of the Roman communities he had to possess certain qualifications. For example, he had to be the founder or the governor, or a relative of the governor or founder of the Roman city or province as stated in *leges Ursonensis, Malacitana*,[83] *Irnitana* and *Salpensana*. Those and other factors were distinctive features of Roman patronage that were not found in Greek εὐεργεσία. Thus, contrary to some scholars' observations, it is evident that even before the first century AD, Roman patronage had the characteristics of a legally and socially encoded and binding system.

As seen above in the discussion on the Greek context, as time progressed, Roman patronage also developed some gross abuses that gave it a negative outlook. The abuses were mainly based on negative reciprocity, where there was pursuit of self-interest at the expense of others. Patronage was a method

---

83. See John Nicols' translation of *Lex Malacitana* in the article, "Patronum cooptare." Lex Ursonensis is also called Lex Coloniae Genetivae Iuliae and is dated 44 BC. Lex Malacitana of about 8AD 2–84, together with Lex Salpensana were also Roman municipal constitutions which among other things inform us about candidates in elections and voting, and the appointment of tutors. Lex Ursonensis and Lex Malacitana mention some regulations laid down for designation of people into patronage and senatorial status in provinces of the ancient Roman world. See also Crawford, *Roman Statutes I*, 431, (statute number CXXX).

through which the rich exploited and controlled the poor. Conversely, it was a method through which the poor tried to protect themselves in a potentially hostile environment where there were inequalities in wealth and status.[84] Some of the benefactors and patrons loved more the honour that they got from the transaction than doing good for the benefit of the recipients. Clients exploited that weakness of the patrons and heaped flatteries on them in false loyalty and friendship to them. For example, there is evidence in Philodemus's Herculaneum Papyri of about 40 or 35 BC. In the papyrus titled *On Flattery (PHerc. 222)* in the section "On Vices and Virtues," he discusses the vice of desire (φιλοτίμια) for fame and honour. In papyri *PHerc. 1675*, *PHerc. 1082*, and *PHerc. 1089* he contrasts between flattery and friendship. Philodemus describes flattery as the enemy of true friendship.[85] Another notorious abuse is that some of the patrons claimed for themselves or eagerly received honour that is befitting for God, from a biblical perspective. It is attested in both extra-biblical and biblical writings that even before the Greek and Roman times, human kings of various kingdoms such as the Medes and Persians received divine honour and worship fit for God. Some of the clients even heaped untrue and inflated praise on the patrons for the sole purpose of getting benefaction. They valued and enjoyed the benefits that they received more than the giver and they sometimes failed to thank him. Another abuse was that some patrons gave only because they were compelled to give, and therefore they gave only the minimum although they were very rich.[86] NT authors recognized such abuses and wrote to counter and correct them.

In the first century AD, Roman patronage closely coexisted with other forms of social exchange relationships such as the family relationships,[87] friendship relationships,[88] charity and εὐεργεσία relationships. By the late

---

84. See also Wallace-Hadrill's comments in *Patronage*, 16–17.

85. Walker, "Benefactor," 157.

86. Walker, 158.

87. Jewish patronage had the features of kinship relationships such that people who belonged to the Judaistic religious association were required to help one another as helping family members. That kind of Jewish patronage was adopted by the Christian association as evidenced in the fictive family references in exhortations in the NT and in extra-biblical material of around the first century AD.

88. For details on friendship relationships, see Peter Marshall, *Enmity in Corinth: Social Conventions in Paul's Relations with the Corinthians* WUNT 2/23 (Tübingen: Mohr

Empire, the Roman ideology of patronage had become so embedded into the social life of people in the Mediterranean G-R world that it could rightly be considered a widespread phenomenon that had usurped all the functions of civic benefaction.[89] Just as the contemporary Greek εὐεργεσία had done, Roman *patronicium* had started with the noble purpose whereby the more privileged parties helped the lesser privileged. In *patronicium*, the transacting parties were supposed to help one another mutually with material and nonmaterial resources and services. The similarities and differences between the two systems are explained further in the following section.

2.3.2.1 Excursus: Similarities and differences between εὐεργεσία and patronicium

In the first century AD in the Mediterranean regions, both εὐεργεσία and *patronicium* worked alongside each other in making various material and nonmaterial resources available to all the parties involved in the transaction. Looking at how the Greeks and Romans understood and practised εὐεργεσία and *patronicium* respectively, we deduce that although there were similarities in their principles of operation, there were significant differences. Their similarities were in the following aspects: (1) Both systems were modes of socioeconomic interdependence relationships which were primarily inaugurated to bring socioeconomic equity among individuals and communities. (2) Although it was more prominent in *patronicium* than in εὐεργεσία, there was an element of socioeconomic asymmetrism between the benefactors and beneficiaries. Neyrey says that human-benefactor-client relationships were "asymmetrical, reciprocal, voluntary, often including favouritism, focused on honor and respect, and held together by 'goodwill' or faithfulness."[90] (3) To make the relationship more friendly between the transacting parties, kinship language was adopted. (4) The central transaction in both systems was the exchange of material and nonmaterial assets and services. (5) Those commodities were exchanged over a period of time in accordance with some definite and generally acknowledged and accepted conventions. (6) The help

---

Siebeck, 1987).

    89. This does not mean that Roman patronage was not a powerful system before the late empire (AD 250–550).

    90. Neyrey, "God," 468.

given was gratuitous, and could not be repaid in kind. (7) The gift was given to enhance the reputation of the giver.

(8) In both systems appropriate response was expected from the recipients. When the client received benefaction, he customarily incurred a debt and a binding obligation to the patron. The client had to repay the debt by being thankful, honourable, faithful and loyal to the patron. He had to give whatever service he was expected to render to the patron in exchange for the benefit he had received from him. Benefits needed to be given and received cheerfully and continuously, just like the ceaseless dance of the three Greek goddesses called Grace (grace of giving, grace of receiving, and grace of gratefulness). The favourable reciprocal response was called χάρις. The ability and willingness to receive help graciously was one of the best virtues and modes of reciprocation. Honour was a common form of reciprocation, such as public gratitude in form of applause, honorary decrees or election to public office.[91] In both systems, the more honour or other kind of reciprocation the benefactor, patron or mediator received, the more indebted he became to give more benefaction or patronage. Other practical forms of reciprocation were that the client provided political support by voting for his patron and offering any other services that might be expected of him.[92]

(9) Failure to reciprocate with thanks was sometimes chided through stern letters of blame. For example, commenting on epistolary styles of the medieval churches (fourth to sixth centuries AD) in sections 6 and 53 of *Pseudo Libanius* on the relationship of the author of a letter and his addressees, Stanley Stowers says that the author of a blame letter, for example, was a benefactor who expected honour from the recipient as appropriate response for benefaction but the recipient had not reciprocated well.[93] That blame feature can also be detected in Christian and non-Christian epistles

---

91. Walker, "Benefactor," 157.

92. For further details on benefaction and reciprocation, see *Seneca III*, I.II.2–4; I.III.1–IV.6; I.X.4–5; III.V.2–VII.2; III.X.1; VII.XXV.3.

93. Stanley K. Stowers, "Social Typification and the Classification of Ancient Letters," in *The social World of Formative Christianity and Judaism: Essays in Tribute to Howard Clark Kee*, eds. Jacob Neusner, Ernest S. Frerichs, Peder Borgen and Richard Horsley (Philadelphia: Fortress, 1988), 80–81. See also Abraham J. Malherbe, *Ancient Epistolary Theorists*, SBL Sources for Biblical Study 19 (Atlanta, GA: Scholars Press, 1988), 69, 75.

of the first century AD.⁹⁴ According to Stowers, the author's relationship to the recipient was that of a superordinate to a subordinate or to an equal friend. In some instances the superordinate person exercised his right and demanded honour from the recipient. When no honour was given, then benefactors blamed the ungrateful recipients and even reprimanded them for dishonouring or insulting them. It is apparent that it was an acceptable thing for a benefactor to question and to chide ungrateful beneficiaries who had either forgotten or carelessly neglected their duty of giving thanks. The ungrateful people proved to be untrustworthy stakeholders in the give-and-take relationship.

Despite the similarities, some of the significant differences in outlook and operations of the two systems were as outlined below in Table 1.⁹⁵

Table 1. Differences between εὐεργεσία and *Patronicium*

Εὐεργεσία	*Patronicium*
1. Benefits were mainly bestowed on all citizens of a specific community in general. For example, Julius Caesar was taken to be the benefactor and saviour of all Greeks, but he was the patron of the city of Pergamus. The benefits that were given mainly consisted of buildings, streets, games and other communal benefits.	1. Benefits were bestowed mainly on few select individuals. The benefits were in form of legal protection, food, money, jobs and other personal benefits.

---

94. For example, Paul's letter to the Galatians, and parts of PE, e.g. 1 Tim 1:6, 20; 5:15; 2 Tim 1:15.
95. See also Walker, "Benefactor," 157–159, and deSilva, "Patronage," 766–771.

2. Favouritism was not preferential. There were generally no special favours to particular people.	2. Favouritism to particular people was preferential and common. Patrons gave special favours to certain clients, often with exploitative motives. In order for the patrons to benefit their clients more than non-clients, they were expected to deliberately give more benefits to the clients than to the other people. In "Precepts of Statecraft" in *Moralia* X.808.C, Plutarch states, "And there are also favours which arouse no ill-will, such as aiding a friend to gain an office, putting into his hands some honourable administrative function or some friendly foreign mission . . ."[96] Similarly, the emperor had special patronage on Roman citizens. For example, he controlled the entire empire through networks of generosity to them.
3. The relationship was kept moving by face-to-face reciprocal exchanges of services.	3. Brokerage (mediatorship) was common. Brokers or mediators usually facilitated the transaction between the patrons and their clients. The broker also acted as a patron but his primary gift to the client was to facilitate access to a more suitable and powerful patron. In the transaction, the broker incurred a debt with his own patron or friend and increased his own honour through the indebtedness of the clients to him.

---

96. See also Richard Saller, "Patronage and Friendship in Early Imperial Rome: Drawing the Distinction," in *Patronage in Ancient Society*, ed. Andrew Wallace-Hadrill, 52–53.

4. As in φιλία networks, in most cases, none of the parties transacting were regarded as inferior. The exchange transaction was carried forth as between equals.	4. Asymmetrism was a core feature. Asymmetrism in social status between the patrons and the clients was emphasized. The patron belonged to a higher social class than the client. For example, patronage relationship existed between former masters and freed slaves. Help was given to clients who were usually considered inferior to the patron. It was not given to social equals or to citizen bodies collectively.
5. As in φιλία, the association was based on *fides* (trust and mutual agreement). It was free and voluntary and therefore its permanence was not guaranteed. DeSilva says that although some forms of beneficence involved mutual loyalty and personal connection, they stood alongside the practice of public benefaction, in which giving brought recognition but did not involve the formation of (permanent) patron-client bonds.[97] However, the transaction of the various forms of public and private εὐεργεσία sometimes led to the establishment of long-term circular relationships of giving and receiving of benefits honour and service respectively between the transactors.	5. In some forms of *patronicium*, permanence of the relationship was guaranteed. In many cases (such as between current/former masters and slaves/freedmen and women) the relationship was more legally bound and permanent than voluntary, free and temporary. In some forms of patronage, failure or unfaithfulness in any of the parties in meeting their respective obligations did not affect much the patron-client relationship.

---

97. deSilva, "Patronage," 766.

7. The relationship was philanthropic. Benefits were given for the collective good of the recipients.	7. The relationship was essentially political. Benefits were given mainly for maintenance of social control. Building of clientele was used to express one's greatness, which helped in the competition for honour. Private control of civic bodies and immense wealth helped in eclipsing peers.
8. There were some abuses in εὐεργεσία but not as prominent as in *patronicium*. There generally was no exploitation.	8. Gross abuses developed in both the patrons and the clients. There was a more pronounced degree of exploitation.[98]
9. Both benefactor and beneficiaries were concerned more about the act of benefaction.	9. The transaction majored on the relationship between the patron and the client.
10. Either the benefactor or beneficiary initiated the transaction. The benefits were bestowed freely by the benefactor.	10. Normally the relationship was entered into from the initiation of the client. The client had to request the patron for benefits. However, in some cases the patron initiated it.[99]
11. The aspect of χάρις dominated the reciprocation.	11. The reciprocation was dominated more or less by legal obligation.
12. Greeks ascribed the title εὐεργέτης to both Greek and Roman benefactors.	12. Romans reserved the title "*patronus*" to Romans only because the primary role of the *patronus* (usually a senator) was representation or legal protection of the clients before Roman authority.
13. All people endowed with resources and abilities were encouraged to help.	13. There was more formality in the appointment of patrons. For someone to be designated as a patron, he or she had to have certain specific qualifications.

---

98. See also Crook, *Reconceptualising Conversion*, 63–66.
99. Crook, *Reconceptualising Conversion*, 6.

14. εὐεργεσία remained operative in the east as *patronicium* as a system declined sharply with the end of the reign of Caesar Augustus (27 BC–AD 14).	14. *Patronicium* as a system declined sharply in the east with the end of the reign of Caesar Augustus (27 BC–AD 14) and it did not revive until the reign of Emperor Trajan (AD 52–117).

According to the preceding list and table, although the differences outnumber the similarities, the similarities were weightier in significance. The similarities often influence some scholars to view the two systems as one. Similarly, as seen earlier, despite some serious abuses by some of the stakeholders in both systems, they were generally good. Both were coexistent, but εὐεργεσία was more widespread and positively accepted and practised in Greek regions at certain times and situations while *patronicium* was more acceptable and practised in the West. There were good and bad benefactors and there were good and bad patrons. An example of a Roman emperor who was considered a good patron of the Greek city of Pergamum and benefactor and saviour of all Greeks is Julius Caesar (according to inscription number IGR 4.303, 305 from Greece). Citing Martial in *Epigrams* 5:19 and 6:2, Crook points out that although Martial's writings make him appear quite bitter about the sorry state of patron-client relationships in the society in general, nevertheless, he considered Caesar's benefactions to humanity as positive.[100] Due to his goodness, the Greeks even regarded him as a god. Among the Greeks, there were social differences among the populace, but the differences were not as emphasized as in the Roman societies.

In the Roman societies the patrons were far above the clients socially and economically. Among the Greeks, the differences were not so salient and emphasized. Nevertheless, they were existent. Walker says that in the Greek world, the closest equivalent to a client was the κόλαξ (flatterer or sycophant) or παράσιτος (parasite).[101] Those terms were used to refer to people who depended on others entirely for daily material provisions. Walker's assertion that there was no equivalent status as that of respectable clients is not entirely

---

100. Crook, 120–121.
101. Walker, "Benefactor," 157.

true. Plutarch says that there were μέτοικοι (resident aliens or immigrants) in Athens. Some of them were wealthy and self-dependent. Nevertheless, as seen earlier, in Greek benefactor-beneficiary relationships there sometimes developed abuse, as in Roman patronage. For example, in Athens, the benefactors called their clients "*thetes*," that is, "hirelings," whereas the Thessalians called theirs "*penestai*," that is, "toilers," reproaching them for their lower socioeconomic status.[102]

In itself, εὐεργεσία was a relationship that was supposed to be voluntary on both the benefactor and beneficiary sides. In *patronicium* some of the patron-client relationships were compulsory. In εὐεργεσία, even where it was not voluntary, the relationship was supposed to look as if it was voluntary.[103] Another feature that was prominent in *patronicium* is that in order for the patrons to benefit their clients more than the non-clients, they were expected to deliberately give more benefits to their clients than to the other people.[104] Thus, the element of favouritism was rampant.

The features of εὐεργεσία and *patronicium* had strong influence on the Mediterranean communities of the first century AD. However, some of those communities adhered strongly to their own traditional social and religious values in the way they related with each other and transacted their interdependence activities. For example, the Jews approached G-R benefaction and patronage with caution mainly based on their religious perspectives on socioeconomic interdependence.

2.3.3 In Jewish Context

As in the case of the Greek world where *patronicium* expressions were not common, in the ancient Jewish context explicit benefaction and patronage terminology is scarce. Possibly, the lack of such vocabulary was partly caused by the negative views that Jews had about some aspects of the Greek and Roman systems of socioeconomic exchange. Nevertheless, the awareness among the Jews in the Mediterranean world of the Intertestamental Period and the NT times about benefaction and patronage is evident, as attested in the NT and some extra-biblical materials. The few explicit expressions are

---

102. deSilva, *Honor*, 103.
103. Westbrook, "Patronage in the Ancient Near East," 211.
104. Neyrey, "God," 467–468.

supported by implicit references to the operations of the systems. Some Jews acknowledged and even carried out their daily socioeconomic operations in accordance with the ideologies of the G-R systems. As Novick points out based on his interpretation of Esther 9:22b ("sending gifts of food to one another and presents to the poor"), together with the practice of צְדָקָה "charity," rabbinic Judaism employed the rhetoric of גמלתחסדים "reciprocation of kindness" to "'come to terms, Jewishly,' with the institutions of reciprocal exchange with which it was, as part of a Mediterranean society, inextricably entwined."[105] For example, in the first century AD, Galilean Jews acknowledged and applauded Josephus as their benefactor and saviour in the G-R sense.[106] However, despite the influence from surrounding systems, from OT times, religious Jews mainly preferred egalitarian kinship benefaction relationships rather than the asymmetrical relationships between socially higher ranked people (patrons) and lower ranked people (clients).

OT documents, for example the Pentateuch, wisdom literature and the prophets, have clear instructions on how the Jews were to treat one another and how they were to treat strangers in their socioeconomic relations and transactions. In Exodus 22:21 and 23:9 the Israelites were exhorted to treat strangers well remembering that they also had been strangers in Egypt. The same injunction was repeated in Deuteronomy 10:18–19 and 16:11, 14 where the Israelites were instructed to include non-Israelite strangers in their festivities. They were explicitly instructed in Exodus 22:25; Leviticus 25:36–37; Deuteronomy 23:19; Psalm 15:5; Proverbs 28:8; Ezekiel 18:8, 13, 17; and 22:12, to lend to fellow Israelites without requiring interest. As Price says, "the charity produced by Jewish society was generally limited to the Jewish poor."[107] However, in Deuteronomy 23:20 Jews were allowed to take interest from foreigners if they wanted to.[108] The result of this re-

---

105. Tzvi Novick, "Charity and Reciprocity: Structures of Benevolence in Rabbinic Literature," *Harvard Theological Review* 105, no. 1 (January 2012): 34–35.

106. Josephus, *Josephus*, 13, paragraphs number 47 and 50.

107. Christopher Price, "Pagans, Christianity, and Charity," *Christian Colligation of Apologetics Debate Research & Evangelism*, accessed 13 July 2012, http://www.christiancadre.org/member_contrib/cp_charity.html

108. See elaboration of this Deuteronomy law in the *Mishnah*, Division on *Neziqin* (Damages) tractate *Baba Metzia*, chapter 5. For example, it is said that " . . . [profits] may be accepted from non-Jews [since], one may borrow from and lend to them with interest."

strictive kinship patronage concept of Judaism in the first century AD was that Judaism had little impact on the wider pagan culture. However, with the rise of Christianity (which we can recognize as an offshoot of Judaism) there developed a benefaction and patronage system that traversed all ethnic communities in the Mediterranean region.[109]

The NT closely followed the views of the Intertestamental writings. For example, in Luke 11:5–8 the story of the midnight friend, in addition to teaching persistence in prayer, it also had the purpose of encouraging the listeners, who were mainly Jews, to help (κίχρημι, "lend")[110] one another as friends. Beyond the OT law that required Jews to lend to fellow Jews without levying any interest, Christians were expected to lend (δανείζω) without expecting anything in return, even the initial amount that they had given out. In 2:1–9 James encouraged that people treat each other as equals across the social and economic levels instead of social discrimination. The Christian community to which he wrote already contained many non-Jews as well as Jews.[111] The friendship that he recommended was friendship between people of all levels in the social, economic and ethnic structures. The patronage that he encouraged in 2:13–17 was that in which the rich helped the poor with necessary provisions based on mercy and in reference to the eschatological judgment (2:13); without looking for immediate merit for their good deeds.

---

109. See also Mumo P. Kisau, *Inclusiveness of Christianity: A Study of the Theme of Inclusiveness in the Acts of the Apostles* (Saabrücken, Deutschland: Lambert Academic, 2010), 179. On universal inclusiveness in the sharing of goods by all believers in Acts, contrary to Hengel's argument that there was no "love communism" in the other communities of believers except in Jerusalem, Kisau says that "the sharing of goods extends to all the communities of believers in Acts."

110. χρῆσον is a hapax in the NT. Here it is 2nd aorist imperative active 2nd person singular from κίχρημι. It is not clear whether it has the idea of loaning with the expectation of refunding or just helping without any expectation of repayment. In other places where the idea of lending is used in the NT and in the apocrypha , a different word, δανείζω, is used. In some instances, δανείζω has a clear nuance of loaning or borrowing with the expectation of refunding, whereas in other instances it is difficult to deduce whether it has that nuance or not. See examples in Luke 6:34; Sir 8:12; 29:2 and 4 Macc 2:8, where it is apparent that it has the sense of lending or borrowing with the expectation of repayment. Its use in Luke 6:35 and Sir 29:1, 7 does not imply that repayment is expected. The form of Christian charity to the needy was mainly with the implication of helping without expectation of repayment.

111. See Peter H. Davids, *The Epistle of James*, NIGTC (Grand Rapids: Eerdmans, 1982), 28–34, about "A POSSIBLE *SITZ IM LEBEN*" on the socioeconomic setting of the epistle in pre-70 Palestine.

Intertestamental writings encouraged mutual benefaction and liberal help for the needy, for example in Sirach 6:14–16: "φίλος πιστὸς σκέπη κραταιά, ὁ δὲ εὑρὼν αὐτὸν εὗρεν θησαυρόν. ¹⁵ φίλου πιστοῦ οὐκ ἔστιν ἀντάλλαγμα, καὶ οὐκ ἔστιν σταθμὸς τῆς καλλονῆς αὐτοῦ. ¹⁶ φίλος πιστὸς φάρμακον ζωῆς, καὶ οἱ φοβούμενοι κύριον εὑρήσουσιν αὐτόν," (A faithful friend is a strong shelter: whoever finds one has found treasure.¹⁵ Of a faithful friend there is no price, and there is no weight equivalent to his goodness.¹⁶ A faithful friend is medicine of life, and those who fear the Lord find him.) In this text Ben Sira writes exalting the benefits of sincere friendship implicitly, in contrast to insincere friendship that sometimes characterized patron-client relationships.[112] 2 Macc 11:13, 14 also supported friendships for mutual benefits far above patron-client relationships.

On first century AD rabbinic literature, referring to Esther 9:22 on the variety of gifts and charity that Jews sent to one another and to the poor respectively during the day of Purim, Novick says that the rabbis depicted relative lack of interest in the practice of Jews sending choice portions (מָנָה) to one another (וּמִשְׁלוֹחַ מָנ). Instead, they preferred sending gifts (מַתָּנָה) to the poor (וּמַתָּנוֹת לָאֶבְיוֹנִים). They did not like it because, compared to charity (sending presents or alms to the poor), "sending gifts" to one another as friends and equals belonged more to the social than to the legal realm.[113] He gives an example from the Palestinian Talmud on Esther (*Yerushalmi Megillah* 1:4 [70d]) that shows how the practice of "sending gifts" to one another had assumed negative outlook. Rabbi Yudan first sent a small gift (one thigh and one bottle of wine) to Rabbi Hoshaya but when Hoshaya characterized it as "a present to the poor" (namely, charity) then Yudan sent a bigger gift (one calf and one jar of wine) to him. Yudan then credited him as having fulfilled the Esther tradition of "and sending gifts to one another."[114] Thus, to some Jews, sending gifts to one another had assumed the negative competitive characteristic of Roman *patronicium* and somehow relegated the giving of charity to the poor to a secondary status in importance.

---

112. See also Henry G. Van Leeuwen, "Sirach," in *International Standard Bible Encyclopedia*, ed. Geoffrey W. Bromiley, vol. 4, Q-Z (Grand Rapids: Eerdmans, 1979–1988), 529.

113. Novick, "Charity and Reciprocity," 35.

114. Novick, 36–37.

On the distribution of tithes from their produce, in the Mishnah, under the Division of Seeds (Agriculture),[115] Jews were required to give to the priests, the Levites, and the poor without fail, for it was a stipulation from God. During harvest, they were to leave a certain corner of their field for the poor to glean.[116] We may view tithing and support for the poor among Jews as a God-instituted patronage system, especially for the benefit of Jews, but also for non-Jews. On the rules of buying and selling among the Israelites, in the Mishnah, under the division of Damages, it was stated that no party at the end of the transaction should have more than what he had at the outset of the transaction. For example, in chapter 4 of *Baba Metzia* in the Division on *Neziqin* (Damages), a shopkeeper was not allowed to reduce the going price of commodities in unfair competition with other shopkeepers. However, the sages encouraged the shopkeeper to sell at a cheap price because the public would benefit from it and thus the shopkeeper would be remembered for doing good. The Mishnah also stipulated that no one should be the victim of a big shift in fortune[117] and social status. Incase there was violation of fairness in dealings, the Mishnah law would restore the circumstance of each party to the original egalitarian status, because the overall aim of the rules in the Division of Damages was to preserve the wholeness of the socioeconomic transactions of the Jews. From this perspective, according to the written and

---

115. The six Divisions of the Mishnah on the day-to-day living of the Jews were: (1) *Zeraim* (Seeds, Agriculture), (2) *Moed* (Set Feasts, Appointed Times), (3) *Nashim* (Women), (4) *Neziqin* (Damages), (5) *Qodashim* (Holy Things), and (6) *Tehorot* (Purities). For detailed exposition of the Mishnah and other rabbinic literature see Jacob Neusner, ed., *Scriptures of the Oral Torah* (San Francisco: Harper & Row, 1987); Jacob Neusner, *The Mishnah: Social Perspectives* (Boston; Leiden: Brill, 1999); and Günter Stemberger, *Introduction to the Talmud and Midrash*, ed. and trans. Markus Bockmuehl (Edinburgh: T & T Clark, 1996); trans. of *Einleitung in Talmud und Midrash*.

116. For example, see chapter 1 of the tractate *Peah* (Corner) in *Zeraim* (Seeds) where it says "You must not fully reap to the corner of your field . . . you must leave them for the poor and the alien" (cf. Lev 19:9–10). In the tractate it is elaborated clearly of which plants must *Peah* be given, what constitutes the corner of a field, how *Peah* is given, on gleaning, the forgotten things, the tithe of the poor, the travelling poor, and who can claim the dues of the poor.

117. Such as a farmer selling his produce to a trader at low price before knowing the market price. In such a case, when the actual price was established, the trader had to pay the farmer the remaining balance. Similarly, if the buyer had bought at higher than the market price, he had the right to negotiate for a lower price. Thus, even in the market setting, no undue advantage was taken against anyone. Egalitarianism was encouraged in the socioeconomic interactions in the Jewish society. See Mishnah Division on *Neziqin*, tractate *Baba Metzia*, chapter 5 for more details.

the oral Torah, and the rabbinic interpretations of the same, it is apparent that the first century AD G-R patronage that was mainly asymmetrical was in disagreement with the egalitarian Jewish benefaction.[118]

In some instances, G-R patron-client and benefactor-beneficiary relationships were only tolerated by the Jews for their survival in the prevailing hostile environment in which they lived in the Diaspora. In OT and NT, Jews adopted and adapted the terms that were used in benefaction and patronage relationships to comply with the familial benefaction terms that they preferred. For example, the term "father" was sometimes used in the patronage setting to refer to someone who only fulfilled the duties of a patron. However, its inferences were derived from its usage in the family setting (for example, Deut 32:6; 2 Kgs 2:12; Matt 5:16, 45; John 8:38–44). The word "father" was sometimes used in reference to a person who was not a biological father.[119] In some extra-biblical materials of around the first century AD, there is evidence of some interpersonal transactions which were patronal in nature. For example, some of the evidence is found in Josephus's and Philo's writings, as indicated earlier in the reviews of their writings in this chapter.

In the early part of the Christian era in the first century, Jewish culture was still respected in the Mediterranean region, such as was the case in Antioch in Pisidia and in Iconium. As indicated in Acts, due to its positive contribution to the welfare of the people, the culture was able to influence the local Gentile population, cf. Acts 13:50; 14:2. Jewish religion has a long and enduring benefaction history, at least in its religious guidance, for example, in spreading knowledge about the true, all-powerful and benevolent God to people of other nations. The religion would not have been so influential if it did not have any significant benefit to the people among

---

118. The situation can be described as Novick does in "Charity and Reciprocity," 33 (citing Seth Schwartz in *Were the Jews a Mediterranean Society? Reciprocity and Solidarity in Ancient Judaism* [Princeton, NJ: Princeton University Press, 2010], 166), that there was tension between the "egalitarian solidarity" of the Jews (as indicated in rabbinic Judaism) and the "competitive reciprocity" of the G-R society in the late Second Temple period.

119. However, the reference to someone as "father" who is not an actual father in the biological sense should not be understood as used in the context of patronage in all instances. For example, feelings of respect between Elisha and Elijah made Elisha refer to Elijah as his father though not in the patronage context. Sometimes, the well-defined Graeco-Roman benefaction and patronage nuances were not in the minds of people as they used terms that were also used in those systems. Nevertheless, various shades of general benefaction have been present from antiquity and still are a widespread phenomenon to this day.

whom the Jews lived and among whom they directly or indirectly spread it as commissioned and empowered by Yahweh. In accordance with the religious injunctions in the Judaistic writings, for example, Jeremiah 29:7, the Jewish communities themselves played a significant part in the holistic welfare of the cities in which they lived as foreigners. That holistic welfare included religious, economic and other types of benefits to the foreign lands.

One of the few episodes that can be considered Jewish political patronage to non-Jews is seen in a stele inscription where Caesar Augustus publicly acknowledged and thanked the Jews for their support to the Roman troops at the end of the Ptolemaic reign. It was a custom of the client to acknowledge and thank the patron through honorary inscriptions. Therefore, one way to view Caesar's inscription in honour of the Jews is to see it a public show of gratitude to the Jews for the good work of patronage that they had done for the benefit of the empire. Another way of viewing Caesar's gesture is that, not only clients made inscriptions in honour to their patrons, but patrons also made them as public acknowledgement and gratitude for the clients' service. Caesar reciprocated the support of the Jews further by making them privileged citizens during his reign. For example, he allowed them to have an ethnarch until AD 11 and exempted them from paying *laographia* (poll tax).[120]

Such support from the Jews can be seen more as an act of endearment by a beneficiary/client to a benefactor/patron in anticipation of future beneficence from the benefactor/patron. This assertion is supported by the fact that the later fate of the Jews under the Roman rule depended on their continuous loyalty to the emperor. For example, according to Josephus's *Contra Apionem* 2.63–64, when a high royal family member, Germanicus Julius Caesar, visited Alexandria in AD 19, the Jews there were deliberately excluded from getting the benefit of corn that was distributed to the other citizens. The reason was that the Jews had taken for granted the earlier benevolence of the Roman authorities.[121] Therefore, their disloyalty led to revocation of their client privileges.

Some of the Jews were benefactors and patrons in the Greek cities where they lived. At the same time, many of the Jews lived as μέτοικοι in those

---

120. See Geoffrey W. Bromiley, ed., *The International Standard Bible Encyclopedia*, ISBE Four (Grand Rapids: Eerdmans, 1988), 471. See also Barclay, *Jews in the Mediterranean*, 48–50.

121. See also Barclay, *Jews in the Mediterranean*, 51.

cities, such as during the reigns of the Ptolemaic rulers.¹²² In some cases, Jews in the foreign cities had to look for patrons to help them to build their synagogues. For Example, the inscription *Monumenta Asiae Minoris Antiqua* (*MAMA*) 6, 264¹²³ from Acmonia in Asia Minor in the mid first century AD shows that Julia Severa, a prominent lady who was most likely a Gentile, donated a synagogue building to the resident Jewish community. In fact, the title ἀρχισυνάγωγος in Acts 18:17 and elsewhere in the NT was an honorific title that was sometimes given to a patron who helped in the building and maintenance of a synagogue from his own resources.¹²⁴ The status of ἀρχισυνάγωγος seems to have been a real role in the synagogue as in Matthew, Mark and Luke. Truly, some evidence that Josephus gave about the relationship between Jews and Romans is questionable because of his inclination to exaggerate Roman favour to the Jews. However, in some records, such as *Ant.* 14.265–67, 323, he provides us with credible evidence on Roman patronage to the Jews in Asia in the first century AD. Josephus's record about the conditions of Jews in Asia Minor in the first century AD is supported by the writing of Apollonius Molon, as in Eusebius's *Praeparatio Evangelica* 9: 19.1–3, and Nicolas, as in *Ant.* 16.31–57. The Jews had patrons in Asia Minor cities who fought on their behalf, for example, by moving motions in their favour in the councils or by reporting injustices against them to the governors. Examples of such patrons are Marcus Alexander in Halicarnassus, as found in *Ant.* 14.256, and Prytanis in Miletus, as in *Ant.* 14.425. At different times, through the emperors, Rome was viewed as the perpetual benefactor of the Jews in Asia Minor.¹²⁵ However, that relationship depended on Caesar's prevailing relationship with the Jews in Judea.

Some of the Jewish μέτοικοι also did patronage acts. An episode in which that happened is in reference to Nicetas son of Jason from Jerusalem. According to Frey, Nicetas and other μέτοικοι contributed one hundred drachmae to a Dionysiac festival.¹²⁶ Because they drew from their own re-

---

122. Margaret H. Ed. Williams, *The Jews among the Greeks & Romans: A Diasporan Sourcebook* (Baltimore, Maryland: John Hopkins University, 1998), 87, 107.

123. *MAMA* 6, 264 is a clearer version of *Corpus Inscriptionum Iudaicarum*, 766.

124. Walker, "Benefactor," 158.

125. See Josephus, *Josephus: Complete Works*, in *Ant.* 16.57.

126. Jean Baptiste Frey, *Corpus Inscriptionum Iudaicarum, Rome*, Pontifical Institute of Biblical Archaeology 1 (New York: Ktav, 1936, 1952, 1975), 749.

sources to sponsor a public festival, they proved to be patrons of some kind. This is despite the fact that as μέτοικοι they themselves had patrons to look up to in order to access the facilities for non-citizens in the city. Thus, it is evident that there were various types and ranks of benefactors/patrons and beneficiaries/clients in the various societies of the ancient Mediterranean world.

Similar to their Greek and Roman counterparts, sometimes Jewish benefaction developed some negative aspects. Jews sometimes abused the benefaction and patronage systems so that they jeopardized their relationships with the other communities living with them. For example, they sought and got more favour from the Roman patrons to the extent that they antagonized their relationship with local Greek authorities and the other local communities in the free Greek cities. According to Philo and Josephus, in the times of the Ptolemies, the Jews in Alexandria were given special freedoms and privileges that were not enjoyed by people of other races who were not citizens in that city. However, their aggressiveness in seeking for favours worked for their advantage as indicated in inscription evidence of the second century AD onwards that Jews continued to receive financial and political patronage from Gentiles. Trebilco gives an example of honorary inscription number 2924 in *Corpus Inscriptionum Graecarum* indicating the participation of Jewish communities in Asia Minor in benefaction and patronage relationships.[127] Another abuse that is recorded in the NT among the Jews in Judea in the first century AD is that some of them did good works of benefaction (such as almsgiving) in order to receive honour for their generosity, cf. Matthew 6:1–4. Almsgiving was a a distinct form of Jewish benefaction. It was different from Greek and Roman benefaction in that: (1) it was not given by wealthy and socially important people, and (2) it had a religious foundation and motivation.[128]

As indicated in the Intertestamental Period writings, in the NT, and in the rabbinic literature of the first century AD, despite the abuses, there was significant goodness of Jewish benefaction. Some examples of its goodness are found in 2 Macc 4:2; 9:25–27; 3 Macc 5:11; 6:24; 4 Macc 8:6; and in

---

127. P. Trebilco, *Jewish Communities in Asia Minor*, SNTSMS 69; (Cambridge: Cambridge University Press, 1991), 157–158.

128. Walker, "Benefactor," 158.

Luke 8:1–3. Christ himself received reciprocal benefaction from Galilean women who themselves had received and were still receiving bigger benefaction from his teaching. It is evident that good benefaction and patronage continued thriving, as recorded in Romans 16:2 where Phoebe was faithful προστάτις to many people, including Paul.

Jewish communities in Asia integrated well with the local communities, accommodating their cultures while at the same time not losing their Jewishness. For example, in Miletus the "God fearers," the Christian and Judaistic Jews, had prominent seats in the theatres (as seen in Ignatius's writing *To the Philadelphians* 6:1; 6:2 and *To the Magnesians* 8:1; 9:1–2; 10:3). Theatres were a central part in the G-R patronage system. To have a prominent seat in a particular theatre indicated that the person was one of its patrons. The Jews in Diaspora assimilated to the G-R customs that they did not find to be against their Jewish distinctiveness, but they abhorred whatever was against their traditions. For example, their abhorrence about regarding Caesar as father, or even as God, is an indication that they did not compromise on their worship of one God. They also did not compromise on the observation of the Sabbath and other sacred festivals, on circumcision of male infants, and other similar aspects, to adhere to G-R culture. Such evidence is found in *The Letter of Aristeas*, in 3 Macc, for example, 3 Macc 2:18 and 6:11, and in Josephus's *Ant.* 16.31–57; 16.14. Thus, in their own terms the Jews played an integral part in the various social systems, including patronage, in the first century AD in the Mediterranean regions. They preferred to receive and give assistance in familial and mutually beneficial settings, on equal social terms. It is evident that Jews participated in the benefaction and patronage systems as of the first century AD as indicated in the biblical and extra-biblical evidence of that time.

2.4 Conclusion

Greek εὐεργεσία, Roman *patronicium* and Jewish mutual kinship benefaction were socio-political and economic modes of interdependence that were in operation in the first century AD. In Greek εὐεργεσία wealthy and able εὐεργετάι (benefactors) did good works by providing goods and services mainly to communities in general, but also to individual fellow citizens. The benefactors considered the citizen beneficiaries as people of equal or near equal status in the society. They also helped people who were not citizens in the various Greek cities. They usually did "good works" expecting to get public honour from the beneficiaries. Gratitude in form of honour and service merited more beneficence. The relationship was usually voluntary, unlike Roman *patronicium* that was typically obligatory. Jews also had their own kinship support system that was mainly guided by their OT Scriptures. There was more egalitarianism in both the Greek and Jewish benefaction systems than in the Roman system.

Unlike Greek εὐεργεσία Roman *patronicium* was usually an asymmetrical relationship between people of more pronounced unequal status and resources. Although it was not always stipulated legally, the Roman system had the characteristics of a legally and socially encoded system. Some principles of the Roman system had acquired permanence. Despite its original good purposes and benefits, similar to Greek εὐεργεσία, the Roman system had acquired negative practices along the way more than the other systems.

On its part, Jewish patronage was more like a kinship or familial relationship of reciprocation. People who ascribed to Judaism were required to help one another as family members. Even while living in the Greek and Roman regimes, Jews mainly preferred the egalitarian relationships of friendship, familial and mutual benefaction above the asymmetrical systems. They adopted G-R features of patronage for survival in the hostile environments that they found themselves in, but they largely retained their religious and familial relationships of mutual help as equals. They also participated in the general welfare of the cities in which they lived in Diaspora.

My preliminary assessment about Christians in the first century AD is that communities generally adopted and enhanced, or Christianized, at least the positive features of Greek εὐεργεσία and Roman *patronicium*, but more so those of the Jewish system. Along the ancient systems, the early church congregations also developed their own principles of Christian socioeconomic interdependence. NT authors, and contemporary extra-biblical authors, portray their support for the good features and practices of the G-R and Jewish benefaction and patronage systems. Simultaneously they also openly wrote against the negative features of the systems. My assessment is that they consciously or subconsciously endeavoured to correct the abuses and to replace them with features that were consistent to the Christian faith. Below, in chapter 3 on exegesis of PE text in view of benefaction and patronage, there is discussion on Paul's support of the good aspects and his opposition and correction of the abuses of the systems.

Because of the closeness of its contents to PE, especially 1 Timothy, *The Didache* is a useful tool on the subject. It gives us evidence of the existence and operations benefaction and patronage systems in the first century AD. As seen in appropriate places later in this writing, its authors and Paul in PE concur on the issues of εὐεργεσία and *patronicium* that we encounter in their writings. Although not strictly in terms of εὐεργεσία or *patronicium* proper, Milavec says that, among its numerous lessons, one encounters the interplay of sharing of resources and the reciprocal gratitude as what provided the mainstay of individual wellbeing within the Christian community.[129] Even before the Christian era, Aristotle (384–322 BC) had indicated that in the G-R benefaction and patronage systems, resource sharing was the central pillar.[130] Overall, although not overtly speaking of benefaction or patronage as such, in some places, such as 13:1–7, the *Didache* gives credible evidence that reciprocal support, such as support for itinerary teachers, was an established system among the Jewish and non-Jewish Christians in the early church. Although it has not been given an independent review in this writing, it is used in the following chapter as a valid reference in support of PE.

---

129. Aaron Milavec, *The Didache: Faith, Hope, & Life of the Earliest Christian Communities, 50–70 C.E.* (Mahwah, NJ: Newman, 2003), vii.

130. See Aristotle, *Rhet* Book I. V.5-9.

CHAPTER 3

Benefaction, Patronage, and Leadership in the Pastoral Epistles Text

3.1 Introduction

The overall quest of my writing is on how Paul interacted with the principles of the Greek, Roman and Jewish benefaction and patronage systems as he issued the instructions for guidance and administration of PE churches. This chapter is the heart of my writing. As indicated in the general introduction at the beginning of my writing, scholars have mainly focused on material benefaction and patronage and given little attention to the nonmaterial counterpart. Similarly, many have focused on the negative aspects of patronage. However, in this chapter, the study examines with impartiality both the positive and negative aspects of material and nonmaterial benefaction and patronage. Paul's interaction with the positive and the negative ideologies of the systems is assessed. Before assessing PE in particular, the discussion dwells briefly on benefaction and patronage in the NT in general.

3.1.1 Benefaction and Patronage in the New Testament

Explicit references to benefaction and patronage are scanty in the NT. This is not a unique phenomenon, because, as Saller also points out, even in secular writing of the Roman Republic and Imperial times, patron-client language was deliberately avoided sometimes because of the negative implications associated with the systems. Nevertheless, we should not jump to the conclusion that patronage was evil or that it existed only where the words *patronus, cliens* and their associates were used explicitly.[1] The phenomenon was widespread and it operated through various principles and was referred to using diverse expressions. Notably, the term προστάτις appears only once in the NT, in Romans 16:2. The literal term for benefaction, εὐεργεσία, and its cognates appear a few times only. Εὐεργεσίᾳ appears once in Acts 4:9; εὐεργέται once in Luke 22:25; εὐεργετῶν once in Acts 10:38, and εὐεργεσίας once in 1 Timothy 6:2. However, despite the scarcity of explicit references, there are numerous implicit expressions that show that Christ, the main character in the NT, and the NT authors were familiar with the positive and negative features of Greek εὐεργεσία, Roman *patronicium*, and Jewish kinship benefaction systems. They interacted with and addressed them candidly in their speech and writing.

3.1.2 God the Father and Christ on Benefaction and Patronage

The OT is replete with benefactory and patronal acts of God to his people, especially Israel. Nevertheless, because this study is not on benefaction and patronage in the OT, the only reference to the OT is used as cross reference to what is being discussed here in the NT in general and later in PE in particular. In the NT, the gospels are a record of the outstanding benefaction of God to all humans in all time, irrespective of social affiliation, or chronological and geographical position. God's benefaction is embodied in the life, teaching, healing and other good works of Christ, culminating in his death. Jesus said that he and the Father are one (John 10:30; 14: 8–11; 17:1), and that he had come to do the will of him (God the Father) who sent him (John 4:34). As stated in Luke 19:10, he said that he came to seek and save the lost. Therefore, everything that he did in his life on earth and what he continues to do after resurrection is God's direct and mediated work of redemption/salvation, which remains as the best form of benefaction for all time.

Apart from what we have in Luke 22:25, ὁ δὲ εἶπεν αὐτοῖς, Οἱ βασιλεῖς τῶν ἐθνῶν κυριεύουσιν αὐτῶν καὶ οἱ ἐξουσιάζοντες αὐτῶν εὐεργέται καλοῦνται, we do not have much explicit evidence of Jesus's view of or interaction with the benefaction systems. Luke records Jesus's apparent

---

1. See Saller, *Personal Patronage*, 5, 7.

abhorrence of the custom of Gentile rulers dominating over their subjects instead of serving them, and those in authority being called benefactors. However, that does not imply that he also abhorred the good practices of the systems. In Matthew 23:9 (cf. 6:2–4) he forbade the listening crowd and his disciples to call anyone "father" for they had only one Father in heaven. As indicated in verse 5, the injunction was given to counter the habit of scribes and Pharisees doing good works to be recognized and honoured as "fathers" or benefactors of the society. Because of their status as leaders and benefactors in the society, such people expected to be honoured and served by their subordinates or their clients. Interpreting Luke 22:25 in the patronage context, Malina and Neyrey say that in the Mediterranean world the wealthy patrons would give benefits to groups of clients who were in turn expected to give praise and other services to them and thus contribute to their public honour.[2] Instead, Jesus urged people to do good without expecting any return from their recipients (Matt 6:1–4). He even encouraged them to do good to those who mistreated them and those who did not do good deeds to them previously or who would repay them subsequently (Luke 6:27–36).

In his life, Jesus exemplified how a good benefactor should act. He also exhorted his followers to exercise their benefaction more nobly. For example, instead of the asymmetrism that dominated *patronicium*, he embodied and promoted egalitarianism and friendship. Although he was far greater than them in all spheres, instead of treating his followers as inferiors and dominating over them, he valued them as his friends and brothers (Matt 12:50; John 15:15). Possibly, he did that in radical opposition to the oppressive and demeaning socioeconomic, political and religious hierarchical systems in which clients and people of lower ranks were regarded as inferior. He also encouraged his followers to treat others with respect, as greater than themselves, especially through service to them (Matt 20:26–28; John 13:13–15).

Crossan observes that Jesus's stance was in direct opposition to the ideologies and practices of the Jewish patriarchal family setups and the Roman patronal and brokerage systems of the day. He says,

---

2. Robert C. Tannehill, *Luke*, ANTC (Nashville: Abingdon, 1996), 317.

> His strategy, implicitly for himself and explicitly for his followers, was the combination of *free healing and common eating*, a religious and economic egalitarianism that negated at once the hierarchical and patronal normalcies of Jewish religion and Roman power. And, lest he himself be interpreted as simply the new broker of a new God, he moved on constantly, settling down neither at Nazareth nor Capernaum. He was neither broker nor mediator but, somewhat paradoxically, the announcer that neither should exist between humanity and divinity or humanity and itself.[3]

Crossan is right in his observation that Jesus's egalitarian treatment of his followers negated the hierarchical and patronal customs of Jewish religion and Roman power. However, his statement would be more correct if he qualified it and said that Jesus opposed the negative features of those systems. He did not oppose their good elements. Similarly, Crossan's statement that Jesus was neither broker nor mediator, and that neither brokerage nor mediatorship should exist between humanity and divinity or within humanity itself, is neither correct nor practical. His statement is contrary to Jesus's statements in John 14:6 in which he depicted himself as the indispensable mediator for facilitation of access to the Father, . . . οὐδεὶς ἔρχεται πρὸς τὸν πατέρα εἰ μὴ δι' ἐμοῦ. In Matthew 10:40 he presented himself as one who had been sent by another, whereby whoever received him received the one who sent him. As such, he was a mediator between the sender and those to whom he was sent.

It is true that when we view Jesus as God incarnate (John 1:14; 10:30; 17:11, 22), and as creator and owner of all things (John 1:3; 16:15), we see him as the chief divine benefactor. Viewed that way, the idea of him being mediator between God and humans may seem paradoxical and unnecessary. Nevertheless, through incarnation, he assumed the role of a secondary or mediatory patron. In the Roman *patronicium* system a secondary patron could be a mediator between clients and a primary patron. Therefore, it was not usual for Christ to be a mediator while remaining a primary patron.

---

3. John Dominic Crossan, *The Historical Jesus: The Life of a Mediterranean Jewish Peasant* (New York: HarperSanFrancisco, 1991), 422.

The reality and necessity of his mediatorship becomes evident when we view him as the human Jesus who died in our place and now stands before God as our advocate. He presented himself as a unique mediator. His mediatorship and patronage were of a much better calibre and were deliberately opposed to the lesser modes that were operating in the G-R and Jewish systems, where limitation in what they could do to the real needs of humans, asymmetry and other weaknesses were apparent.

According to Malina and Rohrbaugh, in the patron-client relationships the role of a broker was very crucial. In their comments on John 5:31–47, they affirm and explain their opinion that Jesus was a legitimate broker.[4] In the G-R patronage system, the broker placed people in touch with each other as he was strategically placed and was accessible to both the clients and the patrons. He was their mediator. On Jesus's status, Neyrey says that, in the gospels and Acts, the story of Jesus's life from birth to death and resurrection is presented as the story of an honourable mediator.[5] As God's mediatorial client, Jesus received client benefactions such as power, commitment, inducement, and influence that he used to draw second-level clients into God's household. As a fitting reward for his loyal mediatorship, his Patron-Father rewarded him with all power in heaven and earth and bestowed on him the highest honour of sitting at his right hand. Thus, Jesus became a co-patron, equal to God the Father. He also became an exclusive and permanent mediator-broker of God's benefaction. Attaining that elevated position, Jesus received the authority to provide the gift (benefaction) of the Holy Spirit to all who believe in him throughout the Christian era. Based on that reality, all believers are members of Jesus's patron-client system.[6] It is true that as a member of the Godhead, Christ was a coequal benefactor/patron with God the Father and the Holy Spirit from eternity. The human Jesus was exalted to the coequal patron status for his exceptional obedience (loyalty) and service to God as a symbolic representative of the human race

---

4. Bruce J. Malina and Richard L. Rohrbaugh, *Social-Science Commentary on the Gospel of John* (Minneapolis: Fortress, 1998), 117–121. See also chapter 6 in Bruce J. Malina, "Patron and Client: The Analogy behind Synoptic Theology," in *The Social World of the New Testament* (London; New York: Routledge, 1996), 143–175.

5. Neyrey, "God," 476, 491.

6. Jerome H. Neyrey, *Render to God: New Testament Understandings of the Divine* (Minneapolis: Fortress, 2004), 30, 90.

(Phil 2:5–11). In reciprocation of Christ's patronage, believers are required to be loyal and courageous witnesses for Christ as they stand in support of him and as they win others to be his followers (clients). Jesus will reward them with more honour for their loyalty at his second coming (Mark 8:38).

In his capacity as a faithful mediator, he propped up the Father's benefaction to humans. For example, in Matthew 7:11 (cf. Luke 11:13), he highlighted God's willingness and ability to give "good things" or benefactions (ἀγαθὰ) to those who ask him[7] as superior to human benevolence and ability: εἰ οὖν ὑμεῖς πονηροὶ ὄντες οἴδατε δόματα ἀγαθὰ διδόναι τοῖς τέκνοις ὑμῶν, πόσῳ μᾶλλον ὁ πατὴρ ὑμῶν ὁ ἐν τοῖς οὐρανοῖς δώσει ἀγαθὰ τοῖς αἰτοῦσιν αὐτόν. Concerning Matthew 7:11, Marshall says that the "good gifts" from God should be understood in a spiritual sense (Rom 3:8; 10:15; Heb 9:11; 10:1; Luke 1:53).[8] That is true. However, as the context in which the statement is uttered suggests, and as implied in Matthew 6:33, the ἀγαθὰ could also include material things.

In Matthew 9:35 and Acts 10:38, Jesus is described as a benefactor "who went about doing good things" (ὃς διῆλθεν εὐεργετῶν).[9] His mode of benefaction was different and stood in contrast to the G-R and Jewish modes of benefaction. The commodities that he transacted with were mainly nonmaterial and others-centred, in contrast to the material and self-centred focus of the prevailing benefaction and patronage systems. His main benefaction was enlightenment of people about the kingdom of God (eternal salvation), forgiveness of sins (the climax of which was his death on the cross), and physical healing (Matt 9:5). Subsequently, his disciples followed his example and gave mainly nonmaterial benefaction, such as Peter to the paralytic at the Beautiful Gate (Acts 3:6).

As stated by Seneca, in the Roman patronage system, class, social status and resources were crucial in how the patron related with his three-tier

---

7. Unlike in εὐεργεσία where the benefactor usually helped communities and individuals without necessarily being asked to, the usual procedure in *patronicium* was for the clients or their mediators to ask the patron for help. Nevertheless, as Crook points out in *Reconceptualising Conversion*, 6, sometimes patrons sought clients to give them benefits.

8. I. Howard Marshall, *Commentary on Luke*, NIGTC (Grand Rapids, MI: Eerdmans, 1978), 470.

9. Note here the use of εὐεργετῶν (cf. εὐεργεσία in Acts 4:9).

hierarchy of friends and clients.¹⁰ In his prescriptions for G-R benefactors, Seneca himself suggested that they should help especially people who were grateful for past benefaction. They were to help the ungrateful only if they had extra resources to spare after helping the virtuous and the grateful.¹¹ Christ is presented as despising such discriminatory benefaction among his followers. Instead, he urged them to be like God who gives generously to all people, even the unrighteous and the ungrateful (Matt 5:42–48; cf. Luke 6:35). He criticized people who only invited friends who could invite them back as repayment for their good deed (Luke 14:12–14). He also reprimanded those who were doing their benefaction mainly for enhancement of their prestige and for the honour and praise that they received for doing it instead of doing it for the honour and glory of God, who is the overall benefactor, or instead of waiting for God to commend and reward them (Matt 6:2–4).¹² Instead, Jesus supported and promoted good benefaction and patronage that benefit others as much as (or more than) self. In Luke 6:30–35 he established the golden rule of doing good things to all people (including enemies) without expecting them to repay in any way. It is not clear whether or not Jesus replaced the existing systems with an entirely new one of reciprocity. It seems that reciprocity is what he had in mind. Nevertheless, it is apparent that he supported the good aspects of the existing benefaction and patronage systems.

Concerning prestige and self-advancement, which many Gentile rulers, benefactors, and patrons were pursuing as they gave their benefaction, Jesus put himself in contrast to them when he said that he did not come to be served but to serve and give his life a ransom for many (Matt 20:25–28). In benefaction and patronage, dying for one's clients was the greatest gift that a patron could give, as dying for a benefactor was also the most profound

---

10. Seneca, *Seneca III*, VI.XXXIV.1–5.

11. Seneca, IV.IX. 3–XI.5.

12. See J. R. Harrison, "Benefaction Ideology and Christian Responsibility for Widows," in *New Documents Illustrating Early Christianity*, vol. 8, *A Review of the Greek Inscriptions and Papyri Published 1984-85*, ed. S. R. Llewelyn (Macquarie University, NSW: Ancient History Documentary Research Centre, 1998), 111n21. For example, in *Inscriptiones Graecae* II(9) 211, in the first century BC, the Greek city of the Eretrians honoured their benefactor, Eunomos Karustios, so that they would be universally recognized and honoured for their πρόνοια (forethought or (high) regard) of him as φίλος (a friend).

gratitude a beneficiary could render (Rom 5:7).[13] Jesus gave his own life freely and entirely for the benefit of humankind (John 10:11; Rom 5:8). When he said that a person who truly loves his friends lays down his life for them, he implied that his disciples should also be ready to do the same for others (John 15:13). Many of them ended up giving their lives for the benefit of others and as fitting response of loyalty and service to their Master-benefactor/patron.

3.1.3 NT Authors on Benefaction and Patronage

NT authors supported what was right and confronted and corrected the wrongs of the systems. Following the example of Jesus, they preferred and promoted egalitarian benefaction in place of asymmetrism. Gowler states that although the patron-broker-client hierarchical system was effective in the world of the gospel authors, the kingdom that Christ and his followers proclaimed depicts a devastating critique against it. He says that the kingdom should be regarded as the criterion for evaluating all social systems.[14] That is true. Nevertheless, as with Crossan's view which is against the hierarchical patronage and household systems, especially against the idea of Jesus being a broker, Gowler's view is not entirely true if he is implying that Jesus and his followers were opposed to the patron-broker-client system as a whole. Looking at their teachings and personal examples as they interacted with the system, it is evident that what they opposed were the abuses, not the entire scheme per se. A significant number of NT authors used the good principles of benefaction and patronage in the promotion of a form of Christian reciprocity whose principles were better than those of the non-Christian systems. The authors urged Christians of all social classes to treat others well and to do good deeds to them based on principles of the saving faith, in sincere love for God and for the neighbour (Luke 10:27; John 13:34, 35; 15:12; Rom 12:10; 13:8), guided by clean conscience (1 Tim 1:5), and godly ethical character (2 Pet 1:7).

As Harrison says, the fact that early Christians did not apply honorific benefactory titles on humans does not mean that they were indifferent

---

13. Seneca, *Epistulae Morales* 81.27 and *Seneca III*, IV.XX.2 and IV.XXIV.2.
14. David B. Gowler, "Text, Culture, and Ideology in Luke 7:1–10," in *Fabrics of Discourse: Essays in Honor of Vernon K. Robbins*, eds. David B. Gowler, L. Gregory Bloomquist, and Duane F. Watson (Harrisburg, PA: Trinity Press International, 2003), 125.

to the terminological opportunities provided by, for example, the soteriological language of the inscriptions.[15] For instance, he views the concept of σωθησόμεθα (in Rom 5:9–10) that Paul used in reference to the salvation accomplished by Christ as reminiscent of a work of beneficence. He compares Christ to Emperor Augustus and says that: (1) like Augustus, Christ had brought peace (Rom 5:1) and hope (Rom 5:2, 4, 5). (2) Similar to Augustus's inception as the first emperor of the Roman imperial regime, the arrival of Christ marked a culminating point in history as it marked the end of the law and the beginning of new life. Augustus's coronation as the first emperor marked the end of the Roman republic era and the beginning of the imperial era. However, Paul elevated the soteriological beneficence of Christ above that of Augustus's soteriological propaganda, in that whereas Augustus restored a world which was collapsing and falling into disarray, Christ is depicted as coming to liberate the groaning creation at the end of time (Rom 8:18ff). Therefore, in contrast to human benefactors, Paul reserves the title σωτηρία for the saving acts of God, where he uses it nineteen times in his writing. It is also important at this point to note that, in his writing, Paul also emphasized much the status of God as saviour. The author of Hebrews also elevated Christ's σωτηρία and χάρις above the χάριτες of the Caesars, in that the divine deliverance that he accomplished is eschatological and permanent, as seen in the expression "eternal salvation" in Hebrews 5:9. Thus, in the propagation of the Christian faith, NT authors used concepts that were common in the benefaction and patronage systems, but with much understanding and great caution.

Unhealthy competition between benefactors and patrons and other abuses in the G-R benefaction systems, such as in the exhibition of good will (εὔνοια), benevolence (φιλανθρωπία), courage (ἀνδρεία), love of glory (φιλοδοξία), love of honour (φιλοτιμία), and greatness of mind (μεγαλοφροσύνη) made them look negative. They competed to outdo one another so that they would receive more honour and power in the society than their fellow benefactors and patrons. Their misguided behaviour made

---

15. J. R. Harrison, "Saviour of the People," in *New Documents Illustrating Early Christianity*, vol. 9, *A Review of the Greek Inscriptions and Papyri Published in 1986-87*, ed. S. R. Llewelyn (Macquarie University, NSW: Ancient History Documents Research Centre, 2002), 4–5.

some NT authors, such as Paul, stand against them. For example, as Harrison points out, Paul deliberately avoided the inscriptional terminology of competition in favour of the different ethical dynamic for Christians, that is, divine χάρις, as in 2 Corinthians 8:1, 9.[16] In Galatians 1:14, he condemned the custom of cleaving to ancestral lineage in order to gain advantage over competitors. He also termed such pursuit as misguided zeal and knowledge of God that displaces Christ's honour as soteriological benefactor and replaces it with one's own (Rom 10:2–4; 2 Cor 11:21–23). In his writing, he avoided negative competition and promoted positive zeal, such as when he encouraged Corinthian Christians to imitate the zeal of the Macedonian Christians (2 Cor 8:1–11). Similar to Paul, one of Luke's most prominent motifs in writing Luke-Acts was the exhortation to share goods to alleviate the suffering urban poor. Citing Philip Esler,[17] Kisau says that one of the purposes of Luke's writing was to rebuke and pressurize some reluctant believers in the primitive church to make them share actively and voluntarily[18] their riches with the poor.[19]

There existed significant social differences between people of the various classes in the society, such as between masters and slaves. In his explanation that the general should have ἔνδοξον "good reputation," Onosander said that the officer had to display such decorum that those who were "inferior to him" would not feel uneasy when submitting to him.[20] This seems to be a noble exhortation, but the problem is that the officer would behave well for the mere purpose of being honoured and for keeping in submission

---

16. Most material in this paragraph is adapted from J. R. Harrison, "Excels Ancestral Honours," in *New Documents Illustrating Early Christianity*, vol. 9, *A Review of the Greek Inscriptions and Papyri Published 1986-87*, ed. S. R. Llewelyn (Macquarie University, NSW: Ancient History Documentary Research Centre, 2002), 20–21.

17. Francis Philip Esler, *Community and Gospel in Luke-Acts: The Social and Political Motivation of Lukan Theology* (Cambridge: Cambridge University Press, 1987).

18. In *Inclusiveness of Christianity*, 176, Kisau says that although the primitive Christian community operated on principles nearly similar to those of the ascetic Essene community, its principle of voluntary sharing was unlike that of the Essenes. In the Essene community, the surrender of one's entire property for communal use was obligatory for one to gain membership in the community. For details, see Qumran document 1QS (also called lQS) VI.18–21a. 1QS is the Qumran document titled *Serek Hayyajadad*, that is, *Rule of the Community*.

19. Kisau, *Inclusiveness of Christianity*, 182.

20. Dibelius, *Pastoral Epistles*, 160.

those under him, not primarily for helping them or raising them to his level or regarding them as his equals. NT authors also promoted equality at least on the spiritual level as they exhorted Christians to treat one another as members of one family of God (2 Tim 4:21; Heb 2:11, 12; and 1 John 3:10). In Ephesians 2:19 Paul says, "So then you are no longer strangers and aliens, but you are citizens with the saints and also members of the household of God" (οἰκεῖοι τοῦ θεοῦ) (cf. Matt 13:52; 24:45; John 8:35, 36; 1 Tim 3:4, 5, 15; Titus 2:5; and 1 Pet 4:17). Such is also found in Acts 2:37; Romans 1:13; 1 Corinthians 1:10; and 1 Timothy 5:1, 2 where Paul exhorts Timothy, "Do not speak harshly to an older man, but speak to him as to a father, to younger men as brothers, to older women as mothers, to younger women as sisters, with absolute purity." The abrasive relationship caused by socioeconomic superiority and inferiority perspectives needed to be replaced by development of a cordial spiritual kinship relationship. From those few examples, it is evident that NT authors supported the good aspects of those systems while at the same time criticizing and remedying the bad.

3.2 Benefaction and Patronage in the Pastoral Epistles

As seen above in the discussion on the other NT writers, Paul made use of the "terminological opportunities" provided by the social systems. He was conscious of and responsive to what was happening around him and to the expectations of the wider society. He made use of the concepts of the social institutions as he gave advice and instructions to Timothy and Titus. For example, it is evident that he acknowledged and esteemed the household institution as the basic unit of the society.[21] Similarly, he displayed knowledge about the operations and expectations of the benefaction and patronage systems, as seen in his extensive use of some concepts of those systems.

The three letters have much in common in matters of literary style and content. They contain an assortment of private and public instruction to Timothy and Titus and, through them, to the wider church communities among which they were serving. Although there were notable differences, the delegates were confronted by comparatively similar situations. As Mounce

---

21. Towner, *Letters to Timothy*, 389.

observes,²² the differences between the situations that Timothy and Titus were facing are that: (1) the church in Ephesus was older and had established problems and structures. However, some members who knew the gospel had strayed from it and therefore Timothy was experiencing severe persecution. Towner says that some matters that needed to be addressed in Ephesus were that there were corrections to be instituted, discipline to be meted out, and leaders to be chosen.²³ Hays says that in 1 Timothy Paul wrote to his younger co-worker and laid down a blueprint characterized by institutional order and stability, as he set forth a series of instructions for organizing and guiding the church in Ephesus.²⁴ (2) Despite some similarity between the problem that Titus was facing in Crete with what Timothy was facing in Ephesus, there were significant differences. As indicated in 1:5, Titus was left at Crete mainly to put in order what remained to be done for the church after Paul left. Titus was to appoint elders in each city (κατὰ πόλιν) in Crete that had a church,²⁵ which means that the church was young. Instead of removing bad leaders, as in Ephesus, Titus was to appoint for the first time new leaders for the Cretan church. The opposition in the Cretan church was not as severe as in Ephesus. The church needed catechetical instruction on basic matters of salvation so that the young Christians would be pure, obedient and ready to do good works pertaining to the Christian faith (Titus 2:15; 3:1, 8). (3) Although Paul was still dealing with opposition in Ephesus, the bulk of 2 Timothy is dealing with personal matters. It is different from 1 Timothy and Titus. For example, it contains encouragement to Timothy to be loyal to Paul²⁶ and to the gospel (1:6, 8, 13–14; 4:1–2), to suffer willingly (1:8; 2:12), to rely on Scripture (2:15), and to visit him in Rome as soon as possible (1:4; 4:9, 13).

The main concern of Paul in 1 Timothy was to urge the addressee to adhere faithfully to the sound doctrine against false teaching (1 Tim 1:3–7).

---

22. In *Pastoral Epistles*, lxxxii–iii.

23. Towner, *Letters to Timothy*, 95.

24. Richard B. Hays, *The Moral Vision of the New Testament: Community, Cross, New Creation; A Contemporary Introduction to New Testament Ethics* (New York: HarperCollins, 1996), 66.

25. Knight III, *Pastoral Epistles*, 288.

26. In benefaction and patronage relationships were based on *fides*, the faithfulness of a benefactor and the loyalty of the beneficiary are what kept the relationship alive.

Timothy was to be true to the prophecies that had been made about him and the right teachings that he had been taught so that by following them he would fight the good fight, having faith and a good conscience (1:18–19; 6:12). As was the case in Titus (1:9–11) and 2 Timothy (2:13–15), the false teachers in 1 Timothy were disloyal to sound teaching (1 Tim 1:10; 4:6–8) and to "the glorious gospel of the blessed God" (1 Tim 1:11). Most perilous of all is that they were causing weak Christians to abandon and be disobedient and thus disloyal to God's gospel that he had entrusted to Paul (1 Tim 1:6–7, 11; cf. 2 Tim 4:3–4). Thus, they were causing people to despise God's benefaction.

Paul wrote to Timothy and Titus to silence false teachers by teaching sound doctrine. He wrote to warn Titus of the bad reputation of those living on the island of Crete and to help him to counter false teachings and practices by being consistent in the right doctrine, Titus 1:9–14; 2:1. From a patronage point of view, the false teachers were equivalent to bad beneficiaries and mediators in that, instead of being loyal to the apostolic doctrine that they had received earlier, they had become rebellious and were rejecting it and drawing people away from the gospel of the true God, who is the Christians' chief patron (Titus 1:9–11, 14, cf. 1 Tim 1:10–11). Some of the prominent themes in Titus are the exhortation to sincere faith, ὑγιαίνοντας τῇ πίστει, "sound in faith," (2:2), cf. πᾶσαν πίστιν ἐνδεικνυμένους ἀγαθήν, "showing complete and perfect fidelity" (2:10), and τὰ ἔργα τὰ καλὰ, "good works," (Titus 2:7, 14; 3:5, 8, 14). BDAG describes πίστις as: (1) that which causes trust and faith, faithfulness, reliability; (2) trust, confidence, faith; and (3) that which is believed, body of faith or belief. It describes ἔργον as "the deeds of men, exhibiting a consistent moral character," which are characterized as good or bad by the context or by an added word. The same themes are also prominent in 1 and 2 Timothy, such as in 1 Timothy 1:5; 2:10; 5:10, 25; 6:18; 2 Timothy 1:5. Faith (πίστις, *fides*, that is, faithfulness and loyalty) and good works were core pillars in the benefaction and patronage systems. However, as seen in chapter 2 above, by deviating from their original good purpose, the systems had largely gone bad. Therefore, throughout PE, Paul advised the church to devote itself to love from a pure heart, good conscience and sincere (good or sound) faith (ἀγάπη ἐκ καθαρᾶς καρδίας καὶ συνειδήσεως ἀγαθῆς καὶ πίστεως ἀνυποκρίτου) and good works (τὰ ἔργα τὰ καλά, which is equivalent to εὐεργεσίαι).

Paul exhorted Timothy, Titus and the other PE Christians to live lives that depicted godliness (εὐσέβεια, "godly living, good religion, good deeds," 1 Tim 2:2; 4:8; 6:6). Notably, the term εὐσέβεια and its derivatives are found ten times in PE (eight in 1 Timothy, and one each in 2 Timothy and Titus), and only five times in the rest of the NT (four in 2 Peter and one in Acts). Θεοσέβεια which is a hapax, is found in 1 Timothy 2:10 only. It means "godliness," "religion," "piety." In the rest of the NT, the equivalent word that is used commonly in reference to godliness is δικαιοσύνη (what God requires; what is right, righteousness, uprightness, justice; religious duties or acts of charity, as in Matt 6:1; 10:41). Connecting it directly with G-R ethics, Hays says that a better translation of εὐσέβεια is "piety" in the root sense of the Latin *pietas*, that connoted dutiful reverence.[27] As used in PE, godly living included active positive participation of Christians in εὐεργεσία (good service to God or acts of kindness to his people), as in 1 Timothy 6:2.

Similar to Spicq,[28] Towner points out that εὐσέβεια in PE does not refer to what some scholars, such as Holtzman and Dibelius, say that it does.[29] They say that PE author used it in reference to a non-theological morality that was based on good works and common respectability, and that such morality was found in a bourgeois Christianity whose main aim was to have peaceful coexistence with various social orders in the world (1 Tim 2:2) to ensure the church's longevity in the world. Their argument is that, "in order to facilitate the transition from the older 'apocalyptic' notion of Christian existence to the new model [peaceful coexistence in the present world], the author employed certain parenetic devices and terminology which played significant role in Greek ethics."[30] Such terms include the εὐσέβεια word-group (1 Tim 2:2; 3:16; 4:7, 8; 5:4; 6:3, 5, 6, 11; 2 Tim 3:5, 12; Titus 1:1; 2:12), the ἀσέβεια group (1 Tim 1:9; 2 Tim 2:16; Titus 2:12), the συνείδησις group (1 Tim 1:5, 19; 3:9; 4:2; 2 Tim 1:3; Titus 1:15), the πίστις group (1 Tim 1:2, 19; 5:12; 6:11; 2 Tim 2:18; 2 Tim 2:2, 22; Titus 1:1,

---

27. Hays, *Moral Vision*, 69.
28. Ceslas Spicq, *Les Epitres Pastorales* (Paris: J. Gabalda, 1969).
29. Towner, *Goal of Our Instruction*, 9–12.
30. Towner, 10.

4; 2:10), σεμνός group (1 Tim 3:8, 11; Titus 2:2); and the δίκαιος group (1 Tim 1:9; 6:11; 2 Tim 2:22; 4:8; 3:16; Titus 1:8; 2:12; 3:5, 7). Their view is that, in conformity with the principles of the social systems of the day (such as basing Christian ethics on them), Christian life had merged with life in the world.[31] However, Towner says that, as it is used in other contexts in the NT, εὐσέβεια (and the other ethical terms) referred to a virtue that the believers were exhorted to exhibit (2 Pet 1:6, 7; 3:11). More broadly, εὐσέβεια was "a term representing the whole Christian life made possible by God" (2 Pet 1:3).[32] Christian εὐσέβεια and the other ethical virtues that Paul encouraged Christians to pursue in this life got their inspiration from the gospel of redemption that had its focus on eschatological expectations.[33] My suggestion is that, as it is used in PE in close connection with other virtues whose focus was the inner life of the believer (as in 1 Tim 6:11–12), it is apparent that the godliness referred to in the epistles was primarily motivated by the desire to please God (1 Tim 2:3; 6:13) and second to be acceptable to the outside world (1 Tim 3:7). It also focused more on the future than the present (Titus 2:13). It was not for conformity with the expectations of the contemporary so-called bourgeois society. The instruction was really targeted against the imposters who were using εὐσέβεια in accordance with the corrupt conventions of the benefaction and patronage systems. For example, the imposters used their "godliness" to impress people for selfish gain (πορισμός, 1 Tim 6:5), for prestige (honour) and money (cf. αἰσχροκερής, 1 Tim 3:8; Titus 1:7, 11).

Paul indicated that Christian piety was higher than its worldly counterpart when he said that godliness was a means of great gain, but only when accompanied by αὐτάρκεια (contentment, satisfaction, 6:6–8). BDAG explains that, in reference to good means of income, πορισμός (gain) is what a person achieves, for example, through farming or by being careful with what he earns (Plutarch, *Cato Major* 25.1). An example of negative πορισμός is what a magician gains by swindling (*Testament of Issachar* 4:5). False teachers were using godliness to swindle naive people (2 Tim 3:1–8). Paul confronted

---

31. Towner, 10, citing Stuhlmacher, "Verantwortung" 184.
32. Towner, *Letters to Timothy*, 173. For fuller elaboration on "godliness and respectability," see Towner's detailed excursus, 171–175.
33. Towner, *Goal of Our Instruction*, 10.

such ungodly practices by encouraging people to work with their own hands, to be self-supportive and to be benefactors to others (Titus 3:13, 14).

Table 2. Customized Outline of the Pastoral Epistles

1 Tim 1:1	Salutation[34]
1:3–11	Warning against False Teachers
1:12–20	**Gratitude for Mercy**
2:1–15	**Instructions on Prayer and Salvation**
3:1–8	**Qualifications of Overseers (Benefactors/Patrons)**
3:8–13	**Qualifications of Deacons (Benefactors/Patrons)**
3:14–16	Purpose of Writing the Instructions
4:1–5	Misguided Asceticism
4:6–16	A Good Minister of Christ
5:1–6:2	Duties towards Others
5:1–2	Right Treatment of Various Age-Groups
5:3–16	**Benefaction for Widows**
5:17–25	**Benefaction for Elders**
6:1–2	**Instructions for Slaves**
6:3–10	Confronting False Teaching
6:11–16	Timothy's Commission: The Good Fight of Faith
6:17–19	**Proper Use of Wealth: Benefaction by the Rich**
6:20–21	Instruction to Avoid Profanity, and Benediction
2 Tim 1:1	Salutation
1:3–18	Thanksgiving and Encouragement
2:1–13	A Good Soldier of Christ
2:14–26	A Worker Approved of God
3:1–9	Godlessness in the Last Days
3:10–4:8	Paul's Charge to Timothy
4:9–18	Personal Instructions

---

34. The sections highlighted in bold print contain significant inferences on benefaction and patronage. In the discussion that follows in this chapter, they are not discussed following the order in which they appear in the outline, but they are discussed appropriately in respective places in the flow of my argument. For example, Titus 1:5–9 is discussed together with 1 Tim 3:1–13 under the qualifications of church officers, and so forth. It does not imply that the sections in light print do not contain expressions related to benefaction. Reflection of the ideologies in those sections are discussed whenever applicable.

4:19–22	Final Greetings and Benediction
Titus 1:1–4	Salutation
1:5–16	Titus' Mission in Crete
1:5–9	**Qualifications of Elders/Overseers (Patrons)**
1:10–16	Silencing False Teachers
2:1–15	Instruction to Teach Sound Doctrine, Proper Character and Duties
2:1, 7–8	Titus' Character and Duties
2:2–6	**Proper Character for Older Men, Women and Younger Women**
2:9–10	**Slaves and Masters**
3:1–11, 13–14	**Instruction to Maintain Good Deeds**
3:12, 15	Final Messages, Greetings and Benediction

Despite the fact that the primary addressees and beneficiaries of PE were singular individuals, as seen in the frequent use of the singular second person pronoun in its various forms (for example, σε in 1 Tim 1:3; σοι in 1:18; σοῦ in 2 Tim 1:3; σύ in Titus 2:1), the main contents of the epistles were instructions given for application to the Ephesian and Cretan congregations in general.[35] It is significant to note that although some ancient manuscripts have the singular second person pronoun σου instead of the plural ὑμῶν, in the benedictions at the end of the two epistles to Timothy, others have plural addressees, Ἡ χάρις μεθ' ὑμῶν, "Grace be with you" (pl) (1 Tim 6:21; 2 Tim 4:22, cf. Col 4:18). The benediction in Titus 3:15 has an undisputed plural address, ἡ χάρις[36] μετὰ πάντων ὑμῶν, "Grace be with all of you."

Amidst challenges from false teaching and ungodly conduct of some Ephesian and Cretan Christians, Paul charged believers to live godly lives being upright and zealous for "good works" (τὰ ἔργα τὰ καλὰ), as in 1 Timothy 5:25; cf. 2:10; 5:10; 6:18; 2 Timothy 2:21; 3:17; and Titus 1:16; 2:7, 14; 3:1, 8. As stated earlier, good interpersonal relationships and involvement in good works were integral parts of the benefaction and patronage systems.

---

35. Knight III, *Pastoral Epistles*, 10.

36. The significance of the term χάρις in the benefaction and patronage systems is discussed later in this chapter.

Similarly, Paul urged Christians strongly to help one another in material and nonmaterial ways. The principle of "good works" in benefaction and patronage is elaborated further in various places in this chapter. For example, it is discussed in relation to enrolment of widows (1 Tim 5:10), in the charge to the wealthy (1 Tim 6:18), and in relation to Christians' commitment in ventures that are profitable to them and others (Titus 3:8).

As seen above, the main purpose of writing the epistles was to instruct Timothy and Titus on how to deal with false teaching. That purpose is apparent especially at the beginning of 1 Timothy. It is also prominent in other sections of PE. Timothy and Titus were to counter false teachers who had become disloyal to God by teaching doctrines that were contrary to what Paul had taught earlier (1 Tim 1:3–11, Titus 1:10–14). In benefaction terms, similar to recipients who responded negatively to their patrons, the apostates had become disloyal because they had received the right teaching but had chosen to turn their loyalty to false teachings, thus distorting and denying the truth (1 Tim 1:3–7; 6:5–11; 2 Tim 4:1–5; Titus 1:7, 10, 11). The overall aim of Paul was not as Verner says, that it was to support the hierarchical structure of the second-generation early church that wanted to keep the rich elites at the top of leadership.[37] Conformity (loyalty) to the true doctrine was the overall purpose, as indicated in 1 Timothy 3:14–15 that the instructions are guidance on how people ought to conduct themselves in the household of God.

As seen in chapter 2 above, giving of advice, for example, through teaching, was regarded as a form of patronage in the first century AD. Seneca viewed gracious reception of advice as the second best virtue.[38] Therefore, as compared to Paul, the false teachers could also be classified as bad patrons for they were giving teaching that was detrimental to their hearers. They were practitioners of the unsocial extreme category of negative reciprocity, for whatever they were teaching they were doing it for self-interest at the expense of their victims.[39] They also were ungrateful recipients of benefaction for they were debasing and repudiating the good gift that they had received. Paul wrote against such negative behaviour and encouraged the various PE

---

37. Verner, *Household of God*, 186.
38. Seneca, *Seneca III*, V.XXV.4.
39. Neyrey, "God," 469.

human characters to observe Christian principles in their benefaction and patronage endeavours.

3.3 Pastoral Epistles Characters as Benefactors and Patrons

In this section, my study begins with discussion on God the Father and Christ respectively in the benefaction and patronage context as found in PE in particular. After that my discussion turns to human benefaction. Under human benefaction, there is a lengthy discussion on the qualifications of various church officers, whom I view as key benefactors and patrons in the church system (1 Tim 3:1–13; Titus 1:5–9). The study examines the qualifications of the officers in comparison with those of patrons in the Roman socio-political leadership context of the first century AD. Following the study on qualifications, the discussion deals with benefaction of the church for widows (1 Tim 5:3–16). Then in connection with the officers, my discussion focuses briefly on the issue of remuneration for some elders (5:17–18). After that the discussion deals briefly with the patronal relationship between masters and slaves (1 Tim 6:1–2; Titus 2:9–10). Finally, the exhortation on generosity of the rich in the church (1 Tim 6:17–19; cf. Titus 3:14) is tackled. In the discussion in these particular sections, there is frequent and appropriate use of other relevant sections of the Pastorals and other NT and OT writings as cross reference.

Various relationships and interactions were on-going between characters in the various NT epistles. Nevertheless, without downplaying the rest, the focus of this writing is on the benefaction and patronage interactions between the main characters (individuals and groups) in PE. The main characters are God the Father, Christ, Paul the author, the main addressees, namely, Timothy and Titus, and the secondary addressees, that is, the other members of the churches, including the false teachers. First, the study examines the relationship between God the Father and humans, starting with Paul. After that the discussion dwells on the relationship between Christ and humans. Discussion on human beings as benefactors and patrons follows, where we examine Paul's relationship with the primary recipients, and, by extension, with the secondary recipients. The discussion in the chapter ends with examination of the benefactory and patronal engagements of the other PE human characters in the first century AD.

3.3.1 God as Benefactor and Patron

As recorded history attests, from the beginning of human existence, good benefactor-beneficiary relationships have always existed between humans and divine supernatural beings. Both biblical and non-biblical records bear witness that from antiquity people everywhere have viewed deities primarily as benefactors or patrons. The benefactor-beneficiary relationship has been the most prominent relationship between humans and the gods. As Danker asserts, the very notion of deity implies beneficent concern.[40] In the divine-human benefaction relationship, it is normally the divine beings who help humans. The gods are believed to give their help impelled by their own will or when petitioned, coerced or even tricked to do so. For example, on deception, a legend states that Prometheus was a wise Greek who tricked the gods for the sake of humans and brought fire to them. He is also said to have deceived the god Zeus into allowing man to keep the best part of the animals sacrificed to the gods and gave the gods the worst parts, that is, the bones and the fat.[41] On their part, humans respond to divine benefaction with thanksgiving in various forms, including veneration and loyalty to them. Concerning that relationship, deSilva states,

> The relationship between human and divine beings, cosmic inferiors and superiors as it were, was expressed in terms of the closest analogy in the world of social interaction, namely patronage, so that we find talk of "patron deities" by individuals and groups (e.g., associations or cities; Saller). This holds true for the way NT authors give expression to the relationship between the one God and the people of God.[42]

On divine-human relationship, Crook states that in G-R setting, the relationship of humans with the gods was understood in the same terms as the human-to-human relationship. He says that the interaction might

---

40. Danker, "Benefactor," 670.

41. David Crystal, ed., *The Cambridge Encyclopedia*, 3rd ed. 1 vol. (Cambridge, UK, New York, and Melbourne: Cambridge University Press, 1992), 969.

42. deSilva, "Patronage," 769.

be called divine patronage and benefaction, since in most cases it involved the exchange of benefactions and reciprocity between humans and their gods.[43] Humans gave honourable names and titles that portrayed their dependency and gratitude to the benefactor/patron deities. Five significant titles that were most frequently used in addition to εὐεργέτης to express benefaction/patronage relationships between deities and human beings are:[44] (1) "King" (βασιλεύς), or "King of Kings" (βασιλεὺς βασιλέων) (equivalent to "Lord of Lords" [κύριος τῶν κυριευόντων]), as used in reference to Zeus for his benefaction (Dio Chrysostom, *Oration* 27.5; 36.35-36). (2) "Father" (πατήρ), frequently used by Greeks and Semites (for example, *Oration* 36.60). (3) "Saviour" (σωτήρ), where the title referred to someone who: (a) rescued another from danger and peril, such as war, illness, judicial condemnation, floods and famines; (b) protected and preserved the city and its citizens; (c) inaugurated a golden age; and (d) benefited others, as used in reference to Zeus (σώζω, *TDNT*, VII). (4) "Creator" (δημιουργός), which was a common description of the creative activities of the gods. Due to its usage in reference to Zeus as a builder and workman, translators of the LXX avoided it totally and used κτίστης, as in Genesis 14:19; Ecclesiastes 12:1. Nevertheless, in the NT, the author of Hebrews used the title δημιουργός in 11:10 in reference to God: ἐξεδέχετο γὰρ τὴν τοὺς θεμελίους ἔχουσαν πόλιν, ἧς τεχνίτης καὶ δημιουργὸς ὁ θεός. (5) δεσπότης, that is, "Sovereign," "Lord" or "Master," which was mainly used of slave-master, and, above all, expressed power and fear, as in Philo's *De Vit Mos* 1.201 and *Rer Div Her* 22–23. The title δεσπότης was adopted and used in Christianity in reference to divine benevolence and power, as in Luke 2:29; Acts 4:24; 2 Timothy 2:21; Revelation 6:10. In Acts 14:17, Luke records Paul as stating that God "has not left himself without a witness in doing good [ἀγαθουργῶν] – giving you rains from heaven and fruitful seasons, and filling you with food and your hearts with joy."

Throughout PE, Paul depicted God the Father, Christ and the Holy Spirit as fully committed mainly to the spiritual salvation of humans (1 Tim 1:1, 2:4, 4:10; 2 Tim 1:10, 14; Titus 1:3–4, 2:10, 13; 3:4–6). Similarly, he also

---

43. Crook, *Reconceptualising Conversion*, 5.
44. See Neyrey, "God," 471–474 for more details on these titles.

portrayed God as fully concerned and involved in humans' common needs, such as giving life to all things (τοῦ θεοῦ τοῦ ζῳογονοῦντος τὰ πάντα, 1 Tim 6:13) and providing all things for their enjoyment (θεῷ τῷ παρέχοντι ἡμῖν πάντα πλουσίως εἰς ἀπόλαυσιν, 6:17). Most of the terms that Paul used in reference to God's personality and relationship with the human characters in PE were also used prominently in reference to the Greek and Roman gods in the divine-human benefaction and patronage relationships. For example, in 1 Timothy 1:1 he described God as σωτῆρος ἡμῶν and Jesus Christ as ἐλπίδος ἡμῶν. Both addresses had much significance in the benefaction and patronage systems. As seen in chapter 2 above, expression of trust and hope in a benefactor or patron highlighted the benefactor's/patron's worth and enhanced his social status. In 2 Timothy 1:12 Paul says he was undergoing suffering in service to God but he was not ashamed for he knew the one in whom he had put his trust, and he was sure that he was able to guard until that day "the deposit" (τὴν παραθήκην)[45] that he had entrusted to him. Similarly, using athletic language metaphorically, in 2 Timothy 4:6–8 Paul said that he was ready to die, after fighting the good fight, finishing the race and keeping the faith (τὴν πίστιν τετήρηκα). As a reward for his commitment and endurance, he knew that a crown of righteousness (ὁ τῆς δικαιοσύνης στέφανος) was reserved for him. He was sure that the Lord, the righteous judge, would give it to him in a future day. He also said that a similar reward was reserved for all who have longed for the Lord's appearing. In Titus 1:2 Paul said that he had hope of eternal life that God, who never lies, promised before the ages began. All these statements had benefaction and patronage overtones.

As seen earlier, in patronage both the patron and the client were expected to be willing to undergo extreme suffering, even death, for the sake of one

---

45. The meaning of the metaphor τὴν παραθήκην μου "my deposit" in 1:12 is not clear. While going for the option that it most appropriately refers to "the life that has been entrusted to his (God's) care," Fee, *1 and 2 Timothy, Titus*, NIBC (Peabody, MA: Hendrickson, 1988), 232, says that it can also mean "'the sound teaching,' that is, 'the gospel faith' that Paul had been entrusted with, or 'Paul's life' or his commitment to Christ and his gospel." Saying that Paul does not limit to just one item what he refers to as "deposit," Mounce (*Pastoral Epistles*, 488, citing Lock, 88) says that it could be the sum total of all that Paul had entrusted to God, namely, his life, apostolic ministry, converts, etc. In *Moral Vision*, 69, Hays says that it includes two sorts of materials, namely, confessional traditions and moral instruction. He adds that if there is any relation between these two elements it remains unclear.

another. The patron was expected to give the ultimate gift, life itself, for the benefit of the client just as Jesus did (. . . ἄνθρωπος Χριστὸς Ἰησοῦς, ὁ δοὺς ἑαυτὸν ἀντίλυτρον ὑπὲρ πάντων, τὸ μαρτύριον καιροῖς ἰδίοις, 1 Tim 2:5b–6). The client was expected to reciprocate in kind in gratitude to his patron. Towards the end of his life, Paul portrayed himself as doing double ultimate commitment. He was giving his life as a sacrifice in ultimate loyalty to God (2 Tim 4:6). Literally, σπένδομαι refers to one's life being poured out as a drink-offering. As a faithful mediator also, he encouraged Timothy to endure suffering and carry his evangelistic work fully (2 Tim 4:5). When Paul said that he knew the one in whom he had put his trust, that he was sure he was able to guard until that day what he had entrusted to him, he was highlighting the "trustworthiness of God" as the basis of his trust and hope. It is similar to when he described him as one who does not lie (ὁ ἀψευδὴς θεός, Titus 1:2). By that description, he was also implying that God was not like some benefactors and patrons who were not faithful and therefore did not fulfil their promises to their clients.

Paul highlighted the Trinity's involvement in benefaction to all humans, especially in the provision of spiritual salvation. Among such statements are:

1. "To the King of the ages, immortal, invisible, the only God, be honour and glory forever and ever" (1 Tim 1:17);
2. ". . . God our Savior, who desires everyone to be saved and to come to the knowledge of the truth" (1 Tim 2:3–4);
3. "For there is one God; there is also one mediator between God and humankind, Christ Jesus, himself human, who gave himself a ransom for all . . ." (2:5–6);
4. ". . . because we have our hope set on the living God, who is the Saviour of all people, especially of those who believe" (4:10);
5. "Guard the good treasure entrusted to you, with the help of the Holy Spirit living in us" (2 Tim 1:14);
6. ". . . while we wait for the blessed hope and the manifestation of the glory of our great God and Saviour, Christ" (Titus 2:13).

There are other statements, such as 1 Timothy 5:5; 6:13, 17; 2 Timothy 1:2, 8; and Titus 1:2 in which Paul highlighted the uniqueness and reliability of God as a helper of the needy.

In the statements, Paul emphasized that God is the only living and eternal God who is the saviour and hope of all people, to whom honour and glory should be given forever. As Towner says in reference to 1 Timothy 1:17 (also 1 Tim 6:15), the description of God as "the King eternal" in the doxology was a traditional Jewish designation of God, which, in the NT, is found in Pauline doxologies.[46] He says that the emphasis on the eternity of God is Paul's distinction between human and divine power. The invisibility of God is paralleled against the materialistic views of gods in pagan idolatry. The statement that he is the only God is intended to emphasize the supremacy of God above the pagan gods. In the OT, we find it in Psalm 24:10; Jeremiah 10:10. Similarly, the statement in 1 Timothy 2:5, εἷς γὰρ θεός "For there is one God," is based on the OT Shema, "the Lord alone is God," Deuteronomy 6:4. Used in the context of salvation (as in 2:3), it meant that God is the only God and saviour (and thus, spiritual benefactor) for all people.

Paul's declaration of God as the only God in 1 Timothy 1:17 and 2:5 could also have been a two-pronged polemical assertion targeting wrong views of members of the Ephesian church. First, as Towner observes cautiously, it is possible that the statement (in 1:17) was an explicit confrontation against the emperors' claim to possession of divine power. He says that Jewish challenges against the claims of pagan rulers were common in their liturgical expressions.[47] Concerning 2:5, if we take the two statements, that "prayers, intercessions, and thanksgivings be made for everyone" (2:1), and that "God desires everyone to be saved" (2:4), as the antecedents to the causal clause ("For there is one God") in 2:5, it is reasonable to view them as having been aimed at telling non-Jews that there is no other God apart from the God of the Jews (Acts 17:23–31; Rom 3:30; 1 Cor 8:6).[48] Second, it is correct to suggest that the statements that "there is one God [*for all people*]; there is also one mediator between God and [*all*] humankind" in 1 Timothy 2:5 and "the grace of God has appeared, bringing salvation to all," in Titus 2:11, were possibly a rejoinder against the claim of exclusive rights on God by the Jews. Paul was telling the separatist Jews that Gentiles also had equal

---

46. Towner, *Letters to Timothy*, 152–153.
47. Towner, 152.
48. See also Knight III, *Pastoral Epistles*, 120.

rights to God's blessings in accordance with the Abrahamic covenant (Gen 12:3; Gal 3:8–29).[49] Some of the Ephesian Gentile Christians seem to have inherited the monopolistic view of the Judaists and they were side-lining non-Christians as targets of God's gift of salvation.

Paul's ascription of honour and glory to God forever (τιμὴ καὶ δόξα εἰς τοὺς αἰῶνας τῶν αἰώνων), in 1 Timothy 1:17 and 6:16, can also be viewed as a competitive comparison between God and the gods. Men gave honour to the gods and to fellow humans for the benefits they had received from them. The gods also bestowed honour to humans for the services that the humans had rendered to them and to fellow humans. For example, in Greek mythology, in Homer's *Iliad* II.1–4, at one time while Achilles, a human hero in the Trojan wars was in a battle field, the god Zeus (Jupiter) is said to have stayed awake thinking of a way to honour him:

ἄλλοι μέν ῥα θεοί τε καὶ ἀνέρες ἱπποκορυσταὶ
εὗδον παννύχιοι, Δία δ' οὐκ ἔχε νήδυμος ὕπνος,
ἀλλ' ὅ γε μερμήριζε κατὰ φρένα ὡς Ἀχιλῆα
τιμήσῃ, ὀλέσῃ δὲ πολέας ἐπὶ νηυσὶν Ἀχαιῶν.

Now all the other gods and men, lords of chariots,
slumbered the whole night through, but Zeus was not holden
of sweet sleep, for he was pondering in his heart how he might
do honour to Achilles and lay many low beside the ships of
the Achaeans.[50]

Similarly, in I.499–505, Achilles's mother, Thetis, is depicted as begging Zeus to honour her son, Achilles. LSJ says that people could also give honour to their elders for the rank they held in society or for the service that they performed for the people.[51] Towner says that in Greek culture, doxologies that gave greatest prominence to the elements of honour and glory were common and that such commendations were given to the rulers. He describes

---

49. See also Knight III, 120.

50. Homer, "Homer, Iliad," *Perseus Collection: Greek and Roman Materials*, edited by Gregory R. Crane of Tufts University, Massachusetts, accessed 25 August 2011. http://www.perseus.tufts.edu/hopper/text?doc=Perseus%3Atext%3A1999.01.0133%3Abook%3D2%3Acard%3D1.

51. Other meanings of τιμή are discussed later in this chapter, for example as it is used in 1 Tim 5:3, 17 and 6:1.

τιμή as a "public acknowledgement of worth."[52] Public acknowledgement of the worth of the person for his status, his resources, and for what he had done for the community was a core principle and practice in the benefaction and patronage systems. We may infer that when Paul proclaimed "eternal honour and glory" to God the Father and to Jesus Christ, whom he also described as God (1 Tim 1:17; 6:15), he highlighted their benefaction and patronage status.

3.3.2 God as Benefactor in the Context of Prayer and Salvation, 1 Tim 2:1–7

This pericope (2:1–7) is set within a wider section on instructions on sound doctrine,[53] faith, conduct, order and organization in the household of God, 1 Timothy 1:3–3:16. The instructions are given especially as countermeasures against the havoc that false teaching was causing in the church at Ephesus. In fact, as seen above, most of the advice and instructions in PE were given to oppose false teaching. At the beginning of the prayer, Paul uses the conjunction οὖν together with the verb παρακαλέω. Witherington III says that, in Pauline epistles, the combination of παρακαλέω with οὖν is often used at the onset of a new argument, as in Romans 12:1 and Ephesians 4:1, and, therefore, whatever is said in 1 Timothy 2:1–15 is not necessarily connected to what is said in chapter 1.[54] However, Towner says that the conjunction connects back to the instructions that Paul left for a while in 1:18–19a, when he detoured briefly in 19b–20.[55] Mounce says that verse 1 of chapter 2 connects 2:1–7 with chapter 1 using an initial οὖν along with the repeated use of παρακαλέω in 1:3 (repeated also in 2:8), and the repetition of ideas (of salvation for sinners) from 1:15. Comparing carefully what is said in chapter 1 with what is said in chapter 2, it is more logical to view the conjunction as a consecutive or inferential connector, not as marker for the beginning of a new argument. The argument that he is raising in 2:1–7

---

52. Towner, *Letters to Timothy*, 153.

53. Meaning of "sound teaching" is discussed later under διδακτικός in section 3.7.3 on "Qualifications of the Church Officers."

54. Ben Witherington III, *Letters and Homilies for Hellenized Christians: A Socio-Rhetorical Commentary on Titus, 1-2 Timothy and 1-3 John* (Downers Grove: InterVarsity Press; Nottingham, UK: Apollos, 2006), 212–213.

55. Towner, *Letters to Timothy*, 165.

is a result of (or inference from) what he said in the preceding section, about Christ saving even the worst of sinners.

In 1 Timothy 1:3–7 and 4:3–4, Paul writes about false teachers who were teaching things about the law that they were not conversant with, and who were forbidding people from marriage and taking certain foods. They were also teaching that the resurrection had taken place (2 Tim 2:18). There is sparse information about the exact type of heresy that they were teaching. However, these and other hints that we have in the letters help us to deduce that their teaching was syncretistic. It exhibited both Judaistic and proto-gnostic elements that reflect tendencies that became more prominent in the second and third-century Gnosticism.[56] Perhaps they were teaching that salvation (the greatest benefaction from God) comes from conformity to the law, instead of faith in God through Christ, thus denying him the honour that he had earned and therefore rightly deserved. In verses 8 to 11, Paul explains the nature and purpose of the law. He says that it is good when used legitimately (1:8), and that it was given to counter whatever was contrary to the sound teaching that conformed to the gospel of the glory of the blessed God (1:10–11). There is implicit indication that false teachers were opposing Paul's apostolic authority and mission by teaching different (false) doctrine (ἑτεροδιδασκαλέω, 1:3). The teachers themselves had deviated from the faith (1:6) and they were corrupting the faith and conduct of some Christians and causing them to turn away from sound doctrine (2 Tim 3:6–7; 4:3–4). Thus, they were leading people away from reverence and loyalty to God to loyalty to Satan (1 Tim 5:15). False teaching was also turning believers away from being loyal to Paul who, possibly, had led them to faith in Christ (2 Tim 1:15). Thus, in benefaction and patronage perspective, the false teachers had become ungrateful clients. Worse than that, they were persuading fellow clients to be disloyal to their patrons.

In 1 Timothy 1:12–17, Paul recounted the testimony about his salvation and call to the evangelistic mission; how Christ strengthened him and appointed him to his service after saving him by his faith, love and mercy (not by the law as the false teachers were purportedly teaching). In the context of salvation, in 1:18–19a he reminded Timothy about the prophecies

---

56. Towner, *Goal of Our Instruction*, 247. More details about the false teaching are given later in this chapter.

made earlier about him, so that by following them he would fight the good fight (enduring suffering while doing work of an evangelist), having faith and a good conscience (contrary to the false teachers). He repeated the reminder in 1 Timothy 4:14; 6:20 and 2 Timothy 1:14; 4:5. In 1 Timothy 1:19b–20, Paul deviated a bit as he specified some of the apostates who had turned against the faith. Therefore, in 2:1–7, he resumed his discussion on the theme of salvation, and introduced a new dimension to it, namely, the universal nature of salvation.

Throughout PE, Paul presented proclamation of God's universal plan of salvation for all people as the primary mission for himself (Paul) (1 Tim 1:11–16; 2:7; 2 Tim 1:11–12), for Timothy (1 Tim 4:6–16; 2 Tim 1:5–13; 4:5) for Titus (2:11–15) and for the church (1 Tim 2:1–7). As Marshall points out, the persistent presentation of God as "'our Saviour God' indicates that the keynote of the letter is the salvific purpose of God who is the source of all blessings."[57] This universal evangelistic mission is what Paul is emphasizing in 1 Timothy 2:1–7 by his repeated use of πᾶς in verses 1, 2, 4 and 6. In addition to the trouble caused by false teaching, the text implies that the secular political authorities also were endangering peace for Christians, possibly through persecution (2 Tim 3:12). Connecting 1 Timothy 2:2 with 2 Timothy 3:12, Mounce says, "everyone desiring to live a religious life will be persecuted because their total consecration to God and outward piety will conflict with this sinful age."[58] Therefore, Paul calls for prayers so that he, Timothy and the other Christians, might lead (διάγω) a calm (ἤρεμος) and quiet (ἡσύχιος) life in complete reverence and dignity (good conduct) (ἐν πάσῃ εὐσεβείᾳ καὶ σεμνότητι).

About the various aspects of the prayer, BDAG says that almost always in the LXX (except 1 Macc 11:49) δέησις refers entreaty or prayer exclusively addressed to God, whereas προσευχή is the more general term that denotes a more specific supplication. BDAG also says that ἔντευξις refers to petition, request, appeal, or intercessory prayer, whereas εὐχαριστία is prayer of thanksgiving. Knight says that δέησις refers to requests for specific needs, προσευχή indicates bringing the needs in view before God, ἔντευξις means

---

57. Marshall, *Pastoral Epistles*, 131. Fuller discussion on God as saviour follows later in this section on "God as Benefactor and Patron."

58. Mounce, *Pastoral Epistles*, 83.

appealing boldly on people's behalf, and εὐχαριστία calls for thankfulness for them. He says that the plural aspect suggests more than one expression of prayer done by a number of believers in the congregation, as τοὺς ἄνδρας in 2:8 indicates.[59] The present tense of the passive infinitive ποιεῖσθαι connotes that the various types of prayers are to be done not once but continuously, as the context also suggests.

Some of Paul's statements in the prayer in 1 Timothy 2:1–7 may be viewed as both corrective and instructive concerning the wrong views and practices of some Christians in the Ephesian church. Paul's emphasis on God's desire that all people be saved implies that it is possible that some of the false teachers, for example, those who based their doctrines on the Torah, were teaching a theology that excluded some people from salvation and thus down-played evangelism to the Gentiles.[60] Another origin of such teaching was the misguided belief that the goal of Christian ethics presented in PE was the church's defence and self-preservation in the present world, rather than focusing on future eschatological judgment.[61] Close to that, others were teaching an exclusivist elitist theology that there will be no bodily resurrection because the spiritual resurrection of believers had already taken place (2 Tim 2:18, as in 1 Cor 15).[62] That meant two things: (1) the central message of the gospel (that Christ had risen bodily from the dead and that believers will rise from the dead in new bodies) was jeopardized, and (2) that there was no need to evangelize the heathen, for they were already locked out. That meant there was no need to pray for the heathen but only for the saved people.[63] That teaching could have arisen from two wrong assumptions: (1) misunderstanding the teaching that Christians have died spiritually and risen in Christ (Rom 6:4), and (2) proto-Gnosticism that taught that

---

59. Knight III, *Pastoral Epistles*, 115.

60. See Towner, *Letters to Timothy*, 177.

61. Towner, *Letters to Timothy*, 167n13. In *Goal of Our Instruction*, 13–14, Towner says that those who see PE author as promoting an ethical teaching based on realized eschatology say that such a view was caused by diminished hope of the second-coming of Christ and future judgment of the church. They see the church as focusing on the past Christ-event and being preoccupied with its existence in the present world. Thus, belief in a future judgment could nolonger influence ethics significantly, because one's eternal standing was ensured by his past salvation achieved through baptism.

62. Mounce, *Pastoral Epistles*, 527–528.

63. Mounce, 78.

spirit is good and body is evil. Paul wrote to correct such misguided notions and guide Christians on the right perspective about their relationship with the Gentiles and pagans, and their mission to them.

Paul urged that prayers and thanksgiving be made for *all* people (v. 1), for heathen kings[64] and *all* in authority (v. 2). He said that praying for all people inclusively is right and pleasing to God who wants *all* to be saved and to come to the knowledge of the truth (v. 4). In 2:5–6, Paul said that there is one God (for all people) and there is one mediator between God and (all) people, who gave himself a ransom for *all*. Coming immediately after such a presentation of the universal scope of God's salvation, his assertion that he was appointed an apostle to the Gentiles (heathen)[65] (2:7) was aimed at correcting the insular thinking[66] of the Ephesian Christians (both Jews and Gentiles). He was directing them back to the original apostolic perspective of the church's mission to the world, namely, evangelism to all people.

We can also view the urgency for prayers for all people, specifically for kings and those in authority, as a tactical opposition to the imperial cult. Greeks and Romans frequently made prayers to their gods on behalf of their human patrons. For example, in inscription number 1063 in *I.Eph. IV*, is a record of "prayer for the *prytanis* [council member] Tullia that the gods [Hestia and Artemis] give her children 'as she accomplished her *prostasia* immaculately in your house.'"[67] Tullia is said to have spent her wealth bountifully in *prostasia* (patronage), and therefore that merited the right to be prayed for by her clients in gratitude for her financial patronage. Romans also had their gods whom they recognized as their patrons, prayed to them

---

64. Citing BAGD, Knight says in *Pastoral Epistles*, 116, that βασιλεύς may refer to "king," "monarch" or any possessor of highest power. Towner (*Letters to Timothy*, 167) also says that the title, "king" had wide usage at this time throughout the Hellenistic world, as it could refer to the Herodian line and the ruler of the Nabateans. However, at Ephesus, where the imperial cult was growing as the fastest religion, the reference would be to the emperor, where the plural, "kings," refers to the successive reigns of emperors. The addition of "and those in authority" could refer to the local or regional representatives of imperial power.

65. BDAG describes ἔθνος as: (1) nation, people; (2) (foreigners [in Greek perspective]), heathen, pagans, Gentiles.

66. Towner, *Letters to Timothy*, 167.

67. G. H. R. Horsley, "Sophia, 'the second Phoibe,'" in *New Documents Illustrating Early Christianity*, vol. 4, *A Review of the Greek Inscriptions and Papyri Published in 1979*, ed. G. H. R. Horsley (Macquarie University, NSW: Ancient History Documentary Research Centre, 1987), 242.

and thanked them for their patronage. For example, they had Jupiter as the patron god of Rome. They worshipped and prayed to him for victory during war. Whenever they succeeded in battle, they celebrated in thanksgiving and praise to him. Similarly, in 31 BC, Augustus attributed his victory at the battle of Actium to Apollo. He dedicated to him a splendid temple on the Palatine Hill in gratitude.[68] Prayers to the gods for patrons in gratitude for their patronage, and thanksgiving to them for their benefaction to people was a common practice. Concerning 2:5, Liefeld says the statement that "there is one God" implies both inclusiveness and exclusiveness. It is exclusive in that God has "no competitors other than in the imagination of pagan idolaters."[69] It is inclusive in that God is God and saviour of all people.

In the Intertestamental Period, the god Apollo was acknowledged as the ancestor and patron of the Seleucid dynasty.[70] At the time of writing, the Greeks in and around Ephesus and Crete were worshippers of many gods, as well as worshippers of the emperor. The most prominent god that they worshipped at Ephesus was Artemis or Diana (Acts 19:23–41). Similarly, Zeus (Jupiter), Hermes and others were gods that the Greeks worshipped in the early church times (Acts 14:11–13). The Greeks regarded those gods as sole providers of life and prosperity and as protectors and they worshipped them. Consequently, the statement in 1 Timothy 2:5 could have been targeted at countering dependence on and allegiance to those false gods. Paul saw God the Father as overall benefactor to all humans and Christ as the overall mediator between God and humans. He therefore urged that prayers and thanksgiving be made to God and not to any other.

A significant grammatical item to note in connection with benefaction and patronage is the preposition that Paul used in reference to the object of

---

68. Higher Education Group, "Commentary: Oxford Classical Mythology Online: Aeneid," *Oxford University Press*, accessed 20 July 2011. http://www.oup.com/us/companion.websites/0195153448/studentresources/chapters/ch26/commentary/?view=usa.

69. Walter L. Liefeld, *1 & 2 Timothy/Titus*, NIVAC (Grand Rapids: Zondervan, 1999), 87.

70. Mark Mercer, "The Benefactions of Antiochus IV Epiphanes and Dan 11:37–38: An Exegetical Note," *The Mater's Seminary Journal* 12, no. 1 (Spring 2001): 90. T. W. Hillard, "Quasi-divine Honours for a Severe Governor," in *New Documents Illustrating Early Christianity*, vol. 9, *A Review of the Greek Inscriptions and Papyri Published in 1986-87*, ed. S. R. Llewelyn (Macquarie University, NSW: Ancient History Documentary Research Centre, 2002), 15. Hillard says that the worship of Apollo was common in the Roman province of Asia (specifically in Lydia).

the prayers. He used ὑπέρ in both 2:1 and 2: ὑπὲρ πάντων ἀνθρώπων (2:1) and ὑπὲρ βασιλέων καὶ πάντων τῶν ἐν ὑπεροχῇ ὄντων (2:2). In both cases, especially when used with words of request or prayer, the right translation of the preposition is "for," "on behalf of" or "for the sake of" (BDAG). Hence, it means that prayers should be made "for the sake of" all people (2:1), and "for the sake of" kings and all those in authority. What is important to note is that Paul did not use the preposition πρός. As Mounce observes, "in contrast to examples of secular prayers, Christians' prayers are ὑπέρ, 'on behalf of,' and not πρός, 'to,' the rulers."[71] This means that instead of viewing and depending on the rulers as their main benefactors and patrons, Christians were to take God as the overall benefactor and patron for all people, including the rulers. In the prayer, in 1 Timothy 2:3, God is presented as being "our saviour," τοῦ σωτῆρος ἡμῶν θεοῦ. As stated earlier in this discussion, the title "saviour" was given to both divine and human benefactors and patrons because of the benefaction they were giving to people.

Coming after the urgency to pray "for all people," ὑπὲρ πάντων ἀνθρώπων, in 2:1, the genitive clause ὑπέρ βασιλέων καὶ πάντων τῶν ἐν ὑπεροχῇ ὄντων in 2:2 is epexegetical. It specifies a subgroup among "all people."[72] Prayers and sacrifices for pagan kings and their families, as a form of thanksgiving for the good things that they had done and were doing for the people, was not a new thing (as in Ezra 6:9–10; *Ep Ar* 45; Philo, *Alleg. Leg.* 157, 317; Josephus, *War* 2.197). D-C says that, among the Jews, the custom of praying for pagan leaders was "the equivalent of the cult of the emperor and thus the most important sign of loyalty."[73] Although sometimes in the pagan setting obedience and prayer for those in authority were acts of slavish subservience in repayment of benefaction, in the context of the church it was obedience and service to God (as in Rom 13:1ff). The practice of prayers for pagan rulers can be traced back to the OT, during Israel's exile. At that time, pagan leaders were seen as God's servants and pagans were gradually viewed as included in God's plan of universal redemption. Therefore, to

---

71. Mounce, *Pastoral Epistles*, 81.

72. See Knight III, *Pastoral Epistles*, 115.

73. Dibelius and Conzelmann, *Pastoral Epistles*, 37. It is more appropriate to say that Jews praying to the LORD for pagan leaders was a godly counteraction against the imperial cult.

Paul, prayer for pagan leaders was a key Christian obligation and it formed part of the rationale for Christian existence, namely, for witness and service in the world.[74] As seen in 2:3, Paul gave the second purpose for the prayer as that "it is right and pleasing to God."

The first purpose of the prayer is found in the ἵνα clause that is used to express wish in 2:2, ἵνα ἤρεμον καὶ ἡσύχιον βίον διάγωμεν ἐν πάσῃ εὐσεβείᾳ καὶ σεμνότητι "so that we may lead a quiet and peaceable life in all godliness and dignity." D-C takes the exhortation for amicable relationship of the church and the secular state as indication of a change of theological perspective of the church. It says that the church was experiencing a "changeover from an eschatological world view to an ecclesiastical existence within an expanding world that provided more room for a Christian life,"[75] meaning that the church was somehow trading its godliness for peaceful coexistence with the world. It is true that this could have been the case with those who had become apostate. Nevertheless, Paul states clearly that the main purpose of the prayers was to ask God to dominate the ruling authorities to the extent that there would be calm and quietness (peace), a concrete discernible condition that was also ideal and understandable in the Hellenistic world.[76] Submission and obedience to the secular authorities and devotion to good works were evidence of the change that Christian faith brings (Titus 3:1–11, also Rom 13:1–7). Paul also knew that suffering was part of Christian life (2 Tim 3:12). Therefore, he encouraged Timothy to excel in all situations (2 Tim 2:3; 4:2). However, as seen in the wish clause, "so that *we* may lead a calm and quiet life in all godliness and dignity," Paul longed for peace, godliness and dignity for the church.[77] For the church, the serene environment would be conducive to the spreading of the gospel.[78] As stated earlier, it is also possible that the plural "we" in the subjunctive verb διάγωμεν also included "all people."[79] In 2:4 Paul said that God desires that all people be

---

74. See Towner, *Letters to Timothy*, 169.
75. Dibelius and Conzelmann, *Pastoral Epistles*, 37.
76. See Towner, *Letters to Timothy*, 169.
77. Towner, 169.
78. See Hays, *Moral Vision*, 67.
79. Knight III, *Pastoral Epistles*, 116.

saved and come to the knowledge of the truth. Therefore, peace and quiet life also were good for all people.

Contrary to Hanson's view, Paul's use of the Hellenistic ethical terms, εὐσεβείᾳ καὶ σεμνότητι, "piety and dignity," does not show his endorsement of a Christian life that sought little more than the goal of respectability similar to the heathen world.[80] Similar to D-C (Dibelius and Conzelmann, *The Pastoral Epistles: A Commentary on the Pastoral Epistles*), in the use of these two terms, εὐσέβεια and σεμνότης, which Paul did not use anywhere in his undisputed letters, Hanson sees an author who was devoid of Paul's insights into the nature of Christian ethics. In PE author's statement, he also sees a church that was focused on conforming to the secular Hellenistic notions and expectations of good citizenship; a church that was settling down "to meet the exigencies of life in the provinces during the opening years of the second century."[81] However, despite his use of terms similar to those currently used in the secular world, Paul placed the Christian ideal of dignity above the Hellenistic standards by basing it on sound theological teaching.[82] He also based Christian piety on salvation and targeted it at pleasing God (2:3–4). It was not to please, pacify or bring honour to the secular authorities or to the society. In fact, as seen above, from the benefaction viewpoint, Paul's statement that prayers and thanksgiving be made *for* all people, including kings and *all* in authority, showed that *all* people (including the pagan rulers) are equally targets of God's benefaction, including salvation.

In addition to the first one in verse 2, other purposes for the urgency for prayers for all people are given in 2:3–7. Paul begins verse 3 with a neuter demonstrative pronoun τοῦτο. The context determines that we refer back particularly to what he has just said in verse 1 and 2. Therefore, in verse 3 he gives the reason as that "this is good and pleasing in the sight of God our saviour" (τοῦτο καλὸν καὶ ἀπόδεκτον ἐνώπιον τοῦ σωτῆρος ἡμῶν θεοῦ). It is not easy to pick the antecedent from verse 1 and 2, for there are two possible referents. (1) It may mean that prayer for all people (including kings and all other leaders) is good and pleasing to God. (2) It can also mean that what

---

80. A. T. Hanson, *The Pastoral Epistles*, NCBC (Grand Rapids, MI: Eerdmeans, 1982), 67.

81. Hanson, *Pastoral Epistles*, 67.

82. See also Towner, *Letters to Timothy*, 163, 170.

is good and pleasing to God is that "we lead a quiet and peaceable life in all godliness and dignity." Nevertheless, what Paul says in verse 4, indicates that the first option most likely was his intended meaning, that prayers for all people is good and pleasing to God our saviour (1 Tim 2:3, also Rom 12:1).

BDAG gives several meanings of καλός as "beautiful, good, useful, pleasant, desirable, morally good, pleasing to God, contributing to salvation." Towner says that καλός means goodness or rightness of behaviour as the Lord measures it.[83] He connects this thought to the OT setting and says that doing good amounted to what was in accordance with the law and thus pleasing to the Lord (Deut 6:18). For ἀπόδεκτος he says that it marks a slight word shift from the term "pleasing," as Paul accesses the OT formula. It calls to mind the use of the word group in Leviticus that describe sacrifice as acceptable to God (as in Rom 15:16; Phil 4:18; 1 Pet 2:5). BDAG says that ἀποδεκτός strictly means "acceptable" and ἀπόδεκτος "pleasing,"[84] and, therefore, it is preferable to translate ἀπόδεκτος in 2:3 (and 5:4) as "pleasing."[85] However, this should not cause a war on words unnecessarily, for in relation to sacrifice, both terms are applicable. Whatever is acceptable to the Lord is also pleasing to him.[86] If it were for pleasing men, as D-C and Hanson accuse PE author of, then it would be very different because whatever is pleasing to men is not always acceptable to God.

In connection with prayer for all people being pleasing to God, Towner observes that Paul "places the church's prayer into an OT cultic framework whereby prayer becomes the latter-day acceptable sacrifice."[87] From the inception of the Jewish nation, various forms of sacrifice were made to God. Many of them were for thanksgiving. Obedient service and thanksgiving to God were a vital positive response to his benefaction. Of course, the views of Stoics, such as Seneca and Philo, were that God does good things to people because of his nature and therefore requires and expects nothing from them

---

83. See Towner, 176, for this and the immediately following references from him.

84. Note the different positions of the accent in ἀποδεκτός and in ἀπόδεκτος.

85. The LXX uses δεκτός in connection with burnt offerings to indicate what is acceptable, welcome or favourable to the Lord (Lev 1:4, cf. Phil 4:18).

86. Compare this with Cain's and Abel's sacrifices in Gen 4:3–7.

87. Towner, *Letters to Timothy*, 175.

in return.[88] Jews also had similar views, as expressed by Josephus "Not by deeds is it possible for men to return thanks to God, for the Deity stands in need of nothing and is above all such recompense."[89] Based on that view, they encouraged benefactors to emulate God by not demanding any return for benefaction. Nevertheless, contrary to the view of the Stoics and the Jews, many Christians in the first century AD operated by rules that were nearly similar to those of the prevailing benefaction and patronage systems in which right response for benefaction (including prayers for the patrons) was seen as appropriate and necessary. We see evidence of that reality in the early extra-biblical writings and in the NT. For example, in *1 Apol.* 13, Justin Martyr stated that the only honour worthy of God is gratitude, not because it adds any worth to him or meets any lack that he has. Honour in form of tangible acts of gratitude was an integral element in the benefaction systems. It served as repayment for benefaction. It enhanced the status of the benefactor or patron in the society. Verner says that rich people took up municipal office and used their resources to help the city and, in so doing, demonstrated their prosperity and generosity, an act that enhanced their own social standing.[90] However, NT authors discouraged self-serving benefaction. Paul also implied that about God in 1 Timothy 1:12–17, that he saved him solely by grace and mercy, not for self-enhancement. He also was very clear that nobody could repay God for the salvation that he had given, as in Romans 5:15–17. Unlike the false teachers, Paul emulated God by charging nothing for the gospel that he was preaching (2 Cor 11:7).

Verse 4 of 1 Timothy 2 resumes the core thesis of the pericope, namely, emphasis on *all*, and connects it with God's plan of salvation, that he desires that all people be saved and come to the knowledge of the truth. This puts the prayer in the context of evangelism. Paul wanted to reinstate in the Ephesian church a prayer practice that had the evangelistic mission to Gentiles as its target.[91] The description of God as σωτῆρος ἡμῶν and ὃς πάντας ἀνθρώπους θέλει σωθῆναι highlights the all-inclusive scope of his

---

88. Seneca, *Seneca III*, IV.III.3; IV.IX.1 & IV.XXV.3, cf. Philo, *De Plant.* 130 & *Det Pot Ins* 161–162; and Cicero, *De Off* I.44.

89. Josephus, *Ant.* 8.111.

90. Verner, *Household of God*, 183.

91. Towner, *Letters to Timothy*, 165.

salvation. Mounce somehow expresses the universal scope of salvation in the context of benefaction, as he says that Paul wishes that the "benefits of God's salvific work" be enjoyed by all.[92] From the very beginning of his first letter to Timothy, and found prominently throughout PE, the title σωτήρ, "saviour" is used more in reference to God the Father (1 Tim 1:1; 2:3; 4:10; 2 Tim 1:8–9; Titus 1:3; 2:10, 13; 3:4) than Christ (2 Tim 1:10; Titus 1:3, 4; 3:6). God is presented as "saviour" in the sense that he is "the architect and initiator of the salvation plan," whereas Jesus is called so because "he is the means by which this salvation plan is implemented in history."[93] Although in 1 Timothy 1:15 Paul introduces the idea that Jesus is saviour, he never addresses him as such anywhere in the entire epistle. In 1 Timothy 4:10 he describes God as the saviour of all people who believe. In the undisputed letters, Paul also says that God saves those who believe. It is only in PE that the concept of God the Father as σωτῆρος ἡμῶν "our saviour" in the spiritual sense is highlighted. Knight says that the purpose of presenting God as saviour was to correct the false teachers' perspective that God was less than the saviour of all people.[94] Towner says that although the designation of God the Father as saviour was common in the Greek OT as it was related to the archetypal exodus salvation, use of the title for Christ was slow to develop in the NT. He suggests that the hesitation was probably caused by the aversion of NT authors against using it on Christ because it was being used in the imperial cult for the deified emperor. He further explains that when it was finally used for Christ, its meaning was drawn from the biblical tradition[95] rather than the imperial cultic convention.

In the NT, the depiction of God as saviour is found only two times in other places outside PE, Luke 1:47 and Jude 1:25. However, it is found six times in PE, in 1 Timothy 1:1; 2:3; 4:10; Titus 1:3; 2:10 and 3:4. Mounce says that the title was used consistently in reference to God in PE as a deliberate assault against the Ephesian worship of redeemer gods and emperors

---

92. Mounce, *Pastoral Epistles*, 84.
93. Towner, *Letters to Timothy*, 97.
94. Knight III, *Pastoral Epistles*, 62.
95. Towner, *Letters to Timothy*, 97. The same can also apply to the usage of μεσίτης in 1 Tim 2:5.

and other humans as saviours.⁹⁶ For example, although this happened in Palestine, Josephus says in his autobiography that at one time when he was standing and speaking to the Galileans they "were all shouting, calling me the patron and rescuer [εὐεργέτης καὶ σωτήρ] of their country . . . While I was still saying these things, there were numerous voices from all sides calling me patron and rescuer."⁹⁷ They did it because of the help that he acquired for them from the Roman authorities. Thus, some Jews and Gentiles viewed fellow humans as saviours. Some Jewish Christians claimed that salvation was not through Christ but through adherence to their mythological reconstruction of the OT genealogies, and therefore their view of salvation was exclusive and sectarian.⁹⁸ In the other epistles, Christ is the one who is consistently presented as the saviour.

The theme of God being saviour of all people is also found in Titus 2:11 where Paul says, "For the grace of God appeared, bringing salvation to all." From the context, cf. 2:14, spiritual salvation is what is implied in this statement. Thus, he showed that all people are potential beneficiaries of God's gift of salvation. It is evident that in the six instances where σωτήρ is used in reference to God in PE, it refers to spiritual deliverance. In 1 Timothy 2:3–4, the emphasis is on God's desire for all people to be saved. 4:10, says that God saves only those who believe, . . . ὅτι ἠλπίκαμεν ἐπὶ θεῷ ζῶντι, ὅς ἐστιν σωτὴρ πάντων ἀνθρώπων, μάλιστα πιστῶν ". . . because we have our hope set on the living God, who is the saviour of all people, namely, of believers."

Following Skeat's interpretation of μάλιστα in 2 Timothy 4:13,⁹⁹ scholars, such as Ngewa, Campbell, Marshall, Knight, and Towner¹⁰⁰ view the

---

96. Mounce, *Pastoral Epistles*, cxxxii–cxxxv, 6. See also Towner, *Goal of Our Instruction*, 73–119.

97. Flavius Josephus, *Life of Josephus*, trans. Steve Mason (Boston; Leiden: Brill, 2003), 114, 117. Paragraphs number (47) 244, and (50) 259.

98. Mounce, *Pastoral Epistles*, cxxxiv.

99. T. C. Skeat, "'Especially the Parchments': A Note on 2 Timothy IV.13," *Journal of Theological Studies* 30, no. 1 (April 1979): 173–177.

100. Samuel M. Ngewa, *1 & 2 Timothy and Titus*, Africa Bible Commentary Series (Grand Rapids: Zondervan, 2009), 99. See also Craig Blomberg's comments in, "1 & 2 Timothy and Titus," review of Samuel M. Ngewa, *1 & 2 Timothy and Titus*, accessed 1 October 2018, https://denverseminary.edu/resources/news-and-articles/1--2-timothy-and-titus/; R. Alastair Campbell, *The Elders: Seniority within Earliest Christianity*, Studies of the New Testament and its World (Edinburgh: Clark, 1994) 200–201; Marshall, *Pastoral*

usage of the adverb μάλιστα in 4:10 as epexegetical to πάντων ἀνθρώπων, thus meaning, "to be precise," "namely," "I mean," "that is," and "in other words," instead of taking it as emphatic, meaning, "especially" as the majority of English Bible versions do. Reading 1 Timothy 4:10 in light of 1 Timohty 2:3–4, where Paul emphasizes God's desire for the salvation of all peoples, translating μάλιστα as "namely" is more appropriate. As stated earlier, Paul's stress on faith as what results in salvation was aimed at denouncing "the extreme exclusivist claims and ascetic rigors" of the opponents of the gospel that Paul was preaching.[101] The universal scope of the God's salvation was in view.

Some scholars have a divergent opinion and say that in PE μάλιστα is used for emphasis rather than for further explanation. Poythress argues that when the authors of the NT, including the authors of the epistles, wanted to make what they were writing more precise, they normally used the phrase τοῦτ' ἔστιν ("that is"), as found in Matthew 27:46; Mark 7:2; Acts 1:19; 19:4; Romans 7:18; 9:8; 10:6, 7, 8; Philemon 12; Hebrews 2:14; 7:5; 9:11; 10:20; 11:16; 13:15; and 1 Peter 3:20.[102] His view is supported by Kim[103] who argues that μάλιστα in 1 Timothy 5:17 and in some other instances in the NT, such as Acts 20:38; 25:26; 26:3; Galatians 6:10; Philippians 4:22; 1 Timothy 4:10; 5:8, 17; 2 Timothy 4:13; Titus 1:10; Philemon 1:16; and 2 Peter 2:10, has the traditional meaning of "especially," rather than explanation, as Skeat argues.

Beyond doubt, in some cases, translating μάλιστα as "especially" is more appropriate than "that is." For example, in 1 Timothy 5:8 the emphasis on helping members of one's immediate household more than helping the wider extended community is understandable. One prominent principle in *patronicium* and kinship benefaction was favouritism towards one's clients and relatives. Paul highlights the element of favouritism among believers in Galatians 6:10: ἄρα οὖν ὡς καιρὸν ἔχομεν, ἐργαζώμεθα τὸ ἀγαθὸν πρὸς

Epistles, 612; Knight III, *Pastoral Epistles*, 203, 204, 232; Towner, *The Letters to Timothy and Titus*, 311–312.

101. Towner, *Letters to Timothy*, 311.

102. Vern Sheridan Poythress, "The Meaning of μάλιστα in 2 Timothy 4:13 and Related Verses," *Journal of Theological Studies* 53, no. 2 (October 2002): 523.

103. Hong Bom Kim, "The Interpretation of μαλιστα in 1 Timothy 5:17," *Novum Testamentum* 46, 4 (October 2004): 360.

πάντας, μάλιστα δὲ πρὸς τοὺς οἰκείους τῆς πίστεως "So then, whenever we have an opportunity, let us work for the good (benefit) of all, *but especially for those of the family of faith*" (italics mine). In view of benefaction and patronage, we may take ἐργαζώμεθα τὸ ἀγαθὸν (to do good) as equivalent to εὐεργεσία. Just as some patrons and benefactors showed favour to their clients based on the clients' loyalty, in matters of spiritual salvation, according to Galatians 6:10, believers were somehow encouraged to show favour to fellow believers. Therefore, the interpretation of μάλιστα as "especially" in 1 Timothy 5:8 is also viable. Nevertheless, doing good to believers only would be going against Jesus's exhortation for his followers to do better than sinners in matters of love (Luke 6:32). Therefore, in 4:10, as used in reference to God's spiritual salvation to all people who believe, the meaning of μάλιστα as "namely" is more appropriate.

Connecting the thought in 4:10 with what is in 2:4–7, we may conclude that Paul was saying that God desires (wills) everyone to know the truth and be saved through believing in Christ[104] because without him, people have no other true God and they have no other mediator who can facilitate access to God's salvation for them. We also can reverse the order of the clauses in 2:4 from "who wills everyone to be saved and to come to knowledge of the truth" to "who wills everyone to come to knowledge of the truth and to be saved."[105] Similar to Hanson, we may confidently suggest that this statement of how God saves people goes against the notion of salvation to the elite only (what seems to have been part of the false teaching in Ephesus), and the Augustinian (and later Calvinist) emphasis on predestination.[106] Likewise, as Mounce,[107] we may argue that when Paul says that God wills all people to know the truth and to be saved he does not imply universalism of salvation.

---

104. See Mounce, *Pastoral Epistles*, 84–85, also Marshall, Oberlinner and Roloff.

105. It is logical to do that even as Roloff says in *Der erste Brief an Timotheus*, 119–120, that only those who have come to the knowledge of the truth, that is, those who have heard the gospel and received it, are saved. See Jürgen Roloff, *Der erste Brief an Timotheus*, Evangelisch-Katholischer Kommentar zum Neuen Testament 15 (Zürich: Benziger Verlag; Neukirchener Verlag, 1988). Nevertheless, we should assume that Paul purposely put σωθῆναι before εἰς ἐπίγνωσιν ἀληθείας ἐλθεῖν. In the Greek syntax, the two infinitive clauses are complementary and have the same weight as objects of the verb θέλω. Therefore, it is more appropriate to translate them as they are without transposing them.

106. Hanson, *Pastoral Epistles*, 68.

107. Mounce, *Pastoral Epistles*, 85.

Knight explains the statement ὃς πάντας ἀνθρώπους θέλει σωθῆναι by saying that it means that "God wishes people to experience that which he would do for them, i.e., save them."[108] He also says that the statement καὶ εἰς ἐπίγνωσιν ἀληθείας ἐλθεῖν "stresses the necessary noetic aspect of salvation, most simply put, knowledge of the person and work of Christ." He views the meaning of ἀλήθεια as "the content of Christianity as the absolute truth," and takes the aorist infinitive ἐλθεῖν as connoting "the personal and experiential response" (cf. 2 Tim 3:7). He concludes by saying that "the phrase as whole is a technical term for conversion." On the same issue, Towner says that salvation in its theological sense means deliverance from sin, and that, although it has an eschatological nuance, Paul's concern is on "building a people of God who incorporate all people regardless of ethnic, social, or economic background, and who are characterized by a manner of life that is qualitatively different from that of society at large (v. 2)."[109] He adds that "knowledge of the truth" "expresses the idea conversion as a rational decision to embrace 'the truth,'" where he defines truth as "the gospel" as opposed to the fallacious competing claims of the false teachers (cf. 1 Tim 6:2). From the above views, it is clear that scholars understand the salvation process differently. Nevertheless, the majority agree that God saves *all* people who believe that Jesus Christ gave himself as ransom for them (ἀντίλυτρον ὑπὲρ πάντων, 2:6).

Concerning the scope of the ransom, in 2:6 Paul changed the adjective from "many" (λύτρον ἀντὶ πολλῶν, "a ransom for *many*"), in Matthew 20:28 and Mark 10:45, to "all" (ἀντίλυτρον ὑπὲρ πάντων "a ransom for *all*.") We may conclude that he changed the adjective to hyperbolize the same truth, making his statement a fitting refutation against the false teachers who were limiting the scope of God's salvation. He said that God saves all, who believe, whatever their ethnic background or social status. He concluded the instruction with a strong affirmation that he was truly appointed a preacher and an apostle, a teacher to Gentiles (2:7, cf. 3:16; 2 Tim 1:11; 4:17), thus

---

108. This and the immediate following allusions are from Knight III, *Pastoral Epistles*, 119–120.

109. This and the immediately following quotations are from Towner, *Letters to Timothy*, 178–179.

taking to them the offer of God's greatest benefaction of salvation through faith in Christ.

3.3.3 Christ as Benefactor, Patron and Mediator

Throughout PE, Paul presented God the Father and Christ mainly in the context of the eternal spiritual salvation (the greatest divine benefaction to humans) (1 Tim 1:1–2; 2 Tim 1:1–2; Titus 1:1–4). In 1 Timothy 1:1, he introduced God (the Father) and Christ as "our saviour" and "our hope" respectively and as his appointing and commissioning authorities: Παῦλος ἀπόστολος Χριστοῦ Ἰησοῦ κατ' ἐπιταγὴν θεοῦ (according to [or because of][110] the command of God) σωτῆρος ἡμῶν καὶ Χριστοῦ Ἰησοῦ τῆς ἐλπίδος ἡμῶν. Knight says that Paul places this designation so prominently at the beginning of his writing to express the authority by which he writes.[111] The description of Christ as "our hope" was in response to the fact that non-Christians had no hope. It was also a critique against the tendency whereby some Christians were placing their hope on temporal things (1 Tim 6:17). Towner says that the hope that is referred to in this verse is eschatological salvation (cf. 1 Thess 5:8).[112] Paul introduced God the Father and Christ in a similar manner, with slight variations in 2 Timothy 1:1, Παῦλος ἀπόστολος Χριστοῦ Ἰησοῦ διὰ θελήματος θεοῦ (because of the will of God) κατ' ἐπαγγελίαν ζωῆς τῆς ἐν Χριστῷ Ἰησοῦ. He said that his commissioning was "through the will of God according to the promise of life in Christ Jesus." In Titus 1:1 he describes himself as Παῦλος δοῦλος θεοῦ, ἀπόστολος δὲ Ἰησοῦ Χριστοῦ κατὰ πίστιν ἐκλεκτῶν θεοῦ καὶ ἐπίγνωσιν ἀληθείας τῆς κατ' εὐσέβειαν, "Paul, a servant of God and an apostle of Christ according/in relation to the faith of God's elect and the knowledge of the truth that is in accordance with godliness." He thus depicted himself as a beneficiary of God's gracious eternal life in Christ.

He ascribed honour to God the Father and Christ, acknowledging their role as benefactors in his life and in the lives of the recipients of his letters.

---

110. Mounce, *Pastoral Epistles*, 4, 6. See also other meanings of the preposition κατά under subsection "J. kata," especially the subsection titled "3. *kata* Denoting Correspondence or Conformity" in *The New International Dictionary of New Testament Theology* 3, ed. Colin Brown (Exeter; Grand Rapids, MI: Paternoster, 1978), 1200–1201. See also BDAG on the use of κατά with the accusative of goal or purpose, meaning "for the purpose of, for (because of), to."

111. Knight III, *Pastoral Epistles*, 58.

112. Towner, *Letters to Timothy*, 98. See further discussion on "hope" in subsection 3.7.7 titled "The Rich and the Needy (1 Tim 6:17–19)."

As a mediator between the addressees and God, he wished for them blessings that he could not give to them, namely, grace (χάρις), mercy (ἔλεος) and peace (εἰρήνη) from God the Father and Christ. In 1 Timothy, Paul described himself as the chief of sinners and portrayed Jesus as having showed him grace (χάρις), mercy (ἔλεος), and "utmost patience," (τὴν ἅπασαν μακροθυμίαν) (1 Tim 1:12–17). He described Christ as "our Lord" (Χριστοῦ Ἰησοῦ τοῦ κυρίου ἡμῶν) and "our hope" (Χριστοῦ Ἰησοῦ τῆς ἐλπίδος ἡμῶν). In that passage, he acknowledged and thanked him specifically for the special mercy that he had showed him by saving him and making him an example to those who would come to believe in him for eternal life. He also thanked Christ for appointing him to his service (1 Tim 1:12). By his gratitude to Christ, Paul presented himself as a loyal beneficiary of Christ's gift of mercy and forgiveness. In an environment where benefaction and patronage principles were operating, it is logical to conclude that Timothy and the Ephesian Christians could have understood his sentiments in the context of those systems.

To express his gratitude to Christ, Paul used the clause χάριν ἔχω in 1:12, whereas in 1:17 he used a statement containing several words exalting him: τῷ δὲ βασιλεῖ τῶν αἰώνων, ἀφθάρτῳ, ἀοράτῳ, μόνῳ θεῷ, τιμὴ καὶ δόξα εἰς τοὺς αἰῶνας τῶν αἰώνων. Prominent among those word are τιμή[113] and δόξα. Δόξα is the glory, estimation or reputation that people have and express about a person. LSJ says that δόξα is mostly the good reputation, honour or praise that a person has. Verbal expression of praise to, or for, a person or something else is expression of glory for the same. In the context of 1 Timothy 1:17, δόξα refers to "the recognition of honour that is owed to a deserving person in high repute."[114] In the epistles, δόξα is especially used in reference to God in general as a fitting means of acknowledgement and enhancement of status or performance. BDAG says that it is used in reference to God as a transcendent or majestic being who deserves honour. Paul had high regard for God because of what he had seen him do for him in Christ Jesus.

As seen in chapter 2, honour and glory for benefactors and patrons were expected from the beneficiaries as favourable reciprocation for the benefits

---

113. The term τιμή is discussed in detail later especially in relation to honouring widows and elders.

114. Towner, *Letters to Timothy*, 153.

received or anticipated. Before its Christianization in the church, especially by reformation and post reformation theologians, χάρις featured prominently in the patronage system. The virtuous response of thanks for benefits received was depicted as one of the three Graces. Malina states that the vocabulary of grace, that is, χαρίζομαι, χάρις, and χάρισμα, belongs to the sphere of favouritism in patronage. He then gives his own interpretation of the three nuances of χάρις in reference to patronage: "I suggest that *charizomai* refers to showing patronage, *charis* to willingness to be a patron, and *charisma* to the outcomes of patronage."[115]

Thanksgiving was a speech act that was directly connected to benefaction and patronage. In fact, reformation and post-reformation Christianity borrowed the term from its secular usage and adapted it for usage in the religious sense. However, in the bulk of its references in the NT, including PE, as in 1 Timothy 1:12 and 2 Timothy 1:3, χάρις is used with the sense of normal thanksgiving, as in the benefaction and patronage context. An alternative word for thanksgiving which also contains χάρις is εὐχαριστία, found in 1 Timothy 2:1; 4:3, 4.[116] It is correct to infer that, when Paul gave his own thanks to Christ and urged other people to give thanks and glory to God, he portrayed himself perfectly as a grateful beneficiary who was loyally serving his patron by encouraging his fellow clients to be thankful to their common benefactor. By encouraging others, his role was that of a client-mediator between the primary patron and the second-level clients.

In 1 Timothy 1:13 and 16, he highlights the fact that he was showed mercy, ἠλεήθην, whereas in 1 Timothy 1:15 he says that he was the chief of sinners whom Christ came into the world to save, Χριστὸς Ἰησοῦς ἦλθεν εἰς τὸν κόσμον ἁμαρτωλοὺς σῶσαι· ὧν πρῶτός εἰμι ἐγώ. The words ἔλεος (mercy) and σωτηρία (salvation) were prominent in the benefaction and patronage systems. These words feature prominently also in this chapter. In the perspective of the prevailing benefaction and patronage systems, Paul was expressing himself as a chief beneficiary of Christ's benefaction. He saw

---

115. Bruce J. Malina, *The Social World of Jesus and the Gospels* (London; New York: Routledge, 1996), 171.

116. The term χάρις is discussed further later in this chapter in section 3.7 titled "Humans as Benefactors and Patrons: Benefaction and Patronage between Various Individuals and Groups."

Christ as his own main benefactor and patron and thus depicted him as one who deserved exclusive continuous honour and glory in recognition of his status as the saviour and as the eternal, immortal, invisible and only God (1 Tim 1:1, 16, 17; 2 Tim 1:10; Titus 1:3, 4; 2:13; 3:6). Thus, he portrayed him as the overall benefactor, far above all human and divine benefactors and patrons. We can safely propose that, that portrayal was in direct contrast to the prevailing trend of regarding humans, especially the emperors, as the ultimate benefactors and patrons.

As stated earlier, favour from a patron to particular clients was common in patronage. When Paul introduced himself as a herald and apostle who was showed extraordinary mercy and appointed by Christ to minister to him especially among the Gentiles, he was thus highlighting Christ's favour for him. Favour indicated exclusiveness and superior regard for particular clients over others. Thus, Paul was thankful to Christ for the special favour of mercy showed to him (1 Tim 1:12–14). If temporal rescue from physical predicament by a mortal being or a lesser god were considered as one of the greatest benefits a benefactor could give to a beneficiary,[117] then the eternal salvation that Christ gave to Paul was a supreme benefit. It inspired gratefulness and ascription of eternal honour and glory from the beneficiary to his supreme patron (1 Tim 1:12–17).

An element that seems contrary to the fact that Paul was strengthened by Christ and appointed to his service based on God's mercy (divine favour) is the statement in verse 12 that says, Χάριν ἔχω τῷ ἐνδυναμώσαντί με Χριστῷ Ἰησοῦ τῷ κυρίῳ ἡμῶν, ὅτι πιστόν με ἡγήσατο θέμενος εἰς διακονίαν. There are variant translations of the subordinate conjunction ὅτι in the clause ὅτι πιστόν με ἡγήσατο θέμενος εἰς διακονίαν. For example, NIV translates ὅτι generally as "that": "I thank Christ Jesus our Lord, who has given me strength, that he considered me faithful (πιστός, 'loyal,' 'trustworthy,' 'reliable'), appointing me to his service." When translated as "that," the conjunction may have the causal nuance, meaning "because." It is also possible to be understood as a conjunction of result or consequence and thus translated as "with the result that." Thus, it could mean that Paul was thanking Christ for giving him strength which helped him to reach a point where he (Christ)

---

117. Steven M. Baugh, "'Savior of All People': 1 Tim 4:10 in Context," *Westminster Theological Journal* 54, no. 2 (1992): 337.

considered him faithful and therefore appointed him to his service. It would then imply that there was no merit on the side of the appointee that influenced or caused Jesus to appoint him to his service. If the conjunction "that" is taken as causal, it could imply that Jesus considered him faithful and appointed him to his service because of his (Paul's) own faithfulness.

NRSV takes the ὅτι as causal and translates the verse as, "I am grateful to Christ Jesus our Lord, who has strengthened me, because he judged me faithful (loyal) and appointed me to his service." On the surface, this statement could be implying that Jesus strengthened and appointed him to his service because he considered him faithful. Thus, the strengthening and appointing were as a result of Paul's effort. However, the statements that follow in verses 13 and 14 negate that interpretation. In those verses, Paul clearly indicates that his salvation, strengthening and appointment into service depended fully on God's mercy. Towner points out, though with some caution, that Paul is "probably much more intent on attributing his calling to Christ than he is of making trustworthiness the condition of his appointment."[118] In the benefaction and patronage context, it is possible that he was thanking God for strengthening him, judging him faithful and appointing him to his service, rather than thanking him for strengthening and appointing him because of his (Paul's) faithfulness, that is, his loyalty as a beneficiary/client.

It is also possible to translate ὅτι as causative in the statement. Taking the soteriological theme that runs through 1 Timothy 1:12–17 as having a patronage outlook, it is possible that Paul was thanking Jesus for saving him solely based on his (Jesus's) mercy, 1:13–14, 16. Nevertheless, he might also have been thanking Christ for appointing him based on the loyalty that he had seen in him (Paul). In patronage, special favours were given to clients who were loyal to the patrons. The more favours were given, the more indebted the client became to the patron. Thus, in verse 17, Paul is exuberant as he exhibits loyalty and pledges more of it to his patron, τῷ δὲ βασιλεῖ τῶν αἰώνων, ἀφθάρτῳ, ἀοράτῳ, μόνῳ θεῷ, τιμὴ καὶ δόξα εἰς τοὺς αἰῶνας τῶν αἰώνων· ἀμήν. As testified by Seneca, in G-R patronage, the patron chose his clients carefully. The faithfulness or loyalty of the client was a determinant

---

118. Towner, *Letters to Timothy*, 138.

factor in the provision of help by the patron. In the same way, it is possible that the subjective faithfulness of Paul played a key role in his appointment. Christ judged him as faithful before he appointed him to his service.

Another issue of interest to note about this verse is that, Paul directed his thanks to Christ Jesus, unlike in 1 Timothy 2:1–4 where he says that prayers and "thanksgiving" are pleasing and acceptable "to God our saviour" (ἐνώπιον τοῦ σωτῆρος ἡμῶν θεοῦ). In 2 Timothy 1:3 he has exactly the same construction as in 1 Timothy 1:12, χάριν ἔχω, but there he directs the thanks to God, τῷ θεῷ. Towner points out that Paul's gratitude to Jesus in 1:12 is based on two factors. First, the passage in which the statement is found is Christological. Second, the statement "looks back on the event of his calling in which Christ Jesus played the decisive role."[119] Knight describes the clause χάριν ἔχω in 1 Timothy 1:12 as a new expression in PE. He argues that Paul used the clause χάριν ἔχω possibly because of influence from the Latin language with which he had some extended contact recently. In Latin, the expression *gratiam habere* (equivalent to χάριν ἔχω) was commonly used.[120] From the patronage viewpoint, Knight's observation is viable because Paul wrote in the context of that system.

In 1 Timothy 2:5 and 6:13, 17, Paul indicated that there is only one God who is saviour and giver of life to all people and provider of all things for our enjoyment. In 2:5 also, he stated that there is only one mediator between God and humankind. Before and during, the writing of the epistles, the term μεσίτης (mediator) was used for particular purposes. In the papyri, the term was used for an arbiter in connection with legal transactions, for a negotiator of business deals, as surety for a debt, and as a trustee in a business venture.[121] For example, in the Oxyrhynchus papyri (from first to sixth century AD), in papyrus number 1241[122] is a legend in which Phoroneus, the founder of Argos (the most important centre on the Greek mainland in

---

119. Towner, 136.

120. Knight III, *Pastoral Epistles*, 93.

121. James Hope Moulton, and George Milligan, *The Vocabulary of the Greek Testament: Illustrated from the Papyri and Other Non-Literary Sources* (Grand Rapids: Eerdmans, 1930), 399.

122. Bernard P. Grenfell and Arthur S. Hunt, *The Oxyrhynchus Papyri: Part X* (London: Egypt Exploration Fund, 1914). http://www.archive.org/stream/oxyrhynchusppt1000grenuoft/oxyrhynchusppt1000grenuoft_djvu.txt.

competition with Sparta) is presented as having been the μεσίτης between Poseidon, the Greek god of the sea and earthquakes, and Hera, the Greek goddess of love and marriage. Phoroneus is said to have decided in favour of Hera against Poseidon, setting her as the divine patron of Argos and establishing her as the god to be worshiped there. In addition, in papyrus number 1298 is a private Intertestamental Period letter in which Ammon appeals to Gonatas as the μεσίτης in a dispute between him (Ammon) and Gunthus on payment for wine.

In the Intertestamental Period, from Polybius[123] onwards, the Greeks used the term μεσίτης for diplomatic, legal and commercial transactions. In *Histories* XXVIII:17:8, Polybius wrote about Quintas Marcius suggesting to Hagepolis that it would have been good for Rhodians to be μεσίται for peace between Antiochus and Ptolemy, possibly because Marcus was afraid that Antiochus would attack Alexandria which was under the Ptolemies.[124] In classical Greek (fifth century BC onwards), μεσίτης was a person who occupied a neutral ground between two parties for the purpose of arbitrating and settling conflicts between them. The concept of a neutral μεσίτης continued into the times of Koine Greek, from the third century BC onwards. According to Plutarch,[125] for Persians,[126] such as Zoroaster,[127] the god Mithra was the mediator between the two gods, Oromazes or God (creator of good) and Areimanius or Daemon (creator of bad things).

Neyrey says that G-R deities often employed intermediaries, such as Hermes, Mercury and prophets, to communicate with and affect humans. On their part, humans had "priests" to sacrifice, petition and consult the

---

123. Polybius was a Greek historian of the Mediterranean Sea region who in his books *The Histories* wrote in detail the Roman history of the period from 220 to the fall of Carthage in 146 BC. When the Roman commissioners left Greece, they authorized Polybius to settle the details for the administration of the surviving cities. Because of doing that delegated work well, he became regarded as a public mediatorial benefactor. Therefore, statues were raised to his honour in Megalopolis, Mantinea, Tegea, Olympia, and several other places (*The Histories* I, trans. W. R. Paton, LCL [Cambridge, MA: Harvard University Press, 1922], ix).

124. See the entire episode in Polybius, *The Histories* VI, LCL (Cambridge, MA: Harvard University Press, 1926), section XXVIII.17.1–15.

125. Plutarch, "Isis and Osiris" in *Plutarch: Moralia: Volume V*, trans. Frank Cole Babbitt, LCL (Cambridge, MA; London: Harvard University Press, 1936), V.369.46.

126. The three Persian empires were: (1) Achaemenid Empire (558–330 BC); (2) Parthian Empire (247 BC–AD 224); and (3) Sassanid Empire (AD 224–651).

127. Zoroaster was a Persian sage whose suggested dates range from 3000 to 400 BC.

deities. For example, Romans had colleges of priests whose head was known as the *pontifex maximus*. In human-to-human relationships, people used go-betweens or brokers in trade, politics, legal matters and patronage. The broker was a person who was trusted by the two parties. In the patronage transaction, the patron expected some return for his patronage. Thus, he received payment for the services that he rendered. Brokers between deities and humans were necessary because the ancient deities were highly-elevated and inaccessible to ordinary mortals. In some cases, the deities were thought to be beyond direct involvement in human affairs. Therefore, they employed angels and minor gods to be mediators between them and humans.[128] In PE, such views about God being unapproachable by humans are found, for example, in 1 Timothy 6:16 where Paul describes him as, "It is he alone who has immortality and dwells in unapproachable light, whom no one has ever seen or can see." The need of a mediator between such a lofty God and humans is highlighted in 1 Timothy 2:5, in the context of prayer and salvation.

In the Greek setting, μεσίτης was a neutral person whom the transacting parties could trust.[129] The Greek notion of μεσίτης as a neutral umpire differed from the OT notion in that in the OT the mediator[130] was not a neutral third party. In the Hebrew OT there is no term for "mediator." In the LXX the word μεσίτης is found only in Job 9:33. Here it is equivalent to the Hebrew hiphil participle masculine singular מוֹכִיחַ that is translated as umpire, or one who judges and decides between two or more parties. In a combat between parties the mediators were the warriors who came between them and decided the war by a single combat, for example, David and Goliath in 1 Samuel 17:4, 23. In the Jewish setting, sometimes the mediators were the rulers of the communities and therefore they were not neutral umpires as in the Greek setting.[131] In some settings, a mediator was

---

128. Neyrey, "God," 475–476.

129. Gerhard Kittel, and Gerhard Freidrich, eds., *Theological Dictionary of the New Testament* 4 (Grand Rapids: Eerdmans, 1967), 599.

130. Although in the OT, the technical term μεσίτης was not explicitly used, the concept of mediation was known and applied. For example, it is found in the episode in which Moses acted as a judge between disputant Israelites (Exod 18:16) and where the commanders of fifties, hundreds, and so forth, mediated in disputes among their fellow Israelites (Deut 1:16).

131. Kittel and Friedrich, *Theological Dictionary*, 602.

a primary client who represented second-level clients to a principal patron. In such a setting, the mediator was a secondary patron to the clients as well as being a primary client to the primary patron. Such was the case where Pliny, himself a friend and primary client to Emperor Trajan, pleaded with Trajan to make Voconius Romanus (Pliny's schoolmate and companion from earlier years) a senator.[132] The good relationship between the mediator and the patron was used as merit for the benefit of secondary clients. Because of the influence of principles of the concurrent social systems on one another, in the NT times, it is most likely that among the Christians the term μεσίτης preserved the Greek, Roman and OT Jewish notions. Either the mediators were neutral third parties, or they belonged either to the benefactor side or to the beneficiary side or both.

In *Ant.* 16.4.3, Josephus records that Caesar (possibly Caligula) was regarded and acted as a mediator during a leadership dispute that had been taken to Rome for arbitration between the Herodian rulers of Palestine.[133] That was non-religious mediation that was found in G-R and Jewish benefaction and patronage systems. In Philo's[134] writings, the term μεσίτης had cosmological and soteriological nuances as it was used in non-religious and religious contexts. For example, in sections 5–6 of "On Flight and Finding,"[135] Philo regarded the angel who appeared to Hagar as a mediator who was sent to arbitrate between her and her mistress, Sarah. In *Questions and Answers on Exodus*, commenting on Exodus 23:20–21, Philo described the angel who was commissioned to guard and lead the Israelites into Canaan as the Logos and mediator of God's gifts and benefaction to the Israelites.

As seen above, the term μεσίτης was used of a person who brokered transaction between two parties. When used in reference to Jesus, it means that, as a mediator, he facilitated smooth relationship between God and

---

132. Pliny the Younger, "Ancient History Sourcebook: Pliny the Younger (61/62-113 CE): Selected Letters, c 100 CE," accessed 31 May 2011. http://www.fordham.edu/halsall/ancient/pliny-letters.html. Translated by William Melmoth (in Harvard Classics series). The mediation is found in Part 1 section III of his letters to Trajan (Book 10 Letter 4 in other records).

133. Josephus, *Josephus*, 342.

134. Philo lived from about 20 BC to about AD 50.

135. Philo, *The Works of Philo: Complete and Unabridged*, new updated ed., trans. C. D. Yonge (Peabody, MA: Hendrickson, 1993), 321.

humankind. As Hebrews says, he was mediator of a new and better covenant between God and humankind (cf. Heb 8:6; 9:15; 12:24). Christ is εἷς . . . μεσίτης, the "one (the only) mediator" between God and humans (1 Tim 2:5). As a fully devoted mediator, he gave himself as ransom ὑπέρ (on behalf of) all humans (1 Tim 2:6; Titus 2:14). Contrary to what some people teach, just as Liefeld says, Jesus did not give himself as a ransom "to" Satan, but he gave himself "for" all people.[136] The genitive case in the word πάντων (an indirect object in the statement) that follows the preposition ὑπέρ supports that view. Jesus gave himself so that *all* who would believe would be saved (1 Tim 1:16; 4:10). It is feasible to concur with Botha and Rousseau, who in their interpretation of τὸν υἱὸν τὸν μονογενῆ in John 3:16 in conjunction with εἷς μεσίτης in 1 Timothy 2:5, say that in the G-R context Jesus was a unique celestial mediator/broker between God and humans. They say he was unique in that he was the only son of God who had come from above, that is, from God, and he was able to ascend there again.[137] In the prevailing Greek, Roman and Jewish contexts, what Jesus did had unique benefaction and patronage implications. We can conclude that Paul was telling the Greeks and Romans that, although they had numerous gods, lords and mediators, none of them was like Jesus in his exceptional divine and human attributes and good deeds. For example, Jesus was exceptional in his mediation that facilitated the exceptional provisions from God, such as eternal salvation and its accompaniments to Paul and to all other believers (1 Tim 1:12–17; 2 Tim 1:9–10), and the provision of the Holy Spirit (Titus 3:4–7, cf. John 14:16, 26; 15:26; 17:7). To the Jews, Paul meant that Jesus's mediation was for the benefit of all people (1 Tim 2:3–7) contrary to their notion that the Messiah would come to help them alone.

As deSilva points out, a mediator could offer his own character as guarantee for the benefit of his clients. He says, "Such considerations in the patron-client exchange have an obvious corollary in the church's Christology and soteriology, wherein God, the patron, accepts Christ's clients (i.e., the Christians) on the basis of the mediator's merit."[138] In reference to Hebrews

---

136. Liefeld, *1 & 2 Timothy/Titus*, 87.

137. J. E. Botha and P. A. Rousseau, "For God Did Not So Love the Whole World – Only Israel! John 3:16 revisited," *HTS Theological Studies* 61, no. 4 (2005): 1161.

138. deSilva, "Patronage," 767.

8:6; 9:15; 12:24, where Jesus is described as διαθήκης καινῆς μεσίτης, deSilva says that, as mediator, Jesus secures favour from God on behalf of those who have committed themselves to him (Jesus) as client dependents.[139] It is true that as a full member of the Godhead, Jesus was a benefactor due to his credentials as creator and provider of life to all humans, John 1:3, 4; 10:30; 16:15; 17:10. However, as mediator he was facilitating reconciliation and provision of life from God to human beings, John 7:16; 14:24. Thus, in the patronage sense, although he could have viewed and represented human beings as his own primary clients, he was more so representing them as clients of God the Father. Based on that perspective, it is correct to argue that when Jesus is presented in 1 Timothy 2:5–6 as the only mediator between God and humankind who gave himself as ransom, it is also right to view him as a benefactor and patron who was representing his own clients, as in the Roman setting. However, as the supreme agent of God's benefaction, his mediatorial function is highlighted more than his benefactory or patronal function. In 2:5 it is God the Father who is presented as the supreme patron.

Another significant issue to note is that, in 1 Timothy 2:5, the context in which the term μεσίτης was used requires that we first of all understand and interpret it from the soteriological context because it is used within a pericope where God is depicted as saviour (1 Tim 2:3, 4). However, it is also necessary to acknowledge the existence of the ideologies of the G-R benefaction and patronage systems that were at work during the writing of the epistles. In the systems, usage of the term μεσίτης was different. As seen above, Jews had their own unique understanding of the role of a mediator, as reflected, for example, in the OT, in Philo and Josephus. Acknowledgement of that reality gives usage of expression εἷς μεσίτης in 1 Timothy 2:5 a broader sense than previously assumed.

Another issue worthy noting is that, by depicting Christ as the only mediator between God and humans Paul did not intend to obliterate the existence and usefulness of secondary human mediators between God and fellow human beings. It is evident that, in his exhortation in 1 Timothy 2:1–2 that Christians offer supplications for their rulers, he implied that Christians could and should represent all people before God in prayer.

---

139. deSilva, 770.

The representation function is a core mediatory mission of the church. It is significant to note that Paul made the declaration that there is only one Mediator between God and humans after indicating the usefulness of human intercessors (Christians) as mediators in the church system. Nevertheless, in relation to Greek and Roman understanding of mediatorship and brokerage, my argument is that the statement that there is only one mediator means that no other mediator can stand between God and humans as Christ does. His uniqueness is highlighted in the Christological formula in 1 Timothy 3:16, "Without any doubt, the mystery of our religion is great: He was revealed in flesh, vindicated in spirit, seen by angels, proclaimed among Gentiles, believed in throughout the world, taken up in glory." On the side of the Jews, Paul was telling them that Jesus was the only mediator of God's salvation for them and the Gentiles, equally; that all people have equal access to God through Christ (1 Tim 2:1–7; 3:16; 2 Tim 4:17), just as Paul says in Romans 1:16.

Still in support of the fact that human mediation was not obliterated, Paul presented himself as having been appointed and authorized by God the Father and Christ to be a servant to the Gentiles, 1 Timothy 1:12; 2:7. As a herald, he thus was a mediator of God's message of spiritual salvation. The authority, capability, credibility and responsibility that he had for educating, guiding and even to urging Timothy, Titus, the church leaders and the church members on their relationships and their transactions with one another, were delegated to him, 1 Timothy 6:13; 2 Timothy 4:1. Paul also described the overseer as οἰκονόμος (steward, manager; treasurer [of a city] or trustee) in the church. He was highlighting the overseer's rank as mediator of God's leadership in the church. In the patronage setting, consideration of social rank in virtually all daily interactions and transactions was prevalent.[140] Therefore, the picture that he depicted about the ranks, roles, relationships and transaction between the various characters in PE, such as God the Father, Christ and human beings could have been understood and accepted as necessary and beneficial for the smooth running and development of the growing church. The instructions that he issued on how humans should view God the Father, Christ and how they should relate with those inside

---

140. Saller, *Personal Patronage*, 3.

and outside the church were based on the ideologies of the prevailing social systems of interrelation, among which were benefaction and patronage. Having discussed God the Father and Christ, we now turn to human-to-human benefaction and patronage interactions.

3.4 Humans as Benefactors and Patrons

In this section, the discussion starts with Paul's interaction with the primary addressees (Timothy and Titus), and then the groups (church leaders, church members, false teachers, and non-Christians) in view of relationships in the G-R and Jewish benefaction and patronage systems. The discussion then moves to interactions between the various groups. Neyrey summarizes Marshall Sahlins' enumeration of three main types of human-to-human patronage relationships as: (1) Generalized reciprocity: the solidarity extreme, where the interests of the other person are primary (Matt 7:11); (2) Balanced reciprocity: the midpoint, in which mutual interests are uppermost (Matt 10:10; 1 Cor 9:3–12); and (3) Negative reciprocity: the unsocial extreme, where there is self-interest at the expense of the other person (Luke 10:30; 19:22).[141] This current study of the human relationships in PE is in light of that categorization. The guiding perspective is similar to Hatch's view that what distinguished Christian associations from pagan voluntary associations is that charity was the heart (the central undertaking) of the church. Hatch said that there were regular contributions from people of different classes, namely, slaves and free, men and women, aliens and citizens.[142] Broadening Hatch's view, based on Acts and the other NT Epistles, it is evident that both material and nonmaterial benefaction were central elements of the early church.

3.4.1 Paul, Timothy, Titus and the Church

As stated earlier, throughout PE, in his address to Timothy, Titus and the churches that they were leading, Paul used expressions that were also common in the benefaction and patronage systems. Although among Christians

---

141. Neyrey, "God," 469. For fuller details see Marshall D. Sahlins, *Stone Age Economics* (Hawthorne, New York: Aldine de Gruyter, 1972), 191–196.

142. Verner, *Household of God*, 6. Cited from E. Hatch, *The Organization of the Christian Churches*, 2nd ed. revised (London: Rivington, 1882).

some of those terms may have acquired new meaning and application, they retained most of their original meaning and usage. For example, during the writing of the NT epistles, it is likely that the term χάρις had acquired special religious connotations close to how it was understood and used during and after the Reformation.[143] Nevertheless, together with other terms, such as faith (πίστις), good works (τὰ ἔργα τὰ καλὰ), salvation (σωτηρία) and others, χάρις still had the nonreligious sense as understood in the G-R benefaction and patronage setting. Therefore, such words still retained the meanings that they had long before their theological usage in Christianity.

Such words and expressions appear numerous times in PE. For example, as BDAG shows, χάρις could mean: (1) The quality of graciousness or attractiveness in general, as used in Homer, Josephus (*Ant* 2, 231), or graciousness in speech, as in Demosthenes,[144] and Demetrius.[145] (2) Favour, grace, gracious care or help, good will; actively, that which one grants to another, and passively, that which one experiences or gets from another. In the Christian context, it is found in epistolary literature, such as in the fixed formulas at the beginning and end of Paul's letters, in which it has the sense of "divine favour." (3) Χάρις also refers to practical application of goodwill, a sign of favour, gracious deed or gift, benefaction from person to person, as in Xenophon,[146] Dionysius of Halicarnassus in *Roman Antiquities* II.XV.4,[147] and also in Acts 24:27. In reference to God and Christ, it may indicate possession of divine grace as a source of blessings for the believer (such as in 1 Tim 1:2, 14), or a store of grace that is given (2 Tim 1:9; Titus 2:11), or a deed of grace done by God, or a work of grace. (4) It also refers to gratitude, as in the LXX, in Josephus (*Ant* 7, 28), and 1 Timothy 1:12; 2 Timothy 1:3. (5) When used in reference to God and the favour that people would

---

143. During the Reformation, the most prominent meaning of χάρις was its redemptive sense, that of being the unmerited favour of God to undeserving sinners. For more details about the meaning(s) of "grace" in Paul, see John M. G. Barclay, *Paul and the Gift* (Grand Rapids: Eerdmans, 2015). Barclay summarizes his extensive 2015 book in a 28 pages booklet titled *Paul and the Subversive Power of Grace*, Grove Biblical Series 80 (Cambridge: Grove Books, 2016) in which he discusses the different facets of grace, highlighting Paul's understanding of grace, and also what it means to the church today.

144. Fourth century BC.
145. First century AD.
146. Fourth century BC.
147. First century BC.

have expected from his word, χάρις also refers to the favour that he shows to his people in various settings or his kind intention toward humanity,[148] as seen in his desire that all people be saved. The point that NT authors make is that God's grace surpasses what they have received from other patrons.

In the Greek world, in the cycle of εὐεργεσία, the benefactor gave benefits (graces) willingly and cheerfully (with grace), and the beneficiary received with thanks (with grace). As seen earlier, in *De Ben* I.III.2, Seneca highlighted that the entire benefaction transaction was portrayed as a dance of the three goddesses, each of which was called Grace. Before Seneca highlighted it, the term was used in reference to the benefactor's good disposition towards the supplicant, as in Aristotle's *Rhet.* 2.7.1–2. It also referred to the gift or the resource that the benefactor gave to the person in need. Similarly, it also referred to the favourable response that was expected from the recipient, that is, gratitude in such forms as public honour, loyalty and other services, as in Demosthenes's *De Cor* 131, where lack of it is criticized. Therefore, before its usage in the NT, χάρις was used in the benefaction and patronage systems. As seen earlier, in PE, it appears mainly in the greetings and benediction that are respectively the formal prologue and epilogue of the epistles. In the prologue it is found in 1 Timothy 1:2; 2 Timothy 1:2 and Titus 1:4. In the epilogue benediction is used in 1 Timothy 6:12; 2 Timothy 4:22 and Titus 3:15. Similar to χάρις, the word ἔλεος and the description of God as θεοῦ πατρὸς (which are also prominently used in PE) were significant concepts in the benefaction and patronage systems.

Since at the time of writing PE there still was general usage of χάρις in the non-Christian world, it is possible that in 1 Timothy 1:2; 2 Timothy 1:2 and Titus 1:4, the word could simply mean that Paul was wishing Timothy and Titus general goodwill, as was common in ancient letter-writing (BDAG). Nevertheless, since Paul and the addressees shared common faith in Christ (1 Tim 1:2, Τιμοθέῳ γνησίῳ τέκνῳ ἐν πίστει, Titus 1:4,Τίτῳ γνησίῳ τέκνῳ κατὰ κοινὴν πίστιν), he could also have been wishing them grace in the Christian divine sense (God's favour/blessings). In common usage in most cases, it was a superior, a father figure, a benefactor or a patron who could

---

148. Towner, *Letters to Timothy*, 102, 141.

pray or wish grace or blessings on a junior (cf. Gen 12:2, 3; 14:18–20;[149] 26:24; Josh 8:33; 1 Sam 2:20; Heb 7:7). However, an equal or even a junior also could wish grace or blessings for a senior (cf. Prov 30:10, 11; Luke 6:28, 29; Rom 12:14; 1 Cor 4:12). Similarly, although it was mainly a senior who gave benefaction to a junior, benefaction was sometimes given by an equal or by a junior to a senior in society.[150] When Paul wished χάρις to be with the addressees, he thus was either depicting himself as their senior or their equal before God. At the same time, he used the notion of χάρις to portray the dependence relationship that he had with God the Father and Christ. He also used it to depict the favourable relationship of dependence that his addressees and all Christians had with God.

As stated briefly in the discussion on Christ as benefactor and patron, Paul introduced himself as an apostle who was authorized by God and by Christ, κατ' ἐπιταγὴν θεοῦ σωτῆρος ἡμῶν καὶ Χριστοῦ Ἰησοῦ τῆς ἐλπίδος ἡμῶν (1 Tim 1:1; 2:7; 2 Tim 2:1, 11; cf. Titus 1:3). From the beginning of the letters, especially to Timothy, Paul asserted that it was God the Father and Christ, who gave him the apostolic authority with which he executed his ministry in the church. As implied in the tone of his statement, some opponents were most likely questioning his authority as an apostle (cf. Gal 1:15–20). By presenting himself as an appointee and emissary of God, who is the founder and owner of the church (1 Tim 3:15, cf. Acts 20:28; 2 Cor 1:1; Gal 1:13), Paul was asserting his legitimacy as a leader and missionary in the early church.

As seen in chapter 2, in the G-R benefaction and patronage contexts, no person could appoint himself as a colonial or municipal patron and be accepted as authentic and authoritative.[151] In that light, Paul was sensitive

---

149. The adjective εὐλογητός in Gen 14:20 has the sense of "a praised one."

150. In *Seneca III*, III.XXIII.1–5, Seneca gives an example of two slaves who hid their owner so that she would not be killed and that way they became her benefactors. After being captured by enemy soldiers, to save himself and his master from more torture, another slave killed the master first and then himself.

151. According to the 97th statute of *Lex Ursonensis*, no one had the right to institute himself or have a decree passed that he be adopted as a patron except only if he was the curator or founder of the colony. Only the founder or his children and descendants could automatically become patrons of the colony. Otherwise, whoever wanted to be adopted as patron in the colony needed to be voted in by a majority of not less than fifty decuriones. (Crawford, *Roman Statutes I*, 407–408, 427).

that he was an ambassador of God and therefore a human mediator taking the message of God's salvation (benefaction) especially to the Gentiles. As leaders, preachers and teachers of the true doctrine who had been appointed by Christ, the apostles were authentic benefactors of the church. Thus, Paul appealed to his divinely given apostolic authority to give advice and charge Timothy, Titus and the churches under their care (1 Tim 1:3; 2:1; 6:2, 13–15; 2 Tim 4:1; Titus 2:6). It was considered virtuous for beneficiaries to accept and adhere to good advice (which was a form of nonmaterial benefaction) from their benefactors.[152] As Paul's protégé-beneficiaries and co-workers, Timothy and Titus had to accept and obey the advice as authoritative directives from their senior. Not only that, but it was critical that the Ephesian and Cretan believers recognize that not only Timothy and Titus were accountable to Paul but also they were accountable to them as the apostle's authorized delegates in the churches.[153]

A factor that made Paul's advice and instructions acceptable to Timothy and Titus is that he had a good relationship with them. Just as was expected in the relationship between benefactors, patrons and their beneficiaries, cordial relationship of trust and loyalty existed between Paul and the recipients of his letters. From the very beginning of each of the three epistles, it is evident that he was on good terms with them. His good relationship with them is evident in the endearing manner in which he addressed them. For example, in 1 Timothy 1:2 he addressed Timothy as γνησίῳ τέκνῳ ἐν πίστει, "[my] loyal child in faith." In 2 Timothy 1:2, he wrote, Τιμοθέῳ γνησίῳ τέκνῳ "To Timothy, [my] loyal child," and in 2:1, τέκνον μου "my child." Paul also addresses Titus in 1:4 as Τίτῳ γνησίῳ τέκνῳ κατὰ κοινὴν πίστιν "To Titus, [my] loyal child in [our] common faith." Just as with the term χάρις, the three words, γνήσιος (true or loyal), τέκνον (child) and πίστις (faith) were common in the benefaction and patronage systems. Trust or loyalty was expected of a friend or companion in mutual reciprocation of various helps (cf. Phil 4:3; 2 Cor 8:8). Loyalty as gratitude in form of honour and other services was highly expected of beneficiaries and clients

---

152. Seneca, *Seneca III*, V.XXV.4.
153. Towner, *Letters to Timothy*, 95.

by the benefactors and patrons respectively, as reciprocation of the benefits they were receiving from them.

In the benefactor/patron-beneficiary/client and friendship relationships, πίστις was a core element. It denoted the firmness, reliability and faithfulness of loyalty that was required of both parties in the transaction, especially the clients.[154] Crook elaborates three types of πίστις as loyalty in the patronage system: (1) the loyalty of client-kings and client-cities to the Emperor (imperial loyalty) (2) loyalty of former slaves to their former masters (manumission loyalty), and (3) loyalty of students of philosophy to their philosopher-patrons (philosophical loyalty).[155] The patrons also were required to be faithful, willing and timely in giving help to their clients. In addition to the conventional meaning, in PE the term πίστις had acquired new nuances in the church setting. On one hand, it was used in reference to the subjective trust that the believer was required to exercise in Christ. On the other hand, it was used in the objective sense in reference to the body of truth that both Paul and the recipients had expressed allegiance to. A more detailed discussion on the objective and subjective aspects of πίστις is found later in this chapter in reference to the qualifications of the deacons and the women in 1 Tim 3:9 (τὸ μυστήριον τῆς πίστεως) and 11 (πιστὰς ἐν πᾶσιν), and of elders/overseers in Titus 1:9.

In PE also, the title τέκνον is used metaphorically because Timothy and Titus were not Paul's children by physical birth. Fee says that the statement "true son in the faith" seems to reflect the authority motif, for although Paul sometimes uses the parent-child imagery, it is not evident that Timothy was his convert. He adds that the phrase "in faith" most likely meant that in his relationship with Paul in his faith in Christ, Timothy was a true, faithful son.[156] An alternative interpretation by Arichea and Hatton is that γνησίῳ τέκνῳ ἐν πίστει can be translated literally as, "who is like a genuine child (to me)."[157] The same is true of Titus. Similarly, in the G-R patronage setting and in the Jewish social setting, people without any filial relationship

---

154. deSilva, "Patronage," 768.

155. Crook, *Reconceptualising Conversion*, 216.

156. Fee, *1 and 2 Timothy*, 36.

157. Daniel C. Arichea and Howard A. Hatton, *A Handbook on Paul's Letters to Timothy and Titus* (New York: United Bible Societies, 1995), 10.

could address one another as πατήρ (father), τέκνον (child) depending on their respective status in the society and in the benefit-giving and receiving hierarchy.[158]

In PE world, there was a transformation of literal references from the G-R household into metaphorical references to the household of God.[159] The church had borrowed the language of reference from the long-established G-R and Jewish social institutions. For example, role names such as κύριος (master), δοῦλος (slave), πατήρ, and τέκνον, which were used literally in the G-R and Jewish households were used metaphorically in the church setting. Those terms were also commonly used in ruler-subject relationships, such as between Roman emperors and citizens, where the ruler was viewed as the overall patron because he provided leadership and material support to his subjects. A similar arrangement was found in the G-R household in which the household head was referred to as *pater familias*, which is Latin for "father of the family" or "master of the household."[160] By virtue of his patronage in the empire, the emperor was also referred to as *pater familias* of the entire empire. Therefore, we may infer that when Paul addressed Timothy and Titus as his loyal children, he could have borrowed that expression from either the household institution or from the benefaction and patronage systems.

Despite their shared features, the household and the other social institutions were entities that were different from the church. For example, the household was based mainly on filial ties and other legal domestic relationships whereas the church was a voluntary association built on faith in Christ. In the case of PE, Paul-recipient relationship was an advisor-advisee

---

158. Neyrey, "God," 467–468.

159. James W. Aageson, *Paul, the Pastoral Epistles, and the Early Church: Library of Pauline Studies* (Peabody, MA: Hendrickson, 2008), 19–20.

160. Verner, *Household of God*, 8–9. August Strobel ("Der Begriff des 'Hauses' im griechischen und römischen Privatrecht" [The Concept of 'Home' in Greek and Roman Private Law], *ZNW* 56 [1965]) said that the Greek οἶκός was equivalent to the Latin *domus* (which designated a group of persons related by blood) and not *familia* (which referred to a household that included family members, slaves and real property). However, Theissen (*The Social Setting of Pauline Christianity: Essays on Corinth* [Eugene, OR: Wipf & Stock, 2004], 83–87) says that although Roman law probably distinguished between *domus* and *familia*, Greek did not know such distinction. Of course, in some cases in the NT οἶκός referred to a household that included slaves as a "whole" or "complete household" (e.g. Acts 18:8). In 1 Tim 3:4f and 3:12, the distinct reference to wife, children and household helps us to conclude that οἶκός also included slaves and other dependents. Therefore, the *pater familias* was more than a biological father.

relationship whereby Paul was giving advice and instructions to Timothy and to Titus respectively in a Christian church setting. The Christian advisor-advisee relationship was cordial as compared to the secular G-R patron-client and benefactor-beneficiary relationships that were sometimes frigid and exploitative, as implied by Seneca.[161] Although it had similarities with the secular relationships, the Christian alternative was built on a premise beyond the social standards. In PE, Paul's relationship with Timothy and Titus was based on faith, love and reverence to God and love for them (cf. 1 Tim 1:2, 14, 18; 4:12; 6:2, 11; 2 Tim 1:2; 2:1; Titus 1:4).

3.4.2 Categories of Benefits in Benefaction and Patronage between Various Individuals and Groups

In the G-R and Jewish societies of the first century AD, benefits were generally exchanged between people of the various social ranks and professions according to the needs that they had. As seen in the review of *De Beneficiis*, in I.XI.5 Seneca says that in the G-R benefaction and patronage systems the benefits that were given were ranked in three categories: the necessary, the useful, and the pleasurable. Public office, such as public leadership, belonged to the "useful" category. An honorary inscription made for Demeas confirms that leaders were regarded as benefactors:

ὁ δῆμος ὁ Μαλλωτῶν	The people of Mallos
Δημέαν Ἑρμοκράτου	(honour) Demeas, son of Hermocrates,
κρινὸν εὐεργέτην γεγενημένον	who has been a public benefactor
καὶ πεπολιτευμένον	and who has held public office
ἐπὶ σωτηρίαι τοῦ δήμου	for the salvation of the people.[162]

According to Seneca, the various church leaders were givers of "useful" (second category) benefits. However, according to this inscription, public leaders were viewed as benefactors or saviours of the people. Thus, their benefaction was of the necessary (first) category.

---

161. See Seneca, *Seneca III*, VI.XXXIII.2–3 especially on the cold relationship between the patron and his third-level friends, the "never true friends" despite being his clients.

162. Harrison, "Saviour of the People," 4. This inscription appears in *Inscriptions de Cilicie* (Paris 1987), no. 69, 113–114 (I. KilikiaDF 69), edited by G. Dagron and D. Feissel.

There were several bequests that were considered as εὐεργεσία and *patronicium*, which benefactors and patrons gave to the beneficiaries.[163] As attested in the inscriptions in Danker's collection,[164] benefits included liberation from oppression and guilt, such as relief from oppressive bureaucracy, forgiveness and official pardon, and liberation from Satan and physical bondage. Another benefit was the provision of stability and common welfare, including restoration of peace, concern for the ruler's welfare, prayers for the welfare of others, disaster relief, and maintenance of the general welfare, for example, improvement of prosperity and good relations with neighbours. Deliverance from physical illnesses was regarded as similar to relief from war, bondage, oppression and natural disasters. Medical benefactors, both deities and human beings, were highly honoured in the G-R world. There are numerous testimonials of gratitude to deities for the benefaction of healing, for example as found in the inscription number 26.9 and 28 in *Benefactor*.

Εὐεργεσία could also be given within the family setting despite the obligatory legal and filial requirement to do good to one's relatives. For example, parents who brought up and cared for their children sincerely and affectionately had to be loved and respected by their children in gratitude for their good parenthood. The same also goes for the mentor who exemplified good character and gave beneficial advice to the protégés, such as Paul to Timothy and Titus and the churches under their care. Another mode of benefaction was the voluntary commitment and acceptance of suffering. Suffering was considered a chance to bestow benefits and a means of receiving benefits. For example, in a letter of encouragement to a philosopher, in *P Oxy* number 42, Aquila encourages Sarapion to go through ascetic suffering as a man, not letting wealth or the charm of youth to distract him, because they bestow no benefit if virtue (ἀρετή) is absent.[165] This means that endurance in suffering, coupled with ethical excellence, brought benefit to the

---

163. Details and specific examples are given earlier in chapter 2 in section 2.3 titled "Benefaction and Patronage in the Greek, Roman and Jewish Contexts."

164. See Danker, *Benefactor*, 393–407 for detailed elaboration of the benefits summarized in this section.

165. P. J. Parsons, "Encouragement to a Philosopher," in *New Documents Illustrating Early Christianity*, vol. 4, *A Review of the Greek Inscriptions and Papyri Published in 1979*, ed. G. H. R. Horsley, trans. S. K. Stowers (Macquarie University, NSW: The Ancient History Documentary Research Centre, 1987), 67–68.

person suffering. The stamina that he acquired through the suffering was considered as benefit from God to him. Likewise, when a person suffered for the sake of others, his suffering was counted as beneficence to the people for whom he was suffering. Thus, Paul encouraged his addressees, especially Timothy, to emulate him and join him in suffering, and endurance (2 Tim 1:8, 12; 2:3, 9:3:11; 4:5). In 1 Timothy 4:7–10, he contrasted the short-term benefits of strenuous physical exercise of the ascetics with the eternal benefits that come from endurance of hard training in godliness. However, although there were various material and nonmaterial forms of benefaction, the commonest benefaction in the secular systems was in form of monetary support. That reality is confirmed by the frequency of the appearance of monetary benefaction in the inscriptions, for example, in inscriptions that Danker numbers as 5.8; 19.5.21.60–63; 43.4.24.49–54. Paul's instruction in 1 Timothy 6:17–19 that the rich be πλουτεῖν ἐν ἔργοις καλοῖς "rich in good works" also indicates that he valued and encouraged monetary benefaction among Christians.

Because of the good that they did during their leadership periods, the various leaders in society were considered as essential benefactors and patrons. They benefitted the societies with their personal character, with their leadership and other various professional skills, and with their material support. For example, the many religious gifts that Antiochus Epiphanes is recorded as having given to Greek cities in the Intertestamental Period are said to have benefitted the cults of the gods of his fathers.[166] Similarly, in the church, leaders such as the Apostles, Paul, Barnabas, Silas, Timothy, Titus and others had positive influence due to their blamelessness and adherence to the right teaching. However, others, such as Demas (2 Tim 4:10), Hymenaeus, Alexander and Philetus (whom Paul presents as prominent among the apostates and false teachers in 1 Tim 1:20; 2 Tim 2:17–18), and Diotrephes (3 John 9–10) affected the church adversely. In fact as Hays

---

166. Mercer, "Benefactions of Antiochus," 92. For details about Antiochus IV's benefactions, see Martin Hengel, *Judaism and Hellenism: Studies in Their Encounter in Palestine during the Early Hellenistic Period* 1, trans. John Bowden (Philadelphia: Fortress, 1974), 285–286; Bezalel Bar-Kochva, *Judas Maccabaeus: The Jewish Struggle against the Seleucids* (Cambridge: Cambridge University Press, 1989) 230–231; Otto Mørkholm, *Antiochus IV of Syria* (Classica et Mediaevalia: Dissertationes, 8 Copenhagen: Gyldendalske Boghandel, 1966), 55–63, 118–122, 131–132.

points out, the instructions in 1 Timothy 3:2–3 suggest that a major function of PE leaders was to serve as role models of Christian character for others in the community.[167] Therefore, there was need for leaders to be vetted carefully before they were entrusted with positions of influence. Thus, the study in this chapter now focuses on the character and proficiency qualifications required of church leaders in comparison to the qualifications of various categories of leaders in the G-R and Jewish societies. Some of the leaders were household heads who also were official benefactors and patrons of voluntary associations. Many such household heads who became Christians also became leaders in the new household of God, the church.

3.4.3 Benefaction and Patronage between Church Officers and the Other People

The Christian church began and progressed as a voluntary association. Although from the beginning Jews were the dominant converts, people of other races and social classes who believed in Christ also became members voluntarily (1 Tim 4:10, cf. Acts 2:5–11, 41–47; 15:1–32). Notably, from its inception the church was involved in benefaction. In fact, the office of deacon was Christianized and instituted in the Jerusalem church as solution to a problem that developed in the benefaction department of the church (Acts 6:1–7). Hellenistic widows were being neglected in the daily distribution of food in the church. That matter was a major problem that had become a hindrance to the core mission of the apostles who were the overseers/elders of the Jerusalem church (6:2, 4). The problem was solved through the choice of seven men who were spoken well of (μαρτυρουμένος, 6:3) to serve as deacons. As a result, the Word of God spread and many people became obedient to the faith (6:7). Similarly, in order for the churches in Ephesus and Crete to develop and function well, various categories of servant-leaders were needed. Timothy and Titus needed good advice on how to get the right people for the various offices. Paul provided such guidance in various sections of PE, as in 1 Timothy 3:1–13; 5:17–19; and Titus 1:5–9.

The various categories of church leaders are referred to by diverse titles, such as ἐπίσκοποι (overseers) (1 Tim 3:1, 2; Titus 1:7, cf. Phil 1:1); πρεσβύτεροι (elders) (1 Tim 4:14; 5:17, 19; Titus 1:5); and διάκονοι

---

167. Hays, *Moral Vision*, 68–69.

(deacons) (1 Tim 3:8, 10, 12, 13, cf. Rom 16:1; Phil 1:1). BDAG says that the word ἐπίσκοπος means "overseer," and that it was in usage in the pre-Christian era, as indicated in Homer, in inscriptions, papyri, LXX, Philo and Josephus.[168] It was used in reference to God and to people. In reference to God, it meant that he was regarded as creator and guardian of every spirit, as in the Apocrypha (1 Cl 59:3). In the Christian era, it was also used in reference to Christ, as 1 Peter 2:25: ἀλλὰ ἐπεστράφητε νῦν ἐπὶ τὸν ποιμένα καὶ ἐπίσκοπον τῶν ψυχῶν ὑμῶν. When used in reference to humans in the G-R world, it referred to someone who had a definite office and function of safeguarding the wellbeing of a group. In the context of the church, the term was used for an overseer or supervisor who had the special duty of guarding the apostolic tradition. BDAG says that Timothy was bishop of the Ephesians, and Titus the bishop of the Cretans.[169] In reference to Titus 1:5, 7, Calvin says that "the title of bishop was held in common by all the presbyters."[170]

Guarding the παραθήκη "property" or "deposit" entrusted to them is the most outstanding charge that the writer gave to both Timothy and Titus in their respective locations of ministry. BDAG describes παραθήκη as "the spiritual heritage entrusted to the orthodox Christian." For example, in 1 Timothy 6:20, Paul charges, Ω Τιμόθεε, τὴν παραθήκην φύλαξον . . ., "O Timothy, guard what has been entrusted to you." This implies that Timothy had to guard the tenets of the Christian faith, both for his own spiritual wellbeing and that of the flock under his care (1 Tim 4:16). It is notable that the conception of Christian doctrine as a fixed body of tradition that must be protected is mentioned in the accepted Paulines (such as in Rom 6:17; 1 Cor 11:2; 15:1–3), but it is given extraordinary emphasis in 1 Timothy (1:3–4; 4:16; 5:21; 6:20) and the other pastorals (2 Tim 1:13–14; 2:2;

---

168. As elaborated by L. Porter in "The Word ἐπίσκοπος in Pre-Christian Usage," *Anglican Theological Review* 21 (1939): 103–112.

169. I concur with Hays when he says in *The Moral Vision of the New Testament*, 67 that the common translation of ἐπίσκοπος as "bishop" "suggests a more developed ecclesiastical structure than is appropriate to the late first century." Therefore I translate it as "overseer" throughout my writing.

170. John Calvin, *The Second Epistle of Paul the Apostle to the Corinthians and the Epistles to Timothy, Titus and Philemon*, trans. T. A. Smail, CNTC (Grand Rapids, MI: Eerdmans, 1973), 228.

Titus 2:1).[171] Therefore, as guardians of the Christian faith, Paul, Timothy and Titus were patrons of the church. In Titus 1:5 and 7, in the list of qualification for church officers, the terms ἐπίσκοπος and πρεσβύτερος are used interchangeably. The overseers, the elders and the deacons who were to be appointed were also required to be loyal guardians, and thus patrons, of the Christian faith.

The title διάκονος was used in reference to a person selected for general ministry in the church. The literal meaning of διάκονος is a servant, a minister, an attendant or a helper. BDAG says that in religious settings outside Christianity, the διάκονοι were officials who performed holy service at the altar. Although outside Christianity, the term was mainly used for male servants, it was also used for both male and female attendants in non-cultic settings, as seen in Pliny's *Epistulae* 10.96.8, of AD 1–2, Porphyry's *De Abstinentia* 81.6 of AD 3.

On the subject of women as servant-leaders, in 1 Timothy 3:2 Paul only states that the overseer should be married once, but he does not elaborate the qualifications of the overseer's wife. Changing the topic abruptly, by use of the adverb ὡσαύτως, and listing the qualifications of γυναῖκες in the middle of those of male deacons implies that it is more likely that he was referring to women by their distinct status as female deacons rather than deacons' wives. It is correct to argue that he did not list them with the overseers because he did not permit any woman to be ἐπίσκοπος or overall leader in the church (1 Tim 2:12). In Titus 2:3–5, there are qualifications for πρεσβύτιδες (older or elderly women), who are portrayed as leaders and advisers of younger women (not men) in the church. In Titus 2:3, the qualifications are nearly similar to what Paul gives for γυναῖκες (women, wives) in 1 Timothy 3:11. In Titus 2:5, he specifies that, in addition to qualifications that are similar to those of the overseers, the elders and the deacons in 1 Timothy 3:1–10, 12–13 and Titus 1:5–9, the πρεσβύτιδες are to be submissive to their own husbands, ὑποτασσομένας τοῖς ἰδίοις ἀνδράσιν. However, he does not give such an instruction for the women in 1 Timothy 3:11. This may help us to conclude that, although deacons' wives also were in the public eye as co-servant-leaders with their husbands, the γυναῖκας (women, wives) referred

---

171. See also Hays, *Moral Vision*, 69.

to in 1 Timothy 3:11 were more likely women deacons rather than deacon's wives. Otherwise, there is no rationale for Paul to have mentioned them alongside the male deacons without having done so with the overseer's wife,[172] and without telling them to be submissive to their husbands.

In the LXX the term διάκονος was generally used of someone who was the servant of a king, for example, in Esther 1:10; 2:2; 6:3, 5. In the NT, the term was sometime used figuratively of those who prioritized other peoples' interests, even sacrificing their own interests, as indicated in Matthew 20:26; 23:11; Mark 9:35; 10:43. Towner says that the word group (διάκονος, διακονία, διακονέω) was used to describe various kinds of ministry and workers, as indicated in Paul's letters. He adds that the title had a central place in describing the role of Jesus, as in Mark 10:43–45[173] (cf. Matt 20:28). In Matthew 20:28, Jesus said that he came to serve (διακονῆσαι) and to give his life a ransom for many. In the early church context, the term διάκονος was used of someone whose official duty was to oversee the distribution of alms in the church and to help in other related ministries.[174] It was used of the servants of God, especially the followers of Christ who were involved in the ministry of spreading the gospel to the lost (John 12:26; Rom 15:8; 16:2; 1 Cor 3:5; 1 Tim 3:12; 4:6). Some of the seven deacons of the Jerusalem church, such as Stephen and Philip, were involved in preaching the gospel and doing great wonders (Acts 6:8–10; 8:40; 21:8). Paul described himself as a servant/minister (διάκονος) of the gospel (Eph 3:7; Col 1:25).[175] The title διάκονοι τοῦ θεοῦ was used of people through whom God carried on his administration on earth, such as government officers (Rom 13:4) and teachers of the Christian faith (1 Cor 3:5; 2 Cor 6:4; 1 Thess 3:2).

BDAG says that, when used in reference to church office, the meaning of the term διάκονος has varied over the years, such that today it cannot be adequately used to identify someone designated for special ministerial service in a Christian community. In the early church, the deacon could have been a man or a woman who was chosen to execute some general short-term or

---

172. So also Roloff, *Der erste Brief an Timotheus*, 165.
173. Towner, *Letters to Timothy*, 260–261.
174. William D. Mounce, *The Analytical Lexicon to the Greek New Testament*, Zondervan Greek Reference Series (Grand Rapids: Zondervan, 1993), 138–139.
175. Paul's authorship of Ephesians and Colossians is debated.

long-term duties in the church. In his capacity as a distributor of the provisions that were given by the church, a διάκονος was a channel or a mediator between the church and the needy. In 1 Timothy 3:1–13 and elsewhere, it is apparent that the ἐπίσκοποι and the πρεσβύτεροι were supervisors of a higher rank than the διάκονοι. However, the overseers, the elders and the deacons, regardless of their gender, were equally guardians and helpers and thus benefactors and patrons of their communities.

3.4.4 Qualifications of the Church Officers (1 Tim 3:1–13; Titus 1:5–9)

In this study about qualifications of the officers, there is an overlap of the principles of the G-R household with those of the benefaction and patronage systems, and of the Jewish kinship systems. As stated earlier, there was borrowing and transmission of vocabulary and organizational structures, especially on roles, from the G-R and Jewish household and benefaction systems to the household of God. As seen below in the table on comparison of the qualifications, people who headed G-R households, the various voluntary associations and even political and military setups were expected to have distinct qualifications in personal character and skills. Similarly, those who were to be in charge of the welfare of the church were expected to have particular moral and professional qualifications that were appropriate for the Christian association. As stated earlier, although there were similarities in some of the qualifications of the G-R and Jewish systems and the church, they were not fully identical for they were based on different domains and they had different purposes. The G-R principles were based on the prevailing cultural norms of the non-Christian world, where moral excellence in outward character (ἀρετή) and competence in execution of leadership duties were pursued to fulfil the requirements of the official task, in keeping with ethical expectations, and for self-satisfaction. The Christian principles of moral uprightness (ἀνεπίλημπτος and ἀνέγκλητος) were to be pursued primarily both in reference and reverence to God (1 Tim 3:5, 15; 6:1; Titus 1:7; 2:5) and especially in reference to and for the benefit of the world outside the church (1 Tim 3:7).[176]

---

176. C. Panagopoulos, "Vocabulaire et mentalite dans les Moralia de Plutarque," *dialogues d'histoire ancienne* 5 (1977): 231.

Benefaction, Patronage, and Leadership 161

At this point, a table on comparison between the G-R and PE qualifications required of leaders is useful to the study of 1 Timothy 3:1–13 and Titus 1:5–9. In Table 3 a few paragraphs below, in the column on G-R officers' qualifications, the qualifications of various leaders are blended, the majority of which come from Onosander's list titled *De Imperatoris Officio 1* (ΠΕΡΙ ΑΙΡΕΣΕΩΣ ΣΤΡΑΤΗΓΟΥ), that is, *The Office of the Emperor 1* (ON THE SECTOR OF THE GENERAL).[177] Onosander's list specifically consists of the qualifications required of the στρατηγός (military general), which also are similar to the qualifications required of other high officers in the Roman Empire. The others qualifications are taken from other sources, especially the sets of laws governing the benefaction and patronage systems, such as from *Lex Irnitana* (cf. *Lex Malacitana*);[178] *Lex Coloniae Genetivae/Lex Ursonensis*;[179] and from Seneca's *De Beneficiis*. Some leaders were the main benefactors and patrons for individuals, for cities and for other organizations in the first century G-R and Jewish world.

Onosander's *De Imperatoris Officio 1* (ΠΕΡΙ ΑΙΡΕΣΕΩΣ ΣΤΡΑΤΗΓΟΥ) list reads:

Φημὶ τοίνυν αἱρεῖσθαι τον στρατηγὸν οὐ κατὰ γένη κρίνοντας, ὥσπερ τοὺς ἱερέας, οὐδὲ κατ' οὐσίας, ὡς τοὺς γυμνασιάρχους, ἀλλὰ σώφρονα· ἐγκκρατῆ, νήπτην, λιτόν, διάπονον, νοερόν, ἀφιλάργυρον, μήτε νέον μήτε πρεσβύτερον, ἂν τύχῃ καὶ πατέρα παίδων, ἱκανὸν λέγειν, ἔνδοξον.[180]

The Office of the Emperor 1 (ABOUT THE SECTOR OF THE GENERAL):

---

177. Dibelius and Conzelmann, *Pastoral Epistles*, 158–160. *De Imperatoris Officio* by Onosander is dated AD 41–54.

178. Gonzalez, and Crawford, "Lex Irnitana," 147–243. The laws were established earlier but they were inscribed on bronze tablets in the reign of Emperor Hadrian (AD 117–138).

179. Crawford, *Roman Statutes I*, 427, 431. *Lex Coloniae Genetivae* and *Lex Ursonensis*, jointly called *Colonia Genetiva Iulia Ursonensis*, also were laws governing Roman provinces and colonies of the Roman Empire.

180. The list and its English translation are taken from Dibelius and Conzelmann, *Pastoral Epistles*, 158. Compare the qualifications with PE lists in 1 Tim 3:1–13 and Titus 1:5–9.

> I believe, then, that we must choose a general, not because of noble birth as priests are chosen, nor because of wealth as the superintendents of the gymnasia, but because he is temperate, self-restrained, vigilant, frugal, hardened to labour, alert, free from avarice, neither too young nor too old, indeed a father of children if possible, a ready speaker, and a man with a good reputation.[181]

Concerning Onosander's list, D-C observes that it has little that is especially appropriate for the general (στρατηγός). Citing Jacobus Wettstein's views on duty codes for specific occupations in the G-R world, D-C says that the qualifications resemble the duties of the overseers in 1 Timothy 2 (sic) (1 Tim 3 is the correct reference) and Titus 1.[182] In the G-R world, especially in the writings of philosophical moralists, there were numerous lists of human virtues and vices. For example, Epictetus listed what brought honour to a person as: the duties of citizenship, marriage, begetting children, reverence to God, and care of parents.[183] Towner points out that the resemblance between the qualifications in PE and those in the secular world "probably reflects the influence of Greek ethics upon Hellenistic Jewish literature."[184]

The rationale for the comparison in this discussion is that, as seen above, in the various sectors of the G-R social world, leaders were often also the patrons of their society.[185] Leaders in the Hellenistic ruler cult and in the Roman imperial cult were regarded as the "saviours" who brought σωτηρία (safety and prosperity) to the community. In the benefaction and patronage context, the title σωτήρ (saviour, deliverer, preserver), was used to refer to philosophers such as Epicurus (in *Epicurus Herc.* 346.4b.7), physicians, wealthy benefactors, priests and priestesses, Roman generals, and other

---

181. Dibelius and Conzelamnn, *Pastoral Epistles*, 158.

182. Dibelius and Conzelmann, 58–59.

183. Raymond F. Collins, *I & II Timothy and Titus: A Commentary* (Louisville: Wesminster John Knox, 2002), 80.

184. Towner, *Letters to Timothy*, 240.

185. For example, from Augustus onwards, the Roman Emperor was regarded as the overall patron in the entire empire. His representatives in the provincial municipalities were his key mediators and local patrons.

dignitaries.[186] Leaders were the custodians of the values of the empire. As such, they were saviours of the people. They transmitted and promoted those principles and guided their fellow citizens in knowing and following them, to keep the society intact, vibrant and progressive. They also guarded them from abuse, such as neglect and manipulation. In addition to their patronage in nonmaterial forms, leaders were also the main patrons of their society in material forms. Although the early church did not credit ordinary human beings with the honorific title of σωτήρ (cf. Luke 22:25–26; Acts 4:12; 12:21–23),[187] church leaders were rightfully patrons of the church organization, mainly in nonmaterial ways. Additionally, some of the leaders, such as Barnabas (Acts 4:36–37; 13:1) also helped with material resources.

As was the case with leaders in the secular society, church leadership candidates also had to be evaluated well before they could be appointed. In Table 3 below, and the discussion that follows, we are comparing the vetting criteria of the church (in Timothy and Titus) with those of contemporary secular systems. The purpose of the discussion of the similarities and differences between qualifications is to assess what Paul endorsed from the secular lists for application in PE churches, what he rejected or/and adjusted, and the new elements he introduced for the faith, conduct, mission and administration of the churches.

---

186. Harrison, "Saviour of the People," 4.
187. Harrison, 4.

Table 3. Qualifications of Church Officers versus Qualifications of Leaders, Benefactors and Patrons in the Graeco-Roman Societies

Church Officers in 1 Timothy 3:1–13 and Titus 1:5–9[188]	Leaders, Benefactors and Patrons in Graeco-Roman Societies
ἀνεπίλημπτος, irreproachable character (1 Tim 3:2); ἀνέγκλητος, blameless, without fault (Titus 1:6, 7); δίκαιον, upright, ὅσιον, holy (Titus 1:8)	ἔνδοξος, of good reputation; ἀρετὰς ἔχοντας τῆς ψυχῆς, having excellent traits of character, as in Onosander's *De Imperatoris*
μιᾶς γυναικὸς ἀνήρ, husband of one wife (1 Tim 3:2; Titus 1:6); cf. ἑνὸς ἀνδρὸς γυνή, wife of one husband (1 Tim 5:8)	Married men were preferred over the unmarried for leadership, as in *Lex Irnitana, Malacitana*, Ch. 56. Marriage to one spouse only[189] and faithfulness to him or her were ideal, as in Xenophon, *Ephesiaca* 1.11.3–5. Men and women were appointed as patrons, as in *Lex Irnitana*, Ch. 97.
νηφάλιος, self-controlled, temperate, clear-minded (1 Tim 3:2, 11)	νήπτην, vigilant; νοερόν, alert or quick, as in *De Imperatoris*. Benefactors were exhorted to select carefully who to help.[190]
σώφρων, of sound mind, with self-control (1 Tim 3:2); μὴ ὀργίλον, not quick-tempered (Titus 1:7); σώφρονα, master of himself, ἐγκρατῆ, self-controlled (Titus 1:8)	σώφρονα, temperate; ἐγκρατῆ, self-restrained, as in *De Imperatoris*
κόσμιος, honourable, respectable (1 Tim 3:2)	ἔνδοξος, of good reputation; ἀρετὰς ἔχοντας τῆς ψυχῆς, having excellent traits of character, as in *De Imperatoris*

---

188. The numbering of the qualifications in 1 Timothy 3:1–13 and Titus 1:5–9 closely follows the sequence in the Greek NT. In the chart, the qualifications on the Graeco-Roman side are not arranged as they are in the original records, but they are arranged to correspond to the lists in 1 Timothy and Titus. Where there is lack of corresponding qualifications on either side, the words "No corresponding qualification" are inserted instead.

189. Wayne A. Meeks, *The First Urban Christians: The Social World of the Apostle Paul* (New Haven; London: Yale University Press, 1983), 228n135.

190. Seneca, *Seneca III*, I.I.1–XV.6.

Church Officers in 1 Timothy 3:1–13 and Titus 1:5–9	Leaders, Benefactors and Patrons in Graeco-Roman Societies
φιλάγαθον, a lover of goodness (Titus 1:8)	In Greek setting a benefactor was called εὐεργέτης, "doer of good" and ἀνὴρ ἀγαθὸς, "good man."
φιλόξενος, lover of strangers, hospitable, generous (1 Tim 3:2; Titus 1:8)	Those appointed had to give 5,000 sesterces to the municipal's common fund and as surety, as in *Irnitana*, Ch. 57. People were prohibited from hoarding.[191]
διδακτικός, skilled in teaching (1 Tim 3:2); ἵνα δυνατὸς ᾖ καὶ παρακαλεῖν ἐν τῇ διδασκαλίᾳ τῇ ὑγιαινούσῃ καὶ τοὺς ἀντιλέγοντας ἐλέγχειν, so that he may be able both to preach with sound doctrine and to refute those who contradict it (Titus 1:9)	ἱκανὸν λέγειν, sufficient to speak, as in *De Imperatoris*
μὴ πάροινον, μὴ οἴνῳ πολλῷ προσέχοντας, not a drunkard, not indulging in much wine (1 Tim 3:3, 8; Titus 1:7)	Whoever displayed bad behaviour when drunk during *collegia*[192] parties was fined, as in *PMich V 243*.[193]
μὴ πλήκτην, ἀλλὰ ἐπιεικῆ, ἄμαχον, not violent but gentle (1 Tim 3:3; Titus 1:7); μὴ αὐθάδη, not arrogant (Titus 1:7)	The general was required to have "good reputation" (ἔνδοξον) so that those inferior to him would not feel uneasy when submitting to him, as in *De Imperatoris*.
ἀφιλάργυρος, not a lover of gold/money (1 Tim 3:3)	ἀφιλάργυρος, not a lover of gold/money; λιτόν, frugal, careful with use of money, as in *De Imperatoris*

---

191. Seneca, *Seneca III*, I.XV.5 & VI.

192. "collegia: Roman organization," accessed 2 October 2018, https://www.britannica.com/topic/collegia. The *collegia* were numerous private associations that had special functions. Such associations were craft or trade guilds, burial societies, and societies dedicated to special religious worship. They carried on their affairs and held property corporately in both the republican times and the imperial times.

193. Richard S. Ascough, "Forms of Commensality in Graeco-Roman Associations," *Classical World* 102, no. 1 (2008): 33–46. *PMich V 243* is *Michigan Papyri V 243*.

Church Officers in 1 Timothy 3:1–13 and Titus 1:5–9	Leaders, Benefactors and Patrons in Graeco-Roman Societies
τοῦ ἰδίου οἴκου καλῶς προϊστάμενον, managing his household well (1 Tim 3:4); εἶναι ὡς θεοῦ οἰκονόμον, being as God's steward (Titus 1:7)	In the G-R household the *pater familias*, "father of the family" or "master of the household" was required to provide leadership and material support to his dependents.[194]
τέκνα ἔχοντα ἐν ὑποταγῇ μετὰ πάσης σεμνότητος, having children in submission with all reverence (1 Tim 3:4); τέκνα ἔχων πιστά, μὴ ἐν κατηγορίᾳ ἀσωτίας ἢ ἀνυπότακτα, having faithful (loyal) children not accused of reckless living or insubordination (Titus 1:6)	πατέρα παίδων, a father of children, as in *De Imperatoris*: Men who had sons were preferred over those without, or those with less, as indicated in *Lex Irnitana*, Ch. 56.
μὴ νεόφυτον, not a recent convert (1 Tim 3:6)	μήτε νέον μήτε πρεσβύτερον, neither too young nor too old, as in *De Imperatoris*; not less than 25 years of age and not above 65, as in *Lex Irnitana*, Ch. 54 & 86
μαρτυρίαν καλὴν ἔχειν ἀπὸ τῶν ἔξωθεν, having a good reputation among outsiders (1 Tim 3:7)	ἔνδοξον, of good reputation, as in *De Imperatoris*
σεμνούς, σεμνάς, worthy of respect, honourable (1 Tim 3:8, 11)	Leaders were chosen from the respected classes of freeborn people only, *Lex Irnitana*, Ch. 54 & 86.

---

194. In Mary Beard, John North, and Simon Price, *Religions of Rome*, vol. 1, *A History*, (Cambridge, UK: Cambridge University Press, 1998), 9, and Mary Beard, John North, and Simon Price, *Religions of Rome*, vol. 2, *A Sourcebook*, (Cambridge, UK: Cambridge University Press, 1998), 140–141, in inscriptions *ILS* 5050 and *CIL* VI.32323 lines 90–168, it is indicated that one of the responsibilities of the *pater familias* was to fund and lead in the sacrificial activities of the *familia*. For example he was to fund and lead in the rituals of sacrifice to *Lares* and *Penates*, who, according to Roman mythology, were groups of deities who protected the family and the Roman state.

Church Officers in 1 Timothy 3:1–13 and Titus 1:5–9	Leaders, Benefactors and Patrons in Graeco-Roman Societies
μὴ διλόγους, not double-tongued (1 Tim 3:8); μὴ διαβόλους, not slanderous (1 Tim 3:11)	Benefactors and the other people were required to delight in justice (*iustitia*) and honesty courage (*fortitudo*) as they gave benefaction and as they expressed their gratitude to God and to the other benefactors.[195] Through their honest eloquent speeches, orators were patrons to the common people.[196]
μὴ αἰσχροκερδεῖς, not greedy for material gain, 1 Tim 3:8. Titus 1:7	διάπονον, hardened for labour, as in *De Imperatoris*: Benefactor was required not to do good deeds to gain benefit.[197]
ἔχοντας τὸ μυστήριον τῆς πίστεως ἐν καθαρᾷ συνειδήσει, holding the mystery of faith with a clear conscience (1 Tim 3:9); ἀντεχόμενον τοῦ κατὰ τὴν διδαχὴν πιστοῦ λόγου holding firm to the trustworthy word as taught (Titus 1:9)	(No corresponding qualification)
πιστὰς ἐν πᾶσιν, faithful in everything (1 Tim 3:11)	Before assuming leadership, a person swore by Jupiter and the deified past emperors that he would be faithful and never do wrong knowingly, as in *Lex Irnitana*, ch. 59, 61, 69, 79.

---

195. Seneca, *Seneca III*, IV.VIII.3.
196. Cicero, *On Duties*, Book II, Section XIX.66, pp. 240, 241.
197. Seneca, *Seneca III*, IV.I.1–3.

Church Officers in 1 Timothy 3:1–13 and Titus 1:5–9	Leaders, Benefactors and Patrons in Graeco-Roman Societies
ὀρέγομαι . . . ἐπιθυμέω, "to aspire . . . desire," καθίστημι, "appoint": Some leaders volunteered for service while others were appointed after being tested (1 Tim 3:1, 10; cf. 5:22; Titus 1:5)	Leaders, for example, patrons and judges, were chosen by casting votes. Judges had to have two thirds of the votes of the decuriones. No senator or son of senator was to be adopted as patron of the *colonia Genetiva* except by votes of three quarters of decuriones in the *colonia*, as in *Lex Irnitana*, chs. 55, 61, 68, 69, and *Lex Genetivae/Ursonensis*, ch. CXXX.
(No corresponding qualification)	The official was required not to have held that position for the last five years, as in *Lex Irnitana*, ch. 54.
Slaves were advised to be respectful, faithful and submissive to their masters (1 Tim 6:2; Titus 2:9–10).	Patrons had rights over freedmen and freedwomen and their property, as in *Lex Irnitana*, ch. 97.
(No corresponding qualification)	To be adopted as patron one had to be a warden who had authority to award or adjudicate about land, one who was the founder of the colony, his children or descendants, as in *Lex Genetivae/Ursonensis*, ch. XCVII.

Paul began chapter 3 of 1 Timothy with a unique formula, πιστὸς ὁ λόγος, which is found five times in PE (1 Tim 1:15; 3:1; 4:9; 2 Tim 2:11; Titus 3:8) and nowhere else in NT. Knight calls it a "quotation-commendation formula" and says that it was used in reference to quoted sayings.[198] Towner calls it "affirmation formula" and says that in 3:1 it was possibly intended for affirming the office of the overseer and thus soliciting and strengthening support for the church. Paul's affirmation was needed at a time when the church's leadership was under attack for failing to deal with the heretical

---

198. Knight III, *Pastoral Epistles*, 99. For more details on the faithful sayings in PE, see Knight's 1968 book titled The Faithful Sayings in the Pastoral Letters.

movement or because some of its members had become apostate and joined the opposition.[199] In 3:1, Paul began with the affirmation: Πιστὸς ὁ λόγος· εἴ τις ἐπισκοπῆς ὀρέγεται, καλοῦ ἔργου ἐπιθυμεῖ, "The saying is trustworthy: If someone aspires to (the) ministry of overseer, he desires good work." The verb ὀρέγομαι means to "be eager for," "aspire to," "long for," or "desire." In the original setting, it could be used positively and negatively.

Positively it was used to mean "aspire" or "strive" for something good.[200] Plutarch used it in *Solon* 29.3; *Phocion* 17.1, and Josephus used it in *Life of Josephus* 13. Philo used it in the religious perspective when he asked in *Life of Abraham* VII.39, "How could anything fail to be great and worthy of our efforts [ὀρέγει] which God offers and gives?" Eagerness or ambition (φιλοτίμια) to render service was a virtue that was recognized and rewarded in the εὐεργεσία system.[201] The author of Hebrews used it positively in 11:16 referring to the good aspiration of the heroes of faith. Paul used it also in the religious perspective, in reference to aspiring for good work of serving and caring for God's church (1 Tim 3:5).[202] In benefaction, being "eager to do good" went along with "sparing no effort" (σπουδάζω, "do one's best," "work hard") in presenting oneself to be an approved workman who had no reason to be ashamed (2 Tim 2:15). Negatively, Hellenists sometimes used ὀρέγομαι to refer to greed. Paul also used its negative sense in 1 Timothy 6:10 referring to the craving for money that caused some people to become apostate.

In view of the benefaction and patronage systems, the adjectival clause καλοῦ ἔργου that describes the overseer's work implies that it was equivalent to the good deeds of the εὐεργέτης or ἀνὴρ ἀγαθός (benefactor, good man or *patronus*). In honorary inscriptions, the title ἀνὴρ ἀγαθός appeared in reference to a civic benefactor. For example, in *Die Inschriften von Smyrna* II.1,[203] an inscription in honour of Dionysius reads:

---

199. Towner, *Letters to Timothy*, 248.

200. Collins, *I & II Timothy and Titus*, 79.

201. Danker, "Benefactor," 670.

202. For more details about ὀρέγομαι, see Spicq, TLNT 2, ed. and trans. by James D. Ernest (Peabody, MA: Hendrickson, 1994), 591–592; and H. W. Heidland, TDNT 5, eds. Gerrard Kittle and Gerhard Friedrich, trans. Geoffrey W. Bromiley (Grand Rapids: Eerdmans, 1964–1976), 447–448.

203. G. Petzl, ed., *Die Inschriften von Smyrna* II (Bonn: Habelt, 1987), 111.

Ὁ δῆμος	The people
Διονύσιον Διονυσίου	(honour) Dionysius, the son
ἄνδρα ἀγαθὸν ὄντα περὶ τὴν	of Dionysius
πολιτείαν	who is a virtuous [literally, "good"]
καὶ εὐεργέτην τοῦ δήμου	man with regard to the
	body of citizens
	and a benefactor of the people.[204]

Paul referred to the good works that he encouraged the various PE believers to do as εὐεργεσία (1 Tim 6:2), ἔργον ἀγαθὸν (1 Tim 2:10; 5:10; Titus 1:16), and καλόν ἔργον (1 Tim 5:25; 6:18; Titus 2:7, 14; 3:8, 14). An example of the connection between good works and benefaction is that, for widows to receive honour (respect and material help) in the church they were required to have been engaged in good works. Elsewhere, in the undisputed letters of Paul, a person who was a doer of good works was given the title ἀνὴρ ἀγαθός (Rom 5:7). In the rest of the NT and the Apocrypha, the title was given to someone who performed beneficial deeds to people, a benefactor (John 7:12; Acts 11:24; Tobit 6:12; 2 Macc 15:12; 4 Macc 4:1). In that perspective, the person who aspired to be a church officer was aspiring for good work. Also as seen earlier, as indicated by Seneca, public office belonged to the second category of "useful benefits."[205] Public officers were viewed as saviours of the people.[206] Therefore, logically, whoever aspired to be an overseer was in effect aspiring to be a benefactor or patron.

Roman officers were required to have ἔνδοξος, "good reputation" and ἀρετὰς τῆς ψυχῆς, "excellent traits of character" (moral excellence). As believers in Christ, the church officers' character and benefaction inclinations were required to be much higher than those of Greek, Roman and even Judaistic benefactors and patrons.[207] As guardians of spiritual values in the church of

---

204. J. R. Harrison, "Benefactor of the People," in *New Documents Illustrating Early Christianity*, vol. 9, *A Review of the Greek Inscriptions and Papyri Published in 1986-87*, ed. S. R. Llewelyn (Macquarie University, NSW: Ancient History Documentary Research, 2002), 6.

205. But my argument is that it belongs to the first category of "necessary" benefits.

206. Harrison, "Saviour of the People," 4.

207. Compare for example Jesus's advice in Matt 5:20 "For I tell you, unless your righteousness exceeds that of the scribes and Pharisees, you will never enter the kingdom of heaven."

God (1 Tim 3:5), the officers were required to be exceptionally faithful and virtuous. Some of the unique qualifications required of them were blamelessness in character, holding strongly to the mystery of the faith with a pure conscience, maturity of faith in Christ, and doing good in reference and reverence to God, in gratitude and obedience to him and for his honour and glory. Most of the qualifications required of church officers were also required of the rest of the Christians, as indicated in various places in PE.

3.4.4.1 ἀνεπίλημπτος (1 Tim 3:2, 10); ἀνέγκλητος (Titus 1:6, 7)

The moral character of the ἐπίσκοπος or πρεσβύτερος (3:1, 2; Titus 1:5, 7), the διάκονος (1 Tim 3:8, 12) and the γυνή (1 Tim 3:11) was to be examined and approved before they could be appointed, or if they were to continue being church leaders. On the appointment of deacons, relating it to the appointment of the overseer, Paul instructs, καὶ οὗτοι δὲ δοκιμαζέσθωσαν πρῶτον, "but these also[208] must be tested first." In Timothy and Titus, the standards for testing were given in form of character and duty codes, with minor differences between the listed items. Depending on the literary context of each statement, in 1 Timothy 3:2, the sentence in which the reason for the requirements are given is introduced with the conjunction οὖν, whereas in Titus 1:7 he uses γάρ. In 1 Timothy the code follows logically from 3:1, while the reason for the list in Titus 1:7 is based on the requirement given in 1:6. The differences in the two lists are occasioned by the respective contexts in each case.[209] The verb of necessity, δεῖ, in 3:2 governs the entire pericope on the qualifications (given mainly in form of adjectives, with a few nouns) of the various officers. In Titus, δεῖ is in verse 7.

In PE, the adverb ὡσαύτως serves as a marker for change of topic (1 Tim 2:9; Titus 2:3, 6). In 1 Timothy 3:8 and 11, the qualifications of deacons

---

208. In the καὶ . . . δέ construction, the interpretation of the conjunction καί in the English sentence is significant. If interpreted as an emphatic conjunction as it is going with the mild adversative δέ, as in NKJV, "But let *these also* first be tested," it implies that the deacons were to be tested before appointment "just as the overseer was tested." Conversely, if translated as "But *also these* must be tested first," there is a possibility that it may mean that the testing is for the deacons only, that the criterion is not applicable to the overseer. NRSV does not translate δέ and translates the καί as a regular coordinating conjunction, "And let them first be tested." The context implies that deacons were to be tested just as the overseer was tested.

209. See Towner, *Letters to Timothy*, 241.

and women follow ὡσαύτως. The adverb in verse 8 ties distinctly the qualifications of deacons to those of the overseer, and those of women in 3:11 to those of deacons. The adjectives that describe the qualifications are in the accusative case but they do not have a verb immediately preceding them. They all share the infinitive verb, εἶναι in 3:2; εἶναι dominates the character qualifications of the three groups of officers (including the teaching skill of the overseer). Therefore, whenever we encounter the series of verbless adjectives in the accusative case in all three lists, we need to go back to the infinitive clause δεῖ . . . εἶναι in 3:2 and take it as the main verb. The construction δεῖ . . . ἔχειν in 3:7 applies to that verse only. Therefore, the entire pericope is one long statement that has its main verb in 3:2. It has several excursive sentences interspersed within it.

In Titus 1:5–9 the main verbs for the first set of qualifications of the elders in verse 6 are the aorist subjunctive verb καταστήσῃς (from καθίστημι) in verse 5, and ἐστιν in verse 6. The accusative adjectives describing the qualifications of the overseers (elders) in verses 7–9 have as their main verb δεῖ accompanied by the infinitive εἶναι, a construction that is exactly similar to the one in 1 Timothy 3:2. The participial clause ἀντεχόμενον τοῦ κατὰ τὴν διδαχὴν πιστοῦ λόγου, "holding firmly to the trustworthy message as it has been taught" in Titus 1:9a is also functioning as the adjectives in the preceding section. The participle is in the accusative case. Therefore, the clause cannot be taken as containing the main verb in that sentence.

The list of qualifications for the overseers is headed by ἀνεπίλημπτος (1 Tim 3:2) and concluded by δεῖ δὲ καὶ μαρτυρίαν καλὴν ἔχειν ἀπὸ τῶν ἔξωθεν (3:7). It consists of aspects of inner and outward behaviour which is observable and measurable by both those within the church and those outside, more so by those outside the church.[210] The overarching requirement for those who were aspiring to be leaders in the household of God was that of being ἀνεπίλημπτος or ἀνέγκλητος, being "irreproachable," "without blame" or "without fault" in all areas of personal character (1 Tim 3:2, 10; cf. 5:7; 6:14; Titus 1:6, 7). BDAG gives the meaning of ἀνεπίλημπτος as "irreproachable conduct," and cites Philo in *De Specialibus Legibus* 3.24 as specifying that it was used in reference to moral standing. LSJ has numerous

---

210. See more details in Towner, *Letters to Timothy*, 249–250.

references: For Thucydides, ἀνεπίλημπτος meant "*not open to attack*"; for Plato, "*less open to criticism*"; and from another set of papyri, "*unassailable, not subject to cancellation.*" LSJ gives the meaning of ἀνέγκλητος (Titus 1:6, 7) as "not accused, without reproach, void of offence." BDAG says that it means "blameless" and "irreproachable."[211] Lock translates it as beyond "any criticism or censure."[212] It means that the overseer was required to be someone against whom nobody was able to sustain an accusation, justly or falsely.[213] In order for someone to be given the responsibility of being a church leader, he had to be exceptionally upright morally.

In Onosander's list, the requirement of being ἔνδοξος, "of good reputation" and "having excellent traits of character," ἀρετὰς ἔχοντας τῆς ψυχῆς, is the overarching qualification that dominates all the others.[214] However, unlike Paul in PE who in 1 Timothy 3 and Titus 1 began his lists with the overarching qualification, ἀνεπίλημπτος and ἀνέγκλητος respectively, Onosander placed the overarching qualification, ἔνδοξος, at the end. Another difference is that although both were to focus on external observable traits, the G-R moral character was based on external rules, whereas for PE leaders it was expected to spring especially from their relationship with Christ. In the epistles, the specific areas in which the overseers, elders, deacons and women were to be blameless are elaborated in 1 Timothy 3:2–13; cf. 5:17; and Titus 1:5–9. In addition to being good servant-leaders in the church, the leaders were required to have such faultless moral character especially so that they would be thought well by outsiders. Good testimony, that is, honourable character was a prerequisite within and outside the leaders' own households, and in and outside the church (1 Tim 3:5, 7). They had to live a life and offer service that entitled them to get honour for their character and service (1 Tim 5:17).

The broad scope of ἀνεπίλημπτος qualifies it to be put at the head of the list. As seen above, in the entire list in 1 Timothy 3:1–13, ἀνεπίλημπτος

---

211. See also Justin in *Dialogue with Trypho* 35 and Josephus in *Antiquities of the Jews* 10 and 17.

212. Walter Lock, *A Critical and Exegetical Commentary on the Pastoral Epistles (I & II Timothy and Titus)* (Edinburgh: T & T Clark, 1978), 36.

213. Collins, *I & II Timothy and Titus*, 81.

214. Dibelius and Conzelmann, *Pastoral Epistles*, 160.

dominates the lists of qualifications for ἐπίσκοπος (1 Tim 3:2), διάκονοι (1 Tim 3:8–10, 12–13), and γυναῖκες (1 Tim 3:11). In 1 Timothy, the overseer and deacons are also called πρεσβύτερος in 1 Timothy 4:14; 5:17, as in Titus 1:5, 7 where the reference starts with πρεσβύτερος in 1:5 and then refers to the same people as ἐπίσκοπος in verse 7. In Titus 1:5–9, ἀνέγκλητος, covers the entire list for the πρεσβύτερος/ἐπίσκοπος. The leaders were required to be blameless in every sphere of their Christian life and service.

3.4.4.2 μιᾶς γυναικὸς ἀνήρ (1 Tim 3:2, 12; 5:9; Titus 1:6)

Paul's elaboration of the officials' blamelessness starts with the most fundamental and most intimate relationship between men and women, namely, sex and marriage. In 1 Timothy 3:2, the ἐπίσκοπος was required to be impeccable in his marital life. As elaborated below in this section, blamelessness in adherence to the conventional standards of marriage in the G-R world earned people, both men and women, much honour in the community, in life and after death. The statement μιᾶς γυναικὸς ἄνδρα "husband of one wife" has received several interpretations. Some English translations, such as the NRSV, render it as "married only once," whereas others, such as Today's New International Version, have "faithful to his wife." Some exegetes take the instruction as aimed at enforcing monogamy and deterring polygamy especially among church leaders.[215] Those who hold the view that μιᾶς γυναικὸς ἄνδρα was aimed at discouraging polygamy are partly right. Although in the first century AD monogamy was the ideal standard that was accepted by both non-Christian and Christian Greeks and Romans, and some Jews, polygamy was common. By the second century AD, polygamy was highly discouraged in the G-R societies, but Jews still practiced and tolerated it. Justin Martyr criticized the Jewish teachers of his time (second century AD), for being unwise, because they allowed each man to have up to five wives simultaneously.[216] Therefore, if the requirement was for

---

215. This is what many contemporary African Christians take it to mean, because, although polygamy is diminishing, it is still common in some traditional ethnic groups, including the Akamba. More of this is discussed in chapter 4 of my research, on African benefaction and patronage.

216. Alexander Roberts and James Donaldson, eds., *Ante-Nicene Fathers*, vol. 1, *The Apostolic Fathers, Justin Martyr, Irenaeus*, The Writings of the Fathers Down to A.D. 325, 10 vols. (Peabody, MA: Hendrickson, 1885), 266–267.

deterring polygamy, it was valid because polygamy was common especially in the Jewish community.

Others see the instruction as a deterrent to divorce, which was also common among the Greeks, Romans and Jews at that time.[217] Close to that interpretation, others take it as prohibition against remarriage after divorce or after the death of a spouse. The relevance of this requirement in relation to benefaction and patronage is that no widow who had been married to more than one husband was honoured or eligible to receive benefaction from the church (1 Tim 5:9).

Compared to the other purposes, faithfulness before marriage and in marriage is most likely what Paul was proposing for the overseer to adhere to. A prominent biblical example of the great significance attached to premarital faithfulness is the relationship of Joseph and Mary in Matthew 1:18–25. A non-biblical equivalent to that requirement is found in Xenophon's second-century AD writing, *Ephesiaca* 1.11.3–5, in which there is a vow of a young couple to remain chaste for each other. Notably also, in the first century AD, marital faithfulness was also portrayed by remaining unmarried after divorce or after the death of a spouse; a practice that was regarded as honourable. There are many inscriptions on tombstones praising women who had been married to one husband only.[218] It was common to find on epitaphs the epithets, *unavira* ("married to one man only"),[219] or *virginius* and *virginia*, meaning respectively "a husband who never had but the one wife" and "a wife who never had but the one husband."[220] Kelly supports that interpretation by saying that it was considered meritorious for one to remain unmarried after the death of a spouse or after divorce because remarriage was viewed as self-indulgence. He supports his argument with Paul's suggestion to abstain from remarriage and even to occasionally abstain from sexual pleasure within marriage (1 Cor 7:1–7, 40). He says that church officers were expected to set a good example to the other people by being satisfied with a single marriage. However, he points out that, second marriages were not absolutely

---

217. Hanson, *Pastoral Epistles*, 75, 78.
218. See Meeks, *First Urban Christians*, 228n135.
219. Hanson, *Pastoral Epistles*, 77.
220. Lock, *Critical and Exegetical Commentary*, 38.

forbidden in the early Christian centuries.[221] Paul supported and encouraged remarriage, especially for young widows, instead of enrolling them for support by the church (1 Tim 5:11–15). Nevertheless, it is likely that those who had remarried could not be chosen to be leaders in the church, just as they could not be enlisted to get benefaction from the church in case they became widows again (1 Tim 5:9).

Another interpretation is that, an unmarried person was not to be appointed as a church leader. Lock says that Paul might have been indicating that it was more preferable to have a person with the experience of the head of a family as leader of the church. However, he also leaves it open that Paul might have meant that "*if* married," the overseer should be married to one wife, and be faithful in marriage.[222] The interpretation that an overseer must be married is less likely to be what he intended because Timothy himself was a young man, possibly unmarried but already a frontline leader, when Paul gave him that instruction (1 Tim 4:12; 5:1, 2). The instruction would be against other teachings in the early church that allowed Christians, such as Paul himself, to be frontline church leaders although they were not married (1 Cor 7:7, 8). Nevertheless, it is a possible interpretation. It is also possible that the injunction for the leaders to be married was aimed at countering the false teachers who were misleading people to abstain from marriage (1 Tim 4:3), thus making them more vulnerable to sensual desires that would lead them away from Christ (5:11). Marshall's view is that the qualification is not aimed at sanctioning a particular form of marriage (monogamy) but rather it is aimed at stressing faithfulness in marriage.[223] Towner holds a similar view when he says that the broader interest of the passage suggests that the husband's fidelity in marriage, faithfulness to his wife, is what was meant.[224]

From this discussion, it is therefore possible that either Paul was (1) exhorting that leaders observe faithfulness before and within marriage, (2) prohibiting them from marriage after death of spouse or after divorce, (3) deterring polygamy, and (4) countering ascetic celibacy. We may conclude

---

221. J. N. D. Kelly, *A Commentary on the Pastoral Epistles: I & II Timothy, Titus*, Black's New Testament Commentaries (London: Black, 1963), 75–76.

222. Lock, *Critical and Exegetical Commentary*, 36.

223. Marshall, *Pastoral Epistles*, 478.

224. Towner, *Letters to Timothy*, 251.

that, among the various options, marital unfaithfulness before and within marriage was most likely the main cause for the injunction. Marital faithfulness was required of all members, more so the leaders. As ethical excellence (ἀρετή) and endurance were some of the highest virtues that earned honour for the benefactor, similarly, marital purity in reference to Christ was integral in the moral, missionary and benefaction constitution of the church (cf. 1 Tim 5:9).

3.4.4.3 φιλόξενος (1 Tim 3:2); φιλάγαθος (Titus 1:8)

Citing Aristotle's *Magna Moralia* 2, 14, 1212b, 18 and other ancient writings, BDAG says that in the G-R world, φιλάγαθος "loving what is good" was a characteristic of an especially respected and responsible citizen. M-M says that it means "a lover of virtue." Citing Philo in *Sacrifices of Abel and Cain* 20ff, D-C says that φιλάγαθος and φιλόξενος are derived from the same rhetorical motif. It says that φιλαγαθία was frequent in honorary inscriptions, such as in W. Dittenberger's *Orientis Graecae Inscriptiones* I.146.1ff, and that it was a quality worthy of honour.[225] Collins says that φιλόξενος "hospitality" was particularly important because in the first-century Christian movement an "open household and a hospitable householder were necessary for the celebration of the Eucharist, the work of catechesis and the task of evangelization."[226] He views φιλάγαθος as an overarching virtue that covers every good work.[227] As stated earlier, ἔργον ἀγαθὸν is a common theme in PE (1 Tim 5:10; 2 Tim 2:21; 3:17; Titus 1:16; 3:1). A benefactor or patron was supposed to excel in ἀρετή, that is, "virtue," "excellence," "goodness," "redemptive acts." This being the case, a person who was φιλάγαθος was equivalent to one who was devoted to pursuing ἀρετή.

The term φιλόξενος is a compound adjective from φίλος (friend) and ξένος (strange, foreign, unusual, stranger, foreigner, or host). The title φιλόξενος was given to a person who was friendly to strangers or hospitable (a host). Being hospitable to strangers was a key virtue, both in εὐεργεσία and *patronicium*, but more so in εὐεργεσία. In εὐεργεσία, help was given to communities without much regard to the recipients' relationship with

---

225. Dibelius and Conzelmann, *Pastoral Epistles*, 133.
226. Collins, *I & II Timothy and Titus*, 324.
227. Collins, 325.

the benefactor. However, in *patronicium*, relationship with the patron was a key determinant before help was offered. As indicated in BDAG, the idea of φιλόξενος was highlighted by Homer in *Odyssey* 6, 198–210. Philo also used it in the *Life of Abraham* 114, and Josephus in *Life* (*Vita*), 142. Hospitality to those in need was a key responsibility and it earned honour for the household heads and community leaders. Concerning hospitality and provision for strangers, in Homer's *Odyssey*, there is a story of Nestor, son of Neleus, ruler of the Achaeans who is said to have welcomed and fed the goddess Athene with her entourage before asking about or knowing who they really were.[228] Welcoming the strangers without first seeking to know who they were helped greatly the individuals and the communities that did so. For example, it facilitated the sharing of good things that each party had. It also helped the generous hosts to avert the potential danger of attack from strangers who were more powerful than them. At the same time, in an honour and shame environment, showing hospitality to strangers helped the hosts to increase their status of honour and avoid the shame of being branded as selfish and unfriendly people. Similarly, a household head and church leader who showed hospitality to strangers and non-believers won immense honour for God, for the church, and for himself.

In the early church, there were people, especially messengers and evangelists who were travelling from church to church, aliens and ordinary people, who needed hospitality in their travels and in their stay in foreign lands. Although there were some inns, people were usually hosted in hospitable households. The church's hospitality was continuity from both the ancient G-R and Jewish hospitality customs.[229] Although the word προσήλυτος that is used for foreigner or stranger in the LXX (Deut 10:19) is different from the NT equivalent ξένος, it conveys a similar idea. From the inception of Israel as a nation, the Lord told his chosen people to be kind to foreigners (Exod 22:21). An archetypal OT example of someone who merited the label φιλόξενος and benefitted much from it is Rahab, an ancestor of Jesus (Josh

---

228. Homer, *The Odyssey of Homer*, with introduction and notes, ed., Charles W. Eliot, trans. S. H. Butcher and A. Lang, The Harvard Classics 22 (New York: P. F. Collier & Son, 1909), Book 3, 34, 35.

229. Andrew Arterbury, *Entertaining Angels: Early Christian Hospitality in its Mediterranean Setting*, New Testament Monographs, 8 (Sheffield: Sheffield Phoenix Press, 2005), 94.

2:1–21). In Matthew 25:35, Jesus said, ξένος ἤμην καὶ συνηγάγετέ με "I was a stranger and you welcomed me." It is possible that Paul was also alluding to that eschatological teaching of Jesus when he issued that requirement.

In some passages in the NT, the same word is used to refer to common "hospitality." For example, when Peter (in 1 Pet 4:9) urges, φιλόξενοι εἰς ἀλλήλους ἄνευ γογγυσμοῦ, the most appropriate translation of his statement is "Be hospitable to one another [both believers and non-believers] without complaining." The reciprocal pronoun ἀλλήλους refers either to people who are familiar with one another or who belong to the same fraternity, that is, people who do not consider each other as "other" or "strange." However, in Romans 12:13, in the statement ταῖς χρείαις τῶν ἁγίων κοινωνοῦντες, τὴν φιλοξενίαν διώκοντες, "sharing in the needs of the saints, practising hospitality," the second clause can either be taken as epexegetical or as independent. This makes the meaning of φιλόξενος or τὴν φιλοξενίαν διώκοντες harder to decipher. If taken as epexegetical, then it means that Christians were encouraged to be hospitable to fellow believers, as RSV says, "Contribute to the needs of the saints, practice hospitality." If taken as independent, it can be understood as focusing on loving strangers, be they saints or strangers in general, as NRSV says, "Contribute to the needs of the saints; extend hospitality to strangers." Whatever may be the correct translation, the message is that a church officer was required to be a benefactor to all types of people, just as God is.

3.4.4.4 διδακτικός (1 Tim 3:2, 9; 2 Tim 2:2, 24; Titus 1:9)

This is the first of the only two skill qualifications; the second is good household management in 1 Timothy 3:4–5. BDAG says that διδακτικός means "skilful in teaching." The word is used that way, for example, in Philodemus's *Rhetorica* II (1892, p. 22) and Philo's "De Præmiis et Pœnis" ("On Rewards and Punishments") 27. M-M gives the equivalent classical adjective as διδασκαλικός as found in *Paris Papyri* 63[51] of 165 BC and *Oxyrhynchus Papyri* II.275[34] of AD 66 in which it reads, κυρία ἡ διδασκαλικὴ, "the contract of apprenticeship is valid." The UBS dictionary gives the meaning of διδακτικός as "able to teach." Knight cites Rengstorf in *TDNT* II, 165 as saying that it means "able to learn."[230] The διδάσκω and διδασκαλία word

---

230. Knight III, *Pastoral Epistles*, 160.

group is very prominent in PE. Paul emphasized the crucial importance of sound teaching (ὑγιαινοῦσα διδασκαλία), that is, good teaching (καλὴ διδασκαλία) in the church (1 Tim 1:10; 4:6, 13, 16; 5:17; 6:1, 3; 2 Tim 1:13; 4:3; Titus 1:9; 2:1, 3, 8).

Closely connected to sound teaching is "sound in the faith" (ὑγιαίνοντας τῇ πίστει) (1 Tim 1:5; 4:6; 6:12; 2 Tim 4:7; Titus 1:13; 2:2). By "sound faith," we mean the objective body of knowledge and principles on which believers exercise their subjective faith. Sound subjective faith is built on sound objective faith. In the undisputed letters of Paul, although he discusses faith as a body of principles (such as in Rom 10:8; 2 Cor 1:24; 13:5; Gal 1:23; 3:23) he mainly talks of subjective faith, such as in Romans 1:8, 12; 1 Corinthians 2:5; Galatians 2:16. However, although Paul also speaks of subjective faith (as in 1 Tim 1:4, 5; 4:12; 6:11; 2 Tim 1:5; 2:18; 3:15; Titus 2:2; 3:15), he focuses on objective faith (1 Tim 1:2; 4:1; 5:8; 6:10; 2 Tim 4:7; Titus 1:1, 4). Concerning the clause ὑγιαίνοντας τῇ πίστει, the verb ὑγιαίνω (that appears twelve times in the NT, eight of them in PE)[231] means "be sound, correct or well-grounded" (in reference to Christian teachings and teachers) and "to be in good health" (in reference to physical state). The adjective ὑγιής (appearing eleven times in the NT, but only once in PE, Titus 2:8) means "whole, sound, healthy; well, cured; sound (teaching)." Paul uses medical language metaphorically to describe the quality of what is said or taught.[232] Mounce says that the medical language is attributable to Luke, who possibly was Paul's amanuensis in writing PE.[233] Paul used the expression "sound teaching" as a polemical contrast against the opponents' lethal practice of ἑτεροδιδασκαλέω "teaching other (different, false) doctrines" that were infectious, diseased and capable of destroying the spiritual health of those who were influenced by them[234] (1 Tim 1:3; 6:3; Titus 1:11).

The most outstanding charge that the writer gave especially to Timothy was to guard the good deposit (τὴν καλὴν παραθήκην) that had been entrusted to him (1 Tim 1:3–4; 4:16; 5:21; 6:20; 2 Tim 1:14). The UBS

---

231. Mounce, *Pastoral Epistles*, 41.

232. Towner, *Letters to Timothy*, 130, citing Malherbe, "Medical Imagery in the Pastorals," in *Paul and the Popular Philosophers*.

233. See Mounce, *Pastoral Epistles*, 41.

234. Towner, *Letters to Timothy*, 130–131.

dictionary interprets παραθήκη as "what is entrusted to one's care." The term also means "property" or "deposit." In reference to the church, BDAG gives its meaning as "the spiritual heritage entrusted to the orthodox Christian." It most likely refers to the gospel for which Paul was appointed.[235] The false teachers were teaching a gospel that was contrary (ἀντίκειμαι, 1 Tim 1:10) to the apostolic gospel. "Sound doctrine" meant teaching that was "in conformity with" the gospel of the glory[236] of the blessed God (κατὰ τὸ εὐαγγέλιον τῆς δόξης τοῦ μακαρίου θεοῦ), which he entrusted to Paul (1 Tim 1:10–11). Paul also calls the true teaching τὸ εὐαγγέλιόν μου, "my gospel" in 2 Timothy 2:8.[237] As used in PE in reference to moral teaching, "sound doctrine" is that which is in keeping with the apostolic teaching that produces sound (healthy) faith (Titus 1:13, 2:2).[238] Mounce contrasts the law that the false teachers were purportedly teaching with the gospel that the genuine teachers were supposed to teach. He says that the law was meant to reveal sin and it was for sinners (1 Tim 1:9–10), whereas the gospel was provided for the righteous person and it revealed the δόξα (glory, importance, power, radiance, dignity) of the blessed (μακάριος) God.[239] Teaching sound doctrine skilfully depended on correct interpretation of the word of truth (ὀρθοτομοῦντα τὸν λόγον τῆς ἀληθείας [2 Tim 2:15]) in harmony with the apostolic gospel.

Calvin equated deacons with the overseers and said that all the leaders were supposed to know "how to apply God's Word to the profit of His people."[240] Nevertheless, Ngewa differs and says that the requirement that the overseers be able to teach is the particular characteristic that distinguishes

---

235. Towner, 431.

236. The term δόξα is a noun, not an adjective (glorious) as NRSV, NIV, NKJV and other English translations render it.

237. Compare the phrase κατὰ τὸ εὐαγγέλιόν μου in 2 Tim 2:8 with Paul's similar phrase in Rom 2:16 and 16:25. It is not found anywhere else in the NT.

238. Towner, *Letters to Timothy*, 130.

239. Mounce, *Pastoral Epistles*, 43. Towner says that μακάριος used here in reference to God means "happy." Citing Spicq, he says that it is used in polemical dialogue with the political powers. In the Greek religion, gods were described as "happy" in that, in contrast to mortal humans, they were immortal. Therefore, Paul is using similar terms to contrast the Christians' immortal God (cf. 1:17 and 6:16) with the false gods.

240. Calvin, *Second Epistle of Paul*, 225.

them from the deacons, "who are not necessarily called to teach."[241] Mounce also says that in the early church context, the term διάκονος was used of someone whose official duty was to oversee the distribution of alms in the church and to help in other related ministries.[242] However, this does not mean that deacons were not involved at all in the teaching and preaching ministry. Among the seven deacons of the Jerusalem church, Stephen and Philip are presented as fully involved in preaching and teaching the gospel, defending the Christian faith and doing great wonders (Acts 6:8–10; 8:40; 21:8).

In the *Didache* 15:1–2 the author listed qualifications for overseers and deacons that are similar to what we have in 1 Timothy 3:1–13 and Titus 1:5–9. He told the church to "appoint overseers and deacons (ἐπισκόπους καί διακόνους) worthy of the Lord, for they too do the ministry of prophets and teachers (προφητῶν καὶ διδασκάλων) in the church." The author instructed the church not to despise them, "for they are your honourable men together with the prophets and teachers." As such, they were viewed and honoured as patrons of the church. Similarly, in PE, the requirement for deacons that they should hold fast to the mystery of the faith with a clear conscience (1 Tim 3:9) implies that they needed to be opposite to the false teachers who distorted the Word of God (1 Tim 1:19–20). As seen earlier in the discussion about the meaning of ἐπίσκοπος, πρεσβύτερος and διάκονος, the term διάκονος was also used to refer to the servants of God, including Christ and Paul, who were involved in the ministry of spreading the gospel to the lost. For example, in Romans 15:8, Paul used the title to refer to Christ. In 1 Corinthians 3:5; Ephesians 3:7 and Colossians 1:25, Paul described himself as διάκονος "according to the gift of God's grace." In 1 Timothy 4:6, Paul told Timothy, "If you put these instructions before the brethren, you will be a good servant (διάκονος) of Christ Jesus, nourished on the words of the faith and of the sound teaching that you have followed." It was through teaching the instructions given to him by Paul that Timothy would prove to be a good deacon of Christ. It is not easy to identify the particular ministry

---

241. Ngewa, *1 & 2 Timothy and Titus*, 64.
242. Mounce, *Analytical Lexicon*, 138–139.

of PE deacons, but one of the main duties of an overseer was to teach sound doctrine and to safeguard it from distortion by false teachers.

Because of its crucial importance in the evangelistic mission of the church, the ability to teach (and preach) the true gospel was given prominence throughout PE (1 Tim 3:2; 2 Tim 2:2, 24). As stated above, Paul listed it as the first of two crucial skills of the overseer, the ability to teach and the ability to manage one's household. The purpose of the requirement for the church officer to be "skilful in teaching" was given in the ἵνα clause in Titus 1:9, ἵνα δυνατὸς ᾖ καὶ παρακαλεῖν ἐν τῇ διδασκαλίᾳ τῇ ὑγιαινούσῃ καὶ τοὺς ἀντιλέγοντας ἐλέγχειν, "so that he may be able both to preach with sound doctrine and to refute those who contradict it." Concurring with Towner, as highlighted in the entire package of instructions to Timothy (and Titus), the fact is it is only through proclamation and the various didactic ministries that the apostolic gospel would be preserved intact within the ministry in Ephesus and Crete and, presumably, in the church of the next generation.[243] In 2 Timothy 2:24–26, the skill of teaching was to be coupled with patience so that the leader would correct the opponents with gentleness. It is significant to note that Paul himself was very stern with some of the opponents. He used a strong verb, ἐγκαταλείπω (which means "forsake, abandon, desert, leave behind, neglect"), to depict their disloyalty to sound faith and good character.[244] As expression of his anger and disdain, he handed over some to Satan to be taught not to blaspheme, (Hymenaeus and Alexander in 1 Tim 1:20). However, he also urged that the skilful teacher should handle opponents with gentleness, hoping that God might perhaps grant that they repent and come to know the truth, and that they might escape from the snare of the devil, who had held them captive (2 Tim 2:24–26). False teachers were using their teaching skill negatively to lead people away from the gospel of God, and thus from God himself (2 Tim 3:6–7; 4:3–4). Therefore, as a means of promoting and protecting the Christian faith, the church leaders' knowledge and skill to impart knowledge was paramount.

D-C says that the requirement that the overseer be able to teach does not mean that he was required to have already assumed, as his regular duty, the

---

243. Towner, *Letters to Timothy*, 431.
244. See also 2 Tim 4:16 for similar use of the verb ἐγκαταλείπω in PE. Elsewhere in the NT it is used in Matt 27:46 (cf. Mark 15:34); 2 Cor 4:9 and Heb 13:5.

office of teaching, but that what was required was some capability in teaching. Viewing the requirement in relation to Greek ethical concerns, D-C says that the term "skilful in teaching" is found twice in Philo's writing (in *Congr.* 35, and *Praem. Poen.* 27), where both times it is used to designate Abraham's διδακτικὴ ἀρετή, that is, virtue attained by means of teaching.[245] It is not clear whether Philo means that Abraham was counted as virtuous because of engaging in teaching, or that he acquired ἀρετή by receiving teaching. Nevertheless, sound teaching of the overseer helped the church to have sound faith and sound character. As seen in chapter 2, advice-giving was regarded as an important nonmaterial benefit in the G-R and Jewish societies.[246] The knowledge that was imparted through teaching was a very important benefit to the trainee for it gave him information and skills that were necessary and helpful for his life and occupation. The early church fathers saw teaching as crucial for the development of the church and devoted their efforts to offer didactic treatises to the church, such as *The Didache*.[247] A general view is that the *Didache* was primarily intended to be an instructional guide for the early church. Many scholars perceive it as describing the earliest stages of the church's order and practice.[248] As Aaron Milavec says in the preface of his commentary, *The Didache* is a record of oral tradition that shows a step-by-step preparation of Gentile converts for initiation into the mid first-century (AD 50 to 70) Christian assemblies.[249] Although his assertion is open to debate, Milavec asserts that it was originally an oral composition which was the property of various Christian "communities of householders"[250] who had received it as a way of life revealed to them by the Father through his servant, Jesus.[251] Just as the Talmud in the OT times, the apostolic doctrines were sacred teachings that had to be passed on by

---

245. Dibelius and Conzelmann, *Pastoral Epistles*, 53.

246. See Seneca, *Seneca III*, I.II.4.

247. The views about its date range from mid first century to the early part of the third century AD.

248. Peter Kirby, "Didache," *Early Christian Writings*, accessed 17 August, 2009. Posted, 2 Februrary, 2006. http://www.earlyChristianwritings.com/didache.html.

249. Milavec, *Didache*, vii.

250. Milavec's view is viable because the early church was a composition of households which were mainly led by house heads, some of whom were benefactors and patrons in the society.

251. Milavec, *Didache*, vii.

people who were gifted and who had the ability to pass them on faithfully without corrupting them in any way.

Starting from the family setting to the wider society, the teacher was regarded as a crucial benefactor. Those who passed on the Word of God carefully and faithfully were counted as deserving great honour. In *The Didache*, for example 4:1–2, the author instructed that the speakers (preachers and teachers) of the Word of God be honoured as the Lord. Verse 1 says, Τέκνον μου, τοῦ λαλοῦντός σοι τὸν λόγον τοῦ Θεοῦ μνησθήσῃ νυκτὸς καὶ ἡμέρας, τιμήσεις δὲ αὐτὸν ὡς Κύριον· ὅθεν γὰρ ἡ κυριότης λαλεῖται, ἐκεῖ Κύριός ἐστιν, "My child, you should remember night and day him that speaks the Word of God to you, and you should honour him as the Lord, for where authority is spoken of, (the) Lord is there." In 11:1–2, the author encouraged the church to receive as the Lord the travelling teacher who was teaching the right doctrine that increases righteousness and knowledge of the Lord, but to reject him who was perverted and was teaching another doctrine to destroy the right doctrine. As seen above, in 13:1–7, the teachers were equated to prophets and high priests (13:3). They were said to be worthy of payment of first fruits of farm produce and livestock, and gifts of money, clothing and all other possessions (cf. 1 Tim 5:17–18). As such, they needed material reciprocation from the church for the nonmaterial benefaction that they were giving to the church (cf. 1 Cor 9:11).[252] As Rabbis who were highly honoured in the Jewish communities for being protectors and promoters of the community values through their teaching, teachers in the church were also honoured and supported.

As seen above, Seneca classified "advice" and "good precepts" in the category of necessary benefits that a friend or a benefactor could give. As such, teachers were benefactors and patrons, who benefited the society mainly with the nonmaterial commodity of helpful advice. Tobit 4:18 exhorts people to seek advice from a wise person and not to despise useful counsel. Custodians of knowledge could benefit people with their knowledge only if they had the skill to pass it on. Guthrie says, "An overseer must certainly have the

---

252. Exhorting the Corinthian believers to be actively involved in supporting itinerant apostles such as himself with material benefaction, in 1 Cor 9:11 Paul asks, "If we have sown spiritual good among you, is it too much if we reap your material benefits?"

propensity to pass on advice and doctrine to the enquirers."²⁵³ Paul instructed Timothy to pass on what he had heard from him to πιστοῖς ἀνθρώποις (faithful, loyal, trustworthy people) who also would teach others (cf. 2 Tim 2:2). He also urged his primary recipients, especially Timothy, to be specifically watchful in his behaviour and teaching so that he would be faithful and true in what he taught. Paul described himself as an apostle and a "teacher" at least twice (1 Tim 2:7; 2 Tim 1:11). As teaching was so crucial for the success of the Christian mission, whoever aspired to be productive in his ministry as an overseer in the church had to have the gift or the ability to teach sound doctrine correctly and faithfully (2 Tim 2:15). As knowledge about the greatest gift of salvation that God desired to give to all people could only be accessed through preaching and teaching, the teaching skill was vital for the church leaders.

3.4.4.5 ἀφιλάργυρος (1 Tim 3:3; cf. 6:10); μὴ αἰσχροκερδής (1 Tim 3:8; Titus 1:7, 11)

The negative compound adjective ἀφιλάργυρος means "not greedy for money" or "not greedy (for money)." In the first century AD, that qualification was required of midwives, as in Soranus the physician's *Gynaecology* 5, 27, and of generals, as in Onosander's *De Imperatoris* 1.8. D-C gives the meaning as "freedom from avarice" and explains that it was a highly-valued virtue, for it was "largely responsible for the incorruptible and large-minded management of affairs."²⁵⁴ BDAG gives the meaning of αἰσχροκερδής (1 Tim 3:8; Titus 1:7, 11) as "shamelessly greedy for money," "avaricious," "fond of dishonest gain." This quality is in contrast to φιλόξενος, "friend of stranger" or "hospitable" (1 Tim 3:2; Titus 1:8) and φιλάγαθος, "lover of goodness" (Titus 1:8). In *Sacrifices of Abel and Cain* 32, Philo listed αἰσχροκερδής with other vices. As indicated by Seneca, the patron's ability, willingness and promptness in helping the needy were the first grace.²⁵⁵ Willingness to give favours was one of the three Graces in the circular dance of benefaction. The patron's benefaction was pegged on his good will and generosity.

---

253. Donald Guthrie, *The Pastoral Epistles*, TNTC, revised ed. (Leicester, England: Inter-Varsity Press, 1990), 92.

254. Dibelius and Conzelmann, *Pastoral Epistles*, 159.

255. Seneca, *Seneca III*, II.I.2.

To be able to give willingly and promptly, patrons had to have money. As pointed out in my review of Seneca, in the G-R municipalities, those who stood as candidates for office as senators or patrons were required to have ample amounts of money so that they would be self-sufficient economically and able to provide for their households and their constituents.[256] As seen above, household heads were required to be generous in helping members of their households and in the hosting of strangers. That being the case, the household heads were benefactors and patrons, at least, to the former slaves who had turned to be their clients, and to their visitors.

Greed or love of material possessions were vices that led to deterioration of the functions of the benefaction and patronage systems. Greed for money and selfish hoarding of material things without wanting to give them away to benefit others was regarded as a detestable vice .[257] In *I.Eph.* IV.1386, avaricious doctors were criticized.[258] As money was a major form of benefaction, and generosity with one's possessions was a key benefaction and patronage virtue, love of money and love for dishonest gain were antithetical to the core rationale of the systems. Even before the first century AD, people were cautioned against the love of money (Eccl 5:10; 2 Macc 4:8). They were warned against getting money through corrupt means and against failing to use it in the right way. Similarly, as seen in chapter 2 of this book, patrons also used their wealth to dominate their clients. Corrupt Roman patrons were reputed as wielding power as rich and powerful patrons to permanently hold their clients in a subservient position and exploit their votes to remain in positions of power and honour.[259] In the extra-biblical materials, for example *The Didache* (4:5–7; 15:1–2), generosity was

---

256. Seneca, *Seneca III*, VI.XIX.4, 5, *n.* a.

257. Seneca, *Seneca III*, VII.VIII.2–XI.2.

258. Horsley, *New Documents Illustrating Early Christianity* 4, 140. See also *The Flinders Petrie Papyri* III.53 of 3rd century BC, and Oxyrhynchus Papyri XIV.1678[12] of third century AD.

259. Wallace-Hadrill, *Patronage*, 16–17. See also Joubert, "One Form of Social Exchange?" 19.

encouraged and greed discouraged.²⁶⁰ Instead of greed for money, the patron was required to provide for his household and his clients from his own treasury.²⁶¹

It is on course to suggest that the injunction not to be lovers of money was a polemic against the false teachers in Ephesus who were teaching primarily for material gain (1 Tim 6:3–5; cf. 2 Tim 3:2; Titus 1:11). The false teachers written about in the epistles and some other Christians had unhealthy love for money and used Christianity to amass wealth wrongly (1 Tim 6:5–10; cf. 2 Tim 3:2–5). The love of money or gold was known to make one greedy and it always led to ruin of the person's life (cf. Sirach 31:5). The injunction also was possibly a challenge and encouragement to rich people in the church who were potential benefactors but were not giving benefaction. Unhealthy love of money also made the leaders intemperate and unkind, thus endangering the good reputation of the church among outsiders (1 Tim 3:2, 7).

Closely related to the injunction ἀφιλάργυρος directed to the overseer (1 Tim 3:3) against loving money are μὴ αἰσχροκερδεῖς (1 Tim 3:8) given to deacons, and αἰσχρός κέρδους (Titus 1:11) against false teachers. Deacons were instructed to have nothing to do with greed for dishonest gain, μὴ αἰσχροκερδεῖς (1 Tim 3:8), which was a vice that characterized the false teachers (1 Tim 6:3, 5–10; Titus 1:7, 11). Knight says that their greed for money did not mean that they did not have an abundance of what they were striving to get.²⁶² In Titus 1:11, Paul said that the false teachers had to be silenced because they were upsetting whole households by their wrong doctrines, all for selfish gain. In OT times, leaders who sought personal gain at the expense of the people whom they were leading were likened to lazy and greedy dogs (Isa 56:10, 11). This metaphorical description is equivalent to Paul's description of false teachers in Crete in Titus 1:12. By their false doctrines and their greed for personal gain, the false teachers were doing the opposite of what a good benefactor was supposed to be doing. They were corrupting the benefaction effort of the church. Instead of greed, Paul

---

260. Kurt Niederwimmer, *The Didache*, ed. Harold W. Attridge, trans. Linda M. Maloney (Minneapolis: Fortress, 1998), 103, 200.

261. Seneca, *Seneca III*, VI.XIX.5.

262. Knight III, *Pastoral Epistles*, 169.

exhorted contentment with whatever a person had (1 Tim 6:6–11) and use of what one had to help others (1 Tim 6:18; Titus 3:8, 14).

In the benefaction and patronage context, benefactors/patrons and clients who sought personal gain at the expense of others corrupted the systems.[263] An example of this bad practice of benefaction is found in *Ant.* 14:247–55,[264] when Judea was co-opted by Rome through Hyrcanus I to be a valuable client against Pompey. That one-sided selection benefitted the Jews in Asia Minor and in other parts of the Mediterranean Diaspora. By their subtlety the Jews got for themselves alone all the help that was supposed to benefit both them and the Greeks. That action ruined good relationship between the Jews and the Greek communities. On the side of the patrons, benefactors or patrons who helped the needy for the sole reason of benefitting them received more honour and good standing in the community than those who served people dishonestly only for the sake of receiving honour and recognition for themselves.[265] Of course, Paul said later that there is great gain in godliness (ἔστιν δὲ πορισμὸς μέγας ἡ εὐσέβεια, 1 Tim 6:6), and that the deacons who served well gained good standing for themselves (3:13).

Verner's interpretation is that Paul's rationale for the church elder's good service was wrong in that the elders were to serve well primarily for gaining a good standing for themselves in the community (cf. 1 Tim 3:13), which was not different from the rationale for secular leaders, for they did good deeds to other people for self-enhancement.[266] In fact he says that the values that PE author promoted were supportive to the leadership circles (bourgeoisie classes of well-off leading citizens) of the Hellenistic-Roman world.[267] But his view is not correct. On the contrary, as Knight points out, the good standing that the church leaders achieved was not primarily before humans but before God in accordance with the Christian faith.[268] Towner says that they would gain

---

263. According to Sahlins, they belonged to the category that practised negative reciprocity: the unsocial extreme, where there is self-interest at the expense of the other person. See *Stone Age Economics*, 191–196, and Neyrey "God," 469.

264. See Josephus, *Josephus*, Book XIV section VIII.1–5. See also Barclay, *Jews in the Mediterranean*, 277.

265. Seneca, *Seneca III*, IV.I.1–XL.5.

266. Verner, *Household of God*, 183.

267. Verner, 182–183.

268. Knight III, *Pastoral Epistles*, 174.

for themselves "excellent standing," that is, to be esteemed or held in high regard in the church setting, and that their faithful service would also deepen their faith and further strengthen their relationship with God and Christ.[269] Mounce also rightly observes that Paul's immediate concern was the reputation of the church before the world that the false teachers' behaviour was ruining. The deacons who served faithfully were building a good reputation for themselves within the community, and they were developing an even deeper confidence in their faith. By so doing, they were acquiring a good standing for themselves before the outside world and that way they were also benefiting the reputation of the church and thus enhancing its cause, especially its evangelistic ministry.[270] Whatever the leaders had to do had to be done for the benefit of others within and outside the church. Whatever they received as honour or honorarium had to be more for their spiritual improvement and for meeting legitimate physical needs (cf. 1 Tim 5:17).

3.4.4.6 τοῦ ἰδίου οἴκου καλῶς προϊστάμενον (1 Tim 3:4, 5, 12; cf. 5:8; Titus 1:6)

Leaving the series of adjectives describing the qualities of personal character in 3:2, 3, Paul focuses on the overseer's second skill, ability to manage the church (1 Tim 3:4, 5). Verse 4 begins with a participial clause, τοῦ ἰδίου οἴκου καλῶς προϊστάμενον. Verse 5 contains a conditional statement that poses a rhetorical question anticipating a negative answer: εἰ δέ τις τοῦ ἰδίου οἴκου προστῆναι οὐκ οἶδεν, πῶς ἐκκλησίας θεοῦ ἐπιμελήσεται; The term προΐστημι in verse 4 and 5 has numerous meanings: "to exercise leadership," "to rule," "to give direction," and "to be at the head." It also means "to have an interest in," "to show concern for," "to care for," and "to give aid." The terms προστάτης (m.) and προστάτις (f.) come from προΐστημι and they were used to refer to someone who "stood out in front" that is, one who looked out for the interests of others, a defender, a guardian, or a benefactor.[271] Good management of one's household involved being a leader, having authority, caring and giving numerous helps adequately to the members of his household.

---

269. Towner, *Letters to Timothy*, 268.
270. Mounce, *Pastoral Epistles*, 205–206.
271. For more details, see BDAG, 180.

In 1 Timothy 3:4b Paul specifies good management of one's children, τέκνα ἔχοντα ἐν ὑποταγῇ μετὰ πάσης σεμνότητος, "keeping his children submissive and respectful in every way." In Titus 1:6c he writes τέκνα ἔχων πιστά, μὴ ἐν κατηγορίᾳ ἀσωτίας ἢ ἀνυπότακτα "having children who are believers, not accused of debauchery and not rebellious." This indicates that the overseer was required first to be a good manager of his nuclear family. However, as 1 Timothy 3:4a, 5 indicate, he was also required to be a good manager of his extended household (οἶκος). Commenting on 1 Timothy 3:4, 5 and 12, Fiore says that households were composed of immediate family members, former slaves who had now become current clients, hired labourers, tenants and business associates who operated in a relationship of subordination rather than kinship.[272] Introducing the benefaction and patronage element into the household metaphor, Towner observes that the instruction on good management of the household goes beyond the care of the nuclear family and includes "management of slaves, property, business interests, and even maintenance of important relationships with benefactors/patrons or clients."[273] DeSilva points out that in the early church household heads often were hosts to house churches (Rom 16:23; 1 Cor 16:19; Phlm 1) and provided hospitality to itinerant missionaries and teachers (Phlm 22; 3 John 5–8, 10b).[274] DeSilva's view is supported by Adams as he observes that in the earliest Christian associations household leaders became leaders of the house churches, thus becoming patrons to the congregations.[275] Thus, benefaction of the Christian household head was crucial in the missionary enterprise of the early church.

Although in Greek culture the protection and other provisions for a freedman were regarded as the responsibility of a god or a magistrate, in the Roman culture the *patronus* assumed legal, moral, political and economic

---

272. Benjamin Fiore, *The Pastoral Epistles: First Timothy, Second Timothy, Titus*, Sacra Pagina 12 Collegeville, MN: Liturgical Press, 2007), 77.
273. Towner, *Letters to Timothy*, 254.
274. deSilva, "Patronage," 770.
275. Edward Adams, "Earliest Christian Meeting Places," (paper presented at British New Testament Conference, St. John's College, Durham University, UK, 6 September, 2008). Proposed book: Edward Adams, *The Earliest Christian Meeting Places: Almost Exclusively Houses?* LNTS 450 (London; New York: Bloomsbury; T & T Clark, 2013).

guardianship over the new freedman-citizen.[276] In that setting, good management of a leader's extensive household was very crucial for the household was perceived as an archetype of the empire. As in the Roman setting, the Christian family was regarded as prototype of the church, with the husband/father as the head of the family, just as Christ was viewed as the overall head and patron of the church (Eph 5:23; Col 1:18). Therefore, as the household head was the primary benefactor or patron of the household, overseers were benefactors and patrons of the church.

It is not clear whether in order for a person to be appointed as overseer he had to be a man who had sufficient means to own household and to manage it.[277] Nevertheless, just as the overseer had to be faithful to his wife, if he had a wife (3:2), if he had a household, he had to be a good manager of the same (3:4). Having a household or households that were managed well in leadership, discipline, and care in material and nonmaterial provisions put the household head in a place of honour above those who did not manage theirs well. In relation to management of the church, the care aspect of good management, καλῶς προϊστάμενον, in 3:4, was highlighted by use of a different verb, ἐπιμελέομαι, at the end of 1 Timothy 3:5. The word means "to take care of" or "to look after." Good management of the basic social institution (the family/household) qualified the household heads to be heads of free associations in the G-R and Jewish worlds. As the household head's success or failure in the management of his household determined his reputation,[278] so his success would determine eligibility for church leadership. The success of the missionary endeavour and reputation of the church of God (ἐκκλησίας θεοῦ, 1 Timothy 3:5, cf. Acts 20:28; 1 Cor 1:2; 10:32; 11:22; 15:1; 2 Cor 1:1; Gal 1:13) was typified by the overseer's skill and reputation. Therefore, the significance of the rhetorical question in verse 5 was immense, given the environment in which the church was operating.

---

276. E. A. Judge and David M. Scholer, eds., *Social Distinctives of the Christians in the First Century: Pivotal Essays by E.A. Judge* (Peabody, MA: Hendrickson, 2008), 168–169.

277. Towner, *Letters to Timothy*, 254. In *Pastoral Epistles*, 840n2, Marshall says that we cannot be certain that PE author ruled out the possibility that women householders could be appointed to serve as overseers. However, from the strong injunction in 1 Tim 2:12, the appointment of a woman as overseer was unlikely. See Köstenberger, *Women in the Church*.

278. Towner, *Letters to Timothy*, 254.

Without ignoring the fact that bad behaviour of slaves could have been the cause of the problem, their running away could be indication of the bad management of some householders. For example, Seneca tells of two slaves who ran away and joined the enemy army of another town.[279] The running away of Onesimus also could be an indication that Philemon, his master, was not taking good care of him (Phlm 1:10–21). Possibly also, some masters were not taking good care of their manumitted slaves who had automatically become their clients and were still counted as members of their household.

The Christian household head's management was especially tested and confirmed in the areas of control and training of his children in godliness. That is possibly why the statement τέκνα ἔχοντα ἐν ὑποταγῇ μετὰ πάσης σεμνότητος, "having (his) children in submission with all reverence," 1 Timothy 3:6, is attached to τοῦ ἰδίου οἴκου καλῶς προϊστάμενον, "one who manages his household well" to specify the meaning of good management. Bestowal of honour to the household head depended on his contribution in the control and welfare his household.[280] The parent who nurtured in young people excellence in moral character, ἀρετή, which was one of the cardinal virtues in the G-R world, was regarded as a benefactor of primary importance, *IPE*, I², 357.6.[281] The parent's contribution to their character was nonmaterial benefaction. Notably, people who provided good parenthood for their offspring were thought of not only as fathers but also as gods. Lines 32–33 of inscription number 26 in *Benefactor*[282] are in praise of the goddess Isis for her gift of familial stability and high regard for parents. They say, συ τιμάσθαι γονεῖς ὑπὸ τέκνων ἐποίησας, οὐ μόνον ὡς πατέρων ἀλλ' ὡς καὶ θεῶν φροντίσασα, "You saw to it that parents were honored by their children, and you thought of them not only as fathers but as gods." Concerning material benefaction, in *IPE* I² 357,[283] the benefactors' good will towards their cities was likened to the benevolence "which good fathers have to affectionate sons": οἷα πατέρων ἀγαθῶν πρὸς υἱοὺς φιλοστόργους.

---

279. Seneca, *Seneca III*, III.xxiii.2–5.
280. Harrison, "Benefaction Ideology," 107–116.
281. Basil Latyschev, *Inscriptiones Antiquae Orae Septentrionalis Ponti Euxini Graecae et Latinae* 1, 2nd ed. (Petersburg: Royal Archaeological Society of Russia, 1916).
282. Danker, *Benefactor*, 181, 407.
283. Danker, "Benefactor," 407.

Material provision for members of one's household, and for strangers, was also regarded as good management of the household. Anyone who failed to provide for his household (such as failing to provide for the widow from her dowry under his management) because of any dishonest reason, was an unfaithful patron. Winter says that Paul was referring to such defaulters in 1 Timothy 5:8.[284] The verb προνοέω means "have in mind to do, try to do; care for, take care of." Mounce chooses the meaning "care for,"[285] whereas Towner says that it can simply mean, "to think of beforehand," whereby in 1 Timothy 5:8 it combines forethought with appropriate material provision, including the equivalent financial support.[286] The implication of Paul's statement in 1 Timothy 5:8 is that, a Christian who did not provide well both material and nonmaterial support for his household had denied the faith (τὴν πίστιν ἤρνηται) and he was described as worse than a nonbeliever (ἄπιστος). Such a person could not have a good testimony and honour in his own household, in the church and among outsiders. Good management of one's household also portrayed maturity in the Christian faith.

3.4.4.7 μὴ νεόφυτος, μαρτυρίαν καλὴν ἔχειν ἀπὸ τῶν ἔξωθεν (1 Tim 3:6, 7)

In verse 6 Paul picked up the prohibitions that he left in verse 3 and introduced a qualification concerning the spiritual maturity of the overseer. Citing D-C, Marshall says that this requirement indicates that at this point the content of the qualifications has become Christian, and that this indicates modification of a secular duty code for leaders.[287] Paul instructed that no νεόφυτος, "novice" was to be appointed as overseer in the church. The word νεόφυτος (1 Tim 3:6) is a hapax in the NT. Highlighting the metaphorical sense, BDAG says that it refers to a person who is "newly planted in the Christian community," meaning one who is "newly converted." Referring to LXX (Job 14:9 and Isa 5:7), Pollux[288] and others, D-C gives the mean-

---

284. Winter, *Roman Wives*, 127.

285. Mounce, *Pastoral Epistles*, 284–285.

286. Towner, *Letters to Timothy*, 343–344.

287. Marshall, *Pastoral Epistles*, 481, cf. See Dibelius and Conzelmann, *Pastoral Epistles*, 53.

288. Pollux 1.231, cf. Aristophanes *Fragments* 828 in the Papyri *BGU* II, 563, I 9.14.16; II 6.12; 565.11;566.3.

ing of νεόφυτος as someone who is "newly baptized," literally or something that is "newly planted."[289] Job 14:9 says, ἀπὸ ὀσμῆς ὕδατος ἀνθήσει, ποιήσει δὲ θερισμὸν ὥσπερ νεόφυτον, "yet at the scent of water it will bud and put forth branches like a young plant." Although the term's literal meaning was "newly-planted," here it was used figuratively to refer to someone who was a new convert to the Christian faith. It could also refer to someone who was "newly-baptized," as D-C suggests, because converts were baptized immediately after professing faith in Christ. However, it is more appropriate to take it as referring to someone who was new or young in the faith.

Johnson also cites LXX (Ps 127:3; 143:12; Isa 5:7 and Job 14:9) and says that the term's literal meaning is "newly planted," and that it is used here figuratively to refer to "a recent convert." He also says that the requirement indicates that the Ephesian Christian community had been in existence for some time, "about two years."[290] The requirement that the overseer be not a new convert was not stipulated for the overseers whom Titus was left to choose in Crete. Scholars assume that the reason for the omission of the requirement for experienced elders for the Cretan church is because the entire church was composed of new Christians when Titus was to appoint elders for it. There were no mature Christians to choose from, as there were in Ephesus where Timothy was in charge, where, according to Mounce, the church was at least ten years old.[291] It is also important to note that the counterpart qualification of the general in the Roman administration focused only on the physical age of the leader; he was not to be too young nor too old, μήτε νέον μήτε πρεσβύτερον.[292] The Christian community felt that it was necessary for those inside and outside the church to approve

---

289. Dibelius and Conzelmann, *Pastoral Epistles*, 53.

290. Luke Timothy Johnson, *The First and Second Letters to Timothy: A New Translation with Introduction and Commentary* (New York: Doubleday, 2001), 216. Mounce (*Pastoral Epistles*, 181) says that the church was at least ten years old when 1 Timothy was written.

291. Mounce, *Pastoral Epistles*, 181. Compare with Johnson's view in the note immediately before this that the church at Ephesus was about two years old when Paul gave the instructions in 1 Timothy.

292. Onosander, *De Imperatoris Officio* in Dibelius and Conzelmann, *Pastoral Epistles*, 158, 159.

the spiritual maturity of the person before he was given responsibility as overseer in the church.[293]

As in the preceding requirement about good management of one's own household, the reasons for not appointing a νεόφυτος are clearly presented at the end of verse 6 and in verse 7. Verse 6 says that if a novice was appointed there was the possibility of him becoming proud and falling into the judgment or condemnation (κρίμα) of the devil. The genitive clause κρίμα . . . τοῦ διαβόλου in the subjunctive clause εἰς κρίμα ἐμπέσῃ τοῦ διαβόλου, "he might fall into the judgment of the devil," has two possible meanings, but one is more appropriate than the other. Taken objectively, it means that the neophyte could receive condemnation from God similar to what the devil himself received when he became conceited (NKJV, NIV, Calvin, A. T. Robertson, Hendriksen, Knight). Subjectively, the meaning is that if appointed too soon, the devil would tempt the neophyte and he would easily fall into the sin of pride as the devil had done (NRSV,[294] Kelly, Lock, Spicq and Ridderboss, Marshall, Mounce, Towner).

Relying on the Genesis episode of God's judgment of the devil, Knight says that the objective sense is more appropriate. Citing BAGD, he says that despite the lack of a definite article before κρίμα, the term rarely means "slander" but rather refers to "judicial verdict" or "condemnation" (cf. Rom 3:8 and in PE, here and in 5:12).[295] Marshall opts for the subjective sense. He says that since elsewhere in PE διάβολος is an adjective meaning slanderous (3:11; Titus 2:3), the subjective genitive sense would imply that the νεόφυτος would fall "into the condemnation pronounced by a slanderer, i.e. the reference is to malicious attacks made on an overseer by other people, whether justified or not (cf. 5.14)."[296] However, he says that the reference here (in 3:6) is to the devil. Citing Scott and Hanson, he says that the neophyte would fall into the "doom which the devil has contrived for him by tempting him to be proud." His interpretation finds support in the parallel

---

293. Dibelius and Conzelmann, *Pastoral Epistles*, 53. See also Marshall, *Pastoral Epistles*, 481–483.

294. NRSV is also ambiguous as it says that the neophyte "may be puffed up with conceit and fall into the condemnation of the devil."

295. Knight III, *Pastoral Epistles*, 164.

296. Marshall, *Pastoral Epistles*, 482.

phrase, παγίδα τοῦ διαβόλου, in 3:7 (cf. 2 Tim 2:26). Nevertheless, he leaves the door open for the objective sense as he combines the subjective sense with the objective and says that "the two references to the devil bring together the complementary ideas of coming under his [devil's] sway and sharing in his condemnation (Mt 25:41; cf. also Oberlinner, 127)."[297] Towner admits that the sense of the genitive clause is ambiguous but little is lost if taken objectively or subjectively. He favours the subjective sense and says that "the active role of the devil in 3:7 favours putting him into an active role in this statement [3:6]."[298] My observation is that, since the rationale of not appointing a neophyte is equivalent to the prohibition on women not to teach or exercise authority over men (2:12–15) because it was Eve who was tempted (by the devil) and fell into sin (Gen 3), the subjective sense is more appropriate. A neophyte should not be appointed for he would fall easily under temptation and condemnation "by" the devil.

The second reason for not choosing a neophyte was that it was necessary for the overseer to have a good reputation/testimony from outsiders (δεῖ δὲ καὶ μαρτυρίαν καλὴν ἔχειν ἀπὸ τῶν ἔξωθεν, 3:7). The requirement for good reputation (μαρτυρίαν καλὴν) was equivalent to τὸν δ' ἔνδοξον (glorious, splendid, fine, honourable, respected reputation) in Onosander's list. The adverb ἔξωθεν preceded by the genitive plural article τῶν (after the preposition ἀπὸ) is used as a substantive and translated as "those from/on the outside," namely, "outsiders." As BDAG puts it, "those on the outside" meant "non-Christians" (as in Herodotus 9, 5; Celsus 3, 4; Josephus, *War* 4, 179 and *Ant.* 15, 316). Collins says that μαρτυρίαν καλὴν ἔχειν was analogous to the contemporary expression, "receive a good recommendation." Good reputation of the overseer would boost the impact of the church on outsiders, whereas lack of it would lead to derision of not only the overseer but of the church community.[299] Failure to maintain good reputation would lead to dishonour (ὀνειδισμός) to both himself and the church. The principal mission of the church was to win followers for Christ from among the outsiders. Therefore, appointing a neophyte as an overseer would be risking the integrity of the gospel. Towner observes that this would further affect

---

297. Marshall, 482–483.
298. Towner, *Letters to Timothy*, 258.
299. Collins, *I & II Timothy and Titus*, 85–86. So also Towner, *Letters to Timothys*, 259.

the evangelistic mandate of the church negatively by association with the sinful overseer, for the church was already affected adversely by association with false teachers.[300]

Mounce takes the conjunction καί that is between ὀνειδισμός and παγίδα τοῦ διαβόλου as epexegetical and thus translates the statement as "lest he fall into reproach, which is [the] snare of the devil."[301] "Snare of the devil" is a metaphor. It stands for both the temptation "by" the devil and the ruin that comes with the fall (cf. 6:9; Rom 11:9).[302] There were numerous snares into which the immature overseer could fall easily. In the Qumran community, three particular snares were highlighted and sternly warned against during the initiation of priests and Levites. The three traps were lust, riches, and defilement of the sanctuary.[303] In addition to those three traps, in the church setting, if a newly converted person was appointed as overseer, he could easily become proud and abuse his prematurely-given high position. As the overseer was the overall human caretaker and patron of the church, his fall would bring disaster to the reputation and mission of the church. Therefore, because of its immense importance, Paul went to great lengths to elaborate this final and crucial qualification for the overseer.

Similar to a few other instructions about the overseer, the injunction that he be not a new convert was also targeted against the behaviour of the false teachers. The teachers were conceited and thought that godliness, for example, the position of a spiritual leader, was a means of gain (1 Tim 6:4; cf. 2 Tim 3:4; Titus 1:11). Focusing on the pursuit of such gains, many weak Christians had become apostate and they were leading others away from the faith (1 Tim 6:10, 20–21). In the patronage context, they had become disloyal to the Lord (the church's benefactor/patron) and caused others to do the same. Instead of honour, they brought disgrace to themselves and jeopardized the core foundation of the church's existence.

---

300. Towner, *Letters to Timothy*, 259.

301. Mounce, *Pastoral Epistles*, 152, 184.

302. See also Mounce, *Pastoral Epistles*, 184.

303. Dibelius and Conzelmann, *Pastoral Epistles*, 54, cf. 1QS II, 11f, 17, and the *Damascus Document* (CD IV, 15.17f).

3.4.4.8 ἔχοντας τὸ μυστήριον τῆς πίστεως *(1 Tim 3:9)*

Similar to maturity in faith that was required of the overseer, the appointment of the deacons was to be based on their grasp of "the mystery of the faith with a pure conscience" (ἔχοντας τὸ μυστήριον τῆς πίστεως ἐν καθαρᾷ συνειδήσει) (cf. τὸ τῆς εὐσεβείας μυστήριον, "the mystery of godliness" [3:16]). BDAG takes the genitive clause, τὸ μυστήριον τῆς πίστεως, "the mystery of the faith" as epexegetical and says that the mystery simply means the "faith," and τὸ τῆς εὐσεβείας μυστήριον in 3:16 means "Christian religion." The clauses would therefore be translated as "the mystery, which is the faith," and "the mystery, which is the Christian religion." Mounce also takes it as epexegetical but interprets the statement a bit differently. He says that the deacons had to "have a firm grasp on the mystery of faith, which is the gospel."[304] Towner interprets the term μυστήριον as "deep truths" and thus translates the genitive clause as "the deep truths [lit. "the mystery"] of the faith." He says that in other sections of Paul's writing the term occasionally stood either alone (Rom 16:25; Eph 3:3, 9; Col 1:25) or in a genitive construction that helps define the mystery (cf. 1 Tim 3:9; 1 Cor 2:1; Eph 3:4).[305] In that case, he also sees the genitive as epexegetical. Similarly, Robertson sees it as appositional or definitive.[306] Taking Ephesians 6:19 "the mystery of the gospel" as the closest parallel to what we have in 3:9, Towner says that the content of what is proclaimed is what is defined as the "mystery of God's plan to save in Christ that was revealed in history."[307] Knight says that μυστήριον refers to "the secret thoughts, plans, and dispensations of God that are hidden from the human reason, as well as from all other comprehension below the divine level, and hence must be revealed." Hence, he translates τὸ τῆς εὐσεβείας μυστήριον attributively as "the revealed truth of the Christian faith," where πίστις refers to what is believed.[308] Of course, in 3:16, assuming that it is referring to the same entity, the meaning of the mystery is given in the relative clause, Ὃς ἐφανερώθη ἐν σαρκί, that

---

304. Mounce, *Pastoral Epistles*, 199.

305. Towner, *Letters to Timothy*, 263.

306. A. T. Robertson, *A Grammar of the Greek New Testament in the Light of Historical Research* (Nashville, TN: Broadman, 1934), 498–499.

307. Towner, *Letters to Timothy*, 263–264.

308. Knight III, *Pastoral Epistles*, 169.

follows the semicolon that punctuates the genitive clause, τὸ τῆς εὐσεβείας μυστήριον. The divine-human Christ and the gospel about him are the basis and object of our faith.

Although it may be different, the mystery mentioned in Colossians 1:25–27 is described specifically as "this mystery, which is Christ in you, the hope of glory." The mystery of salvation through Christ had been hidden from all people, including the Israelites, until the appropriate time God chose to reveal it (1 Tim 2:6; cf. Eph 3:1–12). The mystery of the faith is the mystery of God's plan to save by Christ's blood people of all races who believe in him (cf. 2:3–4; 4:10; Titus 2:11; Rom 16:25–27). Whoever was to be appointed as deacon had to have firm grasp of the mystery of faith "with a clear conscience." Otherwise, he would be a hindrance to the evangelistic mission of the church. Mounce says that the statement ἐν καθαρᾷ συνειδήσει is in contrast to the opponents who had shipwrecked the faith (1:19) and their consciences had been branded.[309] The term καυστηριάζω in 4:2 means "burn with a hot iron so as to deaden to feeling." As Towner says, the attached prepositional clause, ἐν καθαρᾷ συνειδήσει, "with a pure conscience" is aimed at adding "the thought of ethical wholeness to the qualification."[310] For evil reasons, the false teachers had deviated from the apostolic doctrine and consequently no longer had the ethical wholeness needed for preaching the true gospel of salvation.

The requirement that the deacons must be people ἔχοντας τὸ μυστήριον τῆς πίστεως, "who hold fast to the mystery of the faith," that is, having a clear grasp of the tenets of the faith and living it out in practical terms, is a qualification that was not found in the G-R leadership codes. G-R communities had character codes that were not necessarily based on any body of religious faith and they did not necessarily have any spiritual motivation behind the good things that they were doing. However, what may be close to what was expected of Christian officials is that, before assuming leadership, the Roman leader had to swear by Jupiter and by the deified Roman emperors of the past that he would be faithful and never do wrong knowingly.[311] Ἀρετή ("virtue," "excellence," "outstanding merit") was required

---

309. Mounce, *Pastoral Epistles*, 199.
310. Towner, *Letters to Timothy*, 264.
311. Gonzalez and Crawford, "Lex Irnitana," chapters 59, 61, 69, 79.

of Roman leaders. However, the officials were concerned about superficial ethical loyalty, not morals in reference to godliness. Maintaining excellence was not in reference to personal purity of heart or conscience in love and reverence to the supreme God or even to the lesser gods. The swearing in was for commitment to distinguished official service only. Whoever had that virtue earned high honours for himself and for the empire. According to Seneca, benefactors were encouraged to do good deeds simply because it was good to do them.[312] However, the Christian church lifted the standard higher. Whatever good they did had to be in accordance with the faith and in clean conscience (ἐν καθαρᾷ συνειδήσει), all in reverence to God (3:9; cf. 1 Tim 1:5; 2:10; 3:13; 5:10; 6:18, 19; 2 Tim 1:3). Love for God and for humans had to govern the good deeds (1 Tim 1:5; 4:12; 2 Tim 1:13; Titus 2:2).

The dative clause ἐν καθαρᾷ συνειδήσει means "with a pure/clean conscience" is equivalent to the participial clause ἔχων . . . ἀγαθὴν συνείδησιν, "having . . . good conscience" (1 Tim 1:5, 19). Having clean/good conscience means that, the person was not guilty and under condemnation before God because of sin. A clean conscience was an aspect that Paul highlighted repeatedly in PE in connection with the Christian's subjective faith, as in 1 Timothy 1:5 (ἐκ . . . συνειδήσεως ἀγαθῆς καὶ πίστεως ἀνυποκρίτου); 1:19 (ἔχων πίστιν καὶ ἀγαθὴν συνείδησιν); 3:9 (ἔχοντας τὸ μυστήριον τῆς πίστεως ἐν καθαρᾷ συνειδήσει) and 2 Timothy 1:3 (Χάριν ἔχω τῷ θεῷ, ᾧ λατρεύω ἀπὸ προγόνων ἐν καθαρᾷ συνειδήσει). In reference to the false teachers in Crete, in Titus 1:15, he said that their minds and consciences were corrupted and so was their character. Therefore, nothing was pure to them. On the contrary, overseers and deacons were required to be pure in everything.

3.4.4.9 Σεμνός (1 Tim 3:8, 11)

The section on qualifications for deacons in 1 Timothy 3:8–10 begins with Διακόνους[313] ὡσαύτως σεμνούς . . . "Deacons likewise must be of good character (serious, honourable, worthy, or respectable) . . ." As stated earlier,

---

312. Seneca, *Seneca III*, IV.I.1–3.

313. See detailed discussion on the meaning of διάκονος under *Categories of Church Officers* earlier in this chapter.

the adverb ὡσαύτως in verses 8 and 11 marks the beginning of new sets of qualifications, distinguishing the διάκονοι from the ἐπίσκοπος, and the γυναῖκες from the male διάκονοι and the ἐπίσκοπος respectively. After giving instructions on the qualifications of the overseers (3:1–7), similarly using a series of adjectives in the accusative case, in 3:8–13 Paul gives instructions on qualifications of deacons, διακόνους (3:8), and of women, γυναῖκας (3:11). In Titus, although there is no specific statement about deacons, in 2:3–5 he lays out qualifications for older women that are similar to what we have in 1 Timothy 3:11 on women. It is easier to distinguish the overseer's qualifications (3:1–7) from those of the deacons and the women (3:8–13) than distinguishing those of the deacons from those of the women. All the qualifications are tied together under the overarching requirement to be ἀνεπίλημπτος, "blameless" in 1 Timothy 3:2. The syntactical element that ties the qualifications together is the prominent construction in which the verb of necessity, δεῖ, is the main verb in the broad statement from verse 2 to 11. If δεῖ, in 3:2, is taken to be the key verb that controls the syntax of that large section,[314] then it governs the list of qualifications of the overseer, 3:2–7, of deacons, 3:8–10 and of women, 3:11. Verses 12 and 13 have their own main verbs. They conclude the list of qualifications of male deacons which were left off briefly in verse 10, as Paul deviated in verse 11 to speak about the women. Although the adverb ὡσαύτως, "likewise," which precedes the list for deacons (3:8) and for women (3:11) distinguishes the requirements of each group, it also indicates that they are equivalent.

Most of the deacons' qualifications are similar to the overseer's. That is the rationale for discussing some of them (such as the maturity of faith and the love of money) above in concert with the qualifications of the overseers. Similarly, some requirements for the deacons are similar to those of the women that follow. For example, the accusative masculine plural adjective σεμνούς, 3:8, and its feminine counterpart, σεμνάς, 3:11, are translated as "serious," "of good character," "honourable," "worthy," and "respectable." Mounce cites Hawthorne as saying that the word σεμνός "has such a richness about it that it is impossible to equate it with any one English word."

---

314. Marshall, *Pastoral Epistles*, 477.

Nevertheless, he suggests that it means "noble," "worthy" and "esteemed."[315] This characteristic had an important role in the development of Christian existence in the context of Greek ethics, where it depicted seriousness, dignity and respectability in one's character, which was expected of all people in the community. The term and its derivatives appear mainly in PE, but only once elsewhere in the NT, in Philippians 4:8. In Christianity, in addition to its meaning in the Greek setting, it also connoted holiness because it was often associated with the divine and that which is good and of moral worth.[316] Similar to the requirement of being "above reproach" (ἀνεπίλημπτος, 3:2, 10) that dominates the entire list of qualifications in 1 Timothy 3:2–13, the requirement of being σεμνός, "serious" and "worthy of honour," can also be viewed as a general qualification that arches over the sub-lists of qualifications of the deacons and the women respectively. The deacons' and the women's seriousness of faith and character in specific areas of life had to be tested to ensure that they had met the requirements for leadership (3:10).

Equivalent to having excellent traits of character (ἀρετὰς ἔχοντας τῆς ψυχῆς, in Onosander), the serious good character of the deacons put them in a position of honour, worth, and respect. The outer character and deeds of the benefactors and patrons made them worthy people and merited them honour from the society. Blameless outer character of the deacons emanated from their inner Christian character that had matured over time after conversion. Similar to the overseers, the deacons were to be proved in specific areas of personal life and skills; in speech, use of wine, attitude towards money, aptitude and attitude in faith, marital life, and in management of their households, starting with their children. As is evident, most of the qualifications were similar to those of overseers. Nevertheless, three qualifications that were somehow different were that the deacons were not to be double-tongued (3:8), not greedy for material gain (3:8), and that they should hold fast to the mystery of the faith with a clear conscience (3:9).[317]

---

315. Mounce, *Pastoral Epistles*, 198.

316. See Mounce, *Pastoral Epistles*, 199.

317. Apart from the qualification about "not double-tongued," the other two are already discussed above in relation to the overseer. I discuss "double-tongued" in relation to μὴ διαβόλους (not slanderous) about the women below.

3.4.4.10 Qualifications of women, γυνή (1 Tim 3:11; cf. Titus 2:3–6)

Towards the end of the discussion on male deacons, Paul inserted a short list of qualifications of women. The term γυνή is either translated as "woman" or "wife." Over the years, Bible interpreters and scholars have advocated for different views, on whether γυναῖκας (in 3:11) means "wives" of deacons or, simply, "women" (female) deacons. As stated by Misselbrook, prominent scholars, such as Jerome, Calvin, Bengel, Warfield, Jeremias, Riddebos and Mounce prefer the translation, "wives" (similar to the 1973/78 edition NIV), whereas Chrysostom, Ellicott, Hort, Kelly, Ellis, Spicq and Fee go for γυναῖκας as "women" deacons (similar to the NIV edition of 2001 which translates it as "deaconesses"). Misselbrook also views it that way.[318] A third option is given by Lewis who holds the view that the γυναῖκας could be understood as unmarried women who were "committed unconditionally to the service of the church and who in meeting certain character qualities, have been enlisted to aid the deacons in the outworking of their office."[319] Lewis' opinion is based on the positioning of verse 11 in the middle of the discussion on deacons. He says that the positioning indicates some kind of relationship between these women and the deacons. Therefore, to him, the women could have been unmarried assistants to the deacons. Knight combines two options and says that the term refers to "deacons' wives," who were required to manifest the four characteristics in verse 12 because of their special role as "assistants to the deacons," their husbands.[320]

The stance against the appointment of women as deacons with full leadership and teaching authority, as the men, is based on the prohibition in 1 Timothy 2:11–15. The understanding is that married women could not be involved in the ministry of the church for they were required to devote themselves to the home. In Titus 2:3, similar qualifications were required of the πρεσβῦτις (pl. πρεσβύτιδες), that is, "old(er) woman," or "elderly lady," as BDAG interprets it. About 1 Timothy 3:11, Roloff says that what Paul

---

318. Peter Misselbrook, "Notes on the Greek New Testament, Day 291 – October 18th – 1 Timothy 3:1–16," accessed 7 October 2018, http://misselbrook.org.uk/GNT/1018_GNT.pdf.

319. Robert M. Lewis, "The 'Women' of 1 Timothy 3:11," *Bibliotheca Sacra* 136, no. 542 (1979): 171ff.

320. Knight III, *Pastoral Epistles*, 171.

discusses there is applicable to both sexes.[321] In any case, as indicated by the use of feminine adjectives, verse 11 is a brief excursus by Paul to discuss about women, whether deacons' wives, female deacons or female assistants to the male deacons. Verse 12 is resumption of the discussion on male deacons. Then in his conclusion in verse 13, he reverts to what is applicable to both sexes.[322] Mounce admits that both interpretations of γυνή, as wife and as woman, are possible, but prefers "deacon's wives" over "women deacons." The reason he gives is that "the unnatural change of topics, twice in two verses without a clear transition, seems awkward. It is preferable to maintain the connection between v 11 and v 12 by translating γυνή as 'wife.'"[323] Even so, if the awkwardness is what warrants his opinion, then the same should apply to verse 8. On verse 8, he says that the verb construction δεῖ . . . εἶναι ties the paragraph on the overseer with the following one on deacons, and that the adverb ὡσαύτως ties the requirements of a deacon to those of an overseer.[324] If that is the case, then, it is correct to say that the ὡσαύτως in verse 11 similarly ties the qualifications of a female deacon to those of a male deacon and those of an overseer respectively.[325] Although it is a short list that is ensconced between the extensive list for male deacons, the most appropriate interpretation is that the γυναῖκας were female deacons. In Titus 2:3–5 where similar qualifications are given, but there to older women, it is evident that women had prominent roles of teaching (at least guiding young women) in the church. Christian women were influential in the ministry of the church. If for the sake of not being detrimental to the reputation and ministry of the church women in general were required to have outstanding moral character, female deacons would be required to be more impeccable in all spheres of life.

As seen above, the overarching requirement for the overseer (3:1–7) and male deacons (3:8–10, 12–13) was that they be ἀνεπίλημπτος (3:2) or ἀνέγκλητος (3:10; Titus 1:6). The construction δεῖ . . . εἶναι in 3:2 also dominates the adjectives in reference to the female deacons in verse 11. For

---

321. See Roloff, *Der erste Brief an Timotheus*, 164–165.
322. See Marshall, *Pastoral Epistles*, 494.
323. Mounce, *Pastoral Epistles*, 204.
324. Mounce, 197.
325. See also Spicq, *Les Epitres Pastorales*, 1:460–461.

male deacons, the leading qualification was that they needed to be σεμνούς, that is, "dignified" "serious," "of good character," "honourable," "worthy," or "respectable." The equivalent for the γυναῖκες was σεμνάς (3:11). As seen above, because of its unspecific nature, some scholars take σεμνάς as a second-level general qualification that arches over the three specific qualifications in the verse. A general view for the rationale behind this requirement on women is that, most likely influenced by the worship of female gods, in Ephesus they had developed unacceptable excesses in character and, thus, they had become undignified (2:11–12).[326] Therefore, all Christian women, especially the rich women (1 Tim 2:9–10) and women in leadership, needed to be prohibited from participating in particular excesses.

3.4.4.11 μὴ διαβόλους (1 Tim 3:11; cf. Titus 2:3)

Women deacons were required to be of good character in three specific areas. They had to be μὴ διαβόλους (not slanderous), νηφαλίους ("self-controlled" or "temperate," found only twice in NT, only in PE, here and in Titus 2:2 in relation to use of wine, BDAG), and πιστὰς ἐν πᾶσιν, "faithful/trustworthy/ loyal in everything." In other words, they were to be blameless in speech, in temperament and in trustworthiness. The prohibition μὴ διαβόλους is close in meaning to μὴ διλόγους (not double in speech) that was given to the male deacons in 3:8. Nevertheless, it is unique. In 2 Timothy 3:3 it is listed as a characteristic of godless people of the last days. *NIDNTT* says that the label of διάβολος is also used of a person who brings charges with evil intent. Knight interprets the plural adjective διαβόλους as "malicious gossips" or "malicious talkers."[327] In the Intertestamental writings, the devil or the devilish person was someone who through lies and other means tried to disrupt the relationship between God and Israel and also between God and the rest of humankind (1 Enoch 86:1–88:3; Jubilees 5:1–12). In the Qumran writings, a slanderous or devilish person was someone whose heart was filled by the evil spirit called "the angel of darkness" (1QS 1:10). He was a preacher of apostasy and enemy of righteousness (CD 12:2;[328] 1QS 2:16–17; 6:21; 7:4). In the LXX διάβολος was used of Satan or of a person

---

326. Towner, *Letters to Timothy*, 266.
327. Knight III, *Pastoral Epistles*, 172.
328. CD is the Cairo Geniza copy of the *Damascus Document*.

who brought dissentions and sabotaged relationship and operations between groups of people, for example, between ranks of armies (1 Sam 29:4; 1 Kgs 11:23, 25). Satan was called διάβολος because of his character as a deceiver who causes discord between humans and God (their original and supreme benefactor) and among people. The same title is found in 2 Timothy 2:26 in reference to Satan and his old mission of ensnaring people and making them his captives.

The instruction μὴ διαβόλους is striking especially as it was directed mainly to women; (cf. Titus 2:3). Men also could be slanderous as implied in the generic nominative masculine plural adjective διάβολοι in 2 Timothy 3:3 describing ἄνθρωποι in 3:2, but in 1 Timothy 3:11 and Titus 2:3, Paul uses it in reference to women only. In 3:11, he cautioned against malicious talk but he did not give a reason. However, before the instruction in 1 Timothy 3:11, in 2:11–15 he had already given reason for women to be silent in the church. He forbade them to teach or have authority over men. It is notable how he based the reason for the prohibition on the original encounter between Eve and Satan. In the Genesis episode, Satan had used deceptive and slanderous speech to mislead Eve, by tarnishing God's character and intentions. Through it, he made God look like a cunning selfish being who did not want Eve and Adam to be like him. Thus, he caused Eve to see God as a selfish patron. That insinuation gave her a false reason to be disloyal to God. She thus became an embittered client and influenced the only other available client, Adam, to distrust and be disloyal to God, their creator-patron.

Likewise, some of the false teachers caused the Christian faith to seem untrustworthy. They were causing people (for example the naive women) to distrust the sound doctrine that was preached to them (2 Tim 3:6–8). As a result, people became loyal to deceitful demonic teachings, to Satan and to pleasure, rather than loving God and his word (1 Tim 4:12; 5:15; 2 Tim 3:4). In an honour and shame society, tarnishing the reputation of someone through slander resulted in the person losing credibility and honour in the sight of the community. Another faction of false teachers was leading people to be loyal to the law rather than exercising faith in Christ. That group was destroying individual people and families by their wicked doctrines (1 Tim 1:10; 4:1–5; Titus 1:10–14). Women were most likely the primary targets of the false teachers and they were falling victim to their destructive teaching and behaviour (2 Tim 3:6). In Titus 2:3–4, Paul advised Titus to tell older women not to be διαβόλους, but instead, to use their tongues to advise young(er) women (τὰς νέας) to love and be submissive to their husbands, to love their children, and to be good managers of the household. One important aim of the instruction was that there would be love and harmony in the families. False teachers were doing the opposite. Lies and slanderous talk were causing disharmony and destroying homes. They were also discrediting and scandalizing the Word of God (Titus 2:5) and causing it to be distrusted, dishonoured and disobeyed (1 Tim 6:3–5; cf. Eph 4:31; 2 Cor 12:20).

Women were also required to be, νηφαλίους, "temperate," "sober," "self-controlled." On self-control, the closest reference was in relation to excessive use of wine (cf. 3:2, 3, 8) which was highlighted for the overseers and the male deacons. However, there was another distinctive qualification targeted at the women, namely, πιστὰς ἐν πᾶσιν, "faithful (trustworthy or loyal) in all things," as elaborated below.

3.4.4.12 πιστὰς ἐν πᾶσιν *(1 Tim 3:11)*

The feminine accusative adjective πιστὰς has two possible interpretations. It can describe a person who expresses, or is in a state of "belief," someone who is "faithful" or "believing" (substantively, "a believer" [Acts 10:45]). It can also describe a "trustworthy," "reliable," "sure," "true," "unfailing," or "sincere" person or thing (Acts 13:34). As Marshall observes, the πίστις word group plays a central role in PE. Various items on the πίστις vocabulary occur fifty-seven times (plus four times of negative forms), "which is almost three times as high as one would have expected in comparison with the use of the word-group in the earlier epistles of Paul."[329] The adjective πιστός occurs seventeen times, nine times of which it describes the character of a Christian. BDAG gives the passive meaning of πιστός as "trustworthy, faithful, dependable, reliable, inspiring trust or faith" whereas the active meaning is "trusting, cherishing faith or trust, believing, full of faith, faithful, a believer in the Lord, in Christ, in God, a Christian." In an active sense, the meaning of the adjective is "trusting" (or believing) and the object is

---

329. Marshall, *Pastoral Epistles*, Excursus 4, 213–217.

Christ or God (1 Tim 4:3, 10, 12; 5:16; 6:2a, 2b; Titus 1:6).³³⁰ In the active sense, the adjective πιστὰς means that the women were required to be in a believing or trusting state. Additionally, where the cognate infinitive verb, πιστεύειν, is used in 1 Timothy 1:16, it is used in the active sense in speaking about people who would come to believe later. The complementary prepositional dative clause, ἐν πᾶσιν, in 1 Timothy 3:11 makes the requirement in that verse to mean that as Christians the women were required to be in a state of "complete" faith or trust. Paul's complete trust in God may give a clue on what or who the women were to trust in fully (2 Tim 1:12). On the contrary, the apostates, instead of persevering and trusting on God completely to sustain them in everything, they had fallen away in pursuit of personal gain (1 Tim 1:5–7; 6:6, 10).

The passive sense of the adjective πιστὰς is also appropriate. As in the active sense, the complementary clause ἐν πᾶσιν, "in everything," immediately after πιστὰς also strengthens the passive sense. In fact it makes it a better option. Interpreters who go for the passive sense take the adjective πιστὰς as focusing on the aspect of being a trusted person instead of the aspect of being a trusting person.³³¹ They support their argument by stating that if Paul wanted to emphasize the active use he would have used the verb πιστεύω instead of the adjective πιστός. Going for the passive sense leads to the interpretation of the requirement as that the women were to be trusted in everything, they were required to be totally trustworthy and loyal in executing their service. That interpretation is also more feasible because of the context in which the instruction was given. Trustworthiness/loyalty was a virtue that was very essential to both parties, especially in εὐεργεσία, for the relationship to continue. Unlike the false teachers who were not trustworthy, the women were required to be fully trustworthy. Nonetheless, similar to the men, they had to have the same objective truth that the male deacons were required to have (3:9, 13).

As Marshall says, in PE the absence of the definite article before the πίστις word, for example in 1 Timothy 2:7; 3:11, 13 does not automatically make it subjective in meaning. Conversely, the presence of the definite article (for

---

330. Marshall, *Pastoral Epistles*, 215.
331. Towner, *Letters to Timothy*, 267. See also Marshall, *Pastoral Epistles*, 492–495; cf. Excursus 4 on "The πίστις word-group in the Pastoral Epistles," 213–217.

example in 2 Tim 3:10; Titus 2:2) does not automatically make it objective. It is difficult to separate the objective aspect of faith (1 Tim 2:7) from the subjective aspect (1 Tim 2:15).[332] What helps the interpreter to arrive at the most appropriate meaning is the context and the verb or the verbal constructions that relate to the πίστις word in question.[333] However, sometimes even the context and the verbal ideas associated with the πίστις word and its cognates do not shed light on the most appropriate meaning. Thus, in the case of πιστὰς ἐν πᾶσιν in 1 Timothy 3:11, vagueness of meaning still persists. It helps us a bit to know that it is not necessary to separate the subjective faith from the objective, for it is adherence to the gospel (objective faith) (3:9) that produces trustworthiness (subjective faith) in the woman for carrying out her tasks.[334] Women deacons were required to possess the fixed objective tenets of the Christian faith, as was required of their male counterparts (1 Tim 3:9, 13). Since in 3:11 Paul is discussing the character of the female deacons by use of adjectives, the passive subjective sense carries heavier weight.

Women were required to be trustworthy in all things, that is, they had to be completely reliable.[335] Citing Cicero in *De Off* 1.23, Spicq also supports the passive subjective sense and defines it as "that which encompasses good faith, loyalty, and fidelity . . . the basis of all contracts." He contrasts this condition of being faithful with the young widows' lack of it, as seen in the rejection of their first faith (5:12).[336] It is noteworthy that this qualification also was applied to the women but not to the male deacons. Knight, who takes the women as deacons' wives, understands this requirement as meaning that they should be as totally committed and as serious as their husbands, in control of the tongue and attitude, namely, self-controlled and faithful.[337] Additionally, it could also mean that, as recipients of confidences, the female leaders had to be fully dependable in keeping them intact.[338] They

---

332. Marshall, *Pastoral Epistles*, 215.
333. Marshall, 214.
334. See Towner, *Letters to Timothy*, 267.
335. Marshall, *Pastoral Epistles*, 495.
336. Spicq, *Theological Lexicon of the New Testament*, 112–113. See also Livy, *History of Rome* 8.28 and Polybius, *Histories* 7.12.
337. Knight III, *Pastoral Epistles*, 173.
338. An observation by Margaret G. Sim, 12 August, 2010, NEGST.

had to be unlike the idle young widows who were "gossips and busybodies, saying what they should not say" (1 Tim 5:13). As seen in chapter 2, the benefactor-beneficiary, patron-client relationships were mainly relationships which were founded on fides (πίστις), in the sense of trustworthiness and loyalty.³³⁹ Trustworthiness in everything was a crucial virtue. In contrast to lack of trustworthiness of both the benefactors and beneficiaries in the benefaction systems, and as a counter measure against the unfaithfulness of false teachers and their converts (mainly women, including rich women and young widows), Paul wanted Christian women leaders to be fully trustworthy in all their service to the Lord.

Although there were prominent similarities between the character and skill qualifications of the church leaders and their G-R and Jewish counterparts, there were outstanding differences also. In all spheres of their character, skills and tasks, all church leaders had to be better than their non-Christian contemporaries. Their great confidence in faith in Christ (1 Tim 3:13) and the sincere motive and conscience in being righteous and doing good in reference to God³⁴⁰ and for the good of others (not for their advancement) would give them a better standing and enable them to give excellent service. Following the instructions on good qualifications would help the leaders to know how one ought to behave in the household of God (1 Tim 3:15). Similarly, adherence to the sound doctrine would establish the leaders' faith and give them the ability and credibility to refute those who contradicted it (Titus 1:9).

3.4.5 Benefaction for Widows by the Church (1 Tim 5:3–16)

The discussion about widows in the context of benefaction has received significant coverage.³⁴¹ In PE, it is one of the subjects that get much attention from Paul,³⁴² indicating that it was an issue of considerable importance, or

---

339. Joubert, "One Form of Social Exchange," 19.

340. For example, the overseer was to serve as one taking care of God's church (1 Tim 3:5), as God's steward, (Titus 1:7). Women leaders had to serve faithfully so that the Word of God may not be discredited, Titus 2:5.

341. See, for example, Winter, "Providentia,"

342. So also observes Witherington III, *Letters and Homilies*, 265.

of great difficulty[343] in the Ephesian church. 1 Timothy 5:3–16 is the second part of a larger section (1 Tim 5:1–6:2) in which Paul gives instructions on relationships and transactions between members of various groups in the church. The context implies that there was a problem concerning widows. Some scholars, such as Wagener, see the problem as related to a significant order of widows in the church that was agitating for freedom from male domination in church leadership.[344] They say that Paul's reassertion of patriarchalism in church leadership was an attempt at curbing the widows' powers by insisting that, as far as possible, women should devote themselves to domestic duties.[345] Other scholars, such as Rapske,[346] view the problem as related to the church's responsibility towards real needy widows.[347] Yet others see the two problems as going hand in hand. However, the heavier weight goes to the option that the problem was on how the church was to balance its limited resources against the increasing need to provide for the widows.[348] Therefore, 1 Timothy 5:3–16 is one of the passages in PE where Paul evidently guides the church at Ephesus on how to practise good benefaction, by honouring (τιμάω) [349] widows (χῆραι). He directed Timothy on who could/should be put on the list to be honoured by the church (5:3, 5, 9–10), who could/should be supported by family members (5:4, 8, 16), and those who could/should be remarried and be supported by husbands (5:11, 14). The term χήρα may have various meanings, such as "a woman whose husband is dead," "a celibate woman," "a virgin,"[350] or "a woman whose husband abandoned her," or "a woman who separated herself from

---

343. Marshall, *Pastoral Epistles*, 575.

344. Ulrike Wagener, *Die Ordnung des 'Hauses Gottes': der Ort von Frauen in der Ekklesiologie und Ethik der Pastoralbriefe* [The Order of the House of God: The Place of Women in Ecclesiology and Ethics of the Pastoral Epistles], WUNT 2/65 (Tübingen: Mohr Siebeck, 1994).

345. Wagener as cited by Marshall in *Pastoral Epistles*, 575–576.

346. Brian Mark Rapske, *The Widow in the Apostolic Church* (Vancouver, Canada: Regent College, 1987).

347. Rapske as cited by Marshall in *Pastoral Epistles*, 576–577.

348. Johnson, *First and Second*, 178–180.

349. The meaning of τιμάω and τιμή is discussed below.

350. Such as in Ignatius, *Epistle to the Smyrnaeans* 13:1, "I greet . . . the virgins who are called widows."

husband and children for the church."³⁵¹ In this passage, its meaning is partly suggested in 5:9 that, if she was once married, she should only have been married once.

In the larger section (1 Tim 5:1–6:2), Paul uses various principles of the household codes and the benefaction and patronage systems. For example, in each subdivision, he uses a household (and kinship) principle, such as, urging Timothy to treat church members as family members (5:1–2), urging that children and grandchildren help their widowed relatives (5:4, 8, 16), referring to church leaders as elders, as in a household or family setting (5:17), and urging slaves to honour their masters (6:1–2). Related to benefaction, he uses words in the "honour" word-group, either as verb, noun or by implication. It is implied in 5:1–2,³⁵² used as a verb, τιμάω, in 5:3, and as a noun, τιμή, in both 5:17 and 6:1. The present tense aspect in the imperative verb τίμα in 5:3 could imply that the church was urged to continue doing what it was already doing (holding widows with respect and helping them materially).³⁵³ As seen in chapter 2, honour was a prominent feature, especially for reciprocation, in the benefaction and patronage systems. Although the term is not used directly in 5:1–2, it is implied in the instruction on how to treat various people in the church as family members, with courtesy. The chapter begins with instructions addressed to Timothy alone (5:1–2), to apply in his personal relationship with various people in the church (cf. use of the second person singular subjunctive ἐπιπλήξῃς "reprimand," and the imperative παρακάλει "urge" [5:1]). In 5:3 Paul still used the second person singular imperative, τίμα, to address him as an individual, possibly because he was the current overseer. However, it is a bit difficult to know whether the third person subjunctive verb ὦσιν in the purpose clause ἵνα ἀνεπίλημπτοι ὦσιν ("so that 'they' may be above reproach") in 5:7 was targeting the children who were neglecting their needy parents and grandparents (5:4, 8), the widows who were living for pleasure (5:6), or the church members in general. The exact people being referred to in the plural masculine adjective ἀνεπίλημπτοι are not identifiable. Knight's observes that the plural verbs in

---

351. Towner, *Letters to Timothy*, 338.

352. In this case, "honour" is mainly used in reference to general "respect" as in the family setting. But it is applied to people who are not physical blood relatives.

353. See Marshall, *Pastoral Epistles*, 582.

verses 4 and 7 sound an inclusive note and that helps us to conclude that the instruction was targeting the church as a unit.[354] However, that is true of verse 7 only. In verse 4, the plural verb μανθανέτωσαν clearly refers to τέκνα ἢ ἔκγονα only. Based on 5:8, my conclusion is that the most likely targets are the believing children and grandchildren who were neglecting their widowed parents.

Despite being derived from the older benefaction systems, the instruction was given a new dimension in the Ephesian church. In the new perspective, the basic rationale for helping the parents is that it is pleasing to God, τοῦτο γάρ ἐστιν ἀπόδεκτον ἐνώπιον τοῦ θεοῦ. Christians had to do the good deed in reference to God, for his pleasure, not for their own temporal advancement (although that also could have been envisaged). Doing good mainly for self-advancement was acceptable and common in the secular benefaction and patronage systems. However, in the church, doing good mainly for the good of others is what was emphasized (1 Tim 5:10; Titus 3:8). The plural imperative verb μανθανέτωσαν in 4 is meant for the children or grandchildren (τέκνα ἢ ἔκγονα), that is, those who should have been helping the widows in the family setting. The basis of this instruction was also the OT, where in the LXX, Exod 20:12, the same term is given in the commandment about honouring parents. In Matthew 15:4–5, Jesus elaborated the meaning of τιμάω as including material support, as also in 1 Timothy 5:4, 8, 16.

Witherington says that the discussion on support for widows in the church at Ephesus was "not an adaptation of conventional Greco-Roman advice, and it only partially echoes Jewish wisdom on the subject (cf. Exod 22:22–24; Deut 10:18; 24:17–22; 27:19; Ps 68:5; Isa 1:17; Ezek 22:7)"[355] His conclusion is that it was mainly a new idea in the church. However, as discussed in chapter 1, Winter says that in the G-R society, widows were also provided for, although sometimes there was laxity in the care that they were given. Harrison also says that when Paul instructed that children and grandchildren should help their widowed parents, he was endorsing "stock Graeco-Roman norms of good behaviour towards parental benefactors, while subsuming its ethical motivation under traditional Jewish-Christian motifs."[356]

---

354. Knight III, *Pastoral Epistles*, 215.
355. Witherington III, *Letters and Homilies*, 265.
356. Harrison, "Benefaction Ideology," 113.

Thus, he views this injunction as based on both an ancient Jewish religious practice and a G-R ethical custom. After Augustus (63 BC –AD 14), one of the principal functions of the office of the emperor was *providentia*. In his articles based on 1 Timothy 5:3–16, Winter seeks to clarify the puzzling aspects of the G-R and Jewish social and legal context of provision (*providentia*) for widows.[357] He says that in the Greek, Roman, and Jewish social settings of the first century AD, there were clear legal guidelines on how to provide for widows, for example, through the κύριος in charge of her dowry. However, for widows from the lowest economic ladder who had no provision from any household, the church took up the responsibility of taking care of those who had become Christian. Support by children or grand children could not be counted as patronage per se if it was given solely as fulfilment of a filial requirement, but if given as an act of free will, then it qualified to be benefaction. For example, as Seneca proposed, when a child's beneficence surpassed the beneficence that he received from the parents, then he rightly was a better benefactor (patron) than the parents.[358] Likewise, if the parents' good deeds of provision to their children surpassed the legal requirements for parental care, then the deeds qualified to be benefaction. In the G-R and Jewish worlds, poor people in the society, including widows who had no dowry or relatives to rely on were provided for mainly through the benefaction and patronage systems.

The fact that support for widows was not a totally new idea in the church at Ephesus is also highlighted by Knight. He says that "the existence of 'enrolled' widows is implied by the passive imperative of καταλέγω (a NT hapax in v. 9), which has one of its meanings as 'select, enlist, enroll . . . .'"[359] Scholars, such as Dibelius-Conzelmann and Thurston, say that in the Ephesian church there was an "order" of widows who had various duties in the church and who were supported or even "paid" by the church. Other, such as Bernard and Verner, suggest that there were two groups of widows; one made of destitute (genuine) widows, and the other made up of an active order of workers (cf. 5:9–10).[360] Towner admits the possibility of

---

357. Winter, "Providentia," 83–88.
358. Seneca, *Seneca III*, III.XXIX.1–XXXVIII.3.
359. Knight III, *Pastoral Epistles*, 222.
360. For further details see also Marshall, *Pastoral Epistles*, 575.

there being a formal "order or sisterhood of widows" in the church.³⁶¹ Its existence is indicated by: (1) the rule on honouring widows, showing that their payment corresponded with that of an office (cf. payment of elders in 5:17). (2) The similarity between the qualifications required of widows (5:9–10) and of the overseer and deacons (3:1–13) could indicate formal and official recognition of the order. (3) Enrolment on a list might shows evidence of formal acceptance into the order (5:9). (4) The implication of a vow of celibacy (5:12) might indicate an official order. However, feminists who support equality of gender in church leadership read mischief in Paul's instructions on the requirements for enrolment and interpret them as his attempt at suppressing the freedom and ministries of a thriving group of women in the church. It is apparent that there was a widows' list (5:9) and that some of the widows had a private or official ministry of intercession in the church (5:5). However, Paul's greatest concern was for the church to care for those who had no relatives to care for them or dowry to depend on (5:3, 5 and 16).

In the Greek world, the reciprocity custom of πρόνοια, that is, "provision, foresight, care or attention," in kinship relationships, especially in reciprocal help for parents for what they had done for their children, is shown in honorary inscriptions and in writings of ancient authors. For example, in the writings of Pythagoras (c. 580–500 BC), young people were exhorted to regard their parents as benefactors for being responsible for their achievements, for example, in teaching them to honour the gods. Offspring were required to reciprocate by honouring their parents, which would result in pardon from the gods.³⁶² Such honorary reciprocation was through helping the parents in old age and widowhood. Writing to a church in the East where Greek culture was strong, it is likely that Paul was conversant with the Greek philosophy as he gave the instructions that it was the responsibility of offspring to help their widowed parents and grandparents as repayment and honour for their previous parental care (1 Tim 5:4). Polycarp's Epistle to the Philippians³⁶³ discussed about similar requirements, for example, the widow's age limit for eligibility for benefaction by the church. In addition

---

361. Towner, *Letters to Timothy*, 333–334.
362. Harrison, "Benefaction Ideology," 114–115.
363. For example, 4:3; 6:1.

to the other requirements, Paul highlighted the spiritual dimensions needed before someone could be added to the list for benefaction by the church. Therefore, despite support for widows being an old practice, the type of τιμή (both nonmaterial respect and material support) that the church was urged to give to the widows was a new development due to its base on the Christian faith and the *koinonia* spirit of the early church. The support of parents by their children acquired an added value in the church setting because it was to be done based on (or as proof of) the children's Christian faith (5:8). The same goes for support of relatives by believing women (5:16).

3.4.6 Remuneration for Church Officers (1 Tim 5:17–18)

After giving instructions on which particular widows should be supported by the church, Paul revisits the discussion on church officers that he left in 3:13 as he turned his attention to other urgent matters. The issues that he turned to were: (1) giving Timothy the reason for writing the instructions to him (3:14–15); (2) explaining briefly the mystery of our faith (Jesus Christ) (3:16); (3) cautioning Timothy about the prevailing false teachings and exhorting him to remain faithful and active in sound doctrine (4:1–16); (4) advising him how to treat different age-groups in the church (5:1–2); and (5) guiding him on the support for widows (5:3–16). Leaving the discussion about which widows to help, he advised Timothy on which particular elders deserved honour from the church (5:17–18); how he needed to handle accusations against an elder (5:19); how to deal with sinful elders (5:20); charge to avoid partiality in application of the instructions (5:21); charge not to ordain someone hastily as a leader (5:22, cf. 3:6); and charge keep himself pure from the sins of others (5:22). As observed earlier in the section on their qualifications, as leaders in the household of God, church ministers were benefactors and patrons. They helped the church in various ways, especially providing nonmaterial benefaction. Some of them, for example, those who were householders (1 Tim 3:4–5, 12) were benefactors in both ways, giving nonmaterial benefaction (such as, through teaching and guarding the tenets of the Christian faith) and material resources.

Outside PE, in Acts 4:36–37, Barnabas is presented as a benefactor in material things, because he sold his property and gave the proceeds to help the needy. Later on, in Acts 11:23–24, he is described as a good man (ἀνὴρ ἀγαθὸς) because of exhorting new believers in Antioch to remain faithful to the Lord with steadfast devotion. As seen earlier, in the G-R benefaction and patronage systems, the phrase ἀνὴρ ἀγαθός was an honorific title for a benefactor. It appeared regularly in honorary inscriptions which were memorials in reciprocation for benefaction.[364] As implied in Romans 5:7, a beneficiary could die ὑπὲρ . . . τοῦ ἀγαθοῦ, "for the sake of a good person," a benefactor. In *Epistulae Morales* 81.27 and *De Ben* IV.XX.2 and IV.XXIV.2 Seneca said that a beneficiary could exercise intense loyalty to the extent of accepting to be banished from his homeland, risking his reputation, wealth and health (even to death). Therefore, some of the elders in PE could possibly have been double benefactors. On the socioeconomic status of PE officers and their functions in the church, against Verner,[365] Kidd says that not all of the overseers/elders were wealthy, and that just as some were financial providers for the church, others had to live on the good graces of the church.[366] He leaves the door open for the possibility that just as there was social stratification in the community at large, so there also could have been stratification among the church officers. The overseers, were possibly wealthy householders and patrons, while the elders were composed of the wealthy and those who needed financial support by the church.

If philosophers and orators who did their work well were held with honour as benefactors in the secular communities and teachers of the law were highly respected in the Jewish society (for example, Gamaliel, Acts 5:34), Christian counterparts in the church deserved similar treatment. Those who deserved such honour were elders who led well (καλῶς προεστῶτες), specifically those who laboured in preaching and teaching. The perfect tense in the participle προεστῶτες indicates that the elders had been, and still were ruling, leading, directing and caring for the church. Their exceptional leadership was notably in their toiling (κοπιάω) in word ("by word of mouth, preaching") and teaching ministry. Knight says that the adverb καλῶς was used exclusively in PE as the measure of ministry, both in the family (3:4,

---

364. See an example in J. R. Harrison, "Benefactor of the People," 6, citing G. Petzl, *Die Inschriften von Smyrna*, II, 1 (Bonn: Habelt, 1987) no. 616, 111.

365. Verner holds the opinion that PE church leadership was made up of homogeneously well-off people.

366. Kidd, *Wealth and Beneficence*, 108.

12) and in the church (3:13; 5:17).³⁶⁷ In 5:17, it is used to distinguish those are worthy of honour and those who are not. As in Titus, Paul used the title πρεσβύτερος (1:5) interchangeably with ἐπίσκοπος (1:7), we may therefore infer reasonably that they were the same. However, in 1 Timothy 5:17 he did not specify whom he referred to as πρεσβύτεροι, whether or not it was ἐπίσκοπος alone in 3:1 or also to διάκονοι in 3:8 who needed support from the church.

The instruction on honouring certain elders was possibly targeted against the negligence or sins of some of them. Perhaps Paul was distinguishing the elders who managed the church ministry well (cf. 3:4–5) from those who did not, such as those who mismanaged church affairs, lacked some virtues, or even had joined the false teaching that was vexing the church,³⁶⁸ thus failing to teach and preach well. In the two verses that follow the instruction he implies that there were elders who were being suspected or involved in sin and deserved careful examination and/or reprimanding in public: "As for those who persist in sin, rebuke them in the presence of all, so that the rest also may stand in fear" (5:19, 20). Conversely, those who led well deserved special honour.

As seen in chapter 1, Kidd acknowledges that some of the church leaders were themselves financial providers, and thus patrons for the church. He also acknowledges that there were those who might do more "presiding" and some more "teaching and labouring in the word," and that these needed benefaction from the church.³⁶⁹ We argue that these also were patrons of the church, in nonmaterial ways, and, therefore, they needed compensatory (or reciprocal) benefaction, or payment, as honour for what they were doing.³⁷⁰ Paul's statement that they were worthy of double honour, implies that the remuneration was both material and nonmaterial reciprocation for the nonmaterial benefaction that they were giving to the church, just as

---

367. Knight III, *Pastoral Epistles*, 232.

368. Towner, *Letters to Timothy*, 361–362. See also Johnson, *First and Second Letters*, 286–288. Here (5:17, 19) the church officers are generally referred to as πρεσβύτεροι without distinguishing between the overseer, deacons and women.

369. Kidd, *Wealth and Beneficence*, 107.

370. See Knight III, *Pastoral Epistles*, 232 and Towner, *Letters to Timothy*, 362. Similarly, in *Moral Vision*, 68, Hays says that those who did well were to receive financial compensation for their service.

Galatians 6:6 says, "Those who are taught the word must share in all good things with their teacher." Paul instructed that the diligent elders, especially those who laboured in preaching and teaching, were worthy of double honour, διπλῆς τιμῆς ἀξιούσθωσαν (1 Tim 5:17). The idea of hard labour as deserving compensation is from the OT and is also found in Jesus's words in Matthew 10:10, where he used words similar to what we have in 5:17 as he told his disciples not to carry any provisions for themselves as they went about preaching the gospel, ἄξιος γὰρ ὁ ἐργάτης τῆς τροφῆς αὐτοῦ, "for the labourer deserves his food."

The elders who served well deserved διπλή τιμή. Among scholars, there are various views on the meaning of the statement διπλῆς τιμῆς in 1 Timothy 5:17. The majority say that it refers to nonmaterial honour (respect) and material support from the church. Remuneration was part of the honour that the preaching and teaching elders were entitled to receive from those who were benefitting from their ministry. DeSilva says that the early Christian ministry relied on financial support from the richer converts, and thus, such supporters were entitled to receive honour from the church as gratitude (Acts 4:34–37; 1 Cor 16:17, 18; Phil 2:29, 30; Phlm 7).[371] When it is studied within the context of the first-century AD, διπλῆς τιμῆς yields several possible meanings. For example, it can mean double stipend (or "double wages," as BDAG says, or "twice as much"),[372] compared to what those elders were getting previously or compared to what other elders or the widows were getting. Guthrie says that some understand the double honour as referring to honour due to age and honour due to office.[373] Another interpretation is that it refers to two-fold honour, honour due to rank and function and monetary payment for service.[374] BDAG also says that one usage of the term τιμή was in reference to a physician's honorarium, and therefore, double honour in 5:17 meant that the elders were to receive respect and remuneration, honour and honorarium. It could thus indicate respectful recognition of, and submission to, the authority of the elders as servants of God and

---

371. deSilva, "Patronage," 770.
372. Towner, *Letters to Timothy*, 364.
373. Guthrie, *Pastoral Epistles*, 117.
374. Arichea and Hatton, *Handbook on Paul's Letters*, 125–126.

material payment for their good service.[375] Towner refers to G. Schöllgen as saying that it was possible for διπλῆς τιμῆς to refer to double portion at the community meal.[376] Marshall also agrees that it could mean "double portion" and supports his view with examples from the OT and Tertullian.[377]

The instruction in 5:17–18 is based on a prominent OT instruction, Leviticus 19:13; Deuteronomy 24:14–15; 25:4, cf. 1 Corinthians 9:9. There, appropriate and timely payment for work done are envisaged. Likewise, in the benefaction and patronage systems, both material and nonmaterial honour was appropriate for a benefactor/patron. Taking both the OT and benefaction/patronage contexts into account, the interpretation that is most appropriate for διπλῆς τιμῆς in 5:17 is that the elders were worthy of both continuous nonmaterial respect for their status and character, and occasional material remuneration for their service. 1 Timothy 5:18 hints that material payment was part of the honour that the elders were entitled to receive from the church.

3.4.7 Masters and Slaves (1 Tim 6:1–2; Titus 2:9–10)

Still in concurrence with the household codes and benefaction principles, in chapter 6, Paul turned his attention to slaves. It is worthy noting that, for the three groups in focus, he used the verb τιμάω and the noun τιμή with an ascending degree of emphasis. Starting with the widows, he addressed Timothy using the imperative verb, τίμα, without using any adverb to qualify it. He instructed Timothy to "honour widows who are really widows" (1 Tim 5:2). Then, in 5:17, focusing on church elders, he applied the adjective διπλοῦς attributively with comparative force, to qualify the noun τιμή. He instructed that elders who ruled well be considered worthy of "*double* honour." Finally, in 6:1, focusing on the masters, he applied the adjective πᾶς attributively and with superlative force to qualify the noun τιμή as he instructed all those Christian slaves under the yoke to regard their non-Christian masters as worthy of "*all* honour." That must have sounded

---

375. Philip H. Towner, *1–2 Timothy & Titus*, The IVP New Testament Commentary Series (Downers Grove, IL: InterVarsity Press, 1994), 124.

376. Towner, *Letters to Timothy*, 363–364.

377. See Marshall, *Pastoral Epistles*, 614–615.

controversial to those who felt that with their Christian freedom they should not submit to non-Christian masters any more.

Notably also, in 6:1 Paul addressed a particular segment of the slaves, as he did with the widows and the elders. The particular group that he addressed are the slaves under a yoke: Ὅσοι εἰσὶν ὑπὸ ζυγὸν δοῦλοι, τοὺς ἰδίους δεσπότας πάσης τιμῆς ἀξίους ἡγείσθωσαν, "Let all who are under the yoke of slavery regard their masters as worthy of absolute honour." The plural correlative adjective, ὅσοι, that he used encompassed "as many [slaves] as," namely, "all" who were under ζυγός (yoke). The particular slaves addressed in 6:1 were possibly those whose non-Christian masters still treated them as little more than oxen.[378] Towner equates them to the Israelites who were suffering under the yoke of Gentile masters.[379] Bartsch's opinion is that the instruction is addressed to slaves under "the yoke of Christ."[380] However, that opinion is negated by the fact that, in 6:2, Paul contrasts the slaves under a yoke with slaves who have believing (Christian) masters. Therefore, the yoke is not Christian service. Some scholars sense open bias of Paul against all slaves, both those who have non-Christian masters and those with Christian ones, for he instructs that all slaves should regard their masters as worthy of "absolute honour" (πάσης τιμῆς ἀξίους ἡγείσθωσαν) but gives no instruction to the masters to treat their slaves as equals in the faith as in Galatians 3:28; Ephesians 6:5–9 and Colossians 3:22–4:1. Nevertheless, others see it otherwise.

Some scholars, such as Dibelius, view the mode of Christianity that PE author promoted in PE as bourgeois, due to its apparent support for the upper class both in the church and in the non-Christian society. However, Brox holds a different view and says that PE Christianity has no paradox or scandal.[381] He says that the author focused on the slaves because they were the majority in the church at that time. He however criticised the author for his "unimaginative attitude towards slaves," as seen in his overt support

---

378. See Knight III, *Pastoral Epistles*, 244.
379. Towner, *Letters to Timothy*, 383.
380. H. W. Bartsch, *Die Anfänge urchristlicher Rechtsbildungen: Studien zu den Pastoralbriefen* (Hamburg: Reich, 1965), 150.
381. See Norbert Brox, *Die Pastoralbriefe: Timotheus I, Timotheus II, Titus*, RNT 7. Band. Zweiter Teil: Die Pastoralbriefe (Regensburg: Verlag Friedrich Pustet, 1969), 204–207. See also Hanson, *Pastoral Epistles*, 104–105.

for the masters. Hanson acknowledges that the social position of slaves was one of the problems that troubled the early church. However, he does not agree with Bartsch's assertion that we can actually see the outline of a document on the duties of Christian slaves and owners behind Colossians, Ephesians, the Pastorals, 1 Peter, Ignatius, *Didache* and *Barnabas*. He says that in PE there is no evidence of such a document for the epistles do not mention duties of the Christian masters. Nevertheless, we can see more truth in what Bartsch says because there is evidence that for such an old and well-established institution as slavery, there must have been rules for its management. In the OT there were clear rules on the relationships and transactions between slaves and masters.

On the case in PE, Hanson's view is that the basis of the instruction to slaves could have been a situation in which they had stopped being submissive, hinging their behaviour on the Christian teaching that in Christ "there is no longer slave or free" (Gal 3:28; 4:7), a thought implied indirectly by Paul in 1 Timothy 6:2. The present tense of the imperative verb καταφρονείτωσαν indicates that they were already showing disrespect to (literally "looking down on") their masters. Therefore, Paul was urging them, through Timothy, to stop that non-Christian behaviour and, "continue serving" their masters more devotedly (as the present tense in the word δουλευέτωσαν implies). Citing Hasler,[382] Hanson says that there even might have been a group of Christians who were preaching that the church should use its funds to emancipate slaves.[383] That possibly was the case. It finds support in 6:3–4a, where it is apparent that some people were possibly teaching things that were contrary to Paul's recommendation that slaves should be respectful to their Christian and non-Christian masters. In some of his statements, Jesus seems to have accepted the fact that slavery was a perennial reality and that Christians were expected to do the best they could to live with it (cf. Luke 17:10). Nevertheless, he displayed how a Christian master should live with his slaves, at least those who are fellow Christians, no longer regarding them as slaves but as friends (John 15:15).

---

382. V. Hasler, *Die Briefe an Timotheus und Titus*, Zuercher Bible Kommentar (Zürich: Theologischer Verlag Zürich, 1978).

383. For fuller details, read Hanson, *Pastoral Epistles*, 104–105.

Towner also holds a view similar to Hanson as he points out that the instruction in 6:1–2 was possibly a response to a problem with the slaves. Citing BDF, he says that the use of the "present tense imperatives and prohibitions heighten the sense of reality and perhaps stress certain habits, in the case of Christian slaves, that need to be broken."[384] It is possible that Paul wrote that instruction with the aim of breaking those habits. For example, in both cases, whether concerning honouring non-Christian or Christian masters, the slaves' Christian faith was supposed to have made them more obedient. Therefore, first, Paul encouraged them to be submissive and regard the masters as worthy of all honour, so that the name of God and the Christian teaching might not be slandered/spoken against (βλασφημῆται, which is the opposite of being honoured), especially by non-Christians who were potential converts to Christianity (6:1; Titus 2:9, 10b). Peter's counsel to slaves in 1 Peter 2:18–25 is similar to that in PE. Peter advised slaves to follow Christ's example and endure mistreatment from harsh masters, being aware of God (knowing that their good response to mistreatment finds God's approval). Second, Paul urged slaves to serve their masters better (μᾶλλον δουλευέτωσαν, "they must serve them all the more") because those who would benefit (ἀντιλαμβάνομαι) from the good service (εὐεργεσία, "act of kindness") were believers and beloved (dear to God or to the slaves) (6:2).[385] Note that, in this verse we have the only explicit term on benefaction and patronage in PE, that is, εὐεργεσία. Nevertheless, this statement raises the question on whether a slave could be a benefactor to his master.[386]

Lastly, Paul exhorted slaves not to steal from their masters, but, instead, show that they could be fully trusted (Titus 2:10). On this statement, Verner sees a negative view of Paul about the slaves, as he says, "The author is so incapable of reasoning from slave's point of view that he can urge slaves of Christian masters to obedience on the grounds that the latter are paragons of Christian beneficence."[387] Nevertheless, contrary to Verner, Paul was more concerned at safeguarding the godly image of the Christian faith against bad reputation for the sake of the attractiveness of the doctrine of God (word of

---

384. Towner, *Letters to Timothy*, 379.
385. See also Towner, *Letters to Timothy*, 384.
386. This issue is discussed in the second paragraph below.
387. Verner, *Household of God*, 183.

God, gospel) (1 Tim 6:1; Titus 2:10). Mounce says that the motivation for slaves to be faithful, and for women to adorn themselves with what is fitting for godly women, were for the sake of making the gospel attractive.[388] As seen earlier, related to benefaction, more so in εὐεργεσία than *patronicium*, trustworthiness (*fides*), in both benefactor and beneficiary was a core virtue, it was the main thread that held the relationship together.

Hanson says that there are three possible ways to interpret 6:2a:[389] (1) That masters could benefit from slaves' service (so NRSV, NEB, J. B. Philips' translation, Spicq and Donier). His main objection to that view is that in secular Greek, εὐεργεσία never meant a service done to a superior by an inferior. However, he adds immediately that PE author might have used the word deliberately to stress the ultimate equality of slaves and masters in God's eyes. (2) The masters were believers and beloved people who devoted themselves to the well-being of their slaves (as viewed by Bürki, D-C, Brox, Hasler, Holtz). Hanson says that this interpretation may be right but it is over-optimistic to assume that all Christian slave owners were benevolent, as that view suggests. But, taking into account the possibility of translating the participle ἀντιλαμβανόμενοι as "benefit from" or "devotion to," we can interpret it as meaning that at least "some" Christian masters were devoted to the welfare of the slaves, as TNIV states. In that case, then, Paul could have meant that the masters were the ones giving benefaction, rather than the slaves giving it. This would also be in agreement with the prevailing principle that the superior normally gave benefaction to the inferior party. However, instead of taking it that way, Hanson proposes a third (3) interpretation, which is a combination of (1) and (2) above: "since the masters, who share with slaves in Christian service, are believers and beloved." The reason he gives for this new interpretation is that it is in harmony with the Greek secular understanding, and that it fits well with the rather generalized context. It also reminds us of Mark 10:45, where it is indicated that Christian life is service, for both slaves and masters.

Hanson's interpretation, "since the masters, who share with slaves in Christian service, are believers and beloved" depicts lack of consideration

---

388. Mounce, *Pastoral Epistles*, 416.
389. See Hanson, *Pastoral Epistles*, 105–106

about the preceding clause, ἀλλὰ μᾶλλον δουλευέτωσαν, on which the subordinate causal clause ὅτι πιστοί εἰσιν καὶ ἀγαπητοὶ οἱ τῆς εὐεργεσίας ἀντιλαμβανόμενοι is based. For example, it is clearly indicated in the imperative δουλευέτωσαν that it is the slaves (not the masters) who should serve the masters "all the more" (or, "even better") (NIV). Hanson gives much value to the possibility that PE author could have been resolutely going against the status quo and proposing a revolutionary Christian perspective, as he (Hanson) himself acknowledges in the first view that slaves could benefit their masters. On G-R benefaction and patronage, there are vivid examples from history, where non-Christian slaves were benefactors to their non-Christian masters. For example, in *De Ben* III.XIX.1, Seneca makes a statement and asks a logical rhetorical question from it that anticipates an affirmative response, "There is no doubt that a slave is able to give a benefit to anyone he pleases; why not, therefore, also to his master?" In III.XXIII.2–3, he cites an example from the eighteenth book of Claudius Quadrigarius' *Annals* about two slaves who protected their mistress from certain death, a deed that was counted as benefaction. In gratitude, she rewarded the two slaves by manumitting them immediately for their act. That episode, and others similar to it, also teaches us that the idea that slaves could be benefactors to their masters was not an innovation by Paul.

According to the household codes, both current and manumitted slaves were required to show loyalty continually to their current and former masters respectively, because a patron who was a Roman citizen still retained the powers of a patron over freedmen, freedwomen and their goods (*Lex Irnitana*, rubric 97). Moreover, if a master did to a slave (manumitted or not), or a slave did for his master, more good than was required of him by the law, the extra good deed was counted as benefaction. Therefore, a slave could be a benefactor to his master. That is possibly what Paul was encouraging the slaves to do in 1 Timothy 6:2. Although a slave's more diligent service to the master could have been superficial and motivated by the latter's expectation of manumission, what Paul exhorted Christians slaves to do is to serve with more devotion in reference to their common faith and love.

Although slaves' benefaction to masters was not a new thing in the society, there are three things in this instruction that we can view as distinct innovations by Christianity in the interaction between slaves and masters:

(1) The idea that the slaves were not to disrespect their masters because they were their brothers in Christ (ὅτι ἀδελφοί εἰσιν). Calling them brothers was placing the masters at the same level as the slaves, at least in the spiritual sense, which was a revolutionary concept. Jesus had introduced that reversal of the social order earlier when he called his disciples "brothers" and "friends" and told them that in his kingdom the greatest serves the least (Luke 22:25–27). (2) The urgency that slaves should "serve (their masters) all the more" (μᾶλλον δουλευέτωσαν) or "render superior service" because the masters who were to benefit from their εὐργεσία ("good deed," "deed of kindness," or "benefaction") were πιστοί . . . καὶ ἀγαπητοὶ "believers . . . and beloved" (6:2). Instead of failing to respect and serve faithfully or serving from fear or as mere repayment in honour for benefaction given or expected, they were to serve in love for their masters (and for God). (3) The requirement that they should be totally loyal in reference and reverence to God and the Christian teaching: . . . πᾶσαν πίστιν ἐνδεικνυμένους ἀγαθήν, ἵνα τὴν διδασκαλίαν τὴν τοῦ σωτῆρος ἡμῶν θεοῦ κοσμῶσιν ἐν πᾶσιν, "but [they should] show that they can be fully trusted, so that in every way they will make the teaching about God our Savior attractive" (Titus 2:10, NIV). Therefore, unlike the views of some PE scholars (such as Dibelius, Verner and Hanson) that PE author promoted a bourgeois Christianity in the epistles, it is evident that he empowered the lowest class in the society to operate from an egalitarian "position of power; nobility and honor";[390] where they would continue serving as slaves but for advancement of the heavenly economy.

3.4.8 The Rich and the Needy (1 Tim 6:17–19)

After confrontation of false teachers and the lust for material wealth (6:3–10), recapitulation of Timothy's commission (6:11–14) and a brief excursus on a doxology on the epiphany of Jesus (6:15–16), Paul gave instructions on proper use of wealth by the rich (6:17–19). Coming after what seems to be the final doxology in 1 Timothy, this brief passage on instructions to the rich in the Ephesus church seems to be "an afterthought or a displaced piece of teaching."[391] However, if 6:15–16 is taken as another spontaneous eruption

---

390. For more details on this, read Towner, *Letters to Timothy*, 379–390, and "Can Slaves Be."

391. See Towner, *Letters to Timothy*, 424; Burton Scott Easton, *The Pastoral Epistles: Introduction, Translation, Commentary and Word Studies* (New York: Scribner's Sons, 1947),

of praise by Paul, as what has happened previously in the epistle (1:17 and 2:5–6), then 6:17–19 fits well as a continuation and conclusion of the final instructions to Timothy himself on guarding the deposit of faith, and other miscellaneous instructions to various groups in the church. Hanson says, "our study of the author's technique of composition should make us wary of using an abrupt change of subject as a reason for suspecting [6:17–19 as] an interpolation."[392] Coming soon after strong condemnation on false teachers and their greed for material wealth, it is a beautiful piece of advice on what those who were rich already needed to do with their wealth. The instruction in 6:9–10 is warning and guidance on proper attitude towards riches for those who wanted to "get rich" (NIV) or to "be rich" (NRSV) (οἱ δὲ βουλόμενοι πλουτεῖν). These people may be those who were not yet rich but were wishing or desiring to get rich.[393] They may also have been those who were already rich but desired to continue being rich, holding on to the riches that they had already acquired, as supported by the present tense of the participial clause βουλόμενοι πλουτεῖν. However, the first option is more viable, if we take the participle βουλόμενοι as indicating intention or aspiration to have something that those people did not have, and if we take the infinitive πλουτεῖν to be an infinitive of purpose. The term ὀρέγομαι "be eager for, long for, desire" (6:10) also supports this view.

Verner views this injunction (6:9) as PE author's measure to cushion the status of those who were already rich from the potential social-climbers, namely, those who wanted to be rich.[394] However, it is more appropriate to see it as a legitimate caution to Christians not to be taken too much into loving money that they break Christian restraints and shipwreck their faith. The instruction in 6:17–19 is guidance on the right attitude and use of wealth for those who were rich already (τοῖς πλουσίοις ἐν τῷ νῦν αἰῶνι). Verses 17 to 19 are one long sentence with one main verb, παραγγέλω (to command, order, urge) in verse 17, that governs a series of clauses (mainly infinitival clauses in verse 17 and 18) laying out the particular details of the instruction. In 6:17 Paul instructed Timothy to urge the rich to have proper

---

170, and Spicq (1969), 575.
    392. Hanson, *Pastoral Epistles*, 114.
    393. See Towner, *Letters to Timothy*, 401.
    394. Verner, *Household of God*, 184.

perspective and attitude towards riches and God: no conceit or laying hope on riches, but on God alone. After guiding them on the right perspective of and relation with God and riches, he was to guide them on proper use of riches, in good works (v. 18).

In the syntax of verse 17, the articular plural adjective τοῖς πλουσίοις is a substantive that is a dative of indirect object. Paul gives the indirect command in form of two successive negative infinitival clauses: (1) μὴ ὑψηλοφρονεῖν and (2) μηδὲ ἠλπικέναι ἐπὶ πλούτου ἀδηλότητι. He charges Timothy to urge the rich people in the present age, not to be haughty, and not to set their hopes on the uncertainty of riches. He uses the word παραγγέλλω in the present imperative. Mounce says that the word παραγγέλειν in PE means "to urge" rather than "to command," and that in this case its usage "confirms that Paul is speaking not to his opponents but generally to those in the church."[395] The present tense of the infinitive term in the first clause ὑψηλοφρονεῖν (from ὑψηλοφρονέω, another hapax in PE, a compound verb from ὑψηλός (high, proud, arrogant) and φρονέω (think) that means "to think highly of (self)," "to be proud," "arrogant," "conceited," "haughty") indicates that it is a vice that the rich were already involved in and were currently practising. In Titus 1:7, Paul used another word, μὴ αὐθάδη (BDAG, "arrogant, stubborn, self-willed"), for prohibition against arrogance as he gave instructions on the qualifications of elders overseers/elders. But, in 6:17 he used ὑψηλοφρονέω to highlight the haughtiness or negative pride that is a product of wrong self-assessment, as one thinks himself as being above or better than others because of his material possessions. For Christians also, "nothing so generally produces pride and arrogance as wealth."[396] The people who were rich in the present age were arrogant and were basing their hope, ἠλπικέναι (ἐλπίζω, BDAG, "hope, hope for, expect"; UBS, "hope in") on uncertain wealth. Hanson says that the perfect tense in the infinitive, ἠλπικέναι, conveys the sense of action completed.[397] However, as is the normal characteristic of the perfect, the past action has effects in the present, implying that the rich had started relying on the uncertainty of material wealth at a point in the past

---

395. Mounce, *Pastoral Epistles*, 366.
396. Mounce, 366.
397. Hanson, *Pastoral Epistles*, 114.

and were still relying on it.³⁹⁸ By putting their hope in wealth, the rich had technically turned their loyalty from the overall primary benefactor, God, which was the most despicable response of a beneficiary to a benefactor. Instead of responding to God in worshipful thanksgiving (2:1; 4:4), they had acted just as Jesus had visualized, that none can serve two masters equally (Matt 6:24; Luke 16:13).³⁹⁹ Timothy was to insist that they stop and shift to start and continue relying on God instead.

Paul is contrasting the unreliability (ἀδηλότης, "uncertainty," so BDAG, UBS, Polybius, Plutarch, Philo, and others) of material wealth. BDAG also treats the noun ἀδηλότης as an adjective and translates ἠλπικέναι ἐπὶ πλούτου ἀδηλότητι as to hope in "uncertain" wealth. Nonetheless, Paul puts emphasis on the object of the preposition ἐπί, that is, ἀδηλότητι, thus indicating that the clause may read "or to set their hopes on the uncertainty of riches" (NRSV), instead of "nor to trust in uncertain riches" (NKJV), or "nor to put their hope in wealth, which is so uncertain" (NIV). Even so, as Knight says, the construction ἐπὶ πλούτου ἀδηλότητι is equivalent in meaning to ἐπ' ἀδήλῳ πλούτῳ.⁴⁰⁰ Therefore, the clause is also correct if translated as "in/on uncertain riches." The meaning of πλοῦτος is "riches," "wealth," "abundance," and "material possession." In 6:17, it means that the rich people (πλούσιοι) are those who were in "possession of many earthly goods" (BDAG). It is possible that the rich people did not know the uncertainty of the material riches on which they were relying, but Paul knew it. Therefore, with a contrastive clause beginning with a superordinate disjunctive, ἀλλά, he urged Timothy to [advise and] urge them to rely on what is certain, on God (ἐπὶ θεῷ, 6:17), instead on what is variable. The anticipated result would be acquisition of certain/real life that has a future (εἰς τὸ μέλλον, 6:19). The advice in these verses is very similar to what Jesus gave to his disciples

---

398. See also A. T. Robertson, *A Grammar of the Greek New Testament*, 908–909. Robertson says that originally the infinitive did not have tense. However, in indirect discourse the tenses of the infinitive had the element of time, that of the direct, that even when the tense occurs in indirect discourse the time is not changed. Citing Burton, N. T. M. and T., p. 52, he points out that in the NT there is no instance in Perfect infinitive representing a past perfect indicative. He sees the usage of perfect tense in the infinitive as having "intensive" sense, especially when used with a preposition. In 1 Tim 6:17 the verb is used with the two prepositions ἐπί in the verse and has two indirect objects: "uncertainty of riches" and "God."

399. See also Towner, *The Letters to Timothy and Titus*, 426.

400. Knight III, *Pastoral Epistles*, 272–273.

in Matthew 6:19–21, where he advised them not to store their treasure on earth where moth and rust destroy and thieves steal, but in heaven where there is guaranteed eternal safety.

The rich were to be urged to rely on "God who gives us all things richly (abundantly, in full measure) for enjoyment": τῷ παρέχοντι ἡμῖν πάντα πλουσίως εἰς ἀπόλαυσιν. This part of the verse is a repetition of an earlier statement in 1 Timothy 4:4, that "everything created by God is good, and nothing is to be rejected, provided it is received with thanksgiving." In 6:13 also, Paul says that God gives life to everything. Fee interprets the implication of ζῳογονέω (to give life to, to spare life) in 6:13 as meaning that God was able to spare life from martyrdom.[401] That may be one implication of the statement, as Paul follows his statement by citing the example of Jesus who bore testimony of the truth before Pilate without fearing death. Nevertheless, the context indicates that Timothy had to continue holding on to the true faith without abandoning it in pursuit of material gain, as others had done (6:10–12). Paul was speaking of being contented with whatever God was giving to his people for sustenance, such as food and clothing (6:8). Marshall says that the present tense in the participle ζῳογονοῦντος implies the continuous activity of God in giving life (and everything to support it) in the universe (cf. 6:12b).[402] This thought echoes Jesus's words in Matthew 6:33 that if the believer seeks God's kingdom and righteousness first, God will add to him all things (ταῦτα πάντα προστεθήσεται ὑμῖν) that he needs in his life. Paul said that God gives us all things for enjoyment (6:17b). As an indication of his goodness, God provides to us all things lavishly (1 Tim 1:4; Titus 2:7, cf. Ps 52:7) for enjoyment beyond our needs. His statement is contrary to the ascetic tendencies of others who were prohibiting people from enjoyment of food and marriage (cf. 4:3f). The statement is also contrary to the greed of the false teachers who were abandoning the faith in pursuit of material gain. Similarly, by stating that God gives us everything, Paul refuted the self-sufficiency of the rich, which was based on greed for possessions (6:17). Marshall says that the two tendencies (asceticism and

---

401. Fee, *1 and 2 Timothy*, 151.
402. Marshall, *Pastoral Epistles*, 662.

greed) could coexist in the same person.⁴⁰³ It is apparent that they were present in the Ephesian church. Greed was antithetical to benefaction.

Paul says that God gives us everything richly (πλουσίως, richly, in full measure) (6:17), not in the sense of wasteful excess but in gracious sufficiency that meets and continues meeting our needs.⁴⁰⁴ The purpose for which God gives us all things is indicated by the accusative phrase εἰς ἀπόλαυσιν in which the preposition connotes purpose. The feminine term ἀπόλαυσις (enjoyment, pleasure) is used only once elsewhere in the NT, in Hebrews 11:25, where it is used negatively for the transitory pleasures of sin. Nevertheless, here it does not have the negative connotation because Paul has already spoken against that in 5:6; he also wrote against it later in his second letter to Timothy (2 Tim 3:4) concerning sinfulness of people in the last days. The enjoyment that he meant was pure, thankful and responsible enjoyment in reference to God (cf. 4:4; 6:13); an enjoyment that is accompanied by "appropriate behavioural response to God's generosity."⁴⁰⁵ The statement was a direct rejoinder against the ascetic false teaching that forbade people to enjoy marriage and food (4:3). The advice in verse 17 was meant to teach the rich that all that they had (including their life, 6:13) had been provided by God, and that relying on him they would not lose anything, but gain more. Viewed from the benefaction and patronage perspective, Paul presented God as the most generous benefactor, in whom all people, including the rich, should put their trust and hope.

With the infinitival clauses, in verse 18, Paul continues to elaborate the instructions that Timothy is to give to the rich. In addition to the prohibitions, especially on inner personal attitudes, he is to give them positive commands on practical things for the benefit of others. Despite this passage (6:17–19) being viewed as another evidence that Paul compromisingly accommodated the wealthy class in the Ephesian church, on the contrary, it depicts his concerted effort at promoting egalitarianism between all classes of people, such as the rich and the poor, similar to what he also did with the Corinthian church (cf. 2 Cor 8:13–15).⁴⁰⁶ Earlier on, in 5:21, Paul charged

---

403. Marshall, 672.
404. Towner, *Letters to Timothy*, 426.
405. Towner, 425.
406. Towner, 424.

Timothy before God, Christ Jesus and the elect angels to keep the instructions without prejudice, doing nothing based on partiality.

In addition to support for widows by the church, this verse (6:18) is one of the most explicit indicators that Paul supported and promoted the positive aspects of benefaction and patronage. In it, he urged Christians to give benefaction in the church setting. Using language that was common in the benefaction systems, he urged Timothy to command (παραγγέλλω, command, order, give strict orders, cf. Act 5.28) the rich ἀγαθοεργεῖν, "to do good." He wanted them to be rich in good works (πλουτεῖν ἐν ἔργοις καλοῖς, metaphorical use), to be generous or liberal (εὐμεταδότους εἶναι, a hapax), and to be ready to share communally (κοινωνικούς, another hapax, used epexegetically to elaborate εὐμεταδότους, "liberal," "generous"). In noble benefactory spirit, those particular actions were inherently good and they were for the benefit of others.[407] Note the play of words: πλουσίοις . . . πλούτου . . . πλουσίως and πλουτεῖν in 6:17, 18. The πλουσίοις, "rich" Christians were to be urged not to rely on the uncertainty of wealth (πλούτου) but to be πλουτεῖν ἐν ἔργοις καλοῖς "rich in good works" just like God who provides us "richly" (πλουσίως) with everything for enjoyment.

As seen in chapter 2, G-R benefactors and patrons provided various amenities to their clients for good necessary use and for both good and evil pleasure. For example, they built and sponsored the services of temples and operations of theatres for public use, where, people enjoyed various good activities, such as neutral sports. However, sometimes, they also enjoyed evil pastimes, such as watching Christians being mauled to death by wild animals or consumed by fire. Contrary to misuse, in 1 Timothy 3:17–19, the rich people in the church were required to emulate God in sharing their possessions with others in providing good and necessary help. By their active service for the benefit of others, they would be gratefully acknowledging the divine gifts of God (6:17). The attitude of being generous and their disposition to share (εὐμετάδοτος . . . κοινωνικός, which are complementary or synonymous virtues) would be seen in good deeds that are evidence of authentic faith.[408] By setting their hope in God, they would become good

---

407. Knight III, *Pastoral Epistles*, 274.
408. Towner, *Letters to Timothy*, 426.

benefactors. Additionally, putting their hope in God would depict them as loyal beneficiaries/clients of God. On the rich sharing their riches, Hanson is right when, citing Hasler, he says, "there is no suggestion that the rich should share their wealth because all Christians are brothers in Christ."[409] Paul implies that the rich should share because they are Christians who now rely on God, instead of uncertain wealth. Prominently in PE, Paul encourages good deeds for the benefit of all people, both Christians and outsiders (1 Tim 5:4, 8, 10; 6:2; Titus 3:8, 14). The rationale for the charge to share was in keeping with the divine principle of doing good deeds, that it is proper for people who profess reverence for God, 1 Timothy 2:10. As was required of the rich women in the church (5:16), so for the rich men too.

According to Sahlins, if they were to do good exclusively for the benefit of others, they would be benefactors or patrons of the noblest category, who put the interests of others first.[410] The good deeds would be the observable dimension of Christian existence, seen in extraordinary generosity and sharing,[411] giving without expecting anything in return. Nevertheless, Paul seems to suggest that they also would benefit from the good that they were urged to do. In 6:19, he says that by sharing riches with others, they would be storing up for themselves the treasure of a good foundation for the future, and that way they would take hold of the life that really is life. Thus, they would be patrons of the second category, where there was balanced reciprocity and mutual benefits.[412] The concept of sharing so that the giver may benefit the recipient as well as securing a good future for himself was also found in Judaism (Tobit 4:7–10). In the Greek world also, good deeds were seen as guarantee of a good life after death. In mythology, people who did good deeds were ushered into the Elysian Fields (a place or condition of perfect happiness) after death.[413] Therefore, in addition to benefitting others, thus bringing equality/balance in the community (2 Cor 8:13–15), the benefactors participated in good works to secure their future. That could

---

409. Hanson, *Pastoral Epistles*, 114.

410. Sahlins, *Stone Age Economics*, 191-96.

411. Towner, *Letters to Timothy*, 429.

412. Sahlins, *Stone Age Economics*, 191–196. See also Neyrey, "God," 469.

413. "Elysium," *Elysium (Greek Mythology): Britannica Online Encyclopedia: History & Society*, accessed 20 May 2011. http://www.britannica.com/EBchecked/topic/185418/Elysium. See also Towner, *Letters to Timothy*, 427 (citing Spicq, 577).

also have been Paul's thought as he wrote 6:19. The ὄντως ζωῆς "real/true life" that they would get is contrasted with the life that they were presently living (ἐν τῷ νῦν αἰῶνι, 6:17). That which they would get hold of would have both a present and an eternal future dimension, as stated earlier in 6:12 (cf. 4:8; 2 Tim 1:1, 10, eternal life through Christ). Therefore, Paul uses an ἵνα clause primarily to indicate purpose; to show what the rich would get if they used their riches to help the needy: ἵνα ἐπιλάβωνται τῆς ὄντως ζωῆς.

In addition to taking it as an outright purpose clause, it can also be viewed as expressing anticipated result, "that they might (or would) take hold of the life that really is life." In some ἵνα clauses it is not easy to distinguish the purpose from the result because ἵνα is also used to indicate the anticipated result that follows the action of the subject. Citing BD 391[5] Marshall states that in some cases, the ἵνα clause "is equivalent to an infinitive of result."[414] Complicating the situation further, in Jewish thought, purpose and result are sometimes identical. As Margaret Sim points out, in cases where we encounter ambiguity in the translation of the particle ἵνα, such as in a non-purpose usage, the context guides the reader to the right interpretation.[415] The ἵνα clause in 1 Timothy 6:19 presents such ambiguity because the wider context and the theological consistency of the epistle seem to negate interpreting the clause outrightly as expressing the fact that it is the good deed of sharing that would earn salvation for the rich. Elsewhere, Paul has indicated that good deeds do not merit salvation. Instead, eternal life is a result of God's grace and mercy (1:13b–14, 16). That theological thought is amplified in 2 Timothy 1:9 where he says that it is God "who saved us and called us with a holy calling, not according to our works but according to his own purpose and grace. This grace was given to us in Christ Jesus before the ages began." In 2 Timothy 3:15, he says that salvation comes through faith in Christ Jesus. It is the same case in Titus where in 2:14 he says that Christ redeems people from all iniquity and purifies them for himself and that way makes them zealous for good deeds. Therefore, following Paul's lead, we may argue that the sequence is that the believer expresses faith in Christ,

---

414. I. Howard Marshall, *The Epistles of John*, NICNT (Grand Rapids: Eerdmans, 1978), 114n.

415. Margaret Gavin Sim, "A Relevant Theoretic Approach to the Particle ἵνα in Koine Greek," (PhD diss., University of Edinburgh, 2006), 168.

God graciously shows him grace and mercy and gives him salvation, then he becomes zealous for good deeds that are guaranteed to earn him rewards in the real (eternal) eschatological life.

What Paul instructed Timothy to urge the rich to do was not a novel thing. As was the idea of helping widows, the concept of the rich helping the needy had its roots in the OT, as there was also an equivalent practice in the G-R world. As seen above, early church Christians believed that in the life after resurrection there would be physical enjoyment. For example, as BDAG says, Papias and Irenaeus were cited by Photius as having believed that the kingdom of heaven meant enjoyment of certain physical foods. Feasting was an integral pastime of the G-R *collegia* or voluntary associations where benefactors, their friends and the beneficiaries met to eat and enjoy together (cf. Matt 22:2–10; Mark 6:21; Luke 5:29; 14:12). Sometimes, rich people prepared banquets solely for the needy people (2 Macc 2:27). In the G-R systems, benefactors provided banquets for the benefit of the needy and thus guaranteed honour for themselves in life and in death. It is possible that Paul built on the same principle when he encouraged the rich to do good deeds and thus lay for themselves a good foundation for the future. Further still, he could also have been Christianizing the OT practice where rich Jews were commanded to help the poor fellow Israelites and even the aliens.

From the inception of the Israelite nation in the OT, concrete principles were laid down concerning: (1) Relief for the poor, as in the year of jubilee (Lev 25:10–54; 27:17–24; Num 36:4); (2) Kindness to them in material forms (Prov 14:21, 31; 19:17; 21:13; 22:9; 28:8, 27; 31:20); and (3) Payment of ransom for the poor to save them from enslavement (Exod 21:30; 30:12, 16; Job 6:22, 23; 33:23, 24; Isa. 43:3). Wealthy people paid ransom for the poor who could not pay for themselves. As seen in the discussion on Christ as benefactor and patron, the most precious thing that someone could give as ransom to benefit another person is his own life. Payment of ransom through material wealth or life was a form of benefaction that was recognized from the OT times to the NT times (Matt 20:28; Mark 10:45; 1 Tim 2:6). Following the example of Christ who gave himself freely as a ransom, Christians were exhorted to surpass non-Christians in righteousness in their kindness and generosity to the needy (cf. Luke 14:12–14; Matt 5:20). In the Jerusalem church, the rich were helping the needy communally mainly, through the officers of the church (cf. Acts 4:34–37). In reference to the Pauline churches, deSilva says that the congregations were encouraged to act as a collective network of friends who had all things in common.[416] Those who had possessions had to share with those who had nothing. In the same way, Paul urged the rich in PE church to help the needy.

Paul gave the reason for instructing Timothy to urge (παραγγέλλω, "order, command, instruct, direct") the rich to be generous and ready to share as that, by doing so they would be storing up for themselves the treasure of a good foundation for the future, "so that they may take hold of the life that really is life" (1 Tim 6:19). Another implicit reason is that it is possible some of the rich believers were stingy and unwilling to share with the needy. At the same time, in the G-R world, some of the rich people deliberately made the benefaction systems exploitative and suppressive, in order to increase economic inequality among people, for their own selfish ends.[417] Similarly, as was the case of the rich and the corrupt people in the OT (cf. Amos 8:4–7), the false teachers at Ephesus were exploiting people for their own benefit, instead of doing good for the benefit of others (Titus 1:11). Therefore, it is possible that Paul gave the instruction in 6:17–19 as an attempt to correct all those anomalies and salvage the original good purposes of the benefaction systems, now within the church system. He based Christian benefaction on the Christian factor of doing good as a fruit of Christian faith (1 Tim 6:12; 2 Tim 2:22; Titus 2:2), and with the eschatological future in view.

3.5 Conclusion

Contrary to the general opinion, especially in the West, that Greek εὐεργεσία and Roman *patronicium* were generally evil systems, especially *patronicium*, it is correct to conclude that in the first century AD they still contained considerable goodness. Saller rightly observes that, during the Republic, "patron-client relations, far from being thought as evil, were reinforced by law and

---

416. deSilva, "Patronage," 770.
417. Silke Sitzler, "BMCR 2009.03.50, Susan R. Holman, Wealth and Poverty in Early Church," review of *Wealth and Poverty in Early Church: Holy Cross Studies in Patristic Theology and History*, by Susan R. Holman. *Bryn Mawr Classical Reviews* BMCR 2009.03.50 (March 2009), accessed 8 October 2018, http://www.bmcreview.org/2009/03/20090350.html.

religious mores."⁴¹⁸ In the early Imperial era, from Augustus' time, although imperial patronage was used to secure and retain power by the emperor, it was mainly used to secure socio-political cohesion and economic progress in the entire empire, especially through the mediation of the senators and the provincial governors.⁴¹⁹ Therefore, as attested in PE and other NT records, the benefaction systems still retained some of their original goodness and therefore served the communities fairly well. The ancient communities had inaugurated them with the noble objective of helping people to live with one another in a communally supportive way. However, as in any other social system where distribution of resources and powers is involved, those systems also were prone to abuse. It happened that *patronicium* was abused more than εὐεργεσία and kinship benefaction, just as Caragounis observes,

> Roman patronage, according to Dionysios Hal. and Ploutarchos, had its origin in the legislation of Romulus, which attached the poor Romans to the rich Romans. This institution in time deteriorated and the clients were often reduced to abject dependence on their Patronus. This is exemplified by the Roman ἀνδράποδα Martial and Juvenal, who had abjectly surrendered their freedom for a "loaf of bread."⁴²⁰

As attested in the writings of the second-century Greek rhetorician and satirist, Loukianos of Samosata (AD 120–180), due to the abuses in Roman *patronicium*, the Greek communities especially in the Eastern Empire did not accept it readily and practise it much. He viewed it as a despicable institution.⁴²¹ Instead, Greeks preferred εὐεργεσία, which was more amicable and egalitarian. Nevertheless, as seen in chapter 2 of this book, it does not mean that Greeks did not practise *patronicium* at all.

---

418. Saller, *Personal Patronage*, 5.

419. Saller, 42–78.

420. Chrys C. Caragounis, "St. Paul and Corinth: A House Church in Corinth? An Inquiry into the Structure of Early Corinthian Christianity." (Lecture presented at the Corinth Congress. University of Corinth, 2007, 23–25 September), 5.

421. Lucian, *Nigrinus: Lucian to Nigrinus. Health*, trans. H. W. Fowler and F. G. Fowler (Oxford: Clarendon, 1905), 21; Online ed. "Nigrinus," *The Works of Lucian of Samosata I* (Chapel Hill, NC; Project Gutenberg: University of North Carolina, 2006) http://www.sacred-texts.com/cla/luc/wl1/wl109.htm.

Despite the abuses, *patronicium* was not entirely corrupt and some Greeks adopted and practised it. For example, the inscription on the base carrying the statues of three magistrates, situated on the Sacred Way near the temple of Apollo in Lydia (Asia Minor), the language used in it demonstrates the impact of the Roman patron-client phenomenon there. In the inscription, the transliteration of the Latin term, *patronus*, is used instead of the Greek equivalent, εὐεργέτης. The inscription reads:

ὁ δῆμος	The people
Μάνιον Οὐαλέριον	(honour) Manius Valerius
Μεσσάλαν Ποτῖτον	Messala Potitus,
Ταμίαν ἀρετῆς ἕνε-	quaestor, on account of his virtue
κα καὶ πάτρωνα ὄντα τῆ[ς]	and [for] being a patron
πόλεως	of the city.[422]

Comparable to the Greeks in their preference of εὐεργεσία, Jews preferred kinship benefaction, which was mainly mutual and egalitarian. However, they also adopted (but with caution) some practices of Roman *patronicium*. As indicated by Seneca in *De Beneficiis* and by other authors around the first century AD, *patronicium* and εὐεργεσία had bad characteristics that needed to be corrected or discarded and good ones that needed to be cultivated and upheld (similarly so Jewish kinship benefaction). Therefore, the conclusive argument in this chapter is that Paul upheld the good aspects of both the benefaction and patronage systems and opposed the bad ones. As seen in the chapter, his response to the systems is demonstrated in his expressions in the epistles. He did not condemn the systems wholesale nor support them indiscriminately, as various scholars respectively accuse him of doing. In the study, we have examined Paul's prominent presentation of God the Father as the only God and "saviour of all people" and assessed it as a two-pronged polemic, against the monotheistic but exclusivist false teachers and the polytheists. What we have observed is that by presenting him as the provider of life and all things (material and nonmaterial), Paul made the point that God is the unrivalled benefactor of all time. Most significantly, he presented

---

422. T. W. Hillard, "Roman Patronal Practice in the Greek East," in *New Documents Illustrating Early Christianity 9, A Review of the Greek Inscriptions and Papyri Published in 1986-87*, ed. S. R. Llewelyn (Macquarie University, NSW: Ancient History Documentary Research Centre, 2002), 17.

God the Father and Christ as the givers of the greatest nonmaterial gift of spiritual salvation. Contrary to Crossan's view that Jesus was neither broker nor mediator,[423] we have deduced that, in addition to presenting him as a primary benefactor (as "saviour" and "Lord" who showed him mercy, saved him and appointed him to his service), Paul also presents him as the only mediator (second-level patron) between God (the supreme patron) and humans. He presents God as the noblest benefactor and perfect patron and Christ as the most self-giving mediator-benefactor/patron of all time. He also presents the Holy Spirit as an active agent in the facilitation and preservation of the gospel and in effecting salvation to people (2 Tim 1:14; Titus 3:5), thus depicting him as an integral player in the supreme divine benefaction. He thus implicitly presents benefaction as the most significant interaction between all members of the Godhead and humans.

In his writing, Paul has depicted himself as a chief and exemplary beneficiary of God's overall gift of salvation. As a loyal client, he expressed his gratitude and ascribed eternal glory to God as a fitting response that was expected of all beneficiaries. As a faithful beneficiary, he encouraged fellow beneficiaries to be loyal clients to their supreme patron (God). Unlike the false teachers, he encouraged them to receive with gratitude what he gave to them for livelihood and enjoyment. At the same time, Paul also presented himself as a second-level benefactor or patron who responded appropriately to God the primary benefactor/patron and to his (Paul's) second-level beneficiaries/clients. To the faithful ones, such as his primary recipients (Timothy and Titus) he acknowledged their loyalty, thanked them, commended them and continued to give more support to them in form of guidance in personal life, church leadership and evangelistic ministry. However, for the adversarial false teachers, who were disloyal and apostate beneficiaries/clients, he did not hesitate to snub and reprimand them.

Without pressing the point too hard, it is evident in the text that Paul adopted the good principles of the three systems and utilized them as he encouraged benefaction in the church. Similarly, he confronted the abuses of the systems and discouraged the church from practicing them, such as not doing good for personal gain, abusing or failing utilize well and to share

---

423. Crossan, *Historical Jesus*, 422.

what God has graciously given for livelihood and enjoyment. Understanding his wise interaction with their ideologies is particularly helpful for the Africa Inland Church (AIC) and other African churches that confess reliance on PE as their key guide, especially for church administration.

CHAPTER 4

Influences of African Benefaction and Patronage on Africa Inland Church Leadership

4.1 Introduction

In the plethora of social interrelationship systems throughout history in Africa and the whole world, economic ventures and leadership have remained among the most essential and outstanding. Similar to all other human systems, all types of economic and leadership enterprises have positive and negative features in diverse degrees of intensity. As seen in the introduction in chapter 1, the various social systems are essentially and intricately interconnected. They therefore influence each other in significant and unavoidable ways, such as borrowing from each other and sharing each other's positive features, and, regrettably, the negative features too.

The main interest of the discussion in this chapter is to assess the impact of the positive and the negative values of African benefaction and patronage on the appointment and ministry of church leaders in Africa Inland Church, especially in Ūkamba.[1] The founding mission guided the church from its

---

1. A similar situation may be found in other church denominations also in Ūkamba and elsewhere in Kenya, Africa, and the larger world. From here onwards in this chapter, Africa Inland Church is referred to as AIC. As seen in the introduction in chapter 1, AIC is a dominant church in Kenya, Tanzania, eastern Democratic Republic of Congo, and South Sudan. It is also found in Uganda, Rwanda, and Burundi. It was founded originally among the Akamba of eastern Kenya by missionaries of Africa Inland Mission (AIM) in 1895 and became the most dominant church in Ūkamba. From there it spread into other regions of Kenya and the other East African countries. Currently, the Akamba (plural term whose

inception to base its leadership philosophy, its economic ventures, and all other spiritual endeavours on biblical principles, especially as laid out in the Pastoral Epistles.[2] AIC acknowledges full dependence on the Bible for guidance in general administration of the church, in the appointment of leaders, and for instruction on the acquisition and use of material wealth.

The Akamba community in which AIC was originally founded has had its own cultural values of administration in which leadership is closely connected with benefaction and patronage.[3] We therefore discuss the church leadership values laid out especially in 1 Timothy 3:1–13; 5:17–18 and Titus 1:5–9 in juxtaposition with the traditional and modern Akamba cultural principles of benefaction, patronage and leadership. The rationale for doing this comparative study is that, as a member of AIC, I am concerned about the views of some church members, leaders and scholars on the relationship between material patronage and church leadership. The main purpose of the discussion is therefore to provide an objective view on how to link the traditional and the modern Akamba values of benefaction, patronage and leadership with church leadership. Another crucial fact to note from the start of this discussion is that, many Africans, including the Akamba, generally regard their leaders as their exclusive benefactors and patrons.[4] It is also important to note, as Kwenda points out, that in many traditional cultural settings, the rhythms of honourable giving and receiving dictate

---

singular is Mūkamba) are the fifth largest tribe in Kenya. Kĩkamba is their language. Ũkamba is the general region where the Akamba live. Kĩkamba orthography has two unique vowels, ĩ (its capital is Ĩ) and ũ (capital Ũ). Ĩ is pronounced as the i in "hill" and ũ is pronounced as the double o in "look."

2. AIC Central Church Council, *Africa Inland Church Constitution*, (Kijabe, Kenya: AIC Kijabe Printing Press, 1981), 30. See Article IV titled MEMBERSHIP, Section 3 on Officers, Subsections (a) Deacons, (b) Elders, and (d) Ordained Ministers, Sub-subsection 1).

3. As seen especially in chapter 2 of this writing, there are significant differences between the technical meanings of benefaction (εὐεργεσία) and patronage (*patronicium*). Nevertheless, although patronage is the term that suits best the social exchange relationships in Africa, in this discourse the two terms are in some instances used interchangeably in general reference to material and nonmaterial benefaction among the Akamba.

4. See John S. Mbiti, *African Religions & Philosophy* (New York: Praeger, 1969), 182, where Mbiti says that leaders are regarded as God's viceroys and given elevated titles such as "saviour" and "protector," and others; titles that are reserved for benefactors and patrons.

good relationships and interconnection between people, as well as between people and the rest of nature.[5]

The information in this chapter was gathered mainly from AIC respondents, both leaders and lay members of the church. Nevertheless, some significant information was also gained from interviewees who are not necessarily Christian or AIC adherents. The non-AIC interviewees consisted of both retired and serving church leaders of various levels, and lay church members, retired and currently active civic and political leaders, such as location chiefs and county representatives, and a former member of the national assembly who is currently the county governor of Makũenĩ, and lay people from all counties in Ũkamba. Moreover, some of the respondents were drawn from Nairobi and Mombasa cities, where there is a considerable population of the Akamba.[6]

Carefully picked from among many others, in this chapter we discuss only three leadership qualifications that are viewed as having key significance in the discourse on the relationship between patronage and leadership. The qualifications discussed are: faith and moral character of church leaders, their management skill, and their economic status. They are listed here in a descending order, starting from the most prominent to the least prominent, according to my assessment of their importance in church leadership. My special listing is done in counter relation to a prominent unwritten code that is followed by a segment of the secular Akamba community, and some AIC leaders and lay believers, in which the economic proficiency of the leader is prioritized.

4.2 Faith and Moral Character of Church Leaders

Long before the arrival of European and Arab traders, missionaries, settlers, and colonizers to Africa in the fifteenth and nineteenth centuries AD, indigenous Africans were living in well-defined communities, with organized

---

5. Chirevo V. Kwenda, "Beyond Patronage: Giving and Receiving in the Construction of Civil Society," *JTSA* 101 (July 1998): 5.

6. Nairobi is the capital city of Kenya, whereas Mombasa in the main coastal city of the country.

socio-economic, political and religious structures.[7] In regard to religion, they knew about, believed in, and worshipped the Supreme Being (also called the High God) and maintained communion with the ancestors[8] led by community elders.[9] In those communities, the ancestors (the living dead),[10] were acknowledged as the actual leaders and benefactors of the communities because in life they had been the founders, kings and heroes of the communities.[11] The High God, the ancestral spirits and the other spirits were mainly seen as doers of beneficent works to the communities.[12] The ancestors in particular were seen as patrons who provided healing, protection, guidance, rain, and every conceivable blessing, such as provision of wives, knowledge

---

7. For example, see Roland Oliver and Michael Crowder, eds., *The Cambridge Encyclopedia of Africa* (Cambridge; New York: Cambridge University Press, 1981), 125–130 about chiefdoms and Kingdoms in East Africa from 1000–1820. See also Mbiti, *African Religions & Philosophy*, 45–47, 100–101, on societies that have lived in units or clusters and traditionally have had kings, chiefs and other key social leaders.

8. Jomo Kenyatta, *Facing Mount Kenya* (Nairobi: Heinemann Kenya, 1978), 232. The ancestors were and still are regarded by many Africans as the spirits of their dead progenitors, their leaders, and other great people of the community.

9. Although I have used the words "knew," "believed," "worshipped" and "maintained" in the past tense, these realities and others that he has referred to in this article are also existent in the present time because there still are traditional values operating in the African setting. There is an interplay of the ancient and the modern values in people's perspectives of God, such as in worship (cf. Tokunboh Adeyemo, *Salvation in African Tradition* [Nairobi: Evangel, 1979], 33), and in socio-economic transactions among the Akamba. Such fusions are, for example, seen in reliance on modern techniques of trade acquired through formal education, together with reliance on traditional ways of acquiring wealth using magic. See E. Bolaji Idowu, *African Traditional Religion: A Definition* (London: SCM, 1982), 189. See also Matthews Kalola Mwalw'a, "The Power of Witchcraft among Kenyan Akamba," (thesis, Nairobi Evangelical Graduate School of Theology, June 2001), 96.

10. The so-called "living dead" were believed to be the spirits of significant people who had died physically but whose spirits were still hovering around and were involved in the affairs of the living people, as long as they were remembered by the living people. In *African Religions & Philosophy*, 83, Mbiti says that they are the spirits of the departed of up to five generations, who have not yet completed their dying process and are still considered as belonging to the *Sasa* (present) period. In the OT, for example in Deut 18:11; Isa 8:19 and 19:3, these beings are described as ghosts, spirits, familiar spirits or simply as the dead. In the Akamba setting, it is difficult to know whether they are really spirits of dead people or the fallen spirits, demons. Nevertheless, regardless of what they are, God forbids people from consulting them (Deut 18:11–12; Isa 8:19–22). For more details see also Richard J. Gehman, *Who Are the Living Dead? A Theology of Death, Life after Death and the Living Dead* (Nairobi: Evangel Publishing House, 1999).

11. Richard Gehman, *African Traditional Religion in Biblical Perspective* (Nairobi: East African Educational Publishers, 2005), 219.

12. Kenyatta, *Facing Mount Kenya*, 231.

and success in battle, and other blessings, particularly to their offspring.[13] In some communities, it was considered impossible, taboo, and dishonourable to approach the Supreme Being and the other spirit beings directly. Hence, through the traditional medicine-man,[14] seers, other spiritual specialists and the community leaders, the ancestors were also acknowledged and made use of as effective and indispensable mediators[15] between the living humans and the spirit world.

Concerning the provision of leaders for the community, it was believed that it was the Supreme Being and the ancestors who directly identified, appointed and endowed people with the necessary resources for leadership.[16] Hence, leaders were regarded as representatives of the supernatural beings. An alternative method of appointing leaders was by consulting the spirits through traditional seers and medicine-man for guidance.[17] As appointees and representatives of the supernatural beings on earth, the leaders depended fully on them for prosperity in their personal lives and the welfare of the communities. A section of a song which was sang in praise of one famous Akamba leader who was fighting against the colonizers who were taking land by force from the Akamba states, "Na Masamba wanengiwe ũnene nĩ Ngai ũsũvĩe mũthanga. Ĩĩaĩ Masamba ndatonyeka." Its translation is, "And Masamba,[18] you were given authority by God to protect the soil (Akamba

---

13. Gehman, *African Traditional Religion*, 237–238.

14. Commonly known as witchdoctors.

15. Mbiti, *African Religions & Philosophy*, 68–71, 162–163. See also Gehman, *African Traditional Religion*, 238–240.

16. In *African Religions & Philosophy*, 182, Mbiti says that the offices of king, queen and other rulers are regarded as having been instituted by God in the Zamani (ancient) period. Therefore traditional rulers are not regarded as ordinary men and women, but as people who occupy a special office and symbolize the link between God and man.

17. This view concurs with Mbiti's view in *African Religions & Philosophy*, 182, that in communities that had the office of king, it was believed that the office was instituted by God in the ancient times. Thus, there always was very close connection between the leaders and the mystical world. The leaders of the community were regarded not simply as political heads, but as mystical and religious heads of the community. They were seen not as ordinary men and women but as special links between God and humans. Because of their outstanding spiritual and physical endowments, the overall leaders were given elevated titles such as, "saviour," "protector," "child of God," "chief of the divinities," and "lord of earth and life."

18. Masamba was the leader's nickname. His real name was Paul Ngei. The nickname "Masamba" has two possible meanings: (1) It is a transliteration of the Swahili plural word, "Mashamba" which means "agricultural fields," based on the fact that Ngei was fighting to recover land from the colonial powers. (2) It is the immensity (not numerical) plural of

land). Indeed Masamba cannot be defeated." In earlier days, African leaders were regarded as having inherent mystical powers. Therefore, their followers acknowledged their authority fully.[19] They feared and honoured them. To this day, many of the old people, and some of the young, still venerate anyone who exhibits possession of mystical powers. Some of the ancient renowned Akamba leaders who had supernatural gifts and are now considered ancestors of the community are Syokīmaū (a prophetess), Mwatū wa Ngoma (a prophet), Kīvoi and Masakū (traditional community chiefs).

Many other Kenyan communities, such as the Kikuyu, Luo, Luhya, Kalenjin, Maasai, Giriama, and others, also had their mystically-endowed leaders.[20] Some of them, for example Lenana of the Maasai, were even regarded as lord (equivalent to god). He was seen as lord among all the clans of the Maasai due to his supernatural endowment as an invincible warrior who protected their rights.[21] Open communion with the Supreme Being and with the ancestors resulted in most of those leaders being viewed and esteemed as the spiritual and political leaders of their communities. Most were endowed with magical powers to fight and ward off evil powers that were against the society, to lead people in worship of the High God and in communion with the ancestors, and to bring holistic prosperity to the community. Thus, the leaders were regarded as the guardians and providers for their communities.

As protectors of the societies' moral values, the leaders were expected to have exceptional moral uprightness. No immorality or other misdemeanour was tolerated in any of them. For example, no man known to have questionable relationships with other people's wives or with unmarried women

---

"nzamba," that is, a massive and powerful mature "male chicken." The nickname highlighted Ngei's bravery, indicating that he was considered a hero.

19. D. N. Kimilu, *Mūkamba wa W'o* (Nairobi: Kenya Literature Bureau, 1962), 54.

20. See Geoffrey Parrinder, *African Traditional Religion* (Harts, UK: Mayflower Press, 1954), 67, exerpts of the book, including page 67 "VI Divine Rulers" (pages 67–78), accessed 8 October 2018, https://www.questia.com/read/59595010/african-traditional-religion. In the social hierarchy, rulers were sometimes regarded with awe as sons of the gods.

21. Ned, "What's Happ'ning in Maasailand Ngorongoro," *Endulen Maasai Diary* 23, no. 5 (May 2008), accessed 9 April 2009. http://nedmarch.googlepages.com/diarydecember20052.

was appointed as leader.[22] A woman of such questionable character was considered a prostitute and therefore not honoured in the society.[23] Kamende explains that the idiom that says, "Atumĩĩte asũnzũmele" (translated as, "He/She has grown old squatting," which is still used today) was used to describe any elderly person who behaved immaturely, especially in moral matters. For example, if a man was proved as responsible for the illegitimate pregnancy of an unmarried woman, he was totally despised and fined. He was regarded and treated in the same manner as a man or woman who was harming the society through witchcraft.[24] If such an immoral person was a leader already, he or she was removed from leadership[25] or demoted to a lower status.[26] Mũindũ says that, in Mbiũnĩ area, in addition to development consciousness and other leadership capabilities and experience, integrity in all spheres of life is a primary requirement for a community leader.[27] Nevertheless, in some Akamba communities, a man having multiple sexual relationships, even with young girls, was (and still in some communitites is) considered as not morally evil. In fact, it was considered manly, and was condoned,[28] and even encouraged and praised.

---

22. There was an exception for kings in moral uprightness in regard to sexual purity in some African communities. As Mbiti says in *African Religions & Philosophy*, 183, in those communities people considered kings to be holy "mainly in ritual rather than spiritual sense." They therefore allowed the kings to have sexual rights over other people's wives; an act that was not viewed as immoral. Similarly, on page 147, he says that in some communities, people of the same age group were allowed to have sexual relationship with each other's spouses in particular circumstances. In *Mũkamba wa W'o*, 49, Kimilu says that among the Akamba, although sexual contact between young men and women before marriage was sanctioned, it was controlled by the community, and was not viewed as immoral.

23. Paul Nzile Mũngũti, (ex-senior chief, Mboonĩ Location, Mboonĩ West District, Makũenĩ County, Eastern Province; now late), interviewed in 2009. See also Joel Ndolo, (chief of Kyũũ Location, Mboonĩ West District), interviewed in 2009. For interviews with the author in this chapter see appendix B.

24. Benjamin Ndaita Kamende, (Manager, AIC Mboonĩ Children's Home; pastor, AIC Doonholm, Nairobi), interviewed in 2009. Kamende adds that, a witch was loathed although he was feared for his harmful powers.

25. Paul Mũngũti, interview in 2009. Mũngũti's view is also validated in Mbiti's words in *African Religions & Philosophy*, 185, that there were various taboos for rulers. Failure to observe them might disqualify them from office.

26. Joel Ndolo, interview in 2009.

27. Christopher Kĩlonzo Mũindũ, (Councillor until 2012, Mbiũnĩ ward, Mwala constituency, Machakos County), interviewed in 2009.

28. Prof. Kĩvũtha Kibwana, (County Governor of Makũenĩ County), interviewed in 2012. He provided an example of a prominent former political leader in Ũkamba (now late

On social behaviour also, although excessive use of intoxicating drink was highly discouraged for leaders because it could hamper proper execution of leadership duties,[29] moderate use of local alcoholic drinks was permitted. Excessive use could also lower the leaders' dignity. Use of tobacco (especially the fine-ground dark-brown powder inhaled through the nose) was very common and accepted. Nevertheless, the use of other drugs, such as marijuana, was forbidden for it was viewed as destructive.

On speech, although vulgar jokes and insults were allowed among young people, such utterances were taboo and regarded as gross misdemeanour among the elderly, more so the leaders.[30] Mūnyao gave an example of people who insulted him intensely during his political campaigns in 2007 as he was vying for the Upper Mboonī civic ward. However, he says that they came eventually to ask for forgiveness from him when they realized that he was a man of integrity and they were wrong.[31] Although in ancient times among Akamba communities there were no written codes to guide the character and the functions of the leaders, the mores and duties were so entrenched in the psyche of the communities that they were known by every member from very early in life. Kibwana says that it is only the current national constitution that specifically upholds integrity in political leaders, although those who are used to decadence do not readily accept its stipulations.[32] On church leadership, Mūtūnga says that members of the church sometimes do not consider as essential the moral integrity of the people they appoint as leaders.[33]

The requirement for faith and moral values that were expected of the Akamba leaders differ significantly from those expressed in 1 Timothy 3. However, there are similarities. For example, people were aware of the

---

and name withheld) who was notorious for sexual immorality.

29. Francis Kīoko Ngosi (a groceries kiosk keeper) and Joseph Maīthya, (an employee of a secular firm), interviews with author in 2009.

30. Kimilu, *Mūkamba wa W'o*, 43–44.

31. Anthony Mūle Mūnyao, (Councillor until 2012, Upper Mboonī ward, Mboonī Constituency, Makūenī County), interviewed in 2009.

32. Kīvūtha Kibwana, interview in 2012.

33. Dr Joseph Mūtūnga, (Chairman, Makūenī RCC; Principal of AIC Wote Bible Institute in 2012), interviewed in 2012. His view is that, in some cases, the faith and moral status of the prospective leader is given "fifty-fifty" (partial) consideration.

powerful presence and beneficent deeds of the Supreme Being and the ancestors in the community.[34] Therefore, the good behaviour that was required of the leaders was in reference to both the ancestors and the Supreme Being because of their power and benefaction to the community. One negative reality is that, on many occasions, among the Akamba, acknowledgement of and reverence to the ancestors overshadowed reverence to the Supreme Being.[35] For example, most of the prayers, libations, and sacrifices which were offered during supplications and thanksgiving were dedicated to the ancestors of the tribe instead of the Supreme Being. Similar to the Kikuyu, they were given to the Supreme Being only on major occasions of tribal importance.[36] God was not much in the picture.

In antiquity, the good moral standing of the leaders was first of all required for the benefit of the leader himself, second, for the benefit of his immediate family, third, for the benefit of the larger community, and, finally, for the ancestors. Concerning benefitting the leader himself, the good character was aimed at earning good reputation and high position for himself in the community. The leader's good moral standing also saved him from punishment in the present life by the ancestors and by the community for doing wrong.[37] It was also considered as guarantee for a position of honour after life, in the ancestral world.[38] Concerning benefit to the leader's family and the larger community, there is a Kĩkamba proverb that states that "the hind hoof lands exactly where the front hoof has landed."[39] It means that a person usually emulates the character of those who are ahead of him in age and experience. The leader's good character provided good example for his household and earned the family good reputation in the community. About

---

34. Malcolm James McVeigh, "The Interaction of the Conceptions of God of African Traditional Religion and Christianity in the Thought of Edwin W. Smith," (PhD. diss., Boston University Graduate School, 1971), 55.

35. This differs from what Mbiti, *African Religions & Philosophy*, 58, says on sacrifices and offerings to God as form of worship in Africa. He says that although the recipients of these sacrifices are spirits or the living-dead, the ultimate recipient is God, "whether or not the worshippers are aware of that." However, on page 83–84 he also says that men approach the living-dead "more often" for minor needs of life than they approach God.

36. Kenyatta, *Facing Mount Kenya*, 233.

37. Mbiti, *African Religions & Philosophy*, 210.

38. Gehman, *African Traditional Religion*, 235.

39. Mũtĩsya, *Kĩkamba Proverbs and Idioms*, 29.

benefitting the larger community, the leader's character was expected both to attract blessings from the Supreme Being and the ancestors.[40] It also earned and maintained good reputation for the community.

Compared to the orientation of Akamba lay people's and community leaders' religious inclination and moral behaviour that were mainly human-oriented, the Christian faith and moral behaviour of believers were more God-oriented (1 Tim 3:5, 15; 2 Tim 2:14, 15). Although Akamba morality and devotion to the Supreme Being and to the ancestors was partly due to positive respect for the supernatural powers, a large portion of it resulted from the negative fear that they had, and still have, for those powers.[41] They feared punishment from God and the ancestors for failure to honour and obey them and the appointed leaders, and for failure to treat the other members of the society well.[42] As it was with the sacrifices, the moral character of the Akamba, more so the leader, was mainly people-oriented.

As it stands today, strong traces of maintaining good character for fear of punishment and for gaining respect from people in this life still are dominant inclinations of Akamba leaders and lay people. In 1 Timothy 3:13 and 5:17, Paul states that respect comes to leaders because of their behaviour and hard work, as he says, βαθμὸν ἑαυτοῖς καλὸν περιποιοῦνται, "they obtain good standing for themselves," and διπλῆς τιμῆς ἀξιούσθωσαν, "let them be considered as worthy of double honour." Nevertheless, gaining honour is not the only motivation. Acquiring and maintaining good character and doing good works first of all for pleasing and glorifying God and for benefitting others are what Paul emphasized, as stated in 1 Timothy 1:16–19a; 2:3; 5:4; 2 Timothy 2:15; Titus 2:5, 10; 2:11–13; and 3:8. For example, in 1 Timothy 2:3, the good work of praying for all people, including all in authority, is described as, τοῦτο καλὸν καὶ ἀπόδεκτον ἐνώπιον τοῦ σωτῆρος ἡμῶν θεοῦ, "this is right and is acceptable in the sight of God our Savior." In 1 Timothy 4:16, Paul exhorts Timothy to maintain good behaviour and good teaching

---

40. In *African Religions & Philosophy*, 183, Mbiti says that rulers "play the role of priest, rainmaker, intermediary, diviner or mediator between men and God."

41. In *African Traditional Religion*, 151, Gehman tells of a Mūkamba medicine-man who became sick with the same disease that he had cured a certain woman of because he had overcharged her. Punishment by the ancestral spirits forced him to return the goat that he had received from her. He also sacrificed another goat to appease the spirits.

42. Mbiti, *African Religions & Philosophy*, 210.

for that would result in his own salvation and the salvation of his hearers.[43] Thus, the traditional Akamba rationale for good moral character and commitment in ordinary life and in leadership was, and still is, significantly different from the Christian faith and moral character both for the church leaders and lay Christians as laid out in PE. Dedication, gratitude, honour and glory were given to the only God in accordance with what was expected of loyal members of the household of God. Thus, the moral character of the Christian leader and his leadership activities were based on faith in God and oriented towards reverence to him, and for the benefit of his people.

Maina says that many Africans (including Akamba) have the tendency of elevating their leaders to the extent that if the leaders do wrong, everybody in the community is highly disappointed[44] because their collective identity and dignity have been affected. In traditional African communities, high moral character is not demanded of the leaders primarily because it pleases God but because it pleases the community. In keeping with the ancient Akamba culture, since the inception of AIC, there sometimes has been demand for adherence to the collective community's ethos more than honour and obedience to God.[45] In the early church, maturity in faith and good character were required for pleasing God (2 Tim 2:4), for avoidance of falling into the snare and condemnation of the devil (1 Tim 3:6, 7) and for setting a good example before other people (1 Tim 4:12, 16; cf. 2 Tim 2:2). Blamelessness in the church leaders was required, first, for bringing glory to God and earning good reputation among outsiders as 1 Timothy 3:7 says, δεῖ δὲ καὶ μαρτυρίαν καλὴν ἔχειν ἀπὸ τῶν ἔξωθεν, "And he also must have a good testimony from (or among) those who are outside." Together with hard work, maturity in faith and good character were also viewed as ways of earning the leader rewards from God in the present life and in the

---

43. The meaning of "salvation" in this verse is better understood as "spiritual wellbeing." It may also have an "eschatological" nuance because in G-R patronage good ethical behaviour and good works were understood as prime means of meriting salvation in this life and the afterlife.

44. Steve Maina, "When Pastors Fall," *The Church Leader in Africa: A Training Publication of Africa Ministry Resources* 16, no. 1 (January-March 2006): 4.

45. As Mbiti says in *African Religions & Philosophy*, 274, as long as "people [Christians and non-Christians] appreciate and even idolize the traditional present and past," the priority that is given to traditional values above Christian values "will continue to enjoy a comfortable and privileged place in the emotions of African [read Akamba] peoples."

future. The leader's blamelessness was also required for helping the church to mature and to have good reputation in the communities in which it stood as a beacon of truth (1 Tim 3:7, 15; cf. Eph 4:11–13; Matt 5:16; Acts 9:31). Similarly, the leader's blamelessness was regarded as both an indication of present salvation and a catalyst of spiritual and eschatological salvation both for himself and for his observers and hearers (1 Tim 4:12, 16).

All the AIC leaders and members whom I interviewed held the opinion that faith and moral integrity of the Christian leader should be the leading qualifications to be considered. Mũnywokĩ says that maturity of faith, seen in moral character, should the most important requirements in the Christian leader; whereas, in a pastor, effectiveness in preaching should also be prioritized.[46] Peninnah considers salvation, integrity, and training as the most important qualifications for a leader.[47] On whether integrity is upheld during elections, Mũtĩsya says that sometimes it is ignored because of the prioritized social and economic influence of the person in the community.[48] Mbuti's view is that, at the Coast, moral integrity is largely ignored and church elections are not different from political elections.[49] Mũlwa's observation is that, in Nairobi, on most occasions, especially from District Church Council (DCC) to Central Church Council (CCC) elections, instead of faith and moral integrity being given priority, people mainly are more interested in whether the prospective leader comes from their locality in Ũkamba, which Bible school he graduated from, and how economically stable he is.[50] He says that, in Local Church Council (LCC) elections, things are somehow

---

46. Samuel Mũnywokĩ, (Assistant Bishop, AIC Kĩtui Area Church Council, Kĩtui County), interviewed in 2012.

47. Peninnah Kĩvũnzi, (Kĩtui County, wife of former AIC bishop, Titus Kĩvũnzi, and a long-time women leader in AIC, PhD Biblical Studies candidate at AIU), interviewed in 2009.

48. Joyfred Peter Mũtĩsya, (lecturer, Kenyatta University, Kĩtui campus; pastor, AIC Mũtonguni DCC, Kĩtui Area Church Council), interviewed in 2009.

49. John Mbuti, (Former Bishop, AIC Coast Area Church Council), interviewed in 2012. (Note: Mbuti is a Mũkamba. Similarly, the majority of AIC ministers and church members at the Coast are Akamba. Therefore their views are as valid as those of interviewees in Ũkamba.)

50. Abraham Mũlwa, (Bishop, AIC Nairobi Area Church Council), interviewed in 2012. (Note: Mũlwa is a Mũkamba. Similarly, the majority of AIC ministers and church members in Nairobi are Akamba. Therefore, their views are as valid as those of interviewees in Ũkamba.)

different in that, people consider the moral integrity of the person more carefully. On the same matter, Mũema says that in Mboonĩ the faith and moral integrity of the leader are not given priority, but instead, pastors campaign, bribe, and even some consult evil spirits to gain influence over people to vote for them.[51] Nguyo also says that, in many areas in Machakos, political considerations are prioritized above faith and moral status of the prospective leader.[52]

Over time, inevitable developments have occurred and altered the traditional values of the Akamba on faith and moral character in regard to leadership, benefaction and patronage. Some of the changes have occurred inherently. However, most of them are a result of influences by the values of other societies.[53] For example, the high morality of leaders in ancient times that mainly sprang from their acknowledgement, fear of and reverence to the appointing Supreme Being and the ancestors has largely disappeared. With the inception of modern and post-modern values in Africa, such as through secular education, where there is emphasis on secular values against spiritual ones, being morally upright and doing good in reference to supernatural standards have been relegated to the periphery. Spiritual morality has been replaced by immorality and mere humanistic goodness that is motivated by external forces, such as the law and pleasing people. Due to the breakdown of the Akamba society and disregard of spiritual values, many people do good mainly for self-benefit. This attitude has strong influences on leadership in AIC. From the inception of the Christian church to the present, exceptional faith, character, and spiritual endowments are required of overseers, deacons, and the women leaders in the church. According to 1 Timothy 3:1–13 and Titus 1:5–9, church leaders are outstanding benefactors in the church and in the larger society as they exemplify and inspire faith and godly character in the church and the larger society. These values are beneficial to the entire church now and have eternal benefit (1 Tim 4:12, 16).

---

51. Samuel Mũthama Mũema, (Chaplain, Mboonĩ Boys High School; Lecturer, AIC Mboonĩ Bible Institute), interviewed in 2009.

52. Bernard Nguyo, (Bishop, AIC Machakos Area Church Council, Machakos County), interviewed in 2012.

53. See Mbiti, *African Religions & Philosophy*, 271–275, and Kimilu, *Mũkamba wa W'o*, vii–viii, for changing values among the Akamba and other African people groups due to influences of modernity.

4.3 Management Skill

In this section, the management skill is viewed in the sense that "management" entails care, protection and provision for those under one's jurisdiction. It is helpful at this early stage to know that in many traditional African communities, leaders had large households that consisted of several wives, numerous children (preferably sons), other relatives, servants, and various other dependents. Community leaders helped all sorts of people. Some of those people were under the direct authority of the leader while others were not. The people who were under the closest direct management and benefaction of the leader were the wife (or wives) and the children. Next were the other relatives, household servants, and the other people under his civic jurisdiction. Finally, there were others, such as the normal visitors and friends, who were neither relatives or servants; these were not under his authority.

The more members a person had under his care, the more honour he received in his community, and the better chance he had of becoming a prominent leader and benefactor. The palace of the Kabaka (King) of Buganda Kingdom of Uganda is a suitable example of a paramount leader's household before the coming of foreigners to Africa. In addition to relatives, there were many other people, such as pageboys, living with the king in the palace as his servants.[54] All were considered bonafide members of his household. Although some of those people were in charge of various welfare matters of the household, the Kabaka was technically in charge of the overall supervision and management of the palace, and the entire kingdom, especially through the chiefs. The Kabaka was in charge of guiding and providing for his household, for example by collecting portions of material produce and money from the chiefs, landowners, and peasants in the kingdom.[55]

---

54. Encyclopaedia Britannica, "Martyrs of Uganda," *Encyclopaedia Britannica*, accessed 22 October 2009. http://www.britannica.com/EBchecked/topic/612654/Martyrs-of-Uganda.

55. K. M. E. Lillingston, *Glimpses of Uganda* (London: Church Missionary Society, 1939), 4–5. In fact the powers of the Kabaka were so immense that in 1900 under the British colonial government an agreement was reached to limit the jurisdiction of the Kabaka and the chiefs over land. In 1908 a Land Law was put into place to limit those powers further, but the Kabaka still continued to have powers over land ownership as he held the authority to arbitrate between various parties and give approval for land ownership in the kingdom. For further details see A. B. Mukwaya, *Land Tenure in Uganda: Present Day Tendencies* (Nairobi, Kampala, Dar es Salaam: Eagle Press, 1953), 19–20.

The leaders gave both material and nonmaterial help to the community. No person who failed to manage his household, such as having a wayward spouse or disobedient children, was chosen as leader.[56] Generally, the welfare and the conduct of every individual in the community was largely the responsibility of the entire community and vice versa, as stated in the proverb, "I am, because we are; and since we are, therefore I am."[57] It was believed that the behaviour of each community member reflected the image and affected the welfare of the entire community.[58] However, together with that, in many African communities the main responsibility rested on the leader. Similarly, although the discipline of children, youth, and even young and middle aged married women, was the joint responsibility of the elderly members of the community, the chief responsibility lay in the hands of the overall household head. As stated above in connection with immorality, if a person had disobedient dependents under him or if he had failed to provide for his household, he was not eligible for community leadership. If he was a leader already, he was either demoted or removed from leadership. Thus, the ability to manage one's household was a crucial requirement for someone to be chosen or be retained as a community leader. Being a good manager in one's own household was regarded as beneficial to the community.

Some old mainline Christian denominations in Africa were known for their firm stance in support of good management of the Christian household. Good control of one's life and the lives of his dependents was a requirement of all adherents, but more so of the church leaders. In AIC, any church leader who happened to have an unruly wife or children was required to resign from leadership. If he did not resign voluntarily he was forced out by the relevant council, either permanently or until his household members reformed. Although not many ministers were laid off for failure to provide for their households, some suffered that fate for having unruly children. To this day, more have been ousted for lack of self-discipline and for failing to discipline their families than for being too brutal in disciplining them. For

---

56. William Matheka Mbiti, (Retired primary school teacher; serving church elder in AIC Suma, Mboonĩ DCC; Makũenĩ County, interviewed in 2009.

57. Mbiti, *African Religions & Philosophy*, 108–109.

58. In *African Religions & Philosophy*, 205, Mbiti says that any offence (such as stealing a neighbour's sheep) by any individual in the society is "an offence against the community, and its consequences affect not only the thief but also the whole body of his relatives."

example, a certain pastor in the former Machakos Regional Church Council (RCC) in the early 80s had to step down from active ministry and leadership because his children developed the habit of sneaking from his house at night and getting involved in questionable nightlife in town.[59]

In many African communities, physical violence against children, wives and against one's juniors (in age and social rank) are considered normal and legitimate cultural ways of maintaining discipline and authority. In Kenya, Uganda and many other countries, wife-beating is acceptable and therefore common in some communities. For example, among the pastoral Karamojong of Uganda, it is believed that a man dominates over a woman, children and his juniors in every decision in the home and the larger community.[60] To this day, in some African communities, whenever people from junior and subordinate social ranks defy the authority of the superiors, they are punished to deter such behaviour in the future and to safeguard the superiors' authority and reputation. Among the Akamba, beating of wives, children and other junior members to instil good behaviour was, and, in some cases still is, a custom that is commonly tolerated,[61] and even encouraged. Violent dictatorial "management" is applied largely because members of the subordinate groups depend mainly on the dominant senior leaders for material provision.

Boosted by a cultural norm that tolerates and encourages what Christians consider as violent domination,[62] a peculiar interpretation of the leadership instructions in 1 Timothy 3:4, 12 has emerged among the Akamba. Some frontline church leaders are reputed for beating their children and their wives severely and mishandling people who are under them in the veneer of "managing" them.[63] They justify the violence by misinterpreting the state-

---

59. This information is based on the pastor's own testimony during a joint-chapel session between Scott Theological College and Ukamba Bible Institute in the early 1980s. The pastor stepped down voluntarily so that his children might reform.

60. BBC News, "Uganda Tackles Wife-Beating Taboo," *BBC News*, accessed 27 April 2009. Published on Tuesday, 19 March 2002 at 18:28 GMT. http://news.bbc.co.uk/2/hi/africa/1881472.stm.

61. Kimilu, *Mūkamba wa W'o*, 86–87.

62. Although the traditional Akamba culture proponents may not view it as such.

63. In the early 80s in Mboonī, there are certain leaders who broke the limbs of their children and/or wives accusing them of gross disobedience and promiscuity. However, for the sake of preserving the reputation of those leaders, their names are not appropriate here.

ment τοῦ ἰδίου οἴκου καλῶς προϊστάμενον, τέκνα ἔχοντα ἐν ὑποταγῇ μετὰ πάσης σεμνότητος, "one who *rules his own house* well, having his children *in submission* with all reverence" in 1 Timothy 3:4 (NKJV, italics added). As support for their tough household management measures, they also use the statement, "Let deacons be married only once, and *let them manage their children and their households* well," 1 Timothy 3:12 (NRSV, italics added). (At this point, as stated above at the beginning of this subsection, it is helpful for the reader to note that I am interpreting προΐστημι in 3:4 and 12 as meaning, "have authority over," "manage," "care for," "give help," in view of the provision of material and nonmaterial patronage by the household head to his dependents.) Some Akamba Christians interpret these verses wrongly, viewing them as implying that the household head is authorized to use all means possible to keep all members of his household under total submission (ἔχοντα ἐν ὑποταγῇ). What is not taken into account is that the implication of the adverb καλῶς in the participial clauses τοῦ ἰδίου οἴκου καλῶς προϊστάμενον and τέκνων καλῶς προϊστάμενοι καὶ τῶν ἰδίων οἴκων in 1 Timothy 3:4, 12 should be considered as an inseparable and dominant companion of the phrases, "one who rules," "having . . . in submission," and "let them manage their children and households." Managing and disciplining household members should also be done in total harmony with the counsel of the prepositional clause μετὰ πάσης σεμνότητος, "with all dignity/reverence," at the end of 1 Timothy 3:4.

What 1 Timothy 3:2 and 3 propose as proper management is leadership by good example, in blameless character and gentleness. Leadership by example is one of the best modes of nonmaterial patronage; where the household head moulds the lives of his dependents positively for their (not his) present and future benefit. Ngũi says that humility and the counselling skill (especially the ability to listen patiently) are the most important qualifications of a church leader.[64] Mbuti holds a similar view and says that patience, the listening skill, and restraint from making too quick conclusions are the most important qualifications of a leader.[65] Nguyo's view is that the other most important qualifications that the leader should have in addition

---

64. Daniel Ngũi, (Bishop, AIC Makũenĩ Area Church Council, Makũenĩ County), interview with author.

65. John Mbuti, interview in 2012.

to salvation and good moral character are capability in leadership (namely, having a leadership spirit), availability, experience and stability.[66]

My proposition is that violent church management is mainly a result of influence from the violent traditional leadership, and, as stated above in this subsection, is supported by wrong exegesis of the text. In Africa, it is generally known that from antiquity to the postmodern times, some non-Christian leaders, for example dictators, such as the former Ugandan leader, Idi Amin, use both brute power and the powers of malevolent spirits to intimidate their subjects in order to control and exploit them. The exercise of total control over one's household and over those under his jurisdiction is a widespread custom in various African communities. In Ũkamba, some household heads use spirits[67] and magical charms to control and exploit their spouses, other members of their household, and even neighbours. For example, in 1984 some family heads forced their entire households to visit a famous medicine-man, Kajiwe, who had come to our area from the Coast Province to be treated magically so that they would not be bewitched or so that they would not bewitch anybody in the family.[68] Some of these heads were prominent Christians, such as church elders, and even some pastors.[69] Despite the coming of Christianity and the gospel message about the power of Jesus over evil, to this day in Ũkamba, there still exists profound fear and reliance on the powers of darkness, even among Christians.[70] Therefore, it is not surprising to find syncretism in the application of Christian authority and the authority that is derived from malevolent forces in some AIC

---

66. Bernard Nguyo, interview in 2012.

67. Known as ğinn (or djinn) or ğinnī (singular) in Arabic but spelled as genies (plural) in English.

68. See also Kimilu, *Mūkamba wa W'o*, 131, about Akamba people, including Christians, travelling all the way from various parts of Ũkambanī to the Coast to seek magical protection against witchcraft from a famous witchdoctor, Kavwele, (that is, Kabwere, now late, the predecessor of Kajiwe, who also is late) for themselves and their families. This reality is also corroborated by Gehman in *African Traditional Religion*, 80.

69. One Sunday morning in 1984, as I was on my way to lead a church service, I personally met with one community leader coming from treatment by the medicine-man. At that time when the medicine-man was stationed in the home of a prominent politician, I also received many credible reports about prominent Christian household heads, some of who were members of the church that I was leading, who had also consulted the medicine-man to be given some potent magical "water" for healing and protection from subsequent bewitching. The identities of the participants are concealed.

70. Gehman, *African Traditional Religion*, 80–97.

leaders' household and church management. Some leaders misunderstand and misuse the authority that church leaders are given in 1 Timothy 3:4 and 12; they misuse the divine authority in conjunction with malevolent powers that are traditionally accepted as methods of protecting and providing for themselves, their households and the church.

Certainly, in 1 Timothy 3:13 and 5:17 Paul clearly said that the deacons and elders who carry out their duties well, including good management of their households and the church, are entitled to receive double-honour. Therefore, he was in support of personal benefit ensuing from good management. Nevertheless, self-benefit was never his main concern. He emphasized good management for the benefit of all stakeholders, including all in the household, all in the church community, and those outside the church (1 Tim 3:4, 5, 7, 12). Faith-based management most importantly prioritizes and strengthens the church's faith and guarantees its reputation and influence among outsiders (1 Tim 1:3; 3:6, 7, 9; 2 Tim 4:3; Titus 1:9; 2:1). Second, it wins honour for the leader in the church and the larger society (1 Tim 3:13; 5:17). Elevation of traditional African values in leadership and benefaction, and misinterpretation of biblical principles of household and church management have resulted in detrimental syncretism in church management. Paul stipulated that good church management should be based on faith, uprightness in moral character, concern and gentleness towards all people, and leadership skills, including charismatic gifts and natural abilities. Values such as age, gender, and social and economic status that are often given primary importance in traditional African culture are truly important aspects to consider in church leadership. However, they should occupy secondary position.

4.4 Economic Status

As witnessed in various places at various times, even with the inception of the modern styles of leadership and economic independence, some African communities still hold firmly to the indigenous values and practices of traditional leadership and socio-economic interdependence. For example, despite conducting political elections based on modern principles, certain people are still appointed and consecrated as elders, spokesmen, symbolic representatives and sponsors of their community based on the traditional principles.

Both Christians and non-Christians are involved in those traditional appointment methods.[71] Just as the traditional specialists were highly honoured mainly because of the help they gave to their communities,[72] modern leaders are appointed mainly because they are identified as benefactors and patrons of their communities, especially in giving material help. Kĩvũnzi says that a person's wealth should not determine his apointment to leadership, but, unfortunately, it does.[73]

One of the central pillars of African communities is patronage in which there is the dependence of needy people on the propertied members in the community. Kĩsumbĩ says that communal patronage "was part and parcel of every African indigenous society before the colonial times."[74] Traditionally, leaders were chosen to promote the unity and socio-economic progress of the community through interdependence of members. Unity in socio-economic transactions was one of the most distinct markers of the Akamba community.[75] Generosity was an integral virtue in mutual interdependence. It was another distinct marker of a true Mũkamba.[76] Generosity, more so in a leader, was (and still is) valued highly because many in the community depended on it. The idiom that states that "a true Mũkamba family founder (household head) does not have stiff elbows"[77] means that he is not stingy. It encourages leaders to be generous. The leader gains and retains loyal following

---

71. This is confirmed by the many occasions in which certain individuals are instituted as tribal elders and spokespersons through televised ceremonies nearly every time in Kenya as the general elections approach. Some prominent examples are that of William Ruto (the current Deputy President of Kenya) as Kalenjin elder and spokesman and Raila Odinga (the current main opposition leader in Kenya) as a Mijikenda elder at the Coast of Kenya prior to the 2007 elections. The prominent leader of the Akamba, especially in Machakos County for many years, was the nominated MP, Mũlu Mũtĩsya, who was involved in traditional and modern, Christian and non-Christian issues. See also Mbiti, *African Religions & Philosophy*, 182–193, on traditional appointment of kings, queens, other rulers and specialists among various African communities.

72. See Mbiti, *African Religions & Philosophy*, 166–193, on the value of African specialists in the communities, such as medicine-man, rainmakers, kings, priests, and others. See also Gehman, *African Traditional Religion*, 75–78, on the value to those specialists.

73. Titus Mũsili Kĩvũnzi, (former presiding bishop, AIC Kenya; former Head of Pastoral Studies Department, AIU), interviewed in 2009.

74. Charles Kyale Kĩsumbĩ, (church elder at AIC Ngong Road, Makũenĩ County), interviewed in 2009.

75. Kimilu, *Mũkamba wa W'o*, 54.

76. Kimilu, 54.

77. Mũtĩsya, *Kĩkamba Proverbs and Idioms*, 77.

Influences on Africa Inland Church Leadership

for being generous. From antiquity to this day, a person's possession of and ability to access and acquire material wealth, together with his generosity in sharing, are key determinants in his choice as a leader.[78] His ability and willingness to help the community, especially materially, are considered crucial non-negotiable qualifications.

As seen in the discussion on the management skill, the eligibility of the person for leadership is determined and aided by, for example, his ability to acquire, manage and support several wives, numerous children, relatives, servants and various other people in the community.[79] Kĩvũnzi says that the Akamba choose such people because they think that they will get a share of their wealth and thus find their way to a state of prosperity through their help.[80] As seen in the political election patterns in Ũkamba since independence in Kenya in 1963, leaders are chosen mainly because they already are primary patrons or mediators between primary patrons and their clients.[81] Kibwana says that the two main situations that define political leadership in Ũkamba (rural and urban) are money, such as in the widespread solicitation for handouts and donations by individuals and communities, and wave, such as the pressure put on the individual to follow the current popular political party. People mainly seek for material things and sponsorship in various functions.[82] People are also appointed because they are viewed as potential primary patrons or mediators, especially for channelling material benefits to the community. What people consider in the person as they appoint him are what benefits he will bring either to their community as a whole or to the majority in the community. Kibwana says that the society

---

78. Francis Ngosi, interview in 2009.

79. See Mbiti, *African Religions & Philosophy*, 106–107, on the African family, household and the individual. See also Kimilu, *Mũkamba wa W'o*, 86–87, on the responsibilities of elderly men.

80. Titus Kĩvũnzi, interview in 2009.

81. This is indicated by the comments that voters make such as the questions that they ask concerning their prospective MPs and councillors before they elect them, for example, "What good things has he done for us?" These so-called "good things" include provision of tangible support such as monetary support (and other material support) and securing opportunities for the voters or their dependents for jobs and schools locally and overseas.

82. Kĩvũtha Kibwana, interview in 2012.

even consents to the habit of the leader "stealing away from home"[83] to help his own community.

Traditionally, it was considered necessary for the community head to have enough wealth to help the needy. As Mũngũti says, in case a leader became poor or miserly, he was replaced with a wealthy and generous one.[84] No poor, or rich but tight-fisted, person was appointed or honoured in the community. As stated above, although the authenticity of this traditional view may be challenged by postmodern realism, all prominent leaders of the Akamba were believed to have been appointed and empowered by the Supreme Being and the ancestors.[85] These spirit beings are said to have provided their appointees with riches either mysteriously or through provision of gifts by the community.[86] For example, in many places at various times, traditional medicine-man, the people who were closely associated with them and others who had mystical powers were the virtual leaders of their communities.[87] They also were the wealthiest people in the community. They got their wealth from the people whom they healed or to whom they provided divination and other mystical services. It was expected that the wealth and other endowments that they had were to be used for their own benefit and for the benefit of the community in general. Mbiti says, "To African societies the medicine-men are the greatest gift, and the most useful source of help."[88]

---

83. Exploiting other communities.

84. Paul Mũngũti, interview in 2009.

85. As seen above, Mbiti, in *African Religions & Philosophy*, 182, says that African rulers were regarded as having been appointed by God in the Zamani period. On page 184, he also says that in some communities a new ruler was chosen by a council, by chief ministers, or in consultation with the spirits of the departed rulers. On page 183 he says that the spirit of the departed ruler may continue to play an active part in the affairs of the community, such as by possessing and controlling the new successor.

86. In *African Religions & Philosophy*, 167, Mbiti says that honest traditional medicine-man are upright morally, friendly, willing and ready to serve the community without charging exorbitantly for their services. However, on page 171 he also states that in modern towns the strain of modern life has precipitated new situations of need for the services of the traditional medicine-man with the result that some of the medicine-man have become quite prosperous both professionally and economically.

87. Mbiti, in *African Religions & Philosophy*, 182, says that although some of the community leaders had no outstanding talents or abilities, their office was the link between human rule and spiritual government. Therefore, they were regarded as divine and sacral rulers, who were the shadow or reflection of God's rule in the universe.

88. Mbiti, *African Religions & Philosophy*, 166.

Thus, they were regarded as key patrons of their communities. Nevertheless, some medicine-men also became involved in harmful activities against the society, such as deliberately cheating people for unfair gain and publicity.[89] Such corrupt medicine-men also punished recipients of their services, for example when they failed to reciprocate the help they received; clients were punished either by recurrence of the diseases that they had been healed from or worse, or in other ways. Therefore, on most occasions, some of the medicine-men were negative patrons. However, it is believed that such cruel medicine-man never prospered in their profession.

All people, especially leaders, were supposed to share their material wealth and other possessions and talents with members of their community. For example, those who had large tracts of land or many animals were expected to give some away for good or lend them out for some time to those who did not have any until they got their own. Similarly, those who had wealth of knowledge and skills in various fields, such as in herbal medicine, passed it on to help the community. It was believed that occasionally, if any of those leaders fell into disfavour with the Supreme Being, with the ancestors or with the members of the community, their wealth diminished or faded away mysteriously. For example, if any wealthy person became haughty or selfish with his possessions, it was believed that on average he remained rich for about thirty years only and then became poor.[90] As a result, his prestige plummeted and he was finally removed from leadership for he was considered unfit and of little or no benefit.

Among the Akamba, ownership of wealth was predominantly a male domain. If a woman, whether leader or not, wanted to help the needy in the society, she had to get permission from her husband, older brother or any other older or younger male member of the immediate or extended family.[91] The rationale behind that stipulation was that no woman was regarded as owning any property, even if she had worked for it herself.[92] Men

---

89. For further details, see Mbiti, *African Religions & Philosophy*, 170.

90. Silas Misoi Yego, (Presiding Bishop, AIC Kenya Central Church Council), commented in a sermon during a joint church service of the Kipsaina Sub-DCC churches at Kairangi AIC in Kitale North DCC, 1986.

91. Paul Mũngũti, interview in 2009.

92. That fact is also backed-up by an old saying that is normally uttered by men, "Wĩ wakwa ta mbũi ya kĩveti," which is translated as, "You are mine like the goat of a wife."

were regarded as the exclusive owners and dispensers of the wealth, but the wealth was for the benefit of the entire community, starting with members of their immediate families.[93] However, nowadays, with the influences of modernity and post-modernity on the African culture, things are changing and women are increasingly getting recognition as rightful owners of property. Among the Akamba, women are slowly but increasingly becoming autonomous property owners and benefactors. Therefore, they dispense it at their own discretion.

Similarly, although as seen above that in earlier times no poor person was chosen to be a leader, Bernina Kĩsumbĩ's opinion is that a person's possession of wealth and his generosity are not crucial in the appointment to church and community leadership. She states that other key qualifications of the leader are to have "genuine passion to help the community in priority area[s]" and to have "past history of ever [consistently] identifying with the community."[94] Likewise, on economic status and church leadership, Peninnah Kivunzi, states

> A person's access to wealth should not influence his choice into church leadership. Access to material wealth might mean only that, either the church has resources to enable the person access it, or the leader exploits his congregants to have access which would be totally wrong. But if the person happens to have access to material wealth then he should be generous with it as God expects us to share what he has given.[95]

Charles Kĩsumbĩ also holds a similar opinion that possession of or access to wealth should not be a prerequisite for church leadership, for "God is concerned with the person and not the economic goods that he has created."

One meaning of this saying is that all property that belongs to the wife is considered by the husband as his property, because the wife herself also is regarded as his property.

93. For example, my own mother bought a heifer with money that she got from her participation in a women's monthly financial merry-go-round. When the heifer matured and calved and the calves needed to be sold, it was my father who sold them to pay school fees for us and to meet other family needs.

94. Dr. Bernina Kĩsumbĩ, (women's leader at AIC Ngong Road and lecturer at Nairobi University, from Makũeni County), interviewed in 2009.

95. Peninnah Kĩvũnzi, interview in 2009.

Mwenze[96] says that the electorates' inclination in church elections is influenced by the social environment in which the church is found. He says that churchgoers have found themselves in leadership just because they support the church in projects; whereas in mature church environments this would not happen since nomination is done on spiritual basis only.

Although nowadays possession of material wealth and the ability to help others materially are still high in the list of valued qualifications, this is slowly becoming considered as unnecessary.[97] Education (formal and informal training), integrity (uprightness, especially in ethical matters), experience in particular professions, and other endowments that can benefit the community are also considered.[98] Kibwana says that religious teaching and education are producing a changed society.[99] That is why young male and female professionals in various fields are appointed as heads in areas of their expertise in local, national and international enterprises.[100] Mũnyao says that previously material help to individuals was the major qualification that was considered as crucial for election to civic leadership, but nowadays people value other abilities and achievements of the person.[101] He says that voters value projects that the person has initiated to help the community. He gives an example of how the candidate of a popular rival party was giving huge amounts of money to people to vote for him as councillor but the electorate eventually voted Mũnyao back because of what they had seen him do, although he had not given them money.

However, as stated earlier, in the non-church society, leaders are still chosen with high expectation that they will bring both material and other types

---

96. Dickson Mũtukũ Mwenze, (church elder, AIC Ngong Road, Nairobi, from Makũeni County), interviewed in 2009.

97. Bernina Kĩsumbĩ, interview in 2009.

98. William Mbiti, Dr. Paul Mbandi (Deputy Vice-Chancellor, Administration, Scott Christian Unicersity; Machakos County), Charles Kĩsumbĩ, and Bernina Kĩsumbĩ, interviews with author in 2009.

99. Kĩvũtha Kibwana, interview in 2012.

100. In Ũkambanĩ nowadays there are numerous people (male and female) who are chosen based on merit and not wealth to represent and head various institutions of learning, health institutions, civic administration, and in political leadership. For example there now are several women gifted in leadership who have been instituted as chiefs in Makũenĩ County, although they are not necessarily wealthy.

101. Anthony Mũle Mũnyao, interview in 2009.

of benefits to the community.[102] Mũindũ says that in Mbiũnĩ the economic status of the person who wants to be elected as councillor or member of parliament is highly considered. He is expected to be an industrious person who has his own resources so that he will avoid fleecing the community. The leader is even sometimes forced by circumstances to use his own money to help the community, such as in paying school fees for children of poor constituents.[103]

A trend that has been there since antiquity is that some men and women who are endowed with wealth and other natural and supernatural resources have used them for their own benefit at the expense of the poor and needy. For example, as stated above, wealthy and powerful people force the needy to pledge allegiance and render service to them by use of wicked powers.[104] The wicked patronal leaders bind the poor beneficiaries spiritually to provide service to them in return for the benefits they receive. From antiquity to this day, many powerful people have used manipulative tactics on the needy. For example, politicians, and even some church leaders, have used them to compel poor voters to elect and retain them in civic, parliamentary and church leadership positions.[105] Nevertheless, among Christian and non-Christian Akamba, it is believed that such leaders never stay in power for long; and if they do, their leadership tenure is never blissful, because, as stated above, the Supreme Being and the ancestors who endow them with wealth and other gifts do not condone bad use of their endowments.[106] People generally know that benefaction between all stakeholders as equals is

---

102. As Mbiti observes in *African Religions & Philosophy*, 186, in Ũkamba and other African communities the office of the traditional leader has lost its sacredness and become "a political anachronism and an economic debit."

103. Christopher Mũindũ, interview in 2009.

104. In *Mũkamba wa W'o*, 133–134, Kimilu says that Akamba men do not hide their witchcraft, as in the case with women, because they gain honour in the community due to their proficiency in it. They also acquire immense wealth by snatching their opponents' wealth (such as herds of cattle or flocks of goats and sheep or business and leadership opportunities) from them by magic and making it their own.

105. On page 93 of "The Power of Witchcraft among the Kenyan Akamba," Mwalw'a gives an example of a church leader who consulted a medicine-woman, Kakenyi Kamũtĩ, to be helped in leadership. It is alleged that the leader was soon restored to church administration as a result of that help.

106. As Mbiti says in *African Religions & Philosophy*, 170, those who are not intelligent and devoted to the work that they have been gifted to do, do not prosper or get too far in life.

good and valuable.[107] They also know that oppressive patronage is bad and, to Christians, it is non-biblical and evil.

As seen above, as John Mbiti observes, in the secular world political leaders are chosen nowadays mainly with the hope of eliciting material support from them.[108] The disturbing reality is that, in AIC also (and other African churches), people have often been appointed as leaders mainly because of their material wealth or because of their access to sources of wealth and their willingness to share it.[109] The perception that leaders are chosen to be good benefactors to their communities mainly in material forms is dominant even as people choose church leaders. People choose such leaders especially expecting that they will use their wealth to support the church in various projects of physical development.[110] In some cases, the person's moral standing is ignored in the quest for his wealth and generosity.[111] Mbuti says that he knows of a prospective leader who in the 2007/8 AIC church election at the Coast bribed voters by buying mobile phones for them and giving them huge transport allowances so that they would vote for him.[112] Mbuti's sentiment is upheld and amplified by Mũema's view that, in Mboonĩ, overt bribery takes place, especially from DCC to RCC level. Pastors choose as DCC chairmen people from whom they expect to get better salaries and other material favours once they ascend to leadership.[113] Similarly, Nguyo says about Machakos Area Church Council (ACC) that there really are

---

107. That is the meaning of the Akamba proverb, "Kyaa kĩmwe kĩyũaa ndaa" (One finger cannot, on its own, kill a louse.) See Mũtĩsya, *Kikamba Proverbs and Idioms*, 31. Unity and interdependence is encouraged.

108. Mbiti, *African Religions & Philosophy*, 186.

109. Paul Mbandi, of Machakos County, in an interview in 2009, says that in most cases people are elected as church elders "because of their economic capabilities and consequent generosity toward Church ministry."

110. Titus Kĩvunzi and Philip Mũĩa, (Chariman, Mboon RCC; Makũenĩ County), interviews with author in 2009.

111. An example where moral integrity was ignored for a long time in preference for wealth is a case in which someone was retained as the manager of a children's home in Makũenĩ County from the early 70s to early 80s although he was known as a paedophile who was sexually exploiting the vulnerable girls in the home. He was retained for so long because he was clever at soliciting support for the home from overseas donors; some of which he shared with some the executive leaders of the church that had founded the home. A morally upright manager replaced him later.

112. John Mbuti, interview in 2012.

113. Samuel Mũema, interview in 2009.

some incidences when some people bribe voters to elect them into church leadership, but such leaders do not survive long in leadership.[114] He adds that whenever they discover that someone has used dubious means to be elected, they remove him from church leadership.

Charles Kĩsumbĩ says that the church should not imitate the world where election is largely influenced by one's wealth, but it should be determined by the moral standing of the person. Ignorance and deliberate negligence of God's will result in contradiction of the instructions in 1 Timothy 3:2 and 10 that church officers should be blameless (ἀνεπίλημπτος) in all areas of life. Sometimes, church members easily mistake the ill-intentioned generosity of the wealthy as indication of genuine faith.[115] Worse still, according to Mũlinge's view, some local AIC congregations choose as leaders people whom they know clearly as acquiring wealth through dishonest means, such as those who get their wealth by help of evil spirits.[116] Mũema also holds a similar claim that, in past elections in Mboonĩ, some people vying for election have bribed voters with money, and others have consulted evil spirits for empowerment to defeat fellow contestants.[117] They do it despite knowing that the general teaching of the church is that if a rich person is to be appointed or elected into leadership position in the church, if he is wealthy, he needs to have acquired his wealth through virtuous means.

The blamelessness and the good reputation that is required of the overseers, the deacons and the women in 1 Timothy 3:2, 7, 10 include rightful acquisition and use of wealth. In 1 Timothy 3:3, 8 Paul stipulates explicitly that the overseer and the deacons should not be lovers of money (φιλάργυρος) or greedy for material gain (αἰσχροκερδής). In 1 Timothy 6:10 he declares that the love of money is a root of all kinds of evil, and unrestrained pursuit of wealth has caused many to wander away from the

---

114. Bernard Nguyo, interview in 2012.

115. Daniel Kĩlĩli, (Headmaster, AIC Mboonĩ Primary School; Church elder, AIC Kalamanĩ local church, Mboonĩ DCC, Makũenĩ County, interview in 2009.

116. Jeremiah Mũlinge. Mũlinge's view, in an interview in 2009, agrees with Mwalwa's research finding (in "Power of Witchcraft," 96) that many Akamba politicians and business people consult witchdoctors in pursuit of fortune in their endeavours. In some churches in Ũkamba some of such people are chosen as church treasurers and leaders of development programs. John Mbuti also has a similar view about Coast election practices.

117. Samuel Mũema, interview in 2009.

faith. One of the most prominent vices of the false teachers was their love for money. According to Paul, one of the major indicators of the end times is that people will be lovers of money (φιλάργυροι, 2 Tim 3:2).

The requirement that the overseers and deacons be not lovers of money or pursuers of dishonest gain (1 Tim 3:3, 8; 6:5–8; Titus 1:7, 11) was aimed at discouraging meanness and greed for material possessions among Christians, especially church leaders.[118] It was aimed at encouraging contentment if one had few material possessions and generosity if he had enough to share (1 Tim 6:6–8, 18). The exhortation that the church elders who ruled well should be remunerated for their preaching and teaching services (1 Tim 5:17, 18) implies that some of those to be appointed as church leaders were not wealthy and needed material support from the church. They needed it because, in labouring hard (κοπιῶντες) for the church, they had no time to do their own personal work to support themselves. The officers' need for support from the church is evidence that a person's appointment into leadership in the early church was not dependent on his material possessions or his generosity in helping people materially. As seen above in this paragraph, in 1 Timothy, and elsewhere in the Bible, the rich were encouraged to help the needy. It is possible that some of those who already were overseers and those who were to be chosen as overseers were wealthy householders. Nevertheless, possession of wealth was not a precondition for their appointment.

Akamba Christians view possession of wealth and access to it as a distinctive indicator of God's blessing.[119] Of course, it is true that in the OT God is portrayed as the LORD who blessed some people with wealth, such as Abraham, Isaac, Jacob, David and Solomon. It is also true that even from the NT times until today God blesses his people with health and wealth. Nevertheless, it is also true that in OT and NT times God has the final word on who to make rich and who to make poor, as 1 Samuel 2:7 says, "The LORD makes poor and makes rich; he brings low, he also exalts." There were rich and poor godly people in God's chosen nation, Israel. Concerning his time and after, Jesus said that there will always be poor people on earth (Mark 14:7). This would be so among the godly and the ungodly. Therefore,

---

118. See αἰσχροκερδής in BDAG and Didache 4:5–7; 15:1–2.
119. Titus Kĩvunzi, interview in 2009.

the main teaching of the prosperity gospel[120] that has strongly influenced many, especially the majority poor in the Kenyan churches today, is not entirely true. Consequently, those who choose rich people who have no faith and integrity but leave out the godly poor contradict the strong charge in 1 Timothy 5:21, "In the presence of God and of Christ Jesus and of the elect angels, I warn you to keep these instructions without prejudice, doing nothing on the basis of partiality." It is plausible that the prejudice (πρόκριμα) and partiality (πρόσκλισις) that are prohibited in the verse included favouring the wealthy and leaving out the poor and blameless members who were better qualified for church leadership. Concerning partiality, Kĩsumbĩ says that a leader should be "man of all people, . . . Christian or otherwise, in all life issues of giving service to the world."[121]

From ancient times, such as in the Graeco-Roman world of the first century AD, the normal way of life in many communities is involvement in reciprocity transactions. In such settings, "when a person (or persons) is the recipient of good in the form of a favour or a gift, the receiver is obligated to respond to the giver with goodwill and to return a counter-gift or favour to the giver in proportion to the good received."[122] However, a person who helps the needy without requiring repayment is preferred over one who helps in order to receive support from those he helps. That is a principle that has been operating in all human communities from antiquity both in secular and religious circles.[123] Similarly, a rich and active person who helps others

---

120. See Paul Gifford, "Prosperity," *The Oxford Companion to Christian Thought: Intellectual, Spiritual, and Moral Horizons of Christianity*, eds. Adrian Hastings, Alistair Mason and Hugh Pyper (Oxford: Oxford University Press, 2000), 570–571. The prosperity gospel is a popular theological teaching also known as the "health and wealth gospel." It is a Christian religious teaching that claims that the Bible affirms that financial blessing is the will of God for all true Christians. It teaches that faith, positive speech, and donations to Christian ministries (popularly known as "sowing a seed" in Nairobi churches) will always increase one's material wealth and improve one's physical health. Some of the most prominent proponents of this teaching currently in the US are Creflo Dollar and Joel Osteen.

121. Charles Kĩsumbĩ, interview in 2009.

122. G. W. Peterman, *Paul's Gift from Philippi: Conventions of Gift Exchange and Christian Giving*, Society for New Testament Studies: Monograph Series 92 (Cambridge: Cambridge University Press, 1997), 3.

123. In *How to Talk to Christians about Money* (Minneapolis: Augsburg, 1982), 29ff, W. A. Poovey gives examples of the techniques of charitable organizations in soliciting for funds. He also cites John 3:16 and Exod 20:2 about God's gifts that cannot be repaid. On page 30 he says that God never asks anything of humans "until he has first blessed them and

is preferred over one who is perpetually lazy and looks for support from others.[124] My argument is that resourcefulness and generosity are virtues that are fully biblical, as implied in 1 Timothy 6:18; Titus 1:12; 3:14 where Paul abhors indolence and encourages productivity and sharing.

Nevertheless, it is never right when the church ignores people who are morally upright and have special calling and spiritual gifts (who are resourceful and able to help the church to develop spiritually) but have no material wealth in favour of those who can help materially only.[125] Some of the nonmaterial benefits that such people could bring to the church are, most importantly, that their model of Christian faith in personal character and teaching will promote upright life for the church that is consistent with the Christian faith. Such is what Paul exhorted Timothy and Titus to practise and portray for effectiveness of their life and ministry and for the benefit of their hearers and observers (especially for guarantee of present and eschatological salvation, 1 Tim 4:15–16). The instructions in 1 Timothy 3:2–3 suggest that a major function of the PE leaders was to be role models of Christian character for others in the community.[126] This is fundamental patronage in nonmaterial form because if uprightness is revived in the church today through the character of the leaders, it will result in the restoration and empowering of the evangelistic mission of the church.

On this discussion on the economic status of the person, I have arrived at the conclusion that there are varied views on the impact of material wealth on the appointment of leaders in the general Akamba community and the

---

given them more than they can ever repay." In "Inspirational Quote," in *Inspiration Line: The Meaningful Life Magazine* of 18 September, 2008, (http://www.inspirationline.com/EZINE/18SEP006.htm), Glaceta Honeyghan also says, "To give and not expect anything in return; to give for no special time or season; to give, not for any particular recognition; to give, not for a substantial tax refund; to give for the sake of giving – often just between giver and receiver – has a life of its own – an elevated one." This inspirational quotation from Glaceta Honeyghan was also accessed on 8 October 2018 at https://www.abusidiqu.com/an-act-of-kindness-worthy-of-emulation-by-salihu-tanko-yakasai/, and also at http://ariyamagga.net/give-not-expect-anything-return/.

124. Rev Peter Maĩthya Kyũle, (chairman, AIC Mboonĩ District Church Council), interviewed in 2009.

125. For example, in most DCCs in Mboonĩ RCC (and other RCCs in Ũkamba) over the years, those elected as treasurers and secretaries in the church councils are either businessmen or school heads. Pastors and poor church elders are seldom given those "powerful" positions.

126. Hays, *Moral Vision*, 68–69.

church. Concerning community leadership, some interviewees hold the opinion that some leaders are appointed mainly because of their material possessions that the electorate expect them to use for individual and community advantage. Another cluster of the interviewees has the view that the economic status of the person is of little or no significance in the appointment because his other qualities and achievements in the community matter more.[127]

On AIC leadership, some have pointed out that the faith and integrity of the person and other spiritual gifts are what are most necessary. This is in agreement with the PE teaching in 1 Timothy 3:1–13; 5:17 and Titus 1:5–9. Although until now some leaders (such as church treasurers and development chairpersons) are chosen because of their wealth,[128] others are chosen despite the fact that they do not have their own property,[129] or even if they cannot repay if they lose or misuse the property that they are entrusted with.[130] Mūkūū gives an example of himself, that he was elected as DCC vice-chairman in 1985, as RCC chairman in 1996, and eventually as Bishop of Kĩtui ACC in 2009 although he had no considerable material wealth.[131] Ngũi says that in the Makũenĩ church area the financial status of the prospective Christian leader is not given priority because people prioritize God's call and not the financial influence of the person.[132] Therefore,

---

127. Anthony Mũle Mũnyao, interviewed in 2009, says that some political parties still hold the view that they can win voters by giving them money, but that view is becoming obsolete as people are now electing leaders based on merit.

128. The late Daniel Masĩla Mũlemba, (Christian Education Coordinator, AIC Mboonĩ RCC; Senior pastor, AIC Ngaa local church, Kĩkĩma DCC, Mboonĩ RCC; Makũenĩ County), interviewed in 2009, quoted the earlier late Pastor Philip Nguyo of Mboonĩ as saying that for someone to be appointed to take care of another's cassava (manioc) he should have his own. He meant that if a person does not have his own property he should not be entrusted with other people's property. Joyfred Peter Mũtĩsya, interviewed in 2009, says that in some AIC churches, it is more preferable when the person who is to be appointed as treasurer has his own wealth in addition to being a believer and man of integrity.

129. Peninnah Kĩvũnzi, interviewed in 2009, says, if the church demands that the appointee be wealthy, it means that "either the church has resources to enable the person access, or the leader exploits his congregants to have access, which would be totally wrong." Samuel Mũnywokĩ, interview, gives an example of himself that he was appointed into DCC chairmanship in 1989 without any material wealth of his own.

130. Daniel Mwau, (Pastor, AIC Kĩlenge local church, Ũtangwa DCC; Makũenĩ County), interviewed in 2009.

131. Benjamin Mũkũũ, (Bishop, AIC Kĩtui Area Church Council), interviewed in 2012.

132. Daniel Ngũi, interview in 2012.

what we can deduce is that, although as in the secular setting the possession of wealth and the willingness to give material support to the church still have great influence on determining the choice of some church leaders in some AIC churches in Ũkamba,[133] some do not regard wealth as significant. Nevertheless, those who do not regard wealth as significant in the appointment also support the exhortation in 1 Timothy 6:18–19, that those who have material riches should be generous and ready to share sincerely and unselfishly.[134] That view also is in tandem with Titus 3:8 and 14 where Paul says that doing deeds that are excellent and "profitable to everyone" should be a preoccupation of those who have come to believe in God. That includes using material wealth voluntarily and sincerely to help the needy, not exclusively for personal benefit.

4.5 Conclusion

The main issue that the discourse in this chapter has addressed is the influence of ancient and modern African benefaction/patronage and leadership values on the AIC leadership philosophy. The discussion has focused on three main areas, namely, the role that the faith and moral status, management proficiency, and the economic status of the person play in his eligibility for appointment as a church leader. The study has particularly discussed the connection between leadership and material benefaction and patronage in Ũkamba. The conclusion that this writer has arrived at is that, in some places, community leaders are still regarded as integral community benefactors and patrons especially in material support. In those places, benefaction, patronage and leadership are seen as very closely connected. However, in other places, the connection between leadership and material patronage is said to be non-existent and people are said to be appointed especially based on their faith, integrity in moral standing, and their management ability.

In instances where people are influenced by the political trend of electing leaders because of their economic status, the faith and moral integrity of the person are generally ignored. However, based on the outcome of my study, those instances are not found everywhere in Ũkamba. Somehow similar to

---

133. As Mwenze, interviewed in 2009, says about some urban churches.
134. Peninnah Kĩvũnzi, interview in 2009.

the Graeco-Roman systems, some forms of African benefaction and patronage were material whereas others were nonmaterial. Some examples of the non-material forms are, the provision of general leadership; provision of advice and foresight by elders and seers; and the healing of various diseases by medicine-man for the welfare of individuals and the entire community. Therefore, we can logically conclude that, although in Ũkamba leadership and material benefaction and patronage are still closely and strongly connected, people are increasingly basing appointment of church leaders mainly on faith, moral integrity, leadership skill and other nonmaterial endowments of the person.

We can therefore conclude that although there are significant deviations from the PE teachings, AIC in many areas in Ũkamba bases the choice of leaders on the principles of leadership as delineated in 1 Timothy 3:1–13; Titus 1:5–9, other relevant PE passages, and other Bible texts, OT and NT. Realizing that not all people who are fit for church leadership are endowed with material wealth but can adequately contribute to the welfare of the church in nonmaterial ways, they appoint even those who themselves have need of material support from the church, as 1 Timothy 5:17–18 implies. Similarly, those who are rich and have the right perspective on how to use their wealth have been making right use of it, as exhorted in 6:17–19, and in conjunction with the good values of African patronage and leadership.

On faith and moral integrity, my conclusion is that ancient and modern Akamba culture generally upholds moral uprightness. Nevertheless, some of the accepted customs, such as premarital and extramarital sex, polygamy, and stealing for the benefit of the community, are outrightly in conflict with Christian values. Additionally, mainly due to modern patterns of thought and belief, and influences from secular perspectives, some segments of the Akamba society, especially the young educated urbanites, have little regard for supernatural or divine values which were highly honoured and followed in the ancient Akamba societies, and are upheld by Christianity. That lack of prioritization of spiritual and supernatural values has led to a state in which many Christians, both lay members and church leaders have weak faith and low regard for moral values. This weak state of both lay believers and leaders is directly contrary to what Paul advised the PE Christians to strive to acquire and maintain, as he advised and urged them to focus on practical sound faith and impeccable character as they appointed church leaders.

Concerning management, among the Akamba, leadership was given to those who had large households (with many wives, children and other dependents) and were managing them well. Material and nonmaterial patronage, such as giving material support and providing moral guidance to one's dependents, were regarded as good management. In the PE, good management through material and nonmaterial support and leadership are also exhorted, such as in 1 Timothy 3:4–5, 12; 5:8; Titus 1:6; 2:5. However, one area of concern in Akamba management is that sometimes violence and exploitation were applied on the dependents or opponents for negative acquisition and maintenance of power. 1 Timothy 3:3, 4, 12 encouraged good management of one's household and the church through modelling in blamelessness, in love and gentleness. Violence was explicitly and strongly prohibited.

Overall, as seen mainly in the readings about ancient Akamba culture, the Akamba community closely resembles the ancient Jewish community in matters of kinship benefaction,[135] and in the aspect of connection between social leadership and supernatural powers, such as God's commandments and the dictates of the ancestors. However, there are major differences. For example, the Akamba practice of leaders manipulating their dependents and juniors due to their possession of power and authority over them resembles more the negative side of the Roman patronage (*patronicium*) system which was more exploitative than the humanitarian Jewish kinship benefaction.[136] My conclusion is that the ancient Akamba patronage and benefaction system, which still has strong presence in the modern society, had some similarity with the Jewish familial or kinship benefaction, but the exploitative side of

---

135. As implied in Mbiti's famous saying in *African Religions & Philosophy*, 108–109, "I am, because we are; and since we are, therefore I am," and in the idiom in Mũtĩsya's *Kĩkamba Proverbs and Idioms*, 31, "One finger cannot, on its own, pick up and kill a louse." According to Mbiti in *African Religions & Philosophy*, 104, all Akamba are blood-relatives to each other; ". . . each individual is a brother or sister, father or mother, grandmother or grandfather, or cousin, or brother-in-law, uncle or aunt, or something else, to everyone else." As such, the security and prosperity of the community lies in the hands of each member in relation to the others.

136. Nevertheless, among the Jews, as seen in the OT records, sometimes the humanitarian principle was ignored. There were times when leaders manipulated their subjects. For example, Ahab and Jezebel took Naboth's field by force, and David took Uriah's wife because he was the king, 1 Kgs 21; 2 Sam 11.

the modern system is more similar to the corrupted side of the Roman patronage system. On material benefaction and patronage in connection with leadership, what we infer from Paul's instructions is that, although some of those already in church leadership and those who were to be appointed as leaders had material wealth, not all of them had it, nor were they required to have it (1 Tim 5:17–18).[137] That was unlike in the Graeco-Roman setting where patrons were required to be wealthy before they could be appointed as patrons. Nevertheless, honest ardent acquisition of material wealth to support one's dependents and other people who needed support was highly encouraged and required of all PE believers. For example, in 1 Timothy 5:4, believing children and grandchildren were urged to support their parents. In 5:8 believers were exhorted to support relatives, especially family members, and those who neglected doing so were regarded as worse than unbelievers. In 5:16, believing women were encouraged to support their widowed relatives; and in Titus 3:14 believers were urged to learn to devote themselves to good works in order to meet urgent needs of their own and of others instead of being unproductive. Similarly, Paul's exhortation was that the church members and leaders who were wealthy should not base their hope on their wealth or use it only for temporal self-benefit but also for the benefit of the needy, in and outside the church, in view of future eschatological benefits for all parties (1 Tim 6:17–19; cf. 1 Tim 4:16).

---

137. Consider also 1 Tim 5:3, 5 on honouring (supporting materially) real widows, some of whom were probably involved in church leadership.

CHAPTER 5

Summary and Conclusions

5.1 Summary

The main purpose of this treatise has been to assess how Paul interacted with the ideologies of the G-R and Jewish benefaction and patronage systems in the first-century AD as he issued instructions for guidance in Christian life and administration in PE churches. I have responded mainly to the views that: (1) Paul, either deliberately or naively, supported the oppressive hierarchical benefaction and patronage systems (2) the systems, especially *patronicium*, were entirely corrupt, and (3) material benefaction took pre-eminence over nonmaterial benefaction and patronage. In my endeavour to respond to the concerns I have answered two related questions: (1) As reflected in his expressions in the advice and instructions that he issued, how did Paul interact with the various ideologies and practices of the Greek, Roman and Jewish benefaction and patronage systems in the first century AD? (2) On the African scene, in relation to the insights gained from study of PE, how have Christians in the Africa Inland Church interacted with the ideologies of the ancient and the modern African benefaction and patronage systems? I have especially discussed their influences on the church's leadership philosophy.

In chapter 3 of the study especially, I have highlighted what I consider as Paul's application of the good principles for the general guidance of the church in its evangelistic mission, administration and benefaction. I have also discussed what I understand as Paul's response to the anomalies of the systems. Related to that, based on my findings in PE, in chapter 4 I have examined the influences of the ancient and the modern Akamba benefaction and patronage ideologies on the current leadership philosophy of AIC, especially the relationship between benefaction, patronage and leadership. I have presented what I have inferred as the most appropriate way of interpreting and applying PE instructions in AIC in view of the contiguous first century G-R προστασία and *patronicium* ideologies.

5.2 Conclusions

There are detailed conclusions at the end of chapter 2, 3, and 4. Therefore, what is written here is a recap of what has been noted in those previous conclusions. On the background of Greek εὐεργεσία, Roman *patronicium* and Jewish kinship benefaction, my finding is that those systems began operating long before the first century AD. In the first century, various forms of socioeconomic interdependence were still functioning among various Greek, Roman and Jewish communities of the Mediterranean world. Each one of these systems was distinct. Nevertheless, the similarities between their general characteristics and principles of operation were more prominent than their differences, thus influencing some scholars to view and treat them as one. Each began with the noble purpose that the more able members of society should help the less capable. In the systems, various material and nonmaterial resources and services were exchanged between people of various socioeconomic classes and status. The overall assessment is that, although some of their values and modes of operation changed at various times and locations, in the first century AD they still retained their original core value of helping members of the community with various material and nonmaterial assets. Although some of the systems, especially Roman *patronicium* developed gross abuses along the way, such as exploitation of the lower classes by the upper ones in pursuit of power and honour, they still generally retained their goodness and were major means of promoting socioeconomic equilibrium in the societies within which they operated. In fact we can liken them to political democracy in our times. Although it has become largely corrupted, it still retains some of its original noble values and operates well by them regardless of the corruption.

Concerning the PE text, my conclusive argument is that Paul portrays notable familiarity and wise interaction with the ideologies and operations of the G-R and Jewish benefaction and patronage systems. This is evident in his skilful use of explicit and implicit concepts and expressions that were common in those systems. He did not support the systems imprudently nor condemn them indiscriminately. His support for their noble ideologies is evident. It indicates that not everything in them was evil, as some scholars presume. He endorsed for implementation in PE churches whatever elements he viewed as beneficial in the systems. Similarly, his apparent confrontation of their abuses shows that not everything in them was good. That is why he did not support them arbitrarily, as some accuse him of doing. Therefore, I disagree with Dibelius, Verner, Hanson and others whose view is that the PE author[1] gave the instructions in PE with a sinister motive, in naïve support of the repressive bourgeois systems. Instead, what we see in Paul's views is wise selection and careful adoption, adaptation and endorsement of the good principles and strong confrontation of the abuses of the systems.

For example, the outstanding presentation of God as the only God and "saviour of all people," provider of life to all beings and giver of good things to humans, is a plausible indicator that Paul visualized him in terms of positive benefaction and patronage. As such, he depicted him as the unrivalled benefactor of all time, in the provision of eternal and physical, nonmaterial and material help to his dependents. Presenting God the Father, Jesus Christ and the Holy Spirit as the merciful providers of the greatest gift of eternal salvation, Paul relegated the would-be combatant human benefactors and patrons to a low second position in the competitive hierarchy of benefaction and patronage. As he has indicated in 1 Timothy 2:5 concerning the gift of salvation for all people, God is the only provider, Christ is the ransom and only mediator, and the Holy Spirit is the facilitator of that gift to humans. Crossan's view that Jesus was neither broker nor mediator[2] is contrary to Paul's presentation of Jesus as a primary benefactor and patron because Paul presented him as "saviour" and "Lord" who showed him mercy, saved him and appointed him to his service. Because in the first century mediation was more pronounced in the Roman *patronicium* system, by presenting Christ as the "only mediator," Paul highlighted his status as a unique second-level patron who stood between God (the paramount divine patron) and humans

---

1. They do not accept Paul as the PE author.
2. Crossan, *Historical Jesus*, 422.

(God's primary clients). By presenting Jesus as the only mediator who gave his life as ransom for us all, he depicted him polemically and competitively as the unique ideal patron who gave the ultimate gift of his life for the sake of his clients. Similarly, by presenting the Holy Spirit as an active agent in the facilitation and implementation of salvation to humans and in safeguarding the gospel (2 Tim 1:14; Titus 3:5), he thus implicitly depicted him as fully involved in the divine benefaction and patronage enterprise. Thus, in presenting God the Father as the overall saviour, Christ as the ransom and only mediator, and the Holy Spirit as facilitator and caretaker of the new relationship, Paul portrays the Trinity as involved in the most significant benefaction and patronage endeavour of all time.

In the first chapters of 1 Timothy, Paul depicted himself as a chief and exemplary beneficiary of God's overall gift of salvation. As a loyal client, he expressed his gratitude and ascribed eternal glory to God as a fitting response that was expected of all beneficiaries. As a faithful and loyal client, he encouraged fellow beneficiaries to be loyal clients to their supreme patron, God. Throughout the PE, against the false teachers' erratic doctrines and practices, he also encouraged the recipients of his letters to be appreciative to God for what he has richly given to us his creation for livelihood and enjoyment.

Paul also depicted himself as a second-level benefactor and patron.[3] His status is depicted in his relationship with various human characters in PE, which can be summarized as follows: (1) With Timothy and Titus he was like a good father/patron and they were equivalent to loyal children/clients (1 Tim 1:2; Titus 1:4). (2) By encouraging them and the other believers in the PE churches to confirm the genuineness of their salvation by doing good to one another as members of the household of God, he was encouraging the noblest type of patronage between humans. (3) With the false teachers and the apostate believers, Paul presented himself as a faithful patron, while he portrayed them as disloyal clients, who had turned against God their supreme benefactor and patron, against him and against the sound teaching (the true gospel) and instructions that he had given to them. (4) The commodities that Paul was giving out were the gospel of salvation in Christ and the good advice and instructions, which were mainly nonmaterial entities.

---

3. God was the primary or first-level benefactor and patron to Timothy, Titus and the Ephesian and Cretan Christians.

(5) The appropriate response that was expected from the clients was favourable reception of the exhortation and trust in the true gospel, which would be portrayed in obedience to the sound doctrine, leading to faith in Christ and godly Christian conduct in all spheres of life. (6) Paul's legitimate response as a patron to disloyalty by some of his clients is that he mentioned their disloyalty with regret (2 Tim 4:2). He even handed some over to Satan to be taught not to be dishonourable (blasphemous) to the sound doctrine (1 Tim 1:20, cf. 2 Tim 2:17). (7) His response to the loyal clients is that he acknowledged their loyalty to him (1 Tim 1:2; 2 Tim 4:11; Titus 1:4) and continued giving them further patronage, in form of advice and instructions and presenting them to God (the overall primary and eternal patron) in constant prayers and thanksgiving (cf. 2 Tim 1:3).

Stringent maintenance of good character (ἀρετή and δικαιοσύνη) and good works, especially for people's approval and for earning personal honour, was the central pillar in G-R benefaction and patronage. Paul endorsed a Christian alternative for those virtues. By strongly urging those who had become believers in God to maintain impeccable character (such as in 1 Tim 3:1–13; 4:12; Titus 1:5–9; 2:1–15) and be careful to devote themselves to good works which are beneficial to others (1 Tim 2:10; 5:10,25; 6:18; Titus 2:7, 14; 3:8, 14), Paul indicated that good exercise of benefaction and patronage is an integral component of the Christian faith. By labelling failure to help the needy as denial of the faith (1 Tim 5:8), he showed that Christian faith and leadership are or should be inseparable from good benefaction and patronage. In fact, by use of athletic language in 2 Timothy 4:6–8, he concluded his final epistle in PE cluster by stressing the element of personal sacrifice, which was the ultimate gift that a benefactor or patron could give to/for his clients. He was determined to keep the faith until death, which was proof of absolute loyalty. Using military language and in keeping with the rules of good benefaction and patronage, he lived his life and conducted his ministry in such a manner that showed that, just as in the benefaction and patronage systems, he anticipated being rewarded for his endurance and loyalty.

Therefore, it is evident in the text that Paul wisely utilized the good principles of the systems and encouraged both material and nonmaterial benefaction in the church. Understanding his careful adoption of their ideologies is particularly helpful for the churches that use the Pastorals as key guide for Christian life and church leadership. It helps them to identify, assess and adopt wisely the good ideologies and avoid their abuses.

On the relationship between benefaction, patronage and leadership in AIC in Ũkamba, my judgment is that a significant section of members and leaders, regrettably, view material benefaction and patronage as the most important and integral components of leadership. I consider the perspective about the close relationship between leadership and patronage (material and nonmaterial), and about leaders being primary community patrons, as a neutral, natural and indisputable reality. Just as the general Akamba community regards its leaders as its main benefactors and patrons in providing material and nonmaterial help, believers in AIC expect church leaders to be their patrons in similar ways. Whatever the general community expects of its leaders, believers expect that and more from their leaders, including material support. The view by the majority of AIC members and leaders that faith, godly moral character and other nonmaterial spiritual endowments are the most important qualifications required of a church leader is what PE supports. PE urges all capable believers to support the needy members of the household of God, including their blood relatives, based on their faith and in reference to God. Christians who do that have the right perspective about material wealth and make right use of it according to the PE guidelines and in conjunction with the good values of the ancient and the modern African benefaction and patronage ethos.

The goodness or badness of the relationship between leadership and benefaction and patronage depends on its utilization by various regimes and individuals at various times. Both in the non-Christian community and in the church, various stakeholders have utilized it rightly while others have abused it. Particularly, the problem with some church members, both lay people and leaders, is that they purposely and selfishly elevate material benefaction and the Akamba cultural leadership values above Christian values, while others do it unwittingly. That practice has led to the scenario where at times in Ũkamba, church leadership is not different from the contemporary secular leadership. Most disturbing is the fact that they have ignored the crucial aspects of the Christian faith and moral values in pursuit of leadership opportunities that give them temporal material and non-material benefits more than what benefits the church and the non-church communities righteously, holistically and permanently. Nevertheless, a large section of AIC in Ũkamba interprets and applies the instructions on qualifications for church leaders in the PE rightly.

My overall conclusion on the influence of the ancient and the modern African cultural values on leadership, benefaction and patronage is that some of those values are good but others are detrimental to both the church and the non-Christian community. It is true that some of the bad values have crept into the church as a result of misguided interpretation and syncretism of the PE instructions with Akamba culture. Nevertheless, just as was the case with false teachers in the PE churches, mainly, subtle agents who deliberately want to corrupt the values of the church have introduced the non-biblical values to the church. They do it especially in pursuit of social prestige, power and, sometimes, for material gain. Without exonerating it totally from corruption, it is laudable that the ancient Akamba culture valued moral uprightness more than the modern culture that has little regard for divine values. The modern perspective has invaded the church with the result that many Christians, both lay people and leaders, have weak faith and low regard for moral values in reference to spiritual standards. This scenario is directly contrary to the PE principles in which Paul presents sound faith and impeccable character in reference and reverence to God and for benefitting both believers and the surrounding non-Christian community as the most necessary qualifications for all church officers.

In the modern Akamba community, possession of material resources is valued as an integral factor that gives a person the ability and authority to be a leader. However, to Paul, what was required of overseers is maturity of faith, impeccable character and the ability to teach and to manage his household (if he had one) and the church well. Male deacons were required to hold fast to the mystery of the faith with a clear conscience and have impeccable character, whereas their female counterparts were required to have faultless character and be faithful in everything. These were the most important elements for church leadership. Such a person had the ability and credibility to be a leader who could lead by personal example, sound Christian doctrine, and other spiritual leadership capabilities. Concerning economic status that many in the Akamba community view as the most crucial element in the appointment of community leaders, my conclusion is that, although material wealth is indisputably a very useful form of benefaction for both the non-Christian community and the church, it is not the most important. Paul had a clear perspective on the relationship between material and nonmaterial benefaction and patronage and church mission and administration. He exhorted PE Christians to develop and maintain a healthy perspective and balance between material benefaction, patronage and Christian life, keeping an eschatological perspective on both their temporal and eternal values.

5.3 Recommendations

If AIC churches and other churches in Africa, and throughout the world that value the Pastoral Epistles as providing criteria for their church policy and practice, wish to bring their churches more closely into line with what this study has found in these Letters, I recommend that, in the light of this study's findings, they review their practices in relation to, benefaction, patronage, and the appointment of leaders.

5.3.1 Benefaction

Good benefaction, as was encouraged by Paul in Acts and in his epistles, should be one of the most prominent and distinguishing marks of a good Christian leader, not only in church leadership but in all sectors of leadership in Society. This kind of benefactory leadership should be based on and guided by sincere and selfless love for God and for all humans.

5.3.2 Patronage

To redeem the negative view of patronage in general society, all Christians, in AIC and all other churches in Africa and beyond, should embrace and implement the principles of good Christian patronage. Whoever gives any material or non-material support or "*sponsorship*," as it is popularly called (negatively), in Kenya currently, should not give it expecting any selfish dividends from the recipients of the support. Therefore, whoever offers such support in order to be appointed a leader in the church or in the general society, should not be honoured or awarded any leadership position.

5.3.3. Appointment of Leaders

I recommend that the noble exercise of appointing leaders be based not at all on the expectation of material benefits or any other selfish gain, that either those that are led or the leader can get or give from the appointment. Appointment of Christian leaders for the church and for the society should be mainly for the purpose of the enhancement of the divine eternal values in service of society for the glory of God.

APPENDIX A

Questionnaires

Questionnaire on Influences of African Patronage on Church Leadership (Used in 2009)
(*You may also use the back side of this paper for your answers*)

A patron is someone who is chosen, named, or honoured as a special guardian, protector, leader, supporter or provider of resources and services to particular clients. Therefore, patronage is the provision of services and resources in guardianship, protection, leadership and support in particular circumstances.

Some patronage qualities that people consider when choosing a church leader, for example, an elder, pastor, chairman, bishop, etc.

1. What role does the person's Christian faith and moral standing in the church and in the general society play in his/her choice as a patron/leader?

2. Does it matter whether the person is a man or a woman? How?

3. How important is the person's married life status[1] and family leadership as he/she is chosen?

4. Do the person's access to wealth and his/her generosity influence the choice? How?

5. How significant are the person's age and ability to give advice as he/she is chosen?

6. What other qualifications or aspects do you considers necessary in a church leader?

---

1. Does it matter whether the person is married or not? What of the number of wives/concubines and husbands?

Questionnaire on Influences of African Patronage on Civic Leadership (Used in 2009)

(You may also use the back side of this paper for your answers)

A patron is someone who is chosen, named, or honoured as a special guardian, protector, leader, supporter or provider of resources and services to particular clients. Therefore, patronage is the provision of services and resources in guardianship, protection, leadership and support in particular circumstances.

Some patronage qualities that people consider when choosing a civic leader, for example, a village elder, chief, counsellor, member of parliament, etc.

1. Did colonialists introduce or encourage patronage or was it an integral part of African society in pre-colonial times?

2. Does it matter whether the person is a man or a woman? How?

3. How important are the person's marital status,[2] family leadership, and moral character as he/she is chosen?

4. Do the person's access to wealth and his/her generosity influence the choice? How?

5. How significant are the person's age and ability to give advice as he/she is chosen?

6. What other qualifications or aspects do you considers necessary in a community leader?

---

2. Does it matter whether the person is married or not? What of the number of wives/concubines and husbands?

Revised Questionnaire on Influences of African Benefaction/Patronage on Church Leadership (Used in 2012)

1. What do you consider as the most important qualification required of a person as he is appointed as a church leader?

2. On faith and moral character:

   (a) What role does the person's Christian faith play in the appointment?

   (b) What role does his moral standing in the church and in the general society play in the choice?

3. On management skill: How significant are the person's church leadership/management ability as he is chosen?

4. On economic status: Does the person's access to material wealth and his generosity with it or lack of those qualities influence his choice into church leadership? Please elaborate your answer.

5. What other qualifications or characteristics do you consider as necessary in a church leader?

Revised Questionnaire on Influences of African Benefaction/Patronage on Civic Leadership (Used in 2012)

1. In your understanding, did the colonial regime introduce patronage/benefaction (aid/support) in Africa or was it an integral part of the African indigenous society in pre-colonial times?

2. On faith and moral character:

> (a) If at all applicable, what role does the person's connection with the supernatural world play in his choice as community leader?

> (b) Similarly, if at all significant, how important is the person's moral character as he is chosen?

3. On management skill: How significant are the person's community leadership/management ability as he is chosen?

4. On economic status: Does the person's access to material wealth and his generosity with it or lack of those qualities influence his choice into community (civic, political, etc.) leadership? Please elaborate your answer.

5. What other qualifications or aspects do you considers necessary in a civic leader?

APPENDIX B

Interviewees for Chapter 4

1. Kamende, Benjamin Ndaita: Manager, AIC Mboonĩ Children's Home; Pastor, AIC Doonholm, Umoja DCC, Nairobi East RCC; from Makũenĩ County; interviewed in 2009.
2. Kibwana, Prof. Kĩvũtha: Governor, Makũenĩ County, Kenya; interviewed in 2012.
3. Kĩlĩli, Daniel: Headmaster, Ĩthembonĩ Primary School; Mboonĩ West District, Makũenĩ County; interviewed in 2009.
4. Kĩsumbĩ, Charles Kyale: Church elder, AIC Ngong Road, Makũenĩ County; interviewed in 2009.
5. Kĩsumbĩ, Dr. Bernina: Women's leader, AIC Ngong Road; lecturer, Nairobi University, Makũenĩ County; interviewed in 2009.
6. Kĩvũnzi, Peninnah: Kĩtui County; wife of former AIC bishop, Titus Kĩvũnzi, and a long-time women leader in AIC, PhD Biblical Studies candidate at AIU; interviewed in 2009.
7. Kĩvũnzi, Dr. Titus Mũsili: Former presiding bishop, AIC Kenya; former Head of Pastoral Studies Department, AIU; Kĩtui County; interviewed in 2009.
8. Kyũle, Peter Maĩthya: Chairman, Mũthei DCC, AIC Mbooni Region, Makũenĩ County; interviewed in 2009.
9. Maĩthya, Joseph: Peasant farmer and secular company employee, Nairobi, Kenya; Makũenĩ County; interviewed in 2009.
10. Mbandi, Dr Paul Mũindi: Deputy Vice-Chancellor, Administration, Scott Christian University; Machakos County; interviewed in 2009.
11. Mbiti, William Matheka: Retired primary school teacher and serving church elder in AIC Suma, Mboonĩ DCC; Makũenĩ

County; interviewed in 2009.
12. Mbuti, John: Former Bishop, AIC Coast Area Church Council, from Kĩtui County; interviewed in 2012.
13. Mũema, Samuel Mũthama: Chaplain, Mboonĩ Boys High School; Lecturer, AIC Mboonĩ Bible Institute; interviewed in 2009.
14. Mũĩa, Philip Ng'ata: Assistant Bishop, AIC Machakos Area Church Council; interviewed in 2009.
15. Mũindũ, Christopher Kĩlonzo: Director, Wonders of Africa Safaris Limited; interviewed in 2009.
16. Mũkũũ, Benjamin: Bishop, AIC Kĩtui Area Church Council, Kĩtui County; interviewed in 2012.
17. Mũlemba, Daniel Masĩla (now late [October 2018]): Former Christian Education Coordinator, AIC Mboonĩ RCC; Former Senior pastor, AIC Ngaa local church, Kĩkĩma DCC, Mboonĩ RCC; Makũenĩ County; interviewed in 2009.
18. Mũlinge, Jeremiah: Assistant pastor, AIC Ngaa, Mboonĩ DCC; Makũenĩ County; interviewed in 2009.
19. Mũlwa, Abraham: Bishop, AIC Nairobi Area Church Council, from Makũenĩ County; interviewed in 2012.
20. Mũngũti, Paul Nzile (now late [October 2018]): Ex-senior chief, Mboonĩ Location, Mboonĩ West District, Makũenĩ County; interviewed in 2009.
21. Mũnyao, Anthony Mũle: Councilor until 2012, Upper Mboonĩ ward, Mboonĩ Constituency, Makũenĩ County; interviewed in 2009.
22. Mũnywokĩ, Samuel: Assistant Bishop, AIC Kĩtui Area Church Council, Kĩtui County; interviewed in 2012.
23. Mũtiso, Jones: Principal, AIC Mboonĩ Bible Institute; Chairman, Nzevenĩ DCC, Mboonĩ RCC; Makũenĩ County; interviewed in 2009.
24. Mũtĩsya, Joyfred Peter: Lecturer, Kenyatta University, Kĩtui campus; Pastor, AIC Mũtonguni DCC, Kĩtui Area Church Council; interviewed in 2009.
25. Mũtũnga, Joseph: Chairman, AIC Makũenĩ RCC; Principal,

Wote Bible Institute in 2012; interviewed in 2012.
26. Mwau, Daniel (now late [October 2018]): Former Pastor, AIC Kĩlenge local church, Ũtangwa DCC; Makũenĩ County; interviewed in 2009.
27. Mwenze, Dickson Mũtukũ: Local Church Council Chairman, AIC Ngong Road, Nairobi; Makũeni County; interviewed in 2009.
28. Ndolo, Joel: Former Acting chief, Mboonĩ Location, Mboonĩ West District; Makũenĩ County; interviewed in 2009.
29. Ngosi, Francis Kĩoko: Carpenter, peasant farmer, groceries kiosk operator and church elder, AIC Mũtũlu local church, Mboonĩ DCC; Makũenĩ County; interviewed in 2009.
30. Ngũi, Daniel: Bishop, AIC Makũenĩ Area Church Council, Makũenĩ County; interviewed in 2012.
31. Nguyo, Bernard: Bishop, AIC Machakos Area Church Council, Machakos County; interviewed in 2012.
32. Wainaina, Anthony Njuguna: Director, African Rural Trainers project; Nakuru County; interviewed in 2009.
33. Yego, Silas Misoi: Presiding Bishop, AIC Kenya Central Church Council; Trans-Nzoia County. Although not interviewed in 2009 or 2012, the reference to Bishop Yego's 1986 sermon in Chapter 4 may be viewed as being at the same level as the interviews referenced in the chapter.

Bibliography

Primary Sources

Aristotle. *Aristotle: Art of Rhetoric*. Loeb Classical Library XXII: LCL 193. Edited by Jeffery Hendersen and G. P. Goold. Translated by John Henry Freese. Cambridge, MA; London: Harvard University Press; Heinemann, 1926.

———. *Nicomachean Ethics*, edited by Roger Crisp, Cambridge Texts in the History of Philosophy. Cambridge: Cambridge University Press, 2000.

———. *Politics*. Loeb Classical Library XXI. Edited by G. P. Goold. Translated by H. Rackham. Cambridge, MA: Harvard University Press, 1932.

Bromiley, Geoffrey W., ed. *The International Standard Bible Encyclopedia* 4. Grand Rapids: Eerdmans, 1988.

Childs, Brevard S. *The New Testament as Canon: An Introduction*. London: SCM, 1985.

Cicero, Marcus Tullius. *On Duties*. Edited by G. P. Goold. Translated by Walter Miller. Loeb Classical Library 30. Cambridge, MA: Harvard University Press, 1913.

———. *The Verrine Orations I: Against Caecilius. Against Verres, Part 1; Part 2, Books 1–2*. Translated by L. H. G. Greenwood. Loeb Classical Library 221. Cambridge, MA: Harvard University Press, 1928.

Clement, Ignatius, Polycarp, Barnabas, Quadratus, Diognetus and Hermas. *The Apostolic Fathers*. Edited by Jeffery Henderson. Translated by Bart D. Ehrman. Loeb Classical Library. Cambridge, MA; London: Harvard University Press, 2003.

Cloud, Duncan. "The Client-Patron Relationship: Emblem and Reality in Juvenal's First Book." In *Patronage in Ancient Society*, edited by Andrew Wallace-Hadrill, 205–218. London; New York: Routledge, 1990.

Crawford, M. H., ed. *Roman Statutes I*. Bulletin of the Institute of Classical Studies Supplement 64. London: Institute of Classical Studies, University of London, 1996.

Demosthenes. *Demosthenes: Orations XVIII–XIX: De Corona, De Falsa Legatione.* Edited by G. P. Goold. Translated by C. A. Vince and J. H. Vince. Loeb Classical Library 155. Cambridge, MA; London: Harvard University Press, 1939.

Dionysius of Halicarnassus. *Roman Antiquities, Volume I: Books 1–2.* Translated by Earnest Cary. Loeb Classical Library 319. Cambridge, MA; London: Harvard University Press, 1937.

Ehrman, Bart D. *The Apostolic Fathers*, Loeb 1. Cambridge, MA and London: Harvard University Press, 2003.

Flaccus, Quintus Horatius (Horace). "Epistle I.18." *Epistle I.18*. No pages. Accessed 11 June 2008. http://www.humnet.ucla.edu/horaces-villa/poetry/Epistle1.18.html.

Gonzalez, Julian, and Michael H. Crawford. "The Lex Irnitana: A New Copy of the Flavian Municipal Law." *The Journal of Roman Studies* 76 (1986): 147–243.

Hawthorn, Gerald F., Ralph P. Martin, and Daniel G. Reid, eds. *Dictionary of Paul and His Letters: A Compendium of Contemporary Biblical Scholarship.* Downers Grove, IL: InterVarsity Press, 1993.

Hermas. "The Shepherd of Hermas." *Early Christian Writings.* Translated by J. B. Lightfoot. http://www.earlyChristianwritings.com/shepherd.html, 2001–2006.

Homer. *The Odyssey of Homer.* With Introduction and Notes. Edited by Charles W. Eliot. Translated by S. H. Butcher and A. Lang. The Harvard Classics 22. New York: P. F. Collier & Son, 1909.

Josephus, Flavius. *Josephus: Complete Works.* Translated by William Whiston. Grand Rapids: Kregel, 1978.

———. *Life of Josephus.* Translated by Steve Mason. Boston; Leiden: Brill, 2003.

Kent, John Harvey. *The Inscriptions 1926–1950. Corinth: Results of Excavations.* Vol. 8 part 3. Princeton, NJ: Princeton University Press, 1966.

Kirby, Peter. "Artapanus." *Early Jewish Writings: Tanakh, Deuterocanon, Pseudepigrapha, Others.* No pages. Accessed 20 May 2008. http://www.earlyjewishwritings.com/artapanus.html.

———. "Didache." *Early Christian Writings.* No pages. Accessed 17 August 2009. Posted on 2 February 2006. http://www.earlyChristianwritings.com/didache.html.

———. "The Sibylline Oracles." *Early Jewish Writings.* Accessed 20 May 2008. http://www.earlyjewishwritings.com/sibylline.html.

Latyschev, Basil. *Inscriptiones antiquae orae septentrionalis Ponti Euxini graecae et latinae* 1. 2nd edition. Petersburg: Royal Archaeological Society of Russia, 1916.

Livy. *Ab Urbe Condita*. Loeb Classical Library Book 41: Livy Vol. 12. Cambridge, MA: Harvard University Press, 1938.

Lucian. *Nigrinus: Lucian to Nigrinus. Health*. Translated by H. W. Fowler and F. G. Fowler. Oxford: Clarendon, 1905; Online ed. "Nigrinus." *The Works of Lucian of Samosata I*. Chapel Hill, NC; Project Gutenberg: University of North Carolina, 2006. http://www.sacred-texts.com/cla/luc/wl1/wl109.htm.

McCrum, M., and A. G. Woodhead. *Select Documents of the Principates of the Flavian Emperors: Including the Year of Revolution, A.D. 68–96*. Cambridge: Cambridge University Press, 1961.

Mørkholm, Otto. *Antiochus IV of Syria*. Classica et Mediaevalia: Dissertationes 8. Copenhagen: Gyldendalske Boghandel, 1966.

Parsons, Talcott. *Politics and Social Structure*. New York: Free Press, 1969.

Petzl, G., ed. *Die Inschriften von Smyrna*. II. Bonn: Habelt, 1987.

Philo. *On the Confusion of Tongues, On the Migration of Abraham, Who Is the Heir of Divine Things, On Mating with the Preliminary Studies*. Translated by F. H. Colson and G. H. Whitaker. Loeb Classical Library IV. London: William Heinemann, 1968.

———. *On Abraham, On Joseph, On Moses (De Vita Mosis)*. Translated by F. H. Colson. Loeb Classical Library VI. London: William Heinemann, 1966.

———. *Philo Supplement II: Questions and Answers on Exodus*. Translated by Ralph Marcus. Loeb Classical Library. London: William Heinemann, 1953.

———. *The Works of Philo: Complete and Unabridged*. New updated ed. Translated by C. D. Yonge. Peabody, MA: Hendrickson, 1993.

Pliny. "Ancient History Sourcebook: Pliny the Younger (61/62-113 CE): Selected Letters, c 100 CE." *Fordham University*. Harvard Classics Series. Translated by William Melmoth. No pages. Accessed 31 May 2011. http://www.fordham.edu/halsall/ancient/pliny-letters.html.

———. "Pliny, Letters 10.96-97: Pliny and Trajan on the Christians." *Letters - Pliny and Trajan on the Christians*. No pages. Accessed 12 May 2011. http://www.hadrians.com/rome/romans/sources/pliny_letters.html.

Plutarch. *How to Tell a Flatterer from a Friend*. Translated by Mr Tullie of Queen's College. William Goodwin 1878 ed. Boston: Little, Brown & Co., 2006.

———. "Isis and Osiris." In *Plutarch: Moralia: Volume V*, translated by Frank Cole Babbitt, LCL. Cambridge, MA; London: Harvard University Press, 1936.

———. *Lives, Volume II: Themistocles and Camillus, Aristides and Cato Major, Cimon and Lucullus*. Edited by Jeffery Henderson. Translated by Bernadotte Perrin. Loeb Classical Library 47. Cambridge, MA; London: Harvard University Press, 1914.

———. *Moralia: Volume V*. Translated by Frank Cole Babbitt. Cambridge, MA; London: Harvard University Press, 1936.

———. *Moralia: Volume X*. Edited by Jeffery Henderson. Translated by Harold North Fowler. Loeb Classical Library 321. Cambridge, MA; London: Harvard University Press, 1936.
Polybius. *Polybius: The Histories*. Edited by G. P. Goold. Translated by W. R. Paton. Loeb Classical Library I. Cambridge, MA: Harvard University, 1922.
———. *Polybius: The Histories*. Edited by G. P. Goold. Translated by W. R. Paton. Loeb Classical Library III. Cambridge, MA: Harvard University, 1923.
———. *Polybius: The Histories*. Edited by G. P. Goold. Translated by W. R. Paton. Loeb Classical Library V. Cambridge, MA: Harvard University Press, 1926.
———. *Polybius: The Histories*. Edited by G. P. Goold. Translated by W. R. Paton. Loeb Classical Library VI. Cambridge, MA: Harvard University Press, 1927.
Robinson, John A. T. *Redating the New Testament*. London: SCM, 1976.
Seneca, Lucius Annaeus. *Seneca: Ad Lucilium Epistulae Morales*. Edited by E. Capps, T. E. Page, and W. H. D. Rouse. Translated by Richard M. Gummere. Loeb Classical Library. London; New York: Heinemann; G. P. Putnam's Sons, 1918.
———. *Seneca III: Moral Essays III*. Edited by G. P. Goold. Translated by John W. Basore. Loeb Classical Library. Cambridge, MA: Harvard University Press, 1989. Translation of *L. Annaei Senecae Ad Aebutium Liberalem: De Beneficiis*.
Stylow, Armin U. "LA LEX MALACITANA, DESCRIPCIÓN Y TEXTO." *Corpus Inscriptionum Latinum* II (2001): 39–50.

Secondary Sources

Aageson, James W. *Paul, the Pastoral Epistles, and the Early Church: Library of Pauline Studies*. Peabody, MA: Hendrickson, 2008.
Achebe, Chinua. *Things Fall Apart*. New York: McDowell, Obolensky, 1959.
Adams, Edward. "Earliest Christian Meeting Places." Paper presented at British New Testament Conference, St John's College, Durham University, UK, 6 September 2008.
Adams, Merrihew Arthur. *Effective Leadership for Today's Church*. Philadelphia: Westminster, 1978.
Adams, Sean A. "Benefaction in Luke's Gospel." Review of *Jesus, Patrons, and Benefactors: Roman Palestine and the Gospel of Luke*, by Jonathan Marshall. *The Expository Times* 121 (January 2010): 186.

Adeyemo, Tokunboh, ed. *Africa Bible Commentary*. Nairobi, Kenya: WordAlive, 2006.

———. *Salvation in African Tradition*. Nairobi: Evangel Publishing House, 1979.

Allen, David. "Reciprocity & Benefaction in Hebrews." Review of *Enabling Fidelity to God: Perseverance in Hebrews in Light of the Reciprocity Systems of the Ancient Mediterranean World*, by Jason A. Whitlark. *The Expository Times* 121 (January 2010): 210.

Andria, Solomon. "Generosity and Solidarity." In *Africa Bible Commentary*, edited by Tokunboh Adeyemo, 231. Nairobi: WordAlive, 2006.

———. "1 Timothy." In *Africa Bible Commentary*, edited by Tokunboh Adeyemo, 1469–1476. Nairobi: WordAlive, 2006.

Arichea, Daniel C., and Howard A. Hatton. *A Handbook on Paul's Letters to Timothy and Titus*. New York: United Bible Societies, 1995.

Arterbury, Andrew. *Entertaining Angels: Early Christian Hospitality in Its Mediterranean Setting*. New Testament Monographs 8. Sheffield: Sheffield Phoenix, 2005.

Ascough, Richard S. "Forms of Commensality in Graeco-Roman Associations." Draft paper for the SBL Graeco-Roman Meals Consultation. http://www.philipharland.com/meals/AscoughCommensalityiAssociations.pdf 2003?, 1–33.

———. "The Thessalonian Christian Community as a Professional Voluntary Association." *Journal of Biblical Literature* 119, no. 2 (Summer, 2000): 311–328.

Babcock Gove, Philip, and The Merriam-Webster Editorial Staff, eds. *Webster's Third New International Dictionary of the English Language Unabridged*. Springfield, MA: G. & C. Merriam, 1961.

Balch, David L., Everett Ferguson, and Wayne A. Meeks, eds. *Greeks, Romans, and Christians: Essays in Honor of Abraham J. Malherbe*. Minneapolis: Fortress, 1990.

Barclay, John M. G. *Jews in the Mediterranean Diaspora: From Alexander to Trajan (323 BCE–117 CE)*. Edinburgh: T & T Clark, 1996.

———. *Paul and the Gift*. Grand Rapids: Eerdmans, 2015.

———. *Paul and the Subversive Power of Grace*. Grove Biblical Series 80. Cambridge: Grove Books, 2016.

———. "Who Was Considered an Apostate in the Jewish Diaspora?" In *Tolerance and Intolerance in Early Judaism and Christianity*, edited by Graham N. Stanton and Guy G. Stroumsa, 80–98. Cambridge: Cambridge University Press, 1998.

Barrett, C. K., ed. *The New Testament Background: Writings from Ancient Greece and the Roman Empire That Illuminate Christian Origins*. San Francisco: HarperSanFrancisco, 1995.

Bartsch, H. W. *Die Anfänge urchristlicher Rechtsbildungen: Studien zu den Pastoralbriefen*. Hamburg: Reich, 1965.

Bassler, Jouette M. "The Widows' Tale: A Fresh Look at 1 Tim 5:3–16." *Journal of Biblical Literature* 103, no. 1 (March 1984): 23–41.

Batten, Alicia. "God in the Letter of James: Patron or Benefactor?" *New Testament Studies* 50, no. 2 (April 2004): 257–272.

Bauer, Walter. *Die Briefe des Ignatius von Antiochia und der Brief des Polykarp von Smyrna*. Tübingen: Mohr, 1985.

Bauer, Walter, F. W. Danker, W. F. Arndt, and F. W. Gingrich. *A Greek-English Lexicon of the New Testament and Other Early Christian Literature*. 3rd edition. Chicago: University of Chicago Press, 2000.

Baugh, Steven M. "'Savior of All People': 1 Tim 4:10 in Context." *Westminster Theological Journal* 54, no. 2 (Fall, 1992): 331–340.

BBC News. "Uganda Tackles Wife-Beating Taboo." *BBC News*. No pages. Accessed 27 April, 2009. Published on 19 March, 2002 at 18:28 GMT. http://news.bbc.co.uk/2/hi/africa/1881472.stm.

Beard, Mary, John North, and Simon Price. *Religions of Rome. Volume 1: A History*. Cambridge, UK: Cambridge University Press, 1998.

———. *Religions of Rome. Volume 2: A Sourcebook*. Cambridge, UK: Cambridge University Press, 1998.

Betz, Hans Dieter. "Christianity and Antiquity." *Journal of Biblical Literature* 117, no. 1 (1998): 3–22.

Botha, J. E., and P. A. Rousseau. "For God Did Not So Love the Whole World – Only Israel! John 3:16 revisited." *HTS Theological Studies* 61, no. 4 (October 2005): 1149–1168.

Brown, Colin, ed. *The New International Dictionary of New Testament Theology* 3. Exeter, Devon; Grand Rapids, MI: Paternoster, 1978.

Brox, Norbert. *Die Pastoralbriefe: Timotheus I, Timotheus II, Titus*. Regensburger Neues Testament 7. Band. Zweiter Teil: Die Pastoralbriefe. Regensburg: Verlag Friedrich Pustet, 1969.

Buck, Andrew D. "Postsocialist Patronage: Expressions of Resistance and Loyalty." *Studies in Comparative International Development* 41, no. 3 (Fall 2006): 3–24.

Buckwalter, H. Douglas. "The Divine Saviour." In *Witness to the Gospel: the Theology of Acts*, edited by I. Howard Marshall and David Peterson, 107–124. Grand Rapids: Eerdmans, 1998.

Calvin, John. *The Second Epistle of Paul the Apostle to the Corinthians and the Epistles to Timothy, Titus and Philemon*. Translated by T. A. Smail. Calvin's

New Testament Commentaries. Grand Rapids, MI: Eerdmans, Paternoster, 1973.

Campbell, Alastair. *The Elders: Seniority within Earliest Christianity*. Studies of the New Testament and its World. Edinburgh: Clark, 1994.

Capper, Brian. "Reciprocity and the Ethic of Acts." In *Witness to the Gospel: the Theology of Acts*, edited by I. Howard Marshall and David Peterson, 499–518. Grand Rapids: Eerdmans, 1998.

Caragounis, Chrys C. "St. Paul and Corinth: A House Church in Corinth? An Inquiry into the Structure of Early Corinthian Christianity." Lecture presented at the Corinth Congress, University of Corinth, 23–25 September, 2007.

Carter, Brandon. "The Authorship of the Pastoral Epistles." A Senior Honours Thesis in partial fulfilment of the requirements for graduation from the Honours Program of Liberty University. Liberty University, 2007.

Cavazzi, Franco. "Late Republic Chronology." *The Late Roman Republic*. No pages. Accessed April, 2008. http://www.roman-empire.net/republic/laterep-index.html.

Chow, John K. *Patronage and Power: A Study of Social Networks in Corinth*. Sheffield: JSOT, 1992.

Cohick, Lynn. *Women in the World of the Earliest Christians*. Grand Rapids: Baker, 2009.

"Collegia: Roman Organization." Accessed 22 May 2009, http://www.britannica.com/EBchecked/topi/125659/collegia.

Collins, Raymond F. *I & II Timothy and Titus: A Commentary*. Louisville: Westminster John Knox, 2002.

Colvin, Stephen, ed. *The Greco-Roman East: Politics, Culture, Society*. Yale Classical Studies. Cambridge, UK: Cambridge University Press, 2004.

Cordell, Dennis D., and Joel W. Gregory, eds. *African Population and Capitalism: Historical Perspectives*. Madison, WI: University of Wisconsin Press, 1994.

Crawford, Michael H. "Tabula Irnitana." In *The Oxford Classical Dictionary: The Ultimate Reference Work on the Classical World*, edited by Simon Hornblower and Anthony Spawforth, 1467. Oxford: Oxford University Press, 2003.

Crook, Zeba. A. *Reconceptualising Conversion: Patronage, Loyalty, and Conversion in the Religions of the Ancient Mediterranean*. Berlin: Walter de Gruyter, 2004.

Crossan, John Dominic. *The Historical Jesus: The Life of a Mediterranean Jewish Peasant*. New York: HarperSanFrancisco, 1991.

Crystal, David, ed. *The Cambridge Encyclopedia*. 3rd edition. Cambridge, UK; New York; Melbourne: Cambridge University Press, 1992.

Czachesz, István. "The Emergence of Early Christian Religion: A Naturalistic Approach." In *Explaining Christian Origins and Early Judaism: Contributions from Cognitive and Social Science*, edited by Petri Luomanen, Ilkka Pyysiäinen, and Risto Uro, 73–94. Biblical Interpretation Series 89. Leiden: Brill, 2007.

Danker, Frederick W. "Benefactor." In *The Anchor Bible Dictionary* 1: A-C, edited by David Noel Freedman, 669–671. 6 vols. New York: Doubleday, 1992.

———. *Benefactor: Epigraphic Study of a Graeco-Roman and New Testament Semantic Field*. St Louis: Clayton, 1982.

Davids, Peter H. *The Epistle of James*. New International Greek Testament Commentary. Grand Rapids: Eerdmans, 1982.

De Boer, Martinus C. "The Nazoreans: Living at the Boundary of Judaism and Christianity." In *Tolerance and Intolerance in Early Judaism and Christianity*, edited by Graham N. Stanton and Guy G. Stroumsa, 239–262. Cambridge: Cambridge University Press, 1998.

Democratic Underground Administrators. "Swazi King: 12 wives, one other bride-to-be. 27 children." Accessed 27 April 2009. http://www.democraticunderground.com/discuss/duboard.php?az=view_all&address=105x4062402.

deSilva, David A. "Exchanging Favour for Wrath: Apostasy in Hebrews and Patron-Client Relationships." *Journal of Biblical Literature* 115, no. 1 (Spring 1996): 91–116.

———. *Honor, Patronage, Kinship & Purity: Unlocking New Testament Culture*. Downers Grove: InterVarsity Press, 2000.

———. "Patronage." In *Dictionary of New Testament Background*, edited by Craig A. Evans and Stanley E. Porter, 766–771. Downers Grove: InterVarsity Press, 2000.

———. "Patronage and Reciprocity." *Ashland Theological Journal* 31 (1999): 32–84.

Dibelius, Martin. *Die Pastoralbriefe*. Handbuch zum Neuen Testament 13. Tübingen: Mohr Siebeck, 1955.

Dibelius, Martin, and Hans Conzelmann. *The Pastoral Epistles: A Commentary on the Pastoral Epistles*. Philadelphia: Fortress, 1972.

Donahoe, Kate C. "From Self-Praise to Self-Boasting: Paul's Unmasking of the Conflicting Rhetoric-Linguistic Phenomena in 1 Corinthians." PhD dissertation. The University of St Andrews, Scotland, 2008.

Duff, Jeremy. *The Elements of New Testament Greek*. Cambridge: Cambridge University, 2005.

Duling, Dennis C. *The New Testament: History, Literature and Social Context*. 4th edition. Belmont, CA: Thomson/Wadsworth, 2003.

Duncan-Jones, Richard. *The Economy of the Roman Empire: Quantitative Studies*. 2nd edition. Cambridge: Cambridge University Press, 1982.

Dunn, James, D. G. *Romans 9–16*. Word Biblical Commentary 38B. Dallas: Word Books, 1988.

Easton, Burton Scott. *The Pastoral Epistles: Introduction, Translation, Commentary and Word Studies*. New York: Scribner's Sons, 1947.

Ebbinghaus, Susanne. "Protector of the City, or the Art of Storage in Early Greece." *The Journal of Hellenistic Studies* 125 (November 2005): 51–72.

Editors of Encyclopaedia Britannica. "Martyrs of Uganda." *Encyclopædia Britannica*. Accessed 22 October 2009. http://www.britannica.com/EBchecked/topic/612654/Martyrs-of-Uganda.

Eilers, Claude. *Roman Patrons of Greek Cities*. Oxford: Oxford University Press, 2002.

Eisenstadt, S. N., and L. Roniger. *Patron, Clients and Friends: Interpersonal Relations and the Structure of Trust in Society*. Cambridge: Cambridge University Press, 1984.

Encyclopaedia Judaica. 16 vols. Jerusalem, Israel: Encyclopaedia Judaica Jerusalem, and Keter, 1971.

Engberg-Pedersen, Troels. "Gift-Giving and Friendship: Seneca and Paul in Romans 1–8 on the Logic of God's Χάρις and Its Human Response." *Harvard Theological Review* 101, no. 1 (January 2008): 15–44.

Esler, Philip Francis. *Community and Gospel in Luke-Acts: The Social and Political Motivation of Lukan Theology*. Cambridge: Cambridge University Press, 1987.

———. *Modelling Early Christianity: Social-Scientific Studies of the New Testament in Its Context*. London: Routledge, 1995.

Evans, Craig A., and Stanley E. Porter, eds. *Dictionary of New Testament Background*. Downers Grove, IL: InterVarsity Press, 2000.

———. *New Testament Backgrounds: A Sheffield Reader*. Biblical Seminar 43. Sheffield: Sheffield Academic, 1997.

Hatzitsinidou, Evangelia. "Athena, Poseidon and the Patronage of Athens." *Greek-Gods.Info: Gods & Goddesses of Ancient Greece*. Accessed 12 October, 2018. http://www.greek-gods.info/greek-gods/poseidon/stories/poseidon-athena-contest/.

———. "Olympian Gods: Athena." *Greek-Gods.Info: Gods & Goddesses of Ancient Greece*. Accessed 12 October, 2018. Online: http://greek-gods.info/greek-gods/athena/.

Fee, Gordon D. *1 and 2 Timothy, Titus*. New International Biblical Commentary. Peabody, MA: Hendrickson, 1988.

———. Review of *Wealth and Beneficence in the Pastoral Epistles: A Bourgeois Form of Early Christianity?*, by Reggie Kidd. SBL Dissertation Series 122. *Journal of Biblical Literature* 111, no. 2 (Summer 1992): 352–354.

Ferguson, Everett. *Backgrounds of Early Christianity*. Grand Rapids, MI: Eerdmans, 1993.

Field, Eugene, and Roswell Martin Field. "Echoes from the Sabine Farm by Eugene and Roswell Martin Field." *Odes of Horace: by Michael Gilleland*. Accessed 28 April 2008. http://www.mgilleland.com/efechoes.htm.

Fiore, Benjamin. *The Pastoral Epistles: First Timothy, Second Timothy, Titus*. Sacra Pagina 12. Collegeville, MN: Liturgical Press, 2007.

Frey, Jean Baptiste. *Corpus Inscriptionum Iudaicarum, Rome*. Pontifical Institute of Biblical Archaeology 1. New York: KTAV, 1936, 1952, 1975.

Frier, Bruce W. "Urban Praetors and Rural Violence: The Legal Background of Cicero's Pro Caecina." *Transactions of the American Philological Association* 113 (1983): 221–241.

Gehman, Richard. *African Traditional Religion in Biblical Perspective*. Nairobi: East African Educational Publishers, 2005.

Gellner, E., and J. Waterbury, eds. *Patrons and Clients in Mediterranean Societies*. London: Duckworth, 1977.

Georgi, Dieter. "The Early Church – Internal Jewish Migration or New Religion?" *Harvard Theological Review* 88, no. 1 (1995): 35–68.

Gifford, Paul. "Prosperity." In *The Oxford Companion to Christian Thought: Intellectual, Spiritual, and Moral Horizons of Christianity*, edited by Adrian Hastings, Alistair Mason and Hugh Pyper, 570–571. Oxford: Oxford University Press, 2000.

Gill, Malcolm. *Jesus as Mediator: Politics and Polemic in 1 Timothy 2:1–7*. Oxford: Lang, 2008.

Goulder, Michael. "The Pastor's Wolves: Jewish Christian Visionaries behind the Pastoral Epistles." *Novum Testamentum* 38, no. 3 (July, 1996): 242–256.

Gowler, David B. "Text, Culture, and Ideology in Luke 7:1–10." In *Fabrics of Discourse: Essays in Honor of Vernon K. Robbins*, edited by David B. Gowler, L. Gregory Bloomquist, and Duane F. Watson, 89–125. Harrisburg, PA: Trinity Press International, 2003.

Greer, Stephen. "First Century Jewish Culture and Christianity: The Ties That Bind." *Planet Preterist*. Accessed 28 March 2008. http://planetpreterist.com/modules.php?name=News&file=printpdf&sid=5430.

Grenfell, Bernard P., and Arthur S. Hunt. *The Oxyrhynchus Papyri: Part X*. London: Egypt Exploration Fund, 1914.

Grubbs, Judith Evans. *Women and the Law in the Roman Empire*. London: Routledge, 2002.

Guthrie, Donald. *The Pastoral Epistles*. Revised edition. Tyndale New Testament Commentaries. Leicester: InterVarsity Press, 1990.

Hakola, Raimo. "Social Identities and Group Phenomena in Second Temple Judaism." In *Explaining Christian Origins and Early Judaism: Contributions from Cognitive and Social Science*, edited by Petri Luomanen, Ilkka Pyysiäinen, and Risto Uro, 259–276. Biblical Interpretation Series 89. Leiden: Brill, 2007.

Hanson, A. T. *The Pastoral Epistles*. New Century Bible Commentary. Grand Rapids, MI: Eerdmans, 1982.

Harding, Mark. *What Are They Saying about the Pastoral Epistles?* What Are They Saying Series. New York: Paulist, 2000.

Harrison, James R. "Benefaction Ideology and Christian Responsibility for Widows." In *New Documents Illustrating Early Christianity*, vol. 8, *A Review of the Greek Inscriptions and Papyri Published in 1984–85*, edited by S. R. Llewelyn. Macquarie University, NSW: Ancient History Documentary Research, 1998.

———. "Benefactor of the People." In *New Documents Illustrating Early Christianity*, vol. 9, *A Review of the Greek Inscriptions and Papyri Published in 1986–87*, edited by S. R. Llewelyn, 6. Macquarie University, NSW: Ancient History Documentary Research, 2002.

———. "Excels Ancestral Honours." In *New Documents Illustrating Early Christianity*, vol. 9, *A Review of the Greek Inscriptions and Papyri Published 1986–87*, edited by S. R. Llewelyn, 20–21. Macquarie University, NSW: Ancient History Documentary Research Centre, 2002.

———. "Paul and the Gymnasiarchs: Two Approaches to Pastoral Formation in Antiquity." In *Pauline Studies Volume V: Paul: Jew, Greek, and Roman*, edited by S. R. Porter, 141–178. Leiden: Brill, 2008.

———. *Paul's Language of Grace in Its Graeco-Roman Context*. Tübingen: Mohr Siebeck, 2003.

———. "Saviour of the People." In *New Documents Illustrating Early Christianity*, vol. 9, *A Review of the Greek Inscriptions and Papyri Published in 1986–87*, edited by S. R. Llewelyn, 4–5. University, NSW: Ancient History Documents Research Centre, 2002.

Harrison, Percy Neale. *The Problem of the Pastoral Epistles*. London: Oxford University Press, 1921.

Hasler, V. *Die Briefe an Timotheus und Titus (Pastoralbriefe)*. ZürBibelkommentare 12. Zürich: Theologischer Verlag Zürich, 1978.

Hays, Richard B. *The Moral Vision of the New Testament: Community, Cross, New Creation; A Contemporary Introduction to New Testament Ethics*. New York: HarperCollins, 1996.

Heen, Erik M. "Radical Patronage in Luke-Acts." *Currents in Theology and Mission*. Accessed 8 April 2008. Posted on 1 December 2006. http://www.encyclopedia.com/doc/1G1-156274385.html.

Heidland, H. W. *Theological Dictionary of the New Testament*. Vol. 5, edited by Gerrard Kittle and Gerhard Friedrich, translated by Geoffrey W. Bromiley, 447–448. Grand Rapids: Eerdmans, 1964–1976.

Hendrix, Holland. "Benefactor/Patron Networks in the Urban Environment: Evidence from Thessalonica." *Semeia* 56 (1992): 39–58.

Hengel, Martin. *Judaism and Hellenism: Studies in Their Encounter in Palestine during the Early Hellenistic Period*. Translated by John Bowden. Philadelphia: Fortress, 1974.

Herr, Moshe David. "Ancient History: Jews in the Land of Israel from Cyrus to Mohammed." In *Encyclorama of Israel* 1, edited by Arie Serper, 1–47. 7 vols. Jerusalem: Pierre Illouz, 1986.

Higher Education Group. "Commentary: Oxford Classical Mythology Online: Aeneid." *Oxford University Press*. Accessed 20 July 2011, http://www.oup.com/us/companion.websites/0195153448/studentresources/chapters/ch26/commentary/?view=usa.

Hill, Craig C. "The Jerusalem Church." In *Jewish Christianity Reconsidered: Rethinking Ancient Groups and Texts*, edited by Matt Jackson-McCabe, 39–59. Minneapolis: Fortress, 2007.

Hillard, T. W. "Roman Patronal Practice in the Greek East." In *New Documents Illustrating Early Christianity*. Vol. 9, *A Review of the Greek Inscriptions and Papyri Published in 1986-87*, edited by S. R. Llewelyn, 17–18. Macquarie University, NSW: Ancient History Documentary Research Centre, 2002.

Hobbs, T. R. "Reflections on Honor, Shame, and Covenant Relations." *Journal of Biblical Literature* 16, no. 3 (Autumn 1997): 501–503.

Holman, Susan R. *Wealth and Poverty in Early Church and Society*. Holy Cross Studies in Patristic Theology and History. Grand Rapids, MI: Baker Academic, 2008.

Homer. "Homer, Iliad." *Perseus Collection: Greek and Roman Materials*, edited by Gregory R. Crane of Tufts University, Massachusetts. Accessed 25 August 2011, http://www.perseus.tufts.edu/hopper/text?doc=Perseus%3Atext%3A1999.01.0133%3Abook%3D2%3Acard%3D1.

Hondius, J. J. E., ed. *Supplementum Epigrephicum Graecum*. SEG no. 696. Leiden: Brill 1923.

Honeyghan, Glaceta. "Inspirational Quote." *Inspiration Line: The Meaningful Life Magazine*. 18 September 2008. http://www.inspirationline.com/EZINE/18SEP006.htm.

Horrell, David. "Converging Ideologies: Berger and Luckmann and the Pastoral Epistles." In *New Testament Interpretation and Methods*, edited by Stanley E. Porter, and Craig A. Evans, 102–120. Sheffield: Sheffield Academic Press, 1997.

———. "Leadership Patterns and the Development of Ideology in Early Christianity." *Sociology of Religion* 58, no. 4 (1997): 323–341.

———. *Social-Scientific Approaches to New Testament Interpretation*. Edinburgh: T & T Clark, 1999.

Horsley, G. H. R., ed. *New Documents Illustrating Early Christianity*, vol. 4, *A Review of the Greek Inscriptions and Papyri Published in 1979B*. Macquarie University, NSW: The Ancient History Documentary Research Centre, 1987.

———. *New Documents Illustrating Early Christianity*, vol. 5, *Linguistic Essays*. Macquarie University, NSW: Ancient History Documentary Research Centre, 1989.

———. "Sophia, 'the Second Phoibe.'" In *New Documents Illustrating Early Christianity*, vol. 4, *A Review of the Greek Inscriptions and Papyri Published in 1979*, edited by G. H. R. Horsley, 239–244. Macquarie University, NSW: Ancient History Documentary Research Centre, 1987.

Horsley, G. H. R., and S. R. Llewelyn. *New Documents Illustrating Early Christianity*, vol. 2, *A Review of the Greek Inscriptions and Papyri Published in 1977*. Macquarie University, NSW: Ancient History Documentary Research Centre, 1977.

Howell, Justin R. "The Imperial Authority and Benefaction of Centurions and Acts 10.34–43: A Response to C. Kavin Rowe." *Journal for the Study of the New Testament* 31, no. 1 (September 2008) 25–51. Accessed 3 June 2009. http://jnt.sagepub.com/cgi/content/abstract/31/1/25.

Humm, Alan. "Artapanus." *Artapanus*. No pages. Accessed 20 May 2008. http://ccat.sas.upenn.edu/~humm/Resources/OT/Artapanus.html.

Idowu, E. Bọlaji. *African Traditional Religion: A Definition*. London: SCM Press, 1982.

Jackson-McCabe, Matt. "What's in a Name? The Problem of 'Jewish Christianity.'" In *Jewish Christianity Reconsidered: Rethinking Ancient Groups and Texts*, edited by Matt Jackson-McCabe, 7–38. Minneapolis: Fortress, 2007.

Jeffers, James S. *The Greco-Roman World of the NT Era: Exploring the Background of Early Christianity*. Downers Grove, IL: InterVarsity Press, 1999.

Jeremias, Joachim. *Die Briefe an Timotheus und Titus*. Göttingen: Vandenhoeck und Ruprecht, 1934, 1963.

Johnson, Luke Timothy. *The First and Second Letters to Timothy: A New Translation with Introduction and Commentary*. New York: Doubleday, 2001.

———. *Letters to Paul's Delegates: 1 Timothy, 2 Timothy, Titus*. The New Testament in Context. Valley Forge, PA: Trinity Press International, 1996.

Johnstone, Harold Whetstone. *The Private Life of the Romans*. Chicago: Foresman and Co. http://www.forumromanum.org/life/johnston_5.html.176

Johnstone, Patrick. *Operation World: The Day-by-Day Guide to Praying for the World*. 5th edition. Grand Rapids: Zondervan & Dorothea Mission, 1974. Grand Rapids: Zondervan; & OM Publishing, 1993.

Joubert, Stephan J. "Coming to Terms with a Neglected Aspect of Ancient Mediterranean Reciprocity: Seneca's Views on Benefit-Exchange in De Beneficiis as the Framework for a Model of Social Exchange." In *Social Scientific Models for Interpreting the Bible: Essays by the Context Group in Honor of Bruce J. Malina*, edited by John J. Pilch, 47–63. Biblical Interpretation. Leiden: Brill, 2001.

———. "Managing the Household: Paul as Pater Familias of the Christian Household Group in Corinth." In *Modelling Early Christianity: Social-Scientific Studies of the New Testament in Its Context*, edited by Philip F. Esler, 213–223. London: Routledge, 1995.

———. "One Form of Social Exchange or Two? 'Euergesia,' Patronage, and Testament Studies." *Biblical Theology Bulletin* 31, no. 1 (Spring 2001): 17–25.

———. *Paul as Benefactor*. Tübingen: Mohr Siebeck, 2000.

Judge, E. A. *The Social Pattern of Christian Groups in the First Century: Some Prolegomena to the Study of New Testament Ideas of Social Obligation*. London: Tyndale, 1960.

———. "St. Paul and Classical Society." *Jahrbuch für Antike und Christentum* 15 (1972): 19–36.

Judge, E. A., and David M. Scholer, eds. *Social Distinctives of the Christians in the First Century: Pivotal Essays by E. A. Judge*. Peabody, MA: Hendrickson, 2008.

Kalmin, Richard. "Christians and Heretics in Rabbinic Literature of Late Antiquity." *Harvard Theological Review* 87, no. 2 (April 1994): 155–169.

Karanja, James. *The Missionary Movement in Colonial Kenya: The Foundation of Africa Inland Church*. Göttingen: Cuvillier Verlag, 2009.

Kearsley, R. A. "A Civic Benefactor of the First Century in Asia Minor." In *New Documents Illustrating Early Christianity*, vol. 7, *A Review of the Greek Inscriptions and Papyri Published in 1982-83*, edited by S. R. Llewelyn and R. A. Kearsley, 233–241. Macquarie University, NSW: Ancient History Documentary Research Centre, 1994.

Keegan, Timothy. *Colonial South Africa and the Origins of the Racial Order*. Charlottesville: University Press of Virginia, 1996.

Kelly, John Norman Davidson. *A Commentary on the Pastoral Epistles: I & II Timothy, Titus*. Black's New Testament Commentaries. London: Black, 1963.

Kenyatta, Jomo. *Facing Mount Kenya*. Nairobi: Heinemann, 1978.

Keskin, Naci. *Ephesus*. Istanbul: Keskin Color, 2013.

Kidd, Reggie M. *Wealth and Beneficence in the Pastoral Epistles*. SBL Dissertation Series 122. Atlanta, GA: SBL Press, 1990.

Kim, Hong Bom. "The Interpretation of μαλιστα In 1 Timothy 5:17." *Novum Testamentum* 46, no. 4 (October 2004): 360–368.

Kimel, Alvin F. "Who Are the Bishops? Episkope and the Church." *Anglican Theological Review* 77, no. 1 (Winter 1995): 1–14.

Kimilu, D. N. *Mūkamba wa W'o*. Nairobi: Kenya Literature Bureau, 1962.

Kisau, Mumo P. *Inclusiveness of Christianity: A Study of the Theme of Inclusiveness in the Acts of the Apostles*. Saabrücken, Deutschland: Lambert Academic Publishing, 2010.

Kittel, Gerhard, and Gerhard Friedrich, eds. *Theological Dictionary of the New Testament* 4. Translated by Geoffrey W. Bromiley. 10 vols. Grand Rapids: Eerdmans, 1964–1976.

Klauck, Hans-Josef. *The Religious context of Early Christianity: A Guide to Graeco-Roman Religions*. Edited by John Barclay, Joel Marcus and John Riches. Translated by Brian McNeil. Studies of the New Testament and Its World. London; New York: T & T Clark, 2000. Originially published as, *Die Religiose Umwelt des Urchristentums*. Stuttgart: Kohlhammer Verlag, 1996.

———. "The Roman Empire." In *The Cambridge History of Christianity: Volume 1 Origins to Constantine*, edited by Margaret M. Mitchell and Frances M. Young, 69–83. Cambridge: Cambridge University Press, 2006.

Knight, George W., III. *The Pastoral Epistles: A Commentary on the Greek Text*. The New International Greek Testament Commentary. Carlisle: Paternoster, 1992.

Koeller, David W. "Mediterranean Basin Chronology: The Roman Principate, 27 BC–AD 312." *WEBCHRON: The Web Chronology Project*. No pages. Accessed 17 April 2008. http://www.thenagain.info/WebChron/Mediterranean/RomanEmpire.html.

Koester, Helmut. *History and Literature of Early Christianity*. New York: de Gruyter, 1995.

Köstenberger, Andreas J., and Thomas R. Schreiner. *Women in the Church: An Analysis and Application of 1 Timothy 2:9-15*. Grand Rapids: Baker Academic, 2005.

Krause, Deborah. *1 Timothy*. Readings: A New Biblical Commentary. London; New York: T & T Clark, 2004.

Kroll, John H. "The Greek Inscriptions of the Sardis Synagogue." *Harvard Theological Review* 94, no. 1 (January 2001): 5–55. Accessed 30 May 2008. http://journals.cambridge.org/download.php?file=%2FHTR%2FHTR94_01%2FS0017816000022021a.pdf&code=cc7ac658eed1d11600062d1042e9273c.

Kwenda, Chirevo V. "Beyond Patronage: Giving and Receiving in the Construction of Civil Society." *Journal of Theology for Southern Africa* 101 (July 1998): 1–10. http63.136.1.22plseliec.pdfapp. showpdfmyaid=ATLA0001001752.

Laqueur, Richard. *Der jüdische Historiker Flavius Josephus: ein biographischer Versuch auf neuer quellenkritischer Grundlage*. Darmstadt: Wissenschaftliche Buchgesellschaft, 1970 [1920]. http:/www.earlyjewishwritings.com/josephus.html.

Larson, Knute. *I & II Thessalonians, I & II Timothy, Titus, Philemon*. Holman New Testament Commentary. Nashville, TN: Broadman & Holman, 2000.

Lendon, J. E. *Empire of Honor*. Oxford: Oxford University Press, 2001.

Levinsohn, Stephen H. "Some Constraints on Discourse Development in the Pastoral Epistles in S. E. Porter and J. T. Reed (eds.)," In *Discourse Analysis and the New Testament: Approaches and Results*, edited by Stanley E. Porter and Jeffrey T. Reed, 316–333. Journal for the Study of New Testament Supplement Series 170. Sheffield: Sheffield Academic Press, 1999.

Lewins, Frank. "Continuity and Change in a Religious Organization: Some Aspects of the Australian Catholic Church." *Journal for the Scientific Study of Religion* 16, no. 4 (December 1977): 371–382.

Lewis, Robert M. "The 'Women' of 1 Timothy 3:11." *Bibliotheca Sacra* 136, no. 542 (1979): 167–175.

Liddell, Henry George, and Robert Scott. *A Greek-English Lexicon*. Revised supplement edition. Oxford: Clarendon, 1996.

Liefeld, Walter L. *1 & 2 Timothy/Titus*. The NIV Application Commentary. Grand Rapids: Zondervan, 1999.

Lillingston, K. M. E. *Glimpses of Uganda*. London: Church Missionary Society, 1939.

Llewelyn, S. R., ed. *New Documents Illustrating Early Christianity*, vol. 8, *A Review of the Greek Inscriptions and Papyri Published in 1984–85*. Macquarie University, NSW: Ancient History Documentary Research Centre, 1998.

———. *New Documents Illustrating Early Christianity*, vol. 9, *A Review of the Greek Inscriptions and Papyri Published in 1986–87*. Macquarie University, NSW; Grand Rapids, MI; Cambridge, UK: Ancient History Documentary Research Centre; Eerdmans, 2002.

Llewelyn, S. R., and R. A. Kearsley, eds. *New Documents Illustrating Early Christianity*, vol. 6, *A Review of the Greek Inscriptions and Papyri Published in 1980–81*. Macquarie University, NSW: Ancient History Documentary Research Centre, 1992.

———. *New Documents Illustrating Early Christianity*, vol. 7, *A Review of the Greek Inscriptions and Papyri Published in 1982–3*. Macquarie University, NSW: Ancient History Documentary Research Centre, 1994.

———. *New Documents Illustrating Early Christianity*, vol. 9, *A Review of the Greek Inscriptions and Papyri Published in 1986–87*. Macquarie University, NSW; Grand Rapids, MI; Cambridge, UK: Ancient History Documentary Research Centre; Eerdmans, 2002.

Lock, Walter. *A Critical and Exegetical Commentary on the Pastoral Epistles (I & II Timothy and Titus)*. Edinburgh: T & T Clark, 1978.

Lomas, Kathryn, and Tim Cornell, eds. *'Bread and Circuses': Euergesia and Municipal Patronage in Roman Italy*. London: Routledge, 2003.

Longfellow, Brenda. *Roman Imperialism and Civic Patronage: Form, Meaning, and Ideology in Monumental Fountain Complexes*. Cambridge; New York: Cambridge University Press, 2011.

Luomanen, Petri, Ilkka Pyysiäinen, and Risto Uro. "Introduction: Social and Cognitive Perspectives in the Study of Christian Origins and Early Judaism." In *Explaining Christian Origins and Early Judaism: Contributions from Cognitive and Social Science*, edited by Petri Luomanen, Ilkka Pyysiäinen, and Risto Uro, 1–33. Biblical Interpretation Series 89. Leiden: Brill, 2007.

MacGillivray, Erlend D. "Re-evaluating Patronage and Reciprocity in Antiquity and New Testament Studies." *Journal of Graeco-Roman Christianity and Judaism* 6 (2009): 37–81.

MacMullen, Ramsay. *Roman Social Relations, 50 BC to A.D. 284*. New Haven; London: Yale University Press, 1974.

———. "Women in Public in the Roman Empire." *Historia* 29 (1980): 208–218.

Maina, Steve. "When Pastors Fall." *The Church Leader in Africa: A Training Publication of Africa Ministry Resources* 16, no. 1 (January-March 2006): 4–6.

Malherbe, Abraham J. *Ancient Epistolary Theorists*. SBL Sources for Biblical Study 19. Atlanta, GA: Scholars Press, 1988.

Malherbe, Abraham J., Frederick W. Norris, and James W. Thompson, eds. *The Early Church in Its Context: Essays in Honor of Everett Ferguson*. Supplements to Novum Testamentum 90. Leiden: Brill, 1998.

Malina, Bruce J. *The Social World of Jesus and the Gospels*. London and New York: Routledge, 1996.

———. "Patron and Client: The Analogy behind Synoptic Theology." In *The Social World of Jesus and the Gospels*, 143–175. London; New York: Routledge, 1996.

Malina, Bruce J., and John J. Pilch. *Social-Science Commentary on the Letters of Paul*. Minneapolis: Fortress, 2006.

Malina, Bruce J., and Richard L. Rohrbaugh. *Social-Science Commentary on the Gospel of John*. Minneapolis: Fortress, 1998.

Marcus, Joel. "Jewish Christianity." In *The Cambridge History of Christianity: Volume 1 Origins to Constantine*, edited by Margaret M. Mitchell and Frances M. Young, 87–102. Cambridge: Cambridge University Press, 2006.

Marshall, I. Howard. *Commentary on Luke*. New International Greek Testament Commentary. Grand Rapids, MI: Eerdmans, 1978.

———. *The Epistles of John*. The New International Commentary on the New Testament. Grand Rapids: Eerdmans, 1978.

———. *The Pastoral Epistles*. The International Critical Commentary. London: T & T Clark, 1999.

Marshall, Jonathan. *Jesus, Patrons, and Benefactors: Roman Palestine and the Gospel of Luke*. Tübingen: Mohr Siebeck, 2009.

Marshall, Peter. *Enmity in Corinth: Social Conventions in Paul's Relations with the Corinthians*. Wissenschaftliche Untersuchungen Zum Neuen Testament 2/23. Tübingen: Mohr Siebeck, 1987.

Mbiti, John S. *African Religions & Philosophy*. New York: Praeger, 1969.

McVeigh, Malcolm J. "The Interaction of the Conceptions of God of African Traditional Religion and Christianity in the Thought of Edwin W. Smith." PhD dissertation. Boston University Graduate School, 1971.

Meeks, Wayne A. *The First Urban Christians: The Social World of the Apostle Paul*. New Haven; London: Yale University Press, 1983.

———. "Social and Ecclesial Life of the Earliest Christians." In *The Cambridge History of Christianity: Volume 1 Origins to Constantine*, edited by Margaret M. Mitchell and Frances M. Young, 145–173. Cambridge: Cambridge University Press, 2006.

Mercer, Mark. "The Benefactions of Antiochus IV Epiphanes and Dan 11:37–38: An Exegetical Note." *Master's Seminary Journal* 12, no. 1 (Spring 2001): 89–93.

Milavec, Aaron. *The Didache: Faith, Hope, & Life of the Earliest Christian Communities, 50–70 C.E.* Mahwah, NJ: Newman, 2003.

Milco, Michael R. *Ethical Dilemmas in Church Leadership*. Grand Rapids: Kregel, 1997.

Miller, J. Maxwell, and John H. Hayes. *A History of Ancient Israel and Judah*. Philadelphia, PA: Westminster, 1986.

Miller, James D. *The Pastoral Epistles as Composite Documents*. Cambridge: Cambridge University Press, 1997.

Millett, Paul. "Patronage and Its Avoidance in Classical Athens." In *Patronage in Ancient Society*, edited by Andrew Wallace-Hadrill, 15–47. London; New York: Routledge, 1989.

Misselbrook, Peter. "Notes on the Greek New Testament: Weeks 121–129: Paul's Letters to Timothy and Titus." *Paul's Letters to Timothy and Titus*. No pages. Accessed 29 May 2009. http://bijbelstudie.110mb.com/BW/56Tt/Anderen/

Misselbrook%20-%201%20Timothy,%202%20Timothy%20and%20 Titus.pdf Misselbrook's Musings.
Moreschini, Claudio, and Enrico Norelli. *Early Christian Greek and Latin Literature: A Literary History*. Peabody, MA: Hendrickson, 2005.
Moulton, James Hope, and George Milligan. *The Vocabulary of the Greek Testament: Illustrated from the Papyri and Other Non-Literary Sources*. Grand Rapids: Eerdmans, 1930.
Mounce, William D. *The Analytical Lexicon to the Greek New Testament*. Zondervan Greek Reference Series. Grand Rapids: Zondervan, 1993.
———. *Pastoral Epistles*. Word Biblical Commentary 46. Nashville, TN: Nelson, 2000.
Muecke, Frances. Review of *Horace and the Gift Economy of Patronage*, by Phebe Lowel Bowditch. The Classical Journal 98, no. 3 (2001): 334–336. http://www.jstor.org/stable/pdfplus/3298056.pdf.
Mukwaya, A. B. *Land Tenure in Uganda: Present Day Tendencies*. Nairobi; Kampala; Dar es Salaam: Eagle Press, 1953.
Mũtĩsya, Roy M. *Kĩkamba Proverbs and Idioms: Nthimo sya Kĩkamba na Myasyo*. Nairobi: Roma Publishers, 2002.
Mwalw'a, Matthews Kalola. "The Power of Witchcraft among Kenyan Akamba." Thesis, Nairobi Evangelical Graduate School of Theology, June 2001.
Ned. "What's Happ'ning in Maasailand Ngorongoro." *Endulen Maasai Diary* 23, no. 5 (May 2008). No pages. Accessed 9 April 2009. Online: http://nedmarch.googlepages.com/diarydecember20052.
Neste, Ray Van. *Cohesion and Structure in the Pastoral Epistles*. Journal for the Study of the New Testament Supplement Series 280. London: T & T Clark, 2004.
Neusner, Jacob. *The Mishnah: Social Perspectives*. Boston; Leiden: Brill, 1999.
———, ed. *Scriptures of the Oral Torah*. San Francisco: Harper & Row, 1987.
Neusner, Jacob, and William Scott Green, eds. *Dictionary of Judaism in the Biblical Period: 450 B.C.E. to 600 C.E.* 1 vol. Peabody, MA: Hendrickson, 1996 (repr. 2002).
Neusner, Jacob, Ernest S. Frerichs, Peder Borgen, and Richard Horsley, eds. *The Social World of Formative Christianity and Judaism: Essays in Tribute to Howard Clark Kee*. Philadelphia: Fortress, 1988.
Neyrey, Jerome H. "God, Benefactor and Patron: The Major Cultural Model for Interpreting the Deity in Graeco-Roman Antiquity." *Journal for the Study of the New Testament* 27, no. 4 (2005): 465–492.
———. *Render to God: New Testament Understandings of the Divine*. Minneapolis: Fortress Press, 2004.
———., ed. *The Social World of the New Testament: Insights and Models*. Peabody, MA: Hendrickson, 2008.

Ng, Esther Yue L. "Phoebe as Prostatis." *Trinity Journal* NS 25, no. 1 (Spring 2004): 3–13.

———. *Reconstructing Christian Origins?: The Feminist Theology of Elisabeth Schüssler Fiorenza: An Evaluation*. Paternoster Biblical and Theological Monographs. Carlisle: Paternoster, 2002.

Ngewa, Samuel M. *1 & 2 Timothy and Titus*. Africa Bible Commentary Series. Grand Rapids: Zondervan, 2009.

Nicols, John. "Patronum cooptare, patrocinium deferre: lex malacitana, 61." No pages. Accessed 18 April 2008. https://scholarsbank.uoregon.edu/dspace/bitstream/1794/4966/1/LEXMALAC.pdf.

———. "Pliny and the Patronage of Communities." *Hermes* 108 (1980): 365–385.

Njuguna, Anthony Wainaina. "Training Rural Pastors in Africa: Which Way Forward?" A Research Report of the Fraser Peckham Trust, Africa Rural Trainers Project. NEGST, Nairobi, Kenya, 10 February 2009.

Novick, Tzvi. "Charity and Reciprocity: Structures of Benevolence in Rabbinic Literature." *Harvard Theological Review* 105, no. 1 (January 2012): 33–52.

Ó Fearghail, Fearghus. "The Jews in the Hellenistic Cities of Acts." In *Jews in the Hellenistic and Roman Cities*, edited by John R. Bartlett, 39–54. London: Routledge, 2002.

Oberlinner, Lorenz and Anton Vögtle. *Anpassung oder Widerspruch? Von der apostolischen zur nachapostolischen Kirche* [Adaptation or Contradiction: From the Apostolic to the Post-apostolic Church]. Freiberg: Herder, 1992.

Opoku, Kofi Asare. "Death and Immortality in the African Religious Heritage." In *Death and Immortality in the Religions of the World*, edited by Paul Badham and Linda Badham, 9–23. New York: Paragon, 1987.

Oliver, Roland, and Michael Crowder, eds. *The Cambridge Encyclopedia of Africa*. Cambridge: Cambridge University Press, 1981.

Osiek, Carolyn. *Shepherd of Hermas: A Commentary*. Edited by Helmut Koester. Minneapolis: Fortress, 1999.

Panagopoulos, Cécile. "Vocabulaire et mentalite dans les *Moralia* de Plutarque." *Dialogues d'histoire ancienne* 3 (1977): 197–235.

Parrinder, Geoffrey. *African Traditional Religion*. Harts, UK: Mayflower Press, 1954.

Parsons, P. J. "Encouragement to a Philosopher." In *New Documents Illustrating Early Christianity*, vol. 4, *A Review of the Greek Inscriptions and Papyri Published in 1979*. Edited by G. H. R. Horsley. Translated by S. K. Stowers. Macquarie University, NSW: Ancient History Documentary Research Centre, 1987.

Peterman, Gerald W. *Paul's Gift from Philippi: Conventions of Gift Exchange and Christian Giving*. Society for New Testament Studies, Monograph Series 92. Cambridge: Cambridge University Press, 1997.

Pietersen, Lloyd K. *The Polemic of the Pastorals: A Sociological Examination of the Development of Pauline Christianity*. Journal for the Study of the New Testament Supplement Series 264. London: T & T Clark, 2004.

Pilch, John, and Bruce J. Malina, eds. *Handbook of Biblical Social Values*. Peabody, MA: Hendrickson, 1998.

Piper, Ronald A. "Glory, Honor and Patronage in the Fourth Gospel: Understanding the Doxa Given to Disciples in John 17." In *Social Scientific Models for Interpreting the Bible: Essays by the Context Group in Honor of Bruce J. Malina*, edited by John J. Pilch, 281–309. Biblical Interpretation Series. Leiden; Boston: Brill, 2001.

Poovey, W. A. *How to Talk to Christians about Money*. Minneapolis: Augsburg, 1982.

Porter, L. "The Word ἐπίσκοπος in Pre-Christian Usage." *Anglican Theological Review* 21 (1939): 103–112.

Porter, Stanley E. "Pauline Authorship and the Pastoral Epistles: Implications for Canon." *Bulletin for Biblical Research* 5 (1995): 105–123.

Poythress, Vern Sheridan. "The Meaning of μάλιστα in 2 Timothy 4.13 and Related Verses." *Journal of Theological Studies* 53, no. 2 (October 2002): 523–532.

Price, Christopher. "Pagans, Christianity, and Charity." *Christian Colligation of Apologetics Debate Research & Evangelism*. Accessed 13 July 2012, http://www.christiancadre.org/member_contrib/cp_charity.html.

Purcell, Nicholas. "Municipium." In *The Oxford Classical Dictionary: The Ultimate Reference Work on the Classical World*, edited by Simon Hornblower and Anthony Spawforth, 1001. Oxford: Oxford University Press, 2003.

Quinn, Jerome D., and William C. Wacker. *The First and Second Letters to Timothy: A New Translation with Notes and Commentary*. Critical Concepts in Religious Studies. Grand Rapids: Eerdmans, 2000.

Rajak, Tessa. "Synagogue and Community in the Graeco-Roman Diaspora." In *Jews in the Hellenistic and Roman Cities*, edited by John R. Bartlett, 22–38. London: Routledge, 2002.

Rapske, Brian Mark. *The Widow in the Apostolic Church*. Vancouver, BC: Regent College, 1987.

Reed, Jeffrey T. "Cohesive Ties in 1 Timothy: In Defence of the Epistle's Unity." *Neotestamentica* 26, no. 1 (1992): 131–147.

———. "Discourse Features in NT Letters, with Special Reference to the Structure of 1 Timothy." *Journal of Translation and Textlinguistics* 6 (1993): 228–252.

———. "To Timothy or Not? A Discourse Analysis of 1 Timothy." In *Biblical Greek Language and Linguistics: Open Questions in Current Research*, edited by Stanley E. Porter and D. A. Carson, 90–118. Journal for the Study of the New Testament Supplement Series 80. Sheffield: JSOT Press, 1993.

Republic of Kenya. National Constitution Draft. *The Proposed Constitution of Kenya*. Nairobi, Attorney-General, 6 May 2010.

Reynolds, Leighton Durham, Miriam T. Griffin, and Elaine Fantham. "Annaeus Seneca (2), Lucius." In *The Oxford Classical Dictionary* 1, edited by Simon Hornblower and Anthony Spawforth, 96–98. Oxford: Oxford University Press, 2003.

Richardson, Kenneth. *Garden of Miracles: The Story of the Africa Inland Mission*. London: Africa Inland Mission, 1968 (repr. 1976).

Robertson, A. T. *A Grammar of the Greek New Testament in the Light of Historical Research*. Nashville: Broadman Press, 1934.

Robertson, Stuart. "Review of *Josephus on Jesus: The Testimonium Flavianum Controversy from Late Antiquity to Modern Times*, Alice Whealey." *Shofar: An Interdisciplinary Journal of Jewish Studies* 24, no. 3 (2006) 181–184.

Rohrbaugh, Richard L. *The Social Sciences and New Testament Interpretation*. Peabody, MA: Hendrickson, 1996.

Roloff, Jürgen. *Der erste Brief an Timotheus*. Evangelisch-Katholischer Kommentar zum Neuen Testament 15. Zürich: Benziger Verlag; Neukirchener Verlag, 1988.

Romanov, Oleg. "Alexander Polyhistor (ca. 135 BCE–35 BCE)." *Internet Encyclopedia of Philosophy: Alexander Polyhistor*. No pages. Accessed 20 May 2008. http://www.iep.utm.edu/a/alexpoly.htm.

Rowlandson, Jane, ed. *Women & Society in Greek & Roman Egypt: A Sourcebook*. Cambridge: Cambridge University Press, 1998.

Sahlins, Marshall D. *Stone Age Economics*. Hawthorne, NY: Aldine de Gruyter, 1972.

Saldarini, Anthony J. "The Social World of Christian Jews and Jewish Christians." In *Religious and Ethnic Communities in Later Roman Palestine*, edited by Hayim Lapin, 115–154. Bethesda, MD: University of Maryland Press, 1998.

Saller, Richard P. "Patronage and Friendship in Early Imperial Rome: Drawing the Distinction." In *Patronage in Ancient Society*, edited by Andrew Wallace-Hadrill, 52–53. London: Routledge, 1989.

———. *Personal Patronage under the Early Empire*. Cambridge: Cambridge University Press, 1982.

Sampley, J. Paul, ed. *Paul in the Graeco-Roman World: A Handbook*. Harrisburg, PA: Trinity Press International, 2003.

Sanders, E. P. "Judaism and the Grand 'Christian' Abstractions: Love, Mercy, and Grace." *Interpretation* 39, no. 4 (October 1985): 357–372.

Sarah, Robert. *Church Leaders and Christian Life: In the Pastoral Letters*. Nairobi: Paulines Publications Africa, 2001.

Schlatter, Adolf. *The Church in the New Testament Period*. London: SPCK, 1961.

Scholer, David M., ed. *Social Distinctives of the Christians in the First Century: Pivotal Essays by E. A. Judge*. Peabody, MA: Hendrickson, 2008.

———. *Die Kirche Der Griechen im Urteil des Paulus*. Stuttgart: Calwer, 1958.

Schöllgen, Georg. " Die διπλῆ τιμή von 1 Tim 5, 17." *Zeitschrift für die Neutestamentliche Wissenschaft und die Kunde der Älteren Kirche* 80, no. 3–4 (1989): 232–239. Published online, 24 November 2009, accessed 12 October 2018, https://doi.org/10.1515/zntw.1989.80.3-4.232.

Schwartz, Seth. *Were the Jews a Mediterranean Society? Reciprocity and Solidarity in Ancient Judaism*. Princeton, NJ: Princeton University Press, 2010.

Serper, Arie, ed. *Encyclorama of Israel* 1. Jerusalem: Pierre Illouz; Edition et Diffusion Mondiale, 1986.

Sevenster, J. N. *Paul and Seneca*. Supplements to Novum Testamentum 4. Leiden: Brill, 1961.

Sim, Margaret Gavin. "A Relevant Theoretic Approach to the Particle ἵνα in Koine Greek." PhD Dissertation. University of Edinburgh, 2006.

Sitzler, Silke. "BMCR 2009.03.50, Susan R. Holman, Wealth and Poverty in Early Church." (Review of Susan R. Holman, *Wealth and Poverty in Early Church*). Holy Cross Studies in Patristic Theology and History. *Bryn Mawr Classical Reviews* (BMCR-L@brynmawr.edu) BMCR 2009.03.50 (March 2009). Accessed 8 October 2018. http://www.bmcreview.org/2009/03/20090350.html.

Skeat, T.C. "'Especially the Parchments': A Note on 2 Timothy IV. 13." *Journal of Theological Studies* 30 (1979): 173–177.

Smith, Craig A. *Timothy's Task, Paul's Prospect: A New Reading of 2 Timothy*. NT Monographs 12. Sheffield: Sheffield Phoenix Press, 2006.

Smith, Barry D. "Paul's Pastoral Letters." *First Timothy*. No pages. Accessed 28 February 2011. Online: http://www.abu.nb.ca/courses/ntintro/1Timhtm.

Sosin, Joshua D., Roger S. Bagnall, James Cowey, Mark Depauw, Terry G. Wilfong, and Klaas A. Worp, eds. "I. Papyri." *Checklist of Editions of Greek, Latin, Demotic and Coptic Papyri, Ostraca and Tablets: Web Edition*. No pages. Accessed 27 May 2009. Online: http://scriptorium.lib.duke.edu/papyrus/texts/clist_papyri.html. Website updated on 11 September 2008.

Spanneut, M. "Seneca, Lucius Annaeus." (SCU TEX) of *New Catholic Encyclopedia* 13. Edited by John P. Whalen, 80–81. Washington, DC: The Catholic University of America, 1967.

Spicq, Ceslas. *Les Epitres Pastorales*. Paris: J. Gabalda, 1969.

———. *Theological Leixcon of the New Testament* 2, edited and translated by James D. Ernest. Peabody, MA: Hendrickson, 1994.

Spilsbury, Paul. "God and Israel in Josephus: A Patron-Client Relationship." In *Understanding Josephus: Seven Perspectives*, edited by Steve Mason, 172–191. Journal for the Study of the Pseudepigrapha Supplement Series 32. Sheffield: Sheffield Academic Press, 1998.

Stemberger, Günter. *Introduction to the Talmud and Midrash*. 2nd edition. Edited and translated by Markus Bockmuehl. Edinburgh: T & T Clark, 1996. Translation of *Einleitung in Talmud und Midrash*.

Stettler, Hanna. *Die Christologie der Pastoralbriefe*. Wissenschaftliche untersuchungen zum Neuen Testament 105. Tübingen: Mohr Siebeck, 1998.

Stott, John R.W. *Calling Christian Leaders: Biblical Models of Church, Gospel and Ministry*. Leicester: InterVarsity Press, 2002.

———. *The Message of Timothy & Titus*. The Bible Speaks Today. Leicester: InterVarsity Press, 1997.

Stowers, Stanley K. "Social Typification and the Classification of Ancient Letters." In *The Social World of Formative Christianity and Judaism: Essays in Tribute to Howard Clark Kee*, edited by Jacob Neusner, Ernest S. Frerichs, Peder Borgen and Richard Horsley, 78–90. Philadelphia: Fortress, 1988.

Strauch, Alexander. *Biblical Eldership: An Urgent Call to Restore Biblical Church Leadership*. Littleton, CO: Lewis & Roth, 1988.

———. *The NT Deacon: The Church's Ministry of Mercy*. Littleton, CO: Lewis & Roth, 1992.

Strobel, August. "Der Begriff des ‚Hauses' im griechischen und römischen Privatrecht." *Zeitschrift für die neutestamentliche Wissenschaft und die Kunde* 56 (1965): 91–100.

Tannehill, Robert C. *Luke*. Abingdon New Testament Commentaries. Nashville: Abingdon, 1996.

Tate, W. Randolph. *Interpreting the Bible: A Handbook of Terms and Methods*. Peabody, MA: Hendrickson, 2006.

Theissen, Gerd. *Social Reality and the Early Christians: Theology, Ethics, and the World of the NT*. Edinburgh: T & T Clark, 1992.

———. *The Social Setting of Pauline Christianity: Essays on Corinth*. Eugene, OR: Wipf & Stock, 2004.

Tidball, Derek. *The Social Context of the NT*. Biblical Classics Library. Carlisle, UK: Paternoster, 1997.

Thomas, Robert L. *Exegetical Digest of First Timothy*. [California]: Robert L. Thomas, 1985.

Towner, Philip H. "Can Slaves Be Their Masters' Benefactors?" *Current Trends in Scripture Translation* 182/183 (1997): 39–52.

———. *The Goal of Our Instruction: The Structure of Theology and Ethics in the Pastoral Epistles*. Journal for the Study of the NT Supplement Series 34. Sheffield: JSOT Press, 1989.

———. *The Letters to Timothy and Titus*. The New International Commentary on the NT. Grand Rapids, MI: Eerdmans, 2006.

———. "Pauline Theology or Pauline Tradition in the Pastoral Epistles: The Question of Method." *Tyndale Bulletin* 46, no. 2 (1995): 287–314.

———. *1–2 Timothy & Titus*. The IVP NT Commentary Series. Downers Grove, IL: InterVarsity Press, 1994.

Trebilco, Paul. *The Early Christians in Ephesus from Paul to Ignatius*. Wissenschaftliche Untersuchungen zum Neuen Testament 166. Tübingen: Mohr Siebeck, 2004.

———. *Jewish Communities in Asia Minor*. Society for New Testament Studies Monograph Series 69. Cambridge: Cambridge University Press, 1991.

Turismo, Málaga. "Malaga in the Antiquity." *Málaga*. Accessed 12 July 2012. http://www.malagaturismo.com/jsp/quever/historia.jsp?opc=12&id_idioma=2.

Van Leeuwen, Henry G. "Sirach." In *International Standard Bible Encyclopedia* 4, Q–Z, edited by Geoffrey W. Bromiley, 529. Grand Rapids: Eerdmans, 1979–1988.

Verner, David C. *The Household of God: The Social World of the Pastoral Epistles*. SBL Dissertation Series 71. Chico, CA: SBL, 1983.

Veyne, P. *Bread and Circuses: Historical Sociology and Political Pluralism*. London: Allen Lane (Penguin Press), 1990.

Wagener, Ulrike. *Die Ordnung des 'House Gottes': der Ort von Frauen in der Ekklesiologie und Ethik der Pastoralbriefe*. Wissenschaftliche Untersuchungen zum Neuen Testament 65, Reihe 2. Tübingen: Mohr, 1994.

Walker, D. D. "Benefactor." In *Dictionary of New Testament Background*, edited by Craig A. Evans and Stanley E. Porter, 157–159. Downers Grove, IL: InterVarsity Press, 2000.

Wall, R. W. "Pauline Authorship and the Pastoral Epistles: A Response to S. E. Porter." Review of *Pauline Authorship and the Pastoral Epistles: Implications for Canon*, by Stanley E. Porter. *Bulletin for Biblical Research* 5 (1995): 125–128.

Wallace-Hadrill, Andrew, ed. *Patronage in Ancient Society*. London: Routledge, 1989.

Wankel, H., C. Börker, R. Merkelbach, et al., eds. *Die Inschriften von Ephesos* 1–8. Bonn: R. Habelt, 1979–1984.

Westbrook, Raymond. "Patronage in the Ancient Near East." *Journal of the Economic and Social History of the Orient* 48, no. 2 (2005): 210–233.

Whealey, Alice. *Josephus on Jesus: The Testimonium Flaviunum Controversy from Late Antiquity to Modern Times*. Studies in Biblical Literature 36. New York: Lang, 2003.

White, L. Michael, and O. Larry Yarbrough, eds. *The Social World of the First Christians: Essays in Honor of Wayne A. Meeks*. Minneapolis: Fortress, 1995.

Whitlark, Jason A. *Enabling Fidelity to God: Perseverance in Hebrews in Light of Reciprocity Systems in the Ancient Mediterranean World*. Paternoster Biblical Monographs. Milton Keynes: Paternoster, 2008.

Wildman, Joan. "Repetition." *Jazz*. Accessed 12 July 2012. http://hum.lss.wisc.edu/jazz/repetition.html. University Course: Jazz Improvisation 331 and 530.

Williams, Margaret H. Ed. *The Jews among the Greeks & Romans: A Diasporan Sourcebook*. Baltimore, MD: John Hopkins University, 1998.

Winter, Bruce W. "The 'New' Roman Wife and 1 Timothy 2:9–15: The Search for a Sitz im Leben." *Tyndale Bulletin* 51, no. 2 (2000): 285–294.

———. "Providentia for the Widows." *Tyndale Bulletin* 39 (1988): 83–99.

———. "The Public Honouring of Christian Benefactors: Romans 13.3–4 and 1 Peter 2.14–15." *Journal for the Study of the New Testament* 34 (October 1988): 87–103.

———. *Roman Wives, Roman Widows: The Appearance of New Women and the Pauline Communities*. Grand Rapids, MI: Eerdmans, 2003.

———. *Seek the Welfare of the City: Christians as Benefactors and Citizens*. Edited by Clark, A. D. First-Century Christians in the Graeco-Roman World. Grand Rapids, MI: Eerdmans, 1994.

Witherington, Ben, III. *Letters and Homilies for Hellenized Christians, vol. 1, A Socio-Rhetorical Commentary on Titus, 1–2 Timothy and 1–3 John*. Downers Grove, IL: InterVarsity; Nottingham, UK: Apollos, 2006.

Young, Frances M. *The Theology of the Pastoral Letters*. New Testament Theology. Cambridge: Cambridge University Press, 1994.

Langham Literature, with its publishing work, is a ministry of Langham Partnership.

Langham Partnership is a global fellowship working in pursuit of the vision God entrusted to its founder John Stott –

> *to facilitate the growth of the church in maturity and Christ-likeness through raising the standards of biblical preaching and teaching.*

Our vision is to see churches in the majority world equipped for mission and growing to maturity in Christ through the ministry of pastors and leaders who believe, teach and live by the Word of God.

Our mission is to strengthen the ministry of the Word of God through:
- nurturing national movements for biblical preaching
- fostering the creation and distribution of evangelical literature
- enhancing evangelical theological education

especially in countries where churches are under-resourced.

Our ministry

Langham Preaching partners with national leaders to nurture indigenous biblical preaching movements for pastors and lay preachers all around the world. With the support of a team of trainers from many countries, a multi-level programme of seminars provides practical training, and is followed by a programme for training local facilitators. Local preachers' groups and national and regional networks ensure continuity and ongoing development, seeking to build vigorous movements committed to Bible exposition.

Langham Literature provides majority world preachers, scholars and seminary libraries with evangelical books and electronic resources through publishing and distribution, grants and discounts. The programme also fosters the creation of indigenous evangelical books in many languages, through writer's grants, strengthening local evangelical publishing houses, and investment in major regional literature projects, such as one volume Bible commentaries like the *Africa Bible Commentary* and the *South Asia Bible Commentary*.

Langham Scholars provides financial support for evangelical doctoral students from the majority world so that, when they return home, they may train pastors and other Christian leaders with sound, biblical and theological teaching. This programme equips those who equip others. Langham Scholars also works in partnership with majority world seminaries in strengthening evangelical theological education. A growing number of Langham Scholars study in high quality doctoral programmes in the majority world itself. As well as teaching the next generation of pastors, graduated Langham Scholars exercise significant influence through their writing and leadership.

To learn more about Langham Partnership and the work we do visit **langham.org**

www.ingramcontent.com/pod-product-compliance
Lightning Source LLC
Chambersburg PA
CBHW070233240426
43673CB00044B/1771